Stress-Related Disorders

SOURCEBOOK

Fifth Edition

Health Reference Series

Fifth Edition

Stress-Related Disorders SOURCEBOOK

Basic Consumer Health Information about Stress and Stress-Related Disorders, Including Signs, Symptoms, Types, and Sources of Acute and Chronic Stress, the Impact of Stress on the Body, and Mental Health Problems Associated with Stress, Such as Depression, Anxiety Disorders, Bipolar Disorder, Obsessive-Compulsive Disorder, Substance Abuse, Posttraumatic Stress Disorder, and Suicide

Along with Advice about Getting Help for Stress-Related Disorders, Managing Stress and Coping with Trauma, a Glossary of Stress-Related Terms, and a Directory of Resources for Additional Help and Information

OMNIGRAPHICS

615 Griswold, Ste. 901, Detroit, MI 48226

SAYVILLE LIBRARY

Bibliographic Note
Because this page cannot legibly accommodate all the copyright notices, the Bibliographic Note portion of the Preface constitutes an extension of the copyright notice.

* * *

OMNIGRAPHICS
Angela L. Williams, *Managing Editor*

***

Copyright © 2018 Omnigraphics

ISBN 978-0-7808-1634-3
E-ISBN 978-0-7808-1635-0

Library of Congress Cataloging-in-Publication Data

Names: Omnigraphics, Inc., issuing body.

Title: Stress-related disorders sourcebook: basic consumer health information about stress and stress-related disorders, including signs, symptoms, types, and sources of acute and chronic stress, the impact of stress on the body, and mental health problems associated with stress, such as depression, anxiety disorders, bipolar disorder, obsessive-compulsive disorder, substance abuse, posttraumatic stress disorder, and suicide; along with advice about getting help for stress-related disorders, managing stress and coping with trauma, a glossary of stress-related terms, and a directory of resources for additional help and information.

Description: Fifth edition. | Detroit, MI: Omnigraphics, [2018] | Series: Health reference series | Includes bibliographical references and index.

Identifiers: LCCN 2018018797 (print) | LCCN 2018021397 (ebook) | ISBN 9780780816350 (eBook) | ISBN 9780780816343 (hardcover: alk. paper)

Subjects: LCSH: Stress management--Popular works. | Stress (Physiology)--Popular works. | Stress (Psychology)--Popular works.

Classification: LCC RA785 (ebook) | LCC RA785.S78 2018 (print) | DDC 155.9/042--dc23

LC record available at https://lccn.loc.gov/2018018797

Electronic or mechanical reproduction, including photography, recording, or any other information storage and retrieval system for the purpose of resale is strictly prohibited without permission in writing from the publisher.

The information in this publication was compiled from the sources cited and from other sources considered reliable. While every possible effort has been made to ensure reliability, the publisher will not assume liability for damages caused by inaccuracies in the data, and makes no warranty, express or implied, on the accuracy of the information contained herein.

This book is printed on acid-free paper meeting the ANSI Z39.48 Standard. The infinity symbol that appears above indicates that the paper in this book meets that standard.

Printed in the United States

Table of Contents

Part II: How Stress Affects the Body

Part III: How Stress Affects Mental Health

Part IV: Treating Stress-Related Disorders

Part V: Stress Management

Part VI: Additional Help and Information

Preface

About This Book

More than half of U.S. adults report their stress has increased in the last year. The future of the nation, work, and money lead the list of major stressors, followed by concerns about personal health and health problems affecting their family. Stress takes its toll on the body by eroding sleep quality and mental focus, leaving its victims impatient, irritable, fatigued, and prone to overeating and substance abuse. Prolonged stress adversely affects immune system function, worsening conditions such as chronic pain disorders, diabetes, and heart problems. Mental health disorders, including depression, anxiety, and posttraumatic stress disorder, are also linked to serious problems coping with stress. As stress levels in adults rise, so do those in children and adolescents who struggle to cope with worries about family and school.

Stress-Related Disorders Sourcebook, Fifth Edition provides updated information about the origins and types of stress and describes physical and mental health disorders that may develop during and after stressful situations. Readers will learn about how stress worsens asthma, digestive disorders, infertility, and chronic pain. The Sourcebook also discusses how stress contributes to mental health problems, including depression, anxiety disorders, posttraumatic stress disorder, and addiction to tobacco, alcohol, and drugs. Information about trauma, loss, and grief is presented, along with suggestions for managing stressful situations, such as aggressive driving, caregiver stress, economic hardship, and occupational stress. Tips on helping children and teens cope with stress are also offered, along with a glossary of related terms and a directory of resources.

How to Use This Book

This book is divided into parts and chapters. Parts focus on broad areas of interest. Chapters are devoted to single topics within a part.

Part I: Introduction to Stress and Stress-Related Disorders defines and characterizes what stress is. It also gives a brief insight into the common signs and symptoms of stress, and stressful life events. The part also deal with how personality, fatigue, loneliness, childhood, gender differences, and aging are associated with stress.

Part II: How Stress Affects the Body offers facts about how stress is associated with Alzheimer disease, asthma, diabetes, erectile dysfunction, gastrointestinal problems, headache, heart and cardiovascular problems, infertility, weight loss, multiple sclerosis, pain, pregnancy, skin problems, sleep disorders, and teeth grinding.

Part III: How Stress Affects Mental Health discusses depression, anxiety disorders, bipolar disorder, disordered eating, obsessive-compulsive disorder, substance abuse, addiction, bereavement, and other stress-related disorders that develop after trauma. Chapters include information about relationships and traumatic stress and traumatic stress in children and teens. An individual chapter deals exclusively with posttraumatic stress disorder in military personnel returning from the war zone.

Part IV: Treating Stress-Related Disorders includes chapters that deal with warning signs and risk factors for emotional distress, finding a therapist, and coping with traumatic stress reactions. It provides detailed information on the various treatment procedures such as psychotherapy, medications, and complementary and alternative medicine. Individual chapters on treating depression, anxiety disorders, bipolar disorder, posttraumatic stress disorder, and preventing suicide are also discussed.

Part V: Stress Management covers the basics of preventing and managing stress, developing resilience, stress reduction techniques, healthy habits to combat stress, and handling stressful situations. It also discusses tips for coping with stress, and stress management for children, teens, and families.

Part VI: Additional Help and Information includes a glossary of stress-related terms, a directory of organizations that provide information about specific stress-related disorders and how to find a support group to cope with stress.

Bibliographic Note

This volume contains documents and excerpts from publications issued by the following government agencies: Administration for Children and Families (ACF); Agency for Healthcare Research and Quality (AHRQ); Agricultural Research Service (ARS); Centers for Disease Control and Prevention (CDC); Child Welfare Information Gateway; Corporation for National and Community Service (CNCS); *Eunice Kennedy Shriver* National Institute of Child Health and Human Development (NICHD); Federal Bureau of Investigation (FBI); Health Resources and Services Administration (HRSA); National Cancer Institute (NCI); National Center for Complementary and Integrative Health (NCCIH); National Heart, Lung, and Blood Institute (NHLBI); National Institute of Arthritis and Musculoskeletal and Skin Diseases (NIAMS); National Institute of Diabetes and Digestive and Kidney Diseases (NIDDK); National Institute of Mental Health (NIMH); National Institute of Neurological Disorders and Stroke (NINDS); National Institute on Aging (NIA); National Institute on Alcohol Abuse and Alcoholism (NIAAA); National Institute on Drug Abuse (NIDA); National Institutes of Health (NIH); National Oceanic and Atmospheric Administration (NOAA); *NIH News in Health*; Office of Disease Prevention and Health Promotion (ODPHP); Office of Justice Programs (OJP); Office on Women's Health (OWH); Substance Abuse and Mental Health Services Administration (SAMHSA); U.S. Department of Energy (DOE); U.S. Department of Health and Human Services (HHS); U.S. Department of Housing and Urban Development (HUD); U.S. Department of State (DOS); U.S. Department of Veterans Affairs (VA); U.S. Fish and Wildlife Service (FWS); and U.S. National Library of Medicine (NLM).

It may also contain original material produced by Omnigraphics and reviewed by medical consultants.

About the *Health Reference Series*

The *Health Reference Series* is designed to provide basic medical information for patients, families, caregivers, and the general public. Each volume takes a particular topic and provides comprehensive coverage. This is especially important for people who may be dealing with a newly diagnosed disease or a chronic disorder in themselves or in a family member. People looking for preventive guidance, information about disease warning signs, medical statistics, and risk factors for health problems will also find answers to their questions in the *Health Reference Series*. The *Series*, however, is not intended to serve as a tool for diagnosing illness, in prescribing treatments, or as a substitute for the physician/patient relationship. All people concerned about medical symptoms or the possibility of disease are encouraged to seek professional care from an appropriate healthcare provider.

A Note about Spelling and Style

Health Reference Series editors use *Stedman's Medical Dictionary* as an authority for questions related to the spelling of medical terms and the *Chicago Manual of Style* for questions related to grammatical structures, punctuation, and other editorial concerns. Consistent adherence is not always possible, however, because the individual volumes within the *Series* include many documents from a wide variety of different producers, and the editor's primary goal is to present material from each source as accurately as is possible. This sometimes means that information in different chapters or sections may follow other guidelines and alternate spelling authorities.

Medical Review

Omnigraphics contracts with a team of qualified, senior medical professionals who serve as medical consultants for the *Health Reference Series*. As necessary, medical consultants review reprinted and originally written material for currency and accuracy. Citations including the phrase, "Reviewed (month, year)" indicate material reviewed by this team. Medical consultation services are provided to the *Health Reference Series* editors by:

Dr. Vijayalakshmi, MBBS, DGO, MD
Dr. Senthil Selvan, MBBS, DCH, MD
Dr. K. Sivanandham, MBBS, DCH, MS (Research), PhD

Our Advisory Board

We would like to thank the following board members for providing initial guidance on the development of this series:

- Dr. Lynda Baker, Associate Professor of Library and Information Science, Wayne State University, Detroit, MI

- Nancy Bulgarelli, William Beaumont Hospital Library, Royal Oak, MI
- Karen Imarisio, Bloomfield Township Public Library, Bloomfield Township, MI
- Karen Morgan, Mardigian Library, University of Michigan-Dearborn, Dearborn, MI
- Rosemary Orlando, St. Clair Shores Public Library, St. Clair Shores, MI

Health Reference Series *Update Policy*

The inaugural book in the *Health Reference Series* was the first edition of *Cancer Sourcebook* published in 1989. Since then, the *Series* has been enthusiastically received by librarians and in the medical community. In order to maintain the standard of providing high-quality health information for the layperson the editorial staff at Omnigraphics felt it was necessary to implement a policy of updating volumes when warranted.

Medical researchers have been making tremendous strides, and it is the purpose of the *Health Reference Series* to stay current with the most recent advances. Each decision to update a volume is made on an individual basis. Some of the considerations include how much new information is available and the feedback we receive from people who use the books. If there is a topic you would like to see added to the update list, or an area of medical concern you feel has not been adequately addressed, please write to:

Managing Editor
Health Reference Series
Omnigraphics
615 Griswold, Ste. 901
Detroit, MI 48226

Part One

Introduction to Stress and Stress-Related Disorders

Chapter 1

Stress—An Overview

Stress is a reaction to a change or a challenge. In the short term, stress can be helpful. It makes you more alert and gives you the energy to get things done. But long-term stress can lead to serious health problems. Women are more likely than men to report symptoms of stress, including headaches and upset stomach. Women are also more likely to have mental health conditions that are made worse by stress, such as depression or anxiety.

What Is Stress?

Stress is how your body reacts to certain situations, such as sudden danger or long-lasting challenge. During stressful events, your body releases chemicals called hormones, such as adrenaline. Adrenaline gives you a burst of energy that helps you cope and respond to stress. For example, one kind of stress is the jolt you may feel when a car pulls out in front of you. This jolt of adrenaline helps you quickly hit the brakes to avoid an accident. Stress can range from mild and short term to more extreme and long lasting. Long-term (i.e., chronic) stress can affect your mental and physical health.

This chapter includes text excerpted from "Stress and Your Health," Office on Women's Health (OWH), U.S. Department of Health and Human Services (HHS), May 17, 2018.

What Are Some Symptoms of Stress?

Stress affects everyone differently. Some ways that chronic or long-term stress affects women include:

- Pain, including back pain
- Acne and other skin problems, like rashes or hives
- Headaches
- Upset stomach
- Feeling like you have no control
- Forgetfulness
- Lack of energy
- Lack of focus
- Overeating or not eating enough
- Being easily angered
- Trouble sleeping
- Drug and alcohol misuse
- Loss of interest in things you once enjoyed
- Less interest in sex than usual

What Causes Stress?

People can feel stress from many different things. Examples of common causes of short-term stress include:

- Getting stuck in traffic or missing the bus
- An argument with your spouse or partner
- Money problems
- A deadline at work

Examples of common causes of long-term stress include:

- **Poverty and financial worries.** Depression is more common in women whose families live below the federal poverty line. Women in poverty who care for children or other family members, as well as themselves, may experience more severe stress.

- **Discrimination.** All women are at risk for discrimination, such as gender discrimination at work. Some women experience discrimination based on their race, ethnicity, or sexual orientation. Stressful events, such as learning a new culture (for those new to the United States) or experiencing discrimination, put women at higher risk for depression or anxiety.
- **Traumatic events.** Experiencing trauma, such as being in an accident or disaster or going through emotional, physical, or sexual assault or abuse as a child or an adult, may put you at higher risk of depression and other disorders. Women are more likely than men to experience certain types of violence, such as sexual violence, that are more likely to cause mental health conditions, such as posttraumatic stress disorder (PTSD).

Ongoing, low-level stress can be hard to notice, but it can also lead to serious health problems. If you need more help managing stress, talk to a doctor, nurse, or mental health professional.

What Is Posttraumatic Stress Disorder (PTSD)?

PTSD is an illness that some people experience after going through trauma. PTSD can happen to someone who has lived through or witnessed a violent crime or war. It can also happen after a sudden traumatic event like a death of a loved one, physical or sexual abuse, or a severe car crash. Women are about twice as likely as men to develop PTSD. Some PTSD symptoms also are more common in women than in men. For example, women who suffer from PTSD are more likely to:

- Be jumpy
- Have more trouble feeling emotions
- Avoid whatever reminds them of the trauma
- Feel depressed and anxious

*Medications for PTSD**

Medications that have been shown to be helpful in treating PTSD symptoms are some of the same medications also used for symptoms of depression and anxiety.

These are antidepressants, called SSRIs (selective serotonin reuptake inhibitors) and SNRIs (serotonin-norepinephrine reuptake inhibitors). The four antidepressants effective for treating PTSD are:

SSRIs:

- Sertraline (Zoloft)
- Paroxetine (Paxil)
- Fluoxetine (Prozac)

SNRIs:

- Venlafaxine (Effexor)

**Text excerpted from "Medications for PTSD," U.S. Department of Veterans Affairs (VA), December 7, 2017.*

Do Women React to Stress Differently than Men Do?

Yes, studies show that women are more likely than men to experience symptoms of stress. Women who are stressed are more likely than men who are stressed to experience depression and anxiety. Experts do not fully know the reason for the differences, but it may be related to how men's and women's bodies process stress hormones. Long-term stress especially is more likely to cause problems with moods and anxiety in women.

What Can I Do to Help Manage My Stress?

Everyone has to deal with stress at some point in their lives. You can take steps to help handle stress in a positive way.

- **Take deep breaths.** This forces you to breathe slower and helps your muscles relax. The extra oxygen sends a message to your brain to calm and relax the body.
- **Stretch.** Stretching can also help relax your muscles and make you feel less tense.
- **Write out your thoughts.** Keeping a journal or simply writing down the things you are thankful for can help you handle stress.
- **Take time for yourself.** This could be listening to music, reading a good book, or going to a movie.
- **Meditate.** Studies show that meditation, a set time of stillness to focus the mind on a positive or neutral thought, can help lower stress. In addition to traditional medical treatments, meditation also may help improve anxiety, reduce some

menopause symptoms and side effects from cancer treatments, and may lower blood pressure. Meditation is generally safe for everyone, and free meditation guides are widely available online.

- **Get enough sleep.** Most adults need 7–9 hours of sleep each night to feel rested.
- **Eat right.** Caffeine or high-sugar snack foods give you jolts of energy that wear off quickly. Instead, eat foods with B vitamins, such as bananas, fish, avocados, chicken, and dark green, leafy vegetables. Studies show that B vitamins can help relieve stress by regulating nerves and brain cells. You can also take a vitamin B supplement if your doctor or nurse says it is OK.
- **Get moving.** Physical activity can relax your muscles and improve your mood. Physical activity also may help relieve symptoms of depression and anxiety. Physical activity boosts the levels of "feel-good" chemicals in your body called endorphins. Endorphins can help improve your mood.
- **Try not to deal with stress in unhealthy ways.** This includes drinking too much alcohol, using drugs, smoking, or overeating. These coping mechanisms may help you feel better in the moment but can add to your stress levels in the long term. Try substituting healthier ways to cope, such as spending time with friends and family, exercising, or finding a new hobby.
- **Talk to friends or family members.** They might help you see your problems in new ways and suggest solutions. Or, just being able to talk to a family member or friend about a source of stress may help you feel better.
- **Get help from a professional if you need it.** Your doctor or nurse may suggest counseling or prescribe medicines, such as antidepressants or sleep aids. If important relationships with family or friends are a source of stress, a counselor can help you learn new emotional and relationship skills.
- **Get organized.** Being disorganized is a sign of stress, but it can also cause stress. To-do lists help organize both your work and home life. Figure out what is most important to do at home and at work and do those things first.
- **Help others.** Volunteering in your community can help you make new friends and feel good about helping others.

Chapter 2

Characteristics of Stress

Chapter Contents

Section 2.1

Signs and Symptoms of Stress

This section includes text excerpted from documents published by two public domain sources. Text under the headings marked 1 are excerpted from "5 Things You Should Know about Stress," National Institute of Mental Health (NIMH), December 20, 2016; Text under the heading marked 2 is excerpted from "Coping with Stress," Centers for Disease Control and Prevention (CDC), December 4, 2017.

Stress Affects Everyone[1]

Stress is how the brain and body respond to any demand. Every type of demand or stressor—such as exercise, work, school, major life changes, or traumatic events—can be stressful. Stress can affect your health. It is important to pay attention to how you deal with minor and major stress events so that you know when to seek help.

Everyone feels stressed from time to time. Some people may cope with stress more effectively or recover from stressful events more quickly than others. There are different types of stress—all of which carry physical and mental health risks. A stressor may be a one time or short-term occurrence, or it can be an occurrence that keeps happening over a long period of time.

Examples of stress include:

- Routine stress related to the pressures of work, school, family, and other daily responsibilities
- Stress brought about by a sudden negative change, such as losing a job, divorce, or illness
- Traumatic stress experienced in an event like a major accident, war, assault, or a natural disaster where people may be in danger of being seriously hurt or killed. People who experience traumatic stress often experience temporary symptoms of mental illness, but most recover naturally soon after.

Not All Stress Is Bad[1]

Stress can motivate people to prepare or perform, like when they need to take a test or interview for a new job. Stress can even be life-saving in some situations. In response to danger, your body prepares to face a threat or flee to safety. In these situations, your pulse quickens, you breathe faster, your muscles tense, your brain uses more oxygen and increases activity—all functions aimed at survival.

Symptoms of Stress[2]

Common reactions to a stressful event include:

- Disbelief and shock
- Tension and irritability
- Fear and anxiety about the future
- Difficulty making decisions
- Feeling numb
- Loss of interest in normal activities
- Loss of appetite
- Nightmares and recurring thoughts about the event
- Anger
- Increased use of alcohol and drugs
- Sadness and other symptoms of depression
- Feeling powerless
- Crying
- Sleep problems
- Headaches, back pains, and stomach problems
- Trouble concentrating

Long-Term Stress Can Harm Your Health[1]

Health problems can occur if the stress response goes on for too long or becomes chronic, such as when the source of stress is constant, or if the response continues after the danger has subsided. With chronic stress, those same life-saving responses in your body can suppress immune, digestive, sleep, and reproductive systems, which may cause them to stop working normally.

Different people may feel stress in different ways. For example, some people experience mainly digestive symptoms, while others may have headaches, sleeplessness, sadness, anger or irritability. People under chronic stress are prone to more frequent and severe viral infections, such as the flu or common cold.

If You're Overwhelmed by Stress, Ask for Help from a Health Professional[1]

You should seek help right away if you have suicidal thoughts, are overwhelmed, feel you cannot cope, or are using drugs or alcohol to cope. Your doctor may be able to provide a recommendation.

Section 2.2

Types of Stress

This section contains text excerpted from the following sources: Text in this section begins with excerpts from "Stress," MedlinePlus, National Institutes of Health (NIH), August 9, 2016; Text beginning with the heading "Stress Can Be Acute or Chronic" is excerpted from "Self-Regulation and Toxic Stress," U.S. Department of Health and Human Services (HHS), February 2015; Text under the heading "Routine Stress" is excerpted from "5 Things You Should Know about Stress," National Institute of Mental Health (NIMH), December 20, 2016.

Everyone feels stressed from time to time. Not all stress is bad. All animals have a stress response, and it can be life-saving. But chronic stress can cause both physical and mental harm.

There are at least three different types of stress:

- Routine stress related to the pressures of work, family, and other daily responsibilities
- Stress brought about by a sudden negative change, such as losing a job, divorce, or illness
- Traumatic stress, which happens when you are in danger of being seriously hurt or killed. Examples include a major accident, war, assault, or a natural disaster. This type of stress can cause posttraumatic stress disorder (PTSD).

Different people may feel stress in different ways. Some people experience digestive symptoms. Others may have headaches, sleeplessness, depressed mood, anger, and irritability. People under chronic stress get more frequent and severe viral infections, such as the flu or common cold. Vaccines, such as the flu shot, are less effective for them.

Some people cope with stress more effectively than others. It's important to know your limits when it comes to stress, so you can avoid more serious health effects.

Stress Can Be Acute or Chronic

It is important to distinguish between acute and chronic stress. Acute stress involves the body's stress system activating for a short period of time in response to a temporary stimulus. Although such stress can have lasting biological or behavioral effects if it is severe enough, the human stress response system is generally well-equipped to manage acute stress.

In contrast, chronic stress—in which the body's stress system is activated very frequently or for a prolonged period of time or in response to persistent stimuli—may have detrimental effects on the brain and behavior. When a child experiences strong, frequent, and/or prolonged adversity that overwhelms his/her skills or support, the result can create toxic stress response. Stressors that may induce toxic stress responses include physical or emotional abuse, chronic neglect, caregiver substance abuse or mental illness, exposure to violence, and/or the accumulated burdens of family economic hardship (i.e., poverty).

Traumatic Stress

The word "trauma" describes an event or experience where an individual's life or physical well-being (or that of someone important to them) is threatened. Trauma can be either acute(such as a natural disaster or robbery) or chronic (such as child maltreatment). In this regard, it can be considered a stressor, which may create toxic stress in those situations where the child or youth's abilities to cope are overwhelmed. In addition, the aftermath of an acute trauma (for example, sustained homelessness or disruption of social networks after a natural disaster) can itself constitute a chronic stressor; in that way, even acute trauma can have chronic effects if consequences are long lasting.

Routine Stress

Routine stress may be the hardest type of stress to notice at first. Because the source of stress tends to be more constant than in cases of acute or traumatic stress, the body gets no clear signal to return to normal functioning. Over time, continued strain on your body from routine stress may contribute to serious health problems, such as heart disease, high blood pressure, diabetes, and other illnesses, as well as mental disorders like depression or anxiety.

Chapter 3

Stressful Life Events

Stress is a condition of the mind and a factor in the expression of disease that differs among individuals and reflects not only major life events, but also the conflicts and pressures of daily life that elevate physiological systems so as to cause a cumulative chronic stress burden on brain and body. This burden reflects not only the impact of life experiences, but also of genetic variations; individual health-related behaviors such as diet, exercise, sleep patterns, and substance abuse; and epigenetic modifications in development and throughout life that set lifelong patterns of behavior and physiological reactivity

---

This chapter contains text excerpted from the following sources: Text in this chapter begins with excerpts from "Population Health: Behavioral and Social Science Insights," Agency for Healthcare Research and Quality (AHRQ), U.S. Department of Health and Human Services (HHS), July 2015; Text beginning with the heading "Resilience to Major Life Stressors" is excerpted from "Resilience to Major Life Stressors: Conceptual and Methodological Considerations," Office of Behavioral and Social Sciences Research (OBSSR), National Institutes of Health (NIH), July 19, 2016; Text under the heading "The Vicious Cycle of Anxiety, Depression, and Negative Life Events" is excerpted from "Associations between Major Life Events, Traumatic Incidents, and Depression among Buffalo Police Officers," Office of Justice Programs (OJP), 2007. Reviewed June 2018; Text under the heading "Stressful Life Events May Increase Stillbirth Risk" is excerpted from "Stressful Life Events May Increase Stillbirth Risk, NIH Network Study Finds," National Institutes of Health (NIH), March 27, 2013. Reviewed June 2018; Text under the heading "Stressful Life Events Screening Questionnaire (SLESQ)" is excerpted from "Stressful Life Events Screening Questionnaire (SLESQ)," U.S. Department of Veterans Affairs (VA), July 7, 2016.

through both biological embedding and cumulative change. Epigenetics is the now-popular way to describe gene x environment interactions via molecular mechanisms that do not change the genetic code but rather activate, repress, and modulate expression of the code. Indeed, epigenetics denies the notion that "biology is destiny" and opens new opportunities for collaboration between the biological and behavioral and social sciences.

There are many aspects of life experiences that influence physical and mental health, and the brain is central to all of them. Social stressors include trauma and abuse, major life events, and the daily experiences of work, family, neighborhood, and ongoing events in one's city, state, nation, and the world. The brain processes all of this and determines the behavioral and physiological responses. Behavioral responses include quality and quantity of sleep and health-damaging behaviors, such as eating too much, smoking and substance abuse, including alcohol, as well as health promoting behaviors, such as regular physical activity and social integration and social support. Physiological responses that are normally adaptive ("allostasis") can lead to pathophysiology ("allostatic load and overload") when overused or dysregulated. Health behaviors feed into the network of allostasis and can lead to allostatic load (AL) and overload, sleep deprivation being a good example. Socioeconomic status (SES), including both education and income, are reflected in AL and overload and gradients of disease. Again, the brain with its influence on the rest of the body is key because subjective SES, reflecting perceived social position, is reflected in many aspects of physical and mental health. In many societies, the gradient of income is reflected not only in the frequency of diseases, but also in abnormal behavior, including depression, aggression, and violence, which can increase the likelihood of incarceration.

Resilience to Major Life Stressors

What does it mean to lose your spouse or partner, to become unemployed, or to receive a cancer diagnosis? Such events, commonly referred to as major life stressors, result in a qualitative shift in one's life circumstances. The consequences of these major life stressors are not only confined to the individual, but can reverberate through one's family and community. In the case of spousal death, the surviving spouse must adjust to a life without reliance on their partner for tasks of daily living or having to engage in common shared interests alone. Facing unemployment brings up anxieties about where the next paycheck will come from to help support one's family.

Intuition Dictates Major Life Stressors Should Lead to Substantial Declines in Well-Being and Mental Health

Intuition (backed by empirical evidence) may predispose you to believe that these major life stressors should lead to substantial declines in well-being and mental health. However, not all individuals succumb to the detrimental consequences of major life stressors. Resilience is built on the premise that there is a great deal of heterogeneity in individuals' ability to adapt in the face of adversity, with some being able to maintain functioning, whereas others initially decline, but recover over time.

The past 15 years of research in resilience in adulthood and old age has portrayed contrary findings. In fact, research has shown that when confronted with significant adversity (irrespective of type), most individuals are remarkably resilient, defined as showing stable, high levels of functioning. This has been shown for a wide range of adversities, including spousal loss, divorce, unemployment, health adversities such as heart attack and cancer diagnosis, as well as natural disasters and military deployment.

The Vicious Cycle of Anxiety, Depression, and Negative Life Events

According to the American Psychological Association (APA), two-thirds of Americans have reported experiencing at least one stressful life event, such as the death of a family member, divorce, or the birth of a child, in the last two years. As these events accumulate, stress levels increase. Additionally, of those experiencing three or more stressful life events, one-third rated their physical health and 20 percent rated their psychological health as fair or poor. Significant associations between depression and multiple negative life events, such as a loss or separation, have been found in children. The risk for depressive episodes has been shown to be five-fold greater for individuals experiencing a single negative event and nearly eight-fold higher for those experiencing multiple events compared to individuals having no negative events.

The psychological effects of experiencing life events have been well studied. Life events often precede depressive episodes and psychiatric disorders such as anxiety states, alcoholism, bulimia, and schizophrenia contribute to depression, and are associated with greater risk of illnesses.

Stressful Life Events May Increase Stillbirth Risk

Pregnant women who experienced financial, emotional, or other personal stress in the year before their delivery had an increased chance of having a stillbirth, say researchers who conducted a National Institutes of Health (NIH) network study.

Stillbirth is the death of a fetus at 20 or more weeks of pregnancy. According to the National Center for Health Statistics (NCHS), in 2006, there was one stillbirth for every 167 births.

The researchers asked more than 2,000 women a series of questions, including whether they had lost a job or had a loved one in the hospital in the year before they gave birth.

Whether or not the pregnancy ended in stillbirth, most women reported having experienced at least one stressful life event in the previous year. The researchers found that 83 percent of women who had a stillbirth and 75 percent of women who had a live birth reported a stressful life event. Almost 1 in 5 women with stillbirths and 1 in 10 women with live births in this study reported recently experiencing 5 or more stressful life events. This study measured the occurrence of a list of significant life events, and did not include the woman's assessment of how stressful the event was to her.

Women reporting a greater number of stressful events were more likely to have a stillbirth. Two stressful events increased a woman's odds of stillbirth by about 40 percent, the researchers' analysis showed. A woman experiencing five or more stressful events was nearly 2.5 times more likely to have a stillbirth than a woman who had experienced none. Women who reported three or four significant life event factors (financial, emotional, traumatic or partner-related) remained at increased risk for stillbirth after accounting for other stillbirth risk factors, such as sociodemographic characteristics and prior pregnancy history.

Non-Hispanic black women were more likely to report experiencing stressful events than were non-Hispanic white women and Hispanic women. Black women also reported a greater number of stressful events than did their white and Hispanic counterparts. This finding may partly explain why black women have higher rates of stillbirth than non-Hispanic white or Hispanic women, the researchers said.

"We documented how significant stressors are highly prevalent in pregnant women's lives," said study co-author Marian Willinger,

Ph.D., acting chief of the Pregnancy and Perinatology Branch of the *Eunice Kennedy Shriver* National Institute of Child Health and Human Development (NICHD), one of two NIH entities funding the research. "This reinforces the need for healthcare providers to ask expectant mothers about what is going on in their lives, monitor stressful life events and to offer support as part of prenatal care."

The NIH Office of Research in Women's Health (ORWH) also funded the study.

"Because 1 in 5 pregnant women has three or more stressful events in the year leading up to delivery, the potential public health impact of effective interventions could be substantial and help increase the delivery of healthy babies," added lead author Dr. Carol Hogue, Terry Professor of Maternal and Child Health (MCH) at Emory University's Rollins School of Public Health, Atlanta.

Dr. Willinger collaborated with colleagues at the NICHD and Emory University; Drexel University School of Medicine, Philadelphia; University of Texas Medical Branch (UTMB) at Galveston; Children's Healthcare of Atlanta (CHOA); Brown University School of Medicine, Providence, R.I.; University of Texas (UT) Health Science Center at San Antonio; University of Utah School of Medicine and Intermountain Healthcare, Salt Lake City; and RTI International, Research Triangle Park (RTP), N.C.

Their findings appear in the American Journal of Epidemiology (AJE).

The research was conducted by the NICHD-funded Stillbirth Collaborative Research Network (SCRN). The researchers contacted all women delivering a stillbirth as well as a representative portion of women delivering a live birth in defined counties in Georgia, Massachusetts, Rhode Island, Texas, and Utah. The women were enrolled in the study between 2006 and 2008 in 59 community and research hospitals.

Within 24 hours of either a live birth or a stillbirth delivery, the women in the study were asked about events grouped into four categories: emotional, financial, partner-related and traumatic. They answered yes or no to 13 scenarios, including the following:

- I moved to a new address.
- My husband or partner lost his job.
- I was in a physical fight.
- Someone very close to me died.

Some of the stressful events were more strongly associated with stillbirth than were others. For example, the risk of stillbirth was highest:

- For women who had been in a fight (which doubled the chances for stillbirth)
- If she had heard her partner say he didn't want her to be pregnant
- If she or her partner had gone to jail in the year before the delivery

"At prenatal visits, screening is common for concerns such as intimate partner violence and depression, but the questions in our study were much more detailed," said co-author Uma Reddy, M.D., M.P.H., also of NICHD. "This is a first step toward cataloguing the effects of stress on the likelihood of stillbirth and, more generally, toward documenting how pregnancy influences a woman's mental health and how pregnancy is influenced by a woman's mental health."

Stressful Life Events Screening Questionnaire (SLESQ)

The Stressful Life Events Screening Questionnaire (SLESQ) is a 13-item self-report measure for nontreatment seeking samples that assess lifetime exposure to traumatic events. Eleven specific and two general categories of events, such as a life-threatening accident, physical and sexual abuse, witness to another person being killed or assaulted, are examined. For each event, respondents are asked to indicate whether the event occurred ("yes" or "no"), their age at time of the event, as well as other specific items related to the event, such as the frequency, duration, whether anyone died, or was hospitalization, etc. The SLESQ is recommended for research and general screening purposes, and is available in English and Spanish.

Chapter 4

Factors That Influence Response to Stress

Chapter Contents

Section 4.1

Personality and Stress

"Personality and Stress,"
© 2015 Omnigraphics. Reviewed June 2018.

The stress response, sometimes known as the "fight-or-flight" response, mobilizes the body's reserves to overcome a perceived threat. It evolved to protect people from danger and is considered essential to survival. When confronted with a stressful situation, the body increases its production of the chemicals cortisol, adrenaline, and noradrenaline. These chemicals trigger a faster heart rate, rapid breathing, muscle tension, and alertness. At the same time, the chemicals slow down nonessential body functions, such as the digestive and immune systems.

Stress can broadly be classified as physiological or psychological. Physiological stress refers to the adaptive mechanisms the body uses to respond to physical challenges, such as a broken bone or exposure to extreme cold. Psychological stress, on the other hand, refers to a disparity between an external stressor and the person's mental, emotional, or social resources. Examples might include feelings of anxiety about an upcoming test or worry about meeting a work deadline.

Even though the sources of psychological stress may not be life threatening, the body responds to them in much the same way as it responds to physiological stressors. These responses, while designed to protect the body, can actually have harmful effects on both physical and mental health when they recur frequently over prolonged periods of time. Chronic stress has been linked to a multitude of health conditions, including depression, digestive problems, fatigue, headaches, heart disease, high blood pressure, insomnia, muscle aches, and obesity.

Personality Types

The response to stress is a complex and highly personalized mechanism involving many interrelated biological, psychological, and social factors. Studies have shown that an individual's personality—as determined by inherited characteristics, life experiences, and cognitive predispositions—strongly influences how they interpret and deal with stressful situations. People who demonstrate certain personality traits, such as resilience and adaptability, tend to respond better to adversity and be less susceptible to stress.

Researchers have developed the five-factor model (FFM) as a way to classify different personality types. The "Big Five" personality characteristics in this model include:

- Openness to new experiences, as opposed to closed-mindedness
- Conscientiousness, as opposed to disorganization
- Extraversion, as opposed to introversion
- Agreeableness, as opposed to disagreeableness
- Neuroticism, as opposed to emotional stability

Although age, gender, intellect, and other factors can influence a person's sensitivity to stressors, studies have shown that personality type is an important factor in determining an individual's reaction to stress. In fact, personality traits can help explain how some people can handle huge amounts of stress for long periods of time, while others may feel overwhelmed when faced with small amounts of stress on a temporary basis.

An individual's personality influences every stage of the stress response, from evaluating whether or not a situation is stressful to choosing coping methods. In general, individuals with strong scores in extraversion tend to be optimistic and develop good problem-solving and coping strategies. They can reappraise potentially stressful situations in a positive way—for instance, as a challenge and an opportunity for growth and personal development—and effectively seek social support to help them deal with the stressor. On the other hand, individuals with strong scores in neuroticism tend to be pessimistic. They can become overwhelmed by potentially stressful situations, which can take a toll on their life satisfaction and physical health.

Type A and Type B Behavior

The theory of Type A behavior was developed in the 1950s by American cardiologist Meyer Friedman, who noticed a link between a certain personality type and the risk of heart disease. His 1974 book on the theory opened up a new field of research that looked beyond the well-known risk factors of diet and cholesterol and examined the mind-body connection to heart disease. The term "Type A personality" soon became a national buzzword to refer to high-stress personalities who tended to be driven, impatient, and competitive. This personality type was considered to be in opposition to Type B personalities, who tended to be calm, steady, relaxed, and less vulnerable to stress.

Type A personalities are believed to have an overactive sympathetic nervous system pathway. This pathway is responsible for stimulating the "fight-or-flight" response, which is associated with increased secretions of the emergency hormones that elevate the heart and respiratory rates and may contribute to hypertension and heart disease. In Type B personalities, the parasympathetic nervous system pathway is dominant. This pathway is associated with a lower metabolic rate and the release of "feel-good" neurotransmitters like endorphin, melatonin, and serotonin.

Critics argue, however, that human behavior is too complex to be categorized within the narrow parameters outlined by Friedman. Modern-day psychologists generally refrain from drawing a clear distinction between the two extreme personality types, preferring to regard them as points on a continuum. In addition, some psychologists argue that personality and experiences do not necessarily condition people to respond to stress in a certain way. Instead, they claim that people can learn to manage stress effectively through training programs that help them build self-confidence, develop problem-solving skills, and face the everyday challenges of life in a more positive manner.

Reference

McLeod, Saul. "Type A Personality," Simply Psychology, 2011.

Section 4.2

Gender Differences in Stress Response

"Gender Differences in Stress Response,"
© 2015 Omnigraphics. Reviewed June 2018.

It has long been recognized that men and women react differently to stress. Researchers have noted, for example, that women have a higher incidence of stress-related illnesses like posttraumatic stress disorder (PTSD), depression, and anxiety than men. Studies on gender differences in stress response have also shown that the classic, action-oriented "fight-or-flight" response is more typical of men, whereas women are more likely to exhibit a socially oriented "tend-and-befriend" response.

Scientists believe that such differences may have a biological basis. A 2010 study on the brains of rats—which have the same basic neural structure as those of humans—found that females were more sensitive to a certain stress hormone than males, and also less able to adapt to high levels of it. In addition, a 2012 study on humans found that men's and women's brains processed stress differently and suggested that a single gene may be responsible for this gender variation.

Gender Differences in the Brain's Response to Stress

The 2010 study focused on corticotropin-releasing factor (CRF), a hormone released by the hypothalamus region of the brain in response to stress. CRF acts as a neurotransmitter, helping to carry signals between brain cells. In response to a stressor, CRF binds to receptors on cells in the locus coeruleus, a cluster of neurons in the brainstem. The CRF signals the neurons to secrete norepinephrine and cortisol, the main hormones responsible for mobilizing the body's energy reserves and producing the fight-or-flight stress response.

In the presence of these hormones, the nervous system goes into a state of hyperarousal, which is characterized by a faster heart rate, rapid breathing, muscle tension, and alertness. Although hyperarousal is a natural part of the body's stress response, research has shown that long-term and excessive activation of the CRF receptors can lead to stress-related disorders, such as anxiety and PTSD.

In the study of rats, scientists observed that the stress signaling system was more responsive in females than in males, so the receptors in the female brains bound more tightly to CRF. Moreover, the CRF receptors remained activated much longer in response to stress in the female brains, thereby prolonging their exposure to CRF. The male brains, on the other hand, quickly adapted to the higher levels of stress hormones by reducing the number of receptors through a process called internalization, thus limiting their exposure to CRF.

Researchers believe that these gender differences in the stress response may help explain why women have a higher incidence of stress-related mood and anxiety disorders than men. Although the biological mechanism may be different in humans than in animals, the possibility that gender may influence CRF exposure has clinical and therapeutic implications for many psychiatric disorders.

Gender Differences in the Behavioral Response to Stress

In the twenty-first century, many psychologists have begun to question the longstanding belief that humans universally exhibit the fight-or-flight response to stress. A growing number have argued that while this response is common for men, women are more likely to exhibit a tend-and-befriend response. Instead of preparing to fight back or run away when faced with danger, many women demonstrate affiliative social behavior—either by seeking social support to deal with the situation or by trying to defuse the situation through relationship-building.

Research has found that in addition to releasing stress hormones like norepinephrine, women's brains respond to stress by secreting endorphins—so-called "feel-good" chemicals that help alleviate pain and create positive emotions about social interactions. Scientists have theorized that this chemical response may have evolved out of women's historic role in nurturing offspring and affiliating with social groups in times of adversity.

The 2012 study suggested that this gender difference might be connected to the sex-determining region Y (*SRY*) gene, which men carry on the Y chromosome. The *SRY* gene produces proteins that regulate the secretion of norepinephrine and other hormones involved in the fight-or-flight response to stress. Since women do not have the *SRY* gene, their responses to stress are regulated by other genes. Although all of the biological mechanisms involved are not fully understood, recognizing that gender plays a role in the response to stress can help people develop positive coping strategies.

References

1. Goldstein, Jill M., et al. "Sex Differences in Stress Response Circuitry Activation Dependent on Female Hormonal Cycle," *Journal of Neuroscience* 30(2), January 13, 2010, p. 431.

2. Maestripieri, Dario. "Gender Differences in Responses to Stress: It Boils Down to a Single Gene," *Psychology Today*, March 17, 2012.

3. National Institutes of Health (NIH). "Stress Hormone Receptors Less Adaptive in Female Brain," *Science News*, August 9, 2010.

4. "Study: Why Women Are More Sensitive to Stress," *Live Science*, June 18, 2010.

Section 4.3

Resistance Mechanisms in Brain May Prevent Stress-Related Illness

This section includes text excerpted from "Stress: Brain Yields Clues about Why Some Succumb While Others Prevail," National Institute of Mental Health (NIMH), October 18, 2007. Reviewed June 2018.

Stress and Resistance

In humans, stress can play a major role in the development of several mental illnesses, including posttraumatic stress disorder (PTSD) and depression. A key question in mental health research is: Why are some people resilient to stress, while others are not? This research indicates that resistance is not simply a passive absence of vulnerability mechanisms, as was previously thought; it is a biologically active process that results in specific adaptations in the brain's response to stress.

A Study on Resistance Mechanisms

Discovery of resistance mechanisms in mouse brain may lead to help for stress-related mental illness in humans. Results of a new study may one day help scientists learn how to enhance a naturally occurring mechanism in the brain that promotes resilience to psychological stress. Researchers funded by the National Institutes of Health's (NIH) National Institute of Mental Health (NIMH) found that, in a mouse model, the ability to adapt to stress is driven by a distinctly different molecular mechanism than is the tendency to be overwhelmed by stress. The researchers mapped out the mechanisms—components of which also are present in the human brain—that govern both kinds of responses.

Results of the study were published online in *Cell*, on October 18, by Vaishnav Krishnan, Ming-Hu Han, Ph.D, Eric J. Nestler, MD, Ph.D, and colleagues from the University of Texas (UT) Southwestern Medical Center, Harvard University, and Cornell University.

Vulnerability was measured through behaviors such as social withdrawal after stress was induced in mice by putting them in cages with bigger, more aggressive mice. Even a month after the encounter, some mice were still avoiding social interactions with other mice—an indication that stress had overwhelmed them—but most adapted and continued to interact, giving researchers the opportunity to examine the biological underpinnings of the protective adaptations.

"We now know that the mammalian brain can launch molecular machinery that promotes resilience to stress, and we know what several major components are. This is an excellent indicator that there are similar mechanisms in the human brain," said NIMH Director Thomas R. Insel, MD.

Looking at a specific part of the brain, the researchers found differences in the rate of impulse-firing by cells that make the chemical messenger dopamine. Vulnerable mice had excessive rates of impulse-firing during stressful situations. But adaptive mice maintained normal rates of firing because of a protective mechanism—a boost in activity of channels that allow the mineral potassium to flow into the cells, dampening their firing rates.

Higher rates of impulse-firing in the vulnerable mice led to more activity of a protein called brain-derived neurotrophic factor (BDNF), which had been linked to vulnerability in previous studies by the same researchers. With their comparatively lower rates of impulse-firing, the resistant mice did not have this increase in BDNF activity, another factor that contributed to resistance.

The scientists found that these mechanisms occurred in the reward area of the brain, which promotes repetition of acts that ensure survival. The areas involved were the VTA (ventral tegmental area) and the NAc (nucleus accumbens).

In a series of experiments, the scientists extended their findings to provide a progressively larger picture of the vulnerability and resistance mechanisms. They used a variety of approaches to test the findings, strengthening their validity.

"The extensiveness and thoroughness of their research enabled these investigators to make a very strong case for their hypothesis," Insel said.

For example, the researchers showed that the excess BDNF protein in vulnerable mice originated in the VTA, rather than in the NAc. Chemical signals the protein sent from the VTA to the NAc played an essential role in making the mice vulnerable. Blocking the signals with experimental compounds turned vulnerable mice into resistant mice.

The scientists also conducted a genetic experiment which showed that, in resistant mice, many more genes in the VTA than in the NAc went into action in stressful situations, compared with vulnerable mice. Gene activity governs a host of biochemical events in the brain, and the results of this experiment suggest that genes in the VTA of resilient mice are working hard to offset mechanisms that promote vulnerability.

Another component of the study revealed that mice with a naturally occurring variation in part of the gene that produces the BDNF protein are resistant to stress. The variation results in lower production of BDNF, consistent with the finding that low BDNF activity promotes resilience.

The scientists also examined brain tissue of deceased people with a history of depression, and compared it with brain tissue of mice that showed vulnerability to stress. In both cases, the researchers found higher-than-average BDNF protein in the brain's reward areas, offering a potential biological explanation of the link between stress and depression.

"The fact that we could increase these animals' ability to adapt to stress by blocking BDNF and its signals means that it may be possible to develop compounds that improve resilience. This is a great opportunity to explore potential ways of increasing stress-resistance in people faced with situations that might otherwise result in posttraumatic stress disorder, for example," said Nestler.

"But it doesn't happen in a vacuum. Blocking BDNF at certain stages in the process could perturb other systems in negative ways. The key is to identify safe ways of enhancing this protective resilience machinery," Nestler added.

Section 4.4

Chronic Stress and Loneliness Affect Health

"Chronic Stress and Loneliness Affect Health," © 2015 Omnigraphics. Reviewed June 2018.

Since we, human beings, are a social species, forming and maintaining satisfying social relationships is vital to our physical and mental well-being. The lack of such relationships can lead to loneliness, which is a much more complex psychiatric condition than simply "being alone." Studies have shown that chronic loneliness can take a toll on an individual's physical and mental health, compromising the immune system, impairing cognitive performance, and increasing the risk of depression, heart disease, and other conditions. In fact, research suggests that people who experience chronic loneliness have a 45 percent higher risk of early death, while those with strong social connections have a 50 percent lower risk of dying over any given period of time.

Loneliness and Stress

Everyone feels lonely at some point in their lives. Some psychologists claim that people first experience loneliness in infancy, when they are left alone by their parents. Transient loneliness, which is caused by environmental factors like moving to a new city, starting at a new school, or ending a romantic relationship, is a temporary situation that is generally relieved over time. Chronic loneliness, on the other hand, can occur independently of environmental factors and persist over long periods of time. This type of loneliness can affect people even in the absence of social isolation.

Loneliness and stress are closely related, with each condition often contributing to the other. Loneliness can be a significant stressor. Since social relationships are fundamental to human existence, a strain or break in social relationships can rank among the most stressful experiences in life. In addition, healthy and varied social relationships serve as a protective mechanism that increases stress resistance, as people rely on the comforting support of family and friends to help them cope with stressful situations.

As a result of these factors, lonely people experience higher levels of perceived stress as compared to nonlonely people when exposed to the same types of stressors. People who lack social connections tend to react more strongly to the stressors of daily life, which may lead to the development of chronic stress and all of the health problems associated with it.

Health Consequences of Loneliness

Studies have shown that loneliness initiates a series of physiological processes that can negatively affect people's health and well-being. Overwhelming and consistent feelings of loneliness often result in low self-worth, depression, anxiety, irritability, and suicidal behavior. Loneliness can also contribute to the development of such conditions as insomnia, obesity, and substance abuse.

By stimulating the stress response, long-term, persistent loneliness can also lead to a variety of stress-related health issues, including hypertension, cardiovascular disease, and immune system dysfunction. Studies have also shown that loneliness is one of the major causes of motor decline in old age. Elderly people who are lonely are also more likely to experience memory loss and cognitive decline, leading to an increased risk of developing clinical dementia and Alzheimer disease (AD).

Managing Loneliness

Many aspects of modern life—such as technology replacing face-to-face interaction—leave people feeling disconnected, which has made loneliness a growing public health concern. On the plus side, though, loneliness is a treatable condition. Experts have developed methods of behavioral training to help lonely people improve their capacity to socialize. They have also come up with strategies to help people control their expectations and view their situations differently, so that they no longer perceive being alone as stressful.

One of the first steps in managing loneliness involves improving social skills to help people maintain existing relationships or form new ones. For people who experience loneliness due to changing circumstances, such as the loss of a loved one, treatment might include various means of enhancing social support. Individuals can take steps to relieve their own feelings of loneliness by engaging in activities to keep busy, joining groups that share a common interest, volunteering to help others, and sharing feelings or discussing problems with other people.

References

1. Derbyshire, David. "Loneliness Is a Killer," *Daily Mail*, July 28, 2010.
2. Tiwari, Sarvada Chandra. "Loneliness: A Disease?" *Indian Journal of Psychiatry* 55(4), October-December 2013, p. 320.

Section 4.5

Stress and Fatigue

"Stress and Fatigue,"
© 2018 Omnigraphics. Reviewed June 2018.

Stress can affect your body, your emotions, and your behavior. It increases your risk of developing depression, anxiety, substance abuse, and a range of other mental disorders. Fatigue is a feeling of tiredness caused by lack of energy. Fatigue can also cause musculoskeletal disorders as a result of stress.

Fatigue impairs the ability to deal with stressful situations. Changes in circadian rhythm as a result of inadequate sleep cause fatigue and stress. Circadian rhythm changes also cause a series of internal responses that affect both mental and physical health. A familiar example of an external factor that causes fatigue and stress is the experience of jet lag.

Factors That Cause Stress

The aftermath of a traumatic event can cause anxiety, depression, or posttraumatic stress disorder (PTSD), resulting in fatigue that can impair your decision-making skills. The factors that cause stress include:

- Sleep deprivation
- Improper management of time
- Frequent rotating shifts
- Financial problems
- Family and health issues
- Overtime work

Factors That Cause Fatigue

It is important to visit your doctor if you're continually feeling tired. There are a number of factors that may cause fatigue. These include:

- Medicines such as antidepressants, antihistamines, and medicines for nausea and pain
- The aftereffects of medical treatments such as chemotherapy and radiation

- Drinking too much alcohol or too many caffeinated drinks
- Recovering from a major surgery
- Anxiety, stress, or depression
- Staying up too late
- Pregnancy

How Stress and Fatigue Affect Health

The following conditions affect mental health:

- Inability to adapt to certain situations
- Increase in anxiety or depression
- A heightened sense of threat
- Increase in mood swings

Fatigue can also affect physical health:

- The weakening of the cardiovascular system (e.g., causing heart disease, arteriosclerosis, or congestive heart failure)
- Heightened alert response and restlessness
- Gastrointestinal problems (e.g., loss of appetite, abdominal distress, or ulcers)
- Improper hand-eye coordination
- Weight gain

Preventing Stress and Fatigue

Healthy food and regular exercise can help prevent stress and fatigue. Lifestyle changes, yoga, meditation, and relaxation exercises can help reduce feelings of isolation and loneliness. Stress and fatigue can be prevented or alleviated by taking the following actions:

- Consider making changes at your workplace or home in order to reduce your stress level.
- Schedule the most important tasks of each day for times when you are more productive.
- Voice your concerns with your family at home or with the authority concerned at your workplace.

- Exercise regularly and eat a healthy diet.
- Consider meditation and yoga to experience the benefits of relaxation.
- Make sure you have enough free time to yourself every week.
- Avoid excessive drinking and smoking.

References

1. "Officer Work Hours, Stress and Fatigue," National Institute of Justice (NIJ), August 13, 2012.
2. "Why Am I Tired All the Time?" National Health Services (NHS), March 9, 2018.
3. "Fatigue," MedlinePlus, National Institutes of Health (NIH), April 2, 2018.
4. "Work-Related Stress," U.S. Department of Health and Human Services (HHS), June 2012.

Section 4.6

Media Coverage Linked to Stress

This section includes text excerpted from "Media Coverage of Traumatic Events," U.S. Department of Veterans Affairs (VA), September 2, 2015.

Media Coverage of Traumatic Events

Many people find it hard to resist news of traumatic events, such as disasters and terrorist attacks. As awful as it is to watch and read about, many still cannot turn away. Why is this kind of news so hard to resist? Some say it is because people are trying to inform themselves to be prepared in case of future disaster or attacks. Others say that people are watching and reading news in an effort to understand and process the event. Still, others say the media is trying to draw you in with exciting images almost like those from an action movie. Whatever the reason, to understand the effects that this type of news exposure may have.

Watching Traumatic News Is Related to Stress

Research tells us there is a link between watching news of traumatic events, such as terrorist attacks, and stress symptoms. It could be that watching television of the event makes people worse. It could also be that people who have more severe stress reactions are the ones who choose to watch more television about the event. Here are some examples that show the link:

- Research after the September 11, 2001, terrorist attacks found that in the first few days, adults watched an average of eight hours of television related to the attacks. Children watched an average of three hours of television related to the attacks. Older teens watched more than younger children. In both children and adults, those who watched the most coverage had more stress symptoms than those who watched less.
- The Oklahoma City bombing was also widely covered in the news. In adults, watching bomb-related news did not relate to increased posttraumatic stress disorder (PTSD) symptoms. On the other hand, children who watched more bomb-related news did have more PTSD symptoms. Of note, for most Oklahoma school children in the weeks after the bombing, the bulk of their television viewing was bomb-related. Links were seen between PTSD symptoms and bomb-related television for children who did and did not lose a close family member in the bombing.
- In Israel, those who watched television clips of terrorism reported feeling more anxiety than those who watched clips that were not related to terrorism.
- Adults who lost close friends or family in the Mount St. Helens tragedy said that the news coverage made it harder for them to recover. Adults who only lost property said that the news neither hurt nor helped them.
- Children from Kuwait had increased PTSD symptoms after viewing gruesome televised images of violence and death related to the Gulf War.

It is still unclear why this relationship exists. Media might both hurt and help those who experience trauma. Having news media present is sometimes a burden on family members. For example, the media may show their personal grief on television. Also, watching news about a trauma may make the victims feel even more helpless. It may fix even more firmly in their minds the images of death and damage.

Positive Role of the Media

Although there may be negative effects, clearly the media plays a vital role after a disaster. The media provides needed information and alerts. Media outlets can direct the public to services for victims and their families. They are a resource for the community. They can also be a source of hope. In some ways, being involved with the media might give survivors a sense of power. This could help offset their feeling helpless after the trauma.

Recommendations about Viewing

You may want to limit the amount and type of news you are viewing if you:

- Feel anxious or stressed after watching a news program
- Cannot turn off the television
- Cannot take part in relaxing or fun activities
- Have trouble sleeping

Some useful tips include:

- Do not watch the news just before bed
- Read newspapers or magazines rather than watching television
- Inform yourself by talking to other people about the attack

Children and Media Exposure

The research with children shows even more clearly that watching too much trauma-related television can be harmful. Here are some tips for dealing with children and media exposure:

- **Be aware** that children in the household may be exposed to traumatic images. It is common for a television to be on for several hours a day in an American household. Adults should be aware of how much news a child is viewing. This may occur even if no adult has decided that the child can watch trauma-related news.

- **Parents should talk with the child** about what they are seeing on the news. For example, children who watched news about the September 11th attacks may have seen the first plane crash into the building over and over again. These children may have needed it explained to them that they were seeing one single crash that happened on one day, not multiple crashes.
- **Put the news into context.** Explain that:
  - There are many good people who will do their best to keep them safe if something bad happens. Focus on the firemen and rescue teams and not just on the attack.
  - The news often tells us bad things that happen in the world. Most of the time, though, the country is safe. Most people who fly in airplanes land safely on the ground and have no problems at all.
- **Invite children to talk.** Above all, parents need to allow and even invite children to ask questions. Children may have misplaced fears after watching a news report. This may be because they did not understand something. If the child shares those fears or asks questions, parents can help explain and comfort. Parents can tell the child that a lot of people are working hard to make things safer for the future.
- **Limit the child's news viewing.** Some parents do not allow young children to watch the news at all. If news viewing is allowed, experts suggest that parents watch the news with their children. Also, if a child seems to be watching too much trauma-related news, the parent can direct the child to other more positive activities.

Sadly, it is true that most reported news is bad news. We don't hear about the planes that land safely every day. Children need to be reminded that what they see on the news does not reflect the way things are.

Chapter 5

Childhood Stress

Stress is an inevitable part of life. Human beings experience stress early, even before they are born. A certain amount of stress is normal and necessary for survival. Stress helps children develop the skills they need to cope with and adapt to new and potentially threatening situations throughout life. Support from parents and/or other concerned caregivers is necessary for children to learn how to respond to stress in a physically and emotionally healthy manner.

The beneficial aspects of stress diminish when it is severe enough to overwhelm a child's ability to cope effectively. Intensive and prolonged stress can lead to a variety of short- and long-term negative health effects. It can disrupt early brain development and compromise functioning of the nervous and immune systems. In addition, childhood stress can lead to health problems later in life including alcoholism, depression, eating disorders, heart disease, cancer, and other chronic diseases. The purpose of this section is to highlight the research on childhood stress and its implications for adult health and well-being. Of particular interest is the stress caused by child abuse, neglect, and repeated exposure to intimate partner violence (IPV).

This chapter includes text excerpted from "The Effects of Childhood Stress on Health across the Lifespan," Centers for Disease Control and Prevention (CDC), 2008. Reviewed June 2018.

Types of Stress

Following are descriptions of the three types of stress that The National Scientific Council on the Developing Child (NSCDC) has identified based on available research:

Positive stress results from adverse experiences that are short-lived. Children may encounter positive stress when they attend a new daycare, get a shot, meet new people, or have a toy taken away from them. This type of stress causes minor physiological changes including an increase in heart rate and changes in hormone levels. With the support of caring adults, children can learn how to manage and overcome positive stress. This type of stress is considered normal and coping with it is an important part of the development process.

Tolerable stress refers to adverse experiences that are more intense but still relatively short-lived. Examples include the death of a loved one, a natural disaster, a frightening accident, and family disruptions such as separation or divorce. If a child has the support of a caring adult, tolerable stress can usually be overcome. In many cases, tolerable stress can become positive stress and benefit the child developmentally. However, if the child lacks adequate support, tolerable stress can become toxic and lead to long-term negative health effects.

Toxic stress results from intense adverse experiences that may be sustained over a long period of time—weeks, months, or even years. An example of toxic stress is child maltreatment, which includes abuse and neglect. Children are unable to effectively manage this type of stress by themselves. As a result, the stress response system gets activated for a prolonged amount of time. This can lead to permanent changes in the development of the brain. The negative effects of toxic stress can be lessened with the support of caring adults. Appropriate support and intervention can help in returning the stress response system back to its normal baseline.

The Effects of Toxic Stress on Brain Development in Early Childhood

The ability to manage stress is controlled by brain circuits and hormone systems that are activated early in life. When a child feels threatened, hormones are released and they circulate throughout the body. Prolonged exposure to stress hormones can impact the brain and impair functioning in a variety of ways.

- Toxic stress can impair the connection of brain circuits and, in the extreme, result in the development of a smaller brain.

- Brain circuits are especially vulnerable as they are developing during early childhood. Toxic stress can disrupt the development of these circuits. This can cause an individual to develop a low threshold for stress, thereby becoming overly reactive to adverse experiences throughout life.
- High levels of stress hormones, including cortisol, can suppress the body's immune response. This can leave an individual vulnerable to a variety of infections and chronic health problems.
- Sustained high levels of cortisol can damage the hippocampus, an area of the brain responsible for learning and memory. These cognitive deficits can continue into adulthood.

The NSCDC has been studying the effects of toxic stress on brain development.

The Effects of Toxic Stress on Adult Health and Well-Being

Research findings demonstrate that childhood stress can impact adult health. The Adverse Childhood Experiences (ACE) Study is particularly noteworthy because it demonstrates a link between specific:

1. Violence–related stressors, including child abuse, neglect, and repeated exposure to intimate partner violence
2. Risky behaviors and health problems in adulthood

The ACE Study

The ACE Study, a collaboration between the Centers for Disease Control and Prevention (CDC) and Kaiser Permanente's Health Appraisal Clinic in San Diego, uses a retrospective approach to examine the link between childhood stressors and adult health. Over 17,000 adults participated in the research, making it one of the largest studies of its kind. Each participant completed a questionnaire that asked for detailed information on their past history of abuse, neglect, and family dysfunction as well as their current behaviors and health status. Researchers were particularly interested in participants' exposure to the following ten ACE:

Abuse

- Emotional

- Physical
- Sexual

Neglect

- Emotional
- Physical

Household dysfunction

- Mother treated violently
- Household substance abuse
- Household mental illness
- Parental separation or divorce
- Incarcerated household member

The ACE Study findings have been published many times. The following are some of the general findings of the study:

- Childhood abuse, neglect, and exposure to other adverse experiences are common.
- Almost two-thirds of study participants reported at least one ACE, and more than one in five reported three or more.

The short- and long-term outcomes of ACE include a multitude of health and behavioral problems. As the number of ACE a person experiences increases, the risk for the following health outcomes also increases.

- Alcoholism and alcohol abuse
- Chronic obstructive pulmonary disease (COPD)
- Depression
- Fetal death
- Illicit drug use
- Ischemic heart disease (IHD)
- Liver disease
- Risk for intimate partner violence
- Multiple sexual partners

- Sexually transmitted diseases (STDs)
- Smoking
- Suicide attempts
- Unintended pregnancies

ACE are also related to risky health behaviors in childhood and adolescence, including pregnancies, suicide attempts, early initiation of smoking, sexual activity, and illicit drug use. As the number of ACE increases, the number of co-occurring health conditions increases.

Violence-Related ACE Study Findings

Findings from the ACE Study confirm what we already know—that too many people in the United States are exposed early on to violence and other childhood stressors. The study also provides strong evidence that being exposed to certain childhood experiences, including being subjected to abuse or neglect or witnessing intimate partner violence (IPV), can lead to a wide array of negative behaviors and poor health outcomes. In addition, the ACE Study has found associations between experiencing ACE and two violent outcomes: suicide attempts and the risk of perpetrating or experiencing IPV.

The following section will highlight some of the ACE Study findings relevant to violence. Some findings relate to participants' past history of abuse, neglect, and IPV exposure, while others involve the link between ACE and adult behaviors and health status.

Child Maltreatment and Its Impact on Health and Behavior

- 25 percent of women and 16 percent of men reported experiencing child sexual abuse.
- Participants who were sexually abused as children were more likely to experience multiple other ACE.
- The ACE score increased as the child sexual abuse severity, duration, and frequency increased and the age at first occurrence decreased.
- Women and men who experienced child sexual abuse were more than twice as likely to report suicide attempts.

- A strong relationship was found between frequent physical abuse, sexual abuse, and witnessing of IPV as a child and a male's risk of involvement with a teenage pregnancy.
- Women who reported experiencing four or more types of abuse during their childhood were 1.5 times more likely to have an unintended pregnancy at or before the age of twenty.
- Men and women who reported being sexually abused were more at risk of marrying an alcoholic and having current marital problems.

Witnessing Intimate Partner Violence (IPV) as a Child and Its Impact on Health and Behavior

- Study participants who witnessed IPV were two to six times more likely to experience another ACE.
- As the frequency of witnessing IPV increased, the chance of reported alcoholism, illicit drug use, IV drug use, and depression also increased.
- Exposure to physical abuse, sexual abuse, and IPV in childhood resulted in women being 3.5 times more likely to report IPV victimization.
- Exposure to physical abuse, sexual abuse, and IPV in childhood resulted in men being 3.8 times more likely to report IPV perpetration.

The Link between ACE and Suicide Attempts

- 3.8 percent of study participants reported having attempted suicide at least once.
- Experiencing one ACE increased the risk of attempted suicide two to five times.
- As the ACE score increased so did the likelihood of attempting suicide.
- The relationship between ACE and the risk of attempted suicide appears to be influenced by alcoholism, depression, and illicit drug use.

ACE and Associated Health Behaviors

Associations were found between ACE and many negative health behaviors. A partial list of behaviors is included below.

- Participants with higher ACE scores were at greater risk of alcoholism.
- Those with higher ACE scores were more likely to marry an alcoholic.
- Study participants with higher ACE scores were more likely to initiate drug use and experience addiction.
- Those with higher ACE scores were more likely to have 30 or more sexual partners, engage in sexual intercourse earlier, and feel more at risk of contracting acquired immunodeficiency syndrome (AIDS).
- Higher ACE scores in participants were linked to a higher probability of both lifetime and recent depressive disorders.

Implications for Child Maltreatment Prevention

Child maltreatment is one example of toxic stress. CDC works to stop maltreatment, including abuse and neglect, before it initially occurs. Prevention of child maltreatment requires understanding the circumstances and factors that cause it. CDC uses a four-level social ecological model to better understand potential strategies for prevention. This model considers the complex interplay between individual, relationship, community, and societal factors.

Individual Level Strategies

Parent Education

Educational programs that occur in group settings are used to reduce the risk factors and enhance the protective factors that are associated with the perpetration of child maltreatment. Often, these programs contain multiple components that include training on parenting topics (e.g., discipline), moderated discussions with the children, and facilitated parent-child interactions. This model provides parents with new skills and gives them an opportunity to apply the skills in a safe environment. There is some scientific research showing that programs of this type are effective.

The evidence base continues to grow. Some of these parent education programs occur in clinical settings. For example, a hospital-based program has been developed to teach new parents about the dangers of violently shaking an infant. This program was found to reduce the rates of abusive head trauma to infants.

Child Education

Most schools in the United States provide curricula to help children avoid or report abuse. Research has shown that this method is effective in teaching children about safety and providing them with skills that may reduce their risk of abuse. However, the research has also shown that children are less likely to believe they are at risk from parents or caregivers, the same people who are most likely to abuse them. Additional information is needed about how these skills transfer in abusive situations where the perpetrator is someone the child knows well and trusts.

Screening and Treatment

The early identification and treatment of toxic stress, including child maltreatment, can lessen the associated long-term negative health and behavioral outcomes. Daycare providers, teachers, and other adults who interact frequently with children should have sufficient knowledge and skills to identify and care for children who have been exposed to traumatic childhood experiences. They should be familiar with support services to meet the needs of children whose problems cannot be adequately addressed by front-line staff. Social service agencies that are responsible for investigating suspected cases of abuse and neglect should include a thorough assessment of a child's developmental status. This assessment should include the measurement of cognitive, linguistic, emotional, and social competence. Individuals who have experienced ACE should receive help. This may involve psychotherapy, theater workshops, movement therapy, hypnotherapy, expressive writing, diary programs, or some combination.

Relationship Level Strategies

Parent-Child Centers

Parent training and education is often delivered within comprehensive parent-child centers. These centers provide a stable learning environment in which parents and their children can interact. Studies have found that families participating in these centers have lower levels of child maltreatment.

Home Visitation

This type of program involves trained personnel visiting families in their homes to deliver training, education, and support. The trained personnel can be nurses, social workers, paraprofessionals, or peers. Home visits often begin before birth and continue past a child's second birthday. These programs include training on prenatal and infant care as well as child development. They also enhance problem-solving skills, assist with educational and work opportunities, and provide referrals to community services. A systematic review conducted by the nonfederal Community Preventive Services Task Force (CPSTF) found that early childhood home visitation results in a 40 percent reduction in episodes of abuse and neglect. Not all home visitation programs were found to be equally effective. Those deemed to be successful in preventing child maltreatment were specifically aimed at high-risk families, lasted two years or longer, and were conducted by professionals (as opposed to trained paraprofessionals).

Community, Organizational, and Social Level Strategies

Public Awareness Campaigns

Public awareness campaigns have long been used as a prevention strategy for a variety of health issues, including child maltreatment. These campaigns include a variety of public service announcements involving television, radio, the Internet, print media, and billboards. Research has shown that these campaigns are effective in raising awareness about the existence of child maltreatment and its devastating impact on victims. However, there is not yet conclusive evidence to show that public awareness campaigns change the attitudes and behaviors of parents. Research in this area is ongoing.

Using This Information

Many violence prevention practitioners are unaware of the research on toxic stress and ACEs. The following suggestions are meant to help CDC's partners make the case that stopping violence before it occurs can reduce risky behaviors, prevent chronic disease, and foster adult health.

1. **Share knowledge**

   There are many ways you can share the research with your partners and constituents:

   - Incorporate the research into presentations for professional and lay audiences.
   - Invite a Subject Matter Expert (SME) to give a conference keynote address, participate in Grand Rounds, or provide staff training.
   - Work with reporters to highlight the issue on the Internet, television, radio or in print media, including newspapers and magazines.
   - Reference the research in scholarly journal articles.
   - Use the data in a mayoral or gubernatorial proclamation to prevent child maltreatment or intimate partner violence.
   - Work with local colleges and universities to incorporate the research into the curricula of psychology, nursing, medicine, social work, and public health programs.

2. **Collect data**

   Survey instruments are available online. These can be used to assess the prevalence of ACE in populations that are of interest to you. The data can be incorporated into any of the strategies mentioned in "Share Knowledge."

3. **Secure additional resources**

   The data can be incorporated into grant applications or used when other opportunities to secure additional resources become available. Several CDC partners have used the data to demonstrate that violence prevention leads to overall health and well-being.

Chapter 6

Stress and Aging

Stress and Adversity in Aging

All humans are destined to experience adversities throughout their lives that are likely to impact their health and quality of life. However, trajectories of health and function in later life can vary significantly depending on the individual. Typical stressors experienced in the context of aging include chronic illnesses, cognitive impairment, psychosocial stress of caregiving or personal losses of people, independence, and financial. However, individuals react very differently to these adversities: some succumb to depression and early death as a result of these adversities, and some continue to lead a life of personal fulfillment despite those restraints. Models of chronic stress exposure generated mental illness in older adults have been studied in several populations such as the chronically medically ill, those with spousal bereavement, and family dementia caregivers that simply support the stress-health relationships between stress, coping and mental illnesses. Some questions one may consider: What factors define increased risk for disease and mortality and what protective factors lead to successful aging?

This chapter includes text excerpted from "Stress, Inflammation, and Aging," U.S. National Library of Medicine (NLM), September 2012. Reviewed June 2018.

Physiological Mechanisms of Stress Response with Aging

Physiological aging can modify responsivity to stress because of reduced resilience. Individual differences in the aging process can be conceptualized as an accumulation of wear and tear caused by daily experiences and major life stressors that interact with genetic constitution and predisposing early life experiences. The adaptive physiological response to acute stress involves a process, initially referred to as allostasis by Sterling and Eyer, in which the internal milieu varies to meet perceived and anticipated demand. McEwen BS extended this definition to include the concept of a set point that changes because of the process of maintaining homeostasis. The neuroendocrine system, autonomic nervous system, and immune system are mediators of adaptation to challenges of daily life, referred to as allostasis, meaning "maintaining stability through change." Aging process can undermine the process of maintaining homeostasis by invoking changes in the endocrine, autonomic, and immune systems.

Acute stress is known to negatively affect neuroendocrine function via hypothalamic-pituitary-adrenal (HPA) axis. When stimulated this feedback loop results in the secretion sustained during chronic stress of glucocorticoids such as cortisol, enabling, the organism to perform with a heightened sense of alertness. The HPA response to stress is a basic adaptive mechanism in mammals, although an adaptive stress response is essential to survival, sustained elevated levels of glucocorticoids can present a serious health risk including hypertension and suppression of anabolic processes, or hippocampal atrophy. Hippocampal volume loss is well documented in normal and pathological aging. HPA dysregulation has been implicated in several late-life disorders including anxiety, major depression and cognitive impairment and decline. Impaired hippocampal and medial temporal lobe function are implicated in stress-related disorders such as late-life depression and anxiety. McEwen BS suggested that circulating catecholamines constitute another key component of allostasis and can have synergistic and oppositional effects on the actions of glucocorticoids and arousal.

Stress-Related Inflammation

Stress-related inflammation has been implicated in insomnia, late-life depression, anxiety, cognitive decline, and Alzheimer disease (AD). Aging is accompanied by a 2- to 4-fold increase in plasma/serum levels of inflammatory mediators, such as cytokines and acute phase proteins.

In addition, chronic inflammatory processes are implicated in diverse health outcomes associated with aging, such as atherosclerosis, insulin resistance, diabetes, and metabolic syndrome. Furthermore, there is some evidence that aging is associated with a dysregulated cytokine response following stimulation. Consistent with this research, inflammatory mediators are strong predictors of mortality independent of other known risk factors and comorbidity in elderly cohorts. For example, IL-6, a proinflammatory factor whose concentration generally increases in the blood with age, has been linked with AD, osteoporosis, rheumatoid arthritis (RA), cardiovascular disease (CVD), and some forms of cancer, and it is prospectively associated with general disability and mortality in large population-based studies. Anti-inflammatory cytokines interleukin-4 (IL-4) and interleukin-10 (IL-10) may actually confer protective role for the immune system, involving phagocytosis of dying neurons, processing of beta-amyloid and microglia that have been implicated in late-life neuropsychiatric disorders. These cytokines may be particularly important in conferring increased resilience to the inflammatory stress-response. However, prevalence of geriatric depression is higher among those with insomnia, medically ill patients in medical settings and in the long-term care. Additional stress-inducing circumstances of acute medical illness, insomnia, bereavement, or caregiver stress may also be associated with depression. Understanding biomarkers of stress and inflammation in the aging process can lead to the development of preventive and treatment interventions for later-life mood and cognitive disorders.

Sex Differences and Stress

Sex differences may be important in the effects of stress. There is a higher incidence of affective disorders in women with rates above puberty and below menopause approximately twice that of men. This difference appears to equalize or reverse after age 55. Among the strongest candidates for an important role in this gender difference are the gonadal steroids, chiefly estradiol. Alterations in estrogen levels appear to be clearly linked to perimenopausal mood disruptions that occur in approximately 10 percent of women who have not previously had any affective disturbance. Studies of early high-dose oral contraceptives had shown higher rates of depression in young women and female suicide attempts have been associated with higher estrogen phases of the menstrual cycle.

A possible hypothesis for the higher rate of disorders such as depression seen in postpubertal, premenopausal women is that a negative

SAYVILLE LIBRARY

stressful life-event or trauma may have greater impact or salience if it occurs during a high estradiol point in the menstrual cycle. If estrogen sensitizes certain vulnerable women to the impact of stressful life events this may place those women at higher risk for the development of these disorders, especially given genetic vulnerability. However, this could be expected to change after menopause, due to low levels of circulating estrogens. While there have been previous studies that have examined stress reactivity between the genders or in women following postmenopausal hormonal exposure, few investigators have focused on psychological and cognitive effects as results of the studies have generally focused on either physiological or endocrine responsiveness.

Results of studies of gonadal steroids on stress-related measures in animals suggest that estradiol may enhance stress reactivity as measured by HPA activity, prolactin secretion and corticotropin-releasing hormone (CRH) gene expression. Estradiol appears to also modulate a significant gender difference in stress-related differences in classical conditioning with stress enhancing classical conditioning in males but impairing it in females.

Cortisol and Aging

Interestingly estrogen effects on cognition may interact with stress hormones such as cortisol. Cortisol is the classic stress hormone and is reliably elevated in response to psychological and psychosocial stress. Levels rise with aging and are higher in older females than males. Elevated levels of cortisol in aging are associated with higher levels of psychosocial stress, poorer cognitive performance, and atrophy of memory-related structures in the brain such as the hippocampus. Elevations in the stress hormones may negate beneficial effects of estradiol on cognitive performance in normal aging and negatively affect levels and ratios of peptides known to be important in maintaining neuronal integrity and brain health, namely IGF-1 and the ratio of Aβ40/42. Whether normal or excess psychological stress in aging interacts with estradiol status to produce negative effects on cognitive function is unclear, although recent experimental studies suggest a direct interaction between stress hormones and the effects of sex steroids. In the face of acute psychosocial stress, the effects of exogenous estradiol in postmenopausal women may be negative on both mood and cognition; however, the interaction with chronic stress or mood disorders is less well defined. The effects of psychosocial stress and/or elevated cortisol on brain circuits necessary for cognitive performance and mood regulation remain to be more clearly defined.

Understanding how differing endogenous corticosteroid levels modify the effects of estradiol on brain activity and cognitive performance in normal and pathologic aging will require further research as well as understanding the interaction of life stress, medical comorbidity, and estradiol effects on brain function.

Chapter 7

Job Stress

The nature of work is changing at whirlwind speed. Perhaps now more than ever before, job stress poses a threat to the health of workers and, in turn, to the health organizations.

What Is Job Stress?

Job stress can be defined as the harmful physical and emotional responses that occur when the requirements of the job do not match the capabilities, resources, or needs of the worker. Job stress can lead to poor health and even injury. The concept of job stress is often confused with challenge, but these concepts are not the same. Challenge energizes us psychologically and physically, and it motivates us to learn new skills and master our jobs. When a challenge is met, we feel relaxed and satisfied. Thus, challenge is an important ingredient for healthy and productive work. The importance of challenge in our work lives is probably what people are referring to when they say "a little bit of stress is good for you."

What Are the Causes of Job Stress?

Nearly everyone agrees that job stress results from the interaction of the worker and the conditions of work. Views differ, however, on the importance of worker characteristics versus working conditions as the

---

This chapter includes text excerpted from "STRESS...at Work," Centers for Disease Control and Prevention (CDC), June 6, 2014. Reviewed June 2018.

primary cause of job stress. These differing viewpoints are important because they suggest different ways to prevent stress at work.

According to one school of thought, differences in individual characteristics such as personality and coping style are most important in predicting whether certain job conditions will result in stress-in other words, what is stressful for one person may not be a problem for someone else. This viewpoint leads to prevention strategies that focus on workers and ways to help them cope with demanding job conditions.

Although the importance of individual differences cannot be ignored, scientific evidence suggests that certain working conditions are stressful to most people. Such evidence argues for a greater emphasis on working conditions as the key source of job stress, and for job redesign as a primary prevention strategy.

In 1960, a Michigan court upheld a compensation claim by an automotive assembly line worker who had difficulty keeping up with the pressures of the production line. To avoid falling behind, he tried to work on several assemblies at the same time and often got parts mixed up. As a result, he was subjected to repeated criticism from the foreman. Eventually, he suffered a psychological breakdown.

By 1995, nearly one-half of the States allowed worker compensation claims for emotional disorders and disability due to stress on the job (note, however, that courts are reluctant to uphold claims for what can be considered ordinary working conditions or just hard work).

Job Stress and Health

Stress sets off an alarm in the brain, which responds by preparing the body for defensive action. The nervous system is aroused and hormones are released to sharpen the senses, quicken the pulse, deepen respiration, and tense the muscles. This response (sometimes called the fight or flight response) is important because it helps us defend against threatening situations. The response is preprogrammed biologically. Everyone responds in much the same way, regardless of whether the stressful situation is at work or home.

Short-lived or infrequent episodes of stress pose little risk. But when stressful situations go unresolved, the body is kept in a constant state of activation, which increases the rate of wear and tear to biological systems. Ultimately, fatigue or damage results, and the ability of the body to repair and defend itself can become seriously compromised. As a result, the risk of injury or disease escalates.

In the past 20 years, many studies have looked at the relationship between job stress and a variety of ailments. Mood and sleep disturbances, upset stomach and headache, and disturbed relationships with family and friends are examples of stress-related problems that are quick to develop and are commonly seen in these studies. These early signs of job stress are usually easy to recognize. But the effects of job stress on chronic diseases are more difficult to see because chronic diseases take a long time to develop and can be influenced by many factors other than stress. Nonetheless, evidence is rapidly accumulating to suggest that stress plays an important role in several types of chronic health problems—especially cardiovascular disease (CVD), musculoskeletal disorders (MSDs), and psychological disorders.

Stress, Health, and Productivity

Some employers assume that stressful working conditions are a necessary evil-that companies must turn up the pressure on workers and set aside health concerns to remain productive and profitable in the present economy. But research findings challenge this belief. Studies show that stressful working conditions are actually associated with increased absenteeism, tardiness, and intentions by workers to quit their jobs-all of which have a negative effect on the bottom line.

Studies of so-called healthy organizations suggest that policies benefiting worker health also benefit the bottom line. A healthy organization is defined as one that has low rates of illness, injury, and disability in its workforce and is also competitive in the marketplace. National Institute for Occupational Safety and Health (NIOSH) research has identified organizational characteristics associated with both healthy, low-stress work and high levels of productivity. Examples of these characteristics include the following:

- Recognition of employees for good work performance
- Opportunities for career development
- An organizational culture that values the individual worker
- Management actions that are consistent with organizational values

What Can Be Done about Job Stress?

Stress Management

Some companies provide stress management training and employee assistance program (EAP) to improve the ability of workers to cope with difficult work situations. Nearly one-half of large companies in the United States provide some type of stress management training for their workforces. Stress management programs teach workers about the nature and sources of stress, the effects of stress on health, and personal skills to reduce stress. For example; time management or relaxation exercises. (EAPs provide individual counseling for employees with both work and personal problems.) Stress management training may rapidly reduce stress symptoms such as anxiety and sleep disturbances; it also has the advantage of being inexpensive and easy to implement. However, stress management programs have two major disadvantages:

- The beneficial effects on stress symptoms are often short-lived.
- They often ignore important root causes of stress because they focus on the worker and not the environment.

Organizational Change

In contrast to stress management training and EAP programs, some companies try to reduce job stress by bringing in a consultant to recommend ways to improve working conditions. This approach is the most direct way to reduce stress at work. It involves the identification of stressful aspects of work (e.g., excessive workload, conflicting expectations) and the design of strategies to reduce or eliminate the identified stressors. The advantage of this approach is that it deals directly with the root causes of stress at work. However, managers are sometimes uncomfortable with this approach because it can involve changes in work routines or production schedules, or changes in the organizational structure.

As a general rule, actions to reduce job stress should give top priority to organizational change to improve working conditions. But even the most conscientious efforts to improve working conditions are unlikely to eliminate stress completely for all workers. For this reason, a combination of organizational change and stress management is often the most useful approach for preventing stress at work.

Preventing Job Stress—Getting Started

No standardized approaches or simple "how to" manuals exist for developing a stress prevention program. Program design and appropriate solutions will be influenced by several factors—the size and complexity of the organization, available resources, and especially the unique types of stress problems faced by the organization.

Although it is not possible to give a universal prescription for preventing stress at work, it is possible to offer guidelines on the process of stress prevention in organizations. In all situations, the process for stress prevention programs involves three distinct steps: problem identification, intervention, and evaluation. For this process to succeed, organizations need to be adequately prepared. At a minimum, preparation for a stress prevention program should include the following:

- Building general awareness about job stress (causes, costs, and control)
- Securing top management commitment and support for the program
- Incorporating employee input and involvement in all phases of the program
- Establishing the technical capacity to conduct the program (e.g., specialized training for in-house staff or use of job stress consultants)

Bringing workers or workers and managers together in a committee or problem-solving group may be an especially useful approach for developing a stress prevention program. Research has shown these participatory efforts to be effective in dealing with ergonomic problems in the workplace, partly because they capitalize on workers' firsthand knowledge of hazards encountered in their jobs. However, when forming such working groups, care must be taken to be sure that they are in compliance with current labor laws.*

**The National Labor Relations Act (NLRA) may limit the form and structure of employee involvement in worker-management teams or groups. Employers should seek legal assistance if they are unsure of their responsibilities or obligations under the NLRA.*

Steps toward Prevention

Low morale, health and job complaints, and employee turnover often provide the first signs of job stress. But sometimes there are no clues, especially if employees are fearful of losing their jobs. Lack of obvious or widespread signs is not a good reason to dismiss concerns about job stress or minimize the importance of a prevention program.

Step One: Identify the Problem

The best method to explore the scope and source of a suspected stress problem in an organization depends partly on the size of the organization and the available resources. Group discussions among managers, labor representatives, and employees can provide rich sources of information. Such discussions may be all that is needed to track down and remedy stress problems in a small company. In a larger organization, such discussions can be used to help design formal surveys for gathering input about stressful job conditions from large numbers of employees.

Regardless of the method used to collect data, information should be obtained about employee perceptions of their job conditions and perceived levels of stress, health, and satisfaction.

- Hold group discussions with employees
- Design an employee survey
- Measure employee perceptions of job conditions, stress, health, and satisfaction
- Collect objective data
- Analyze data to identify problem locations and stressful job conditions

The list of job conditions that may lead to stress and the warning signs and effects of stress provide good starting points for deciding what information to collect.

Regardless of the method used to collect data, information should be obtained about employee perceptions of their job conditions and perceived levels of stress, health, and satisfaction. The list of job conditions that may lead to stress and the warning signs and effects of stress provide good starting points for deciding what information to collect.

Objective measures such as absenteeism, illness and turnover rates, or performance problems can also be examined to gauge the presence and scope of job stress. However, these measures are only rough indicators of job stress—at best.

Data from discussions, surveys, and other sources should be summarized and analyzed to answer questions about the location of a stress problem and job conditions that may be responsible—for example, are problems present throughout the organization or confined to single departments or specific jobs?

Survey design, data analysis, and other aspects of a stress prevention program may require the help of experts from a local university or consulting firm. However, overall authority for the prevention program should remain in the organization.

Step Two: Design and Implement Interventions

Once the sources of stress at work have been identified and the scope of the problem is understood, the stage is set for design and implementation of an intervention strategy.

In small organizations, the informal discussions that helped identify stress problems may also produce fruitful ideas for prevention. In large organizations, a more formal process may be needed. Frequently, a team is asked to develop recommendations based on analysis of data from Step 1 and consultation with outside experts.

- Target source of stress for change
- Propose and prioritize intervention strategies
- Communicate planned interventions to employees
- Implement Interventions

Certain problems, such as a hostile work environment, may be pervasive in the organization and require company-wide interventions. Other problems such as excessive workload may exist only in some departments and thus require more narrow solutions such as redesign of the way a job is performed. Still, other problems may be specific to certain employees and resistant to any kind of organizational change, calling instead for stress management or employee assistance interventions. Some interventions might be implemented rapidly (e.g., improved communication, stress management training), but others may require additional time to put into place (e.g., redesign of a manufacturing process).

Step Three: Evaluate the Interventions

Evaluation is an essential step in the intervention process. Evaluation is necessary to determine whether the intervention is producing desired effects and whether changes in direction are needed.

Time frames for evaluating interventions should be established:

- Conduct both short- and long-term evaluations
- Measure employee perceptions of job conditions, stress, health, and satisfaction

- Measure employee perceptions of job conditions, stress, health, and satisfaction
- Include objective measures
- Refine the intervention strategy and return to Step One (Identify the Problem)

Interventions involving organizational change should receive both short- and long-term scrutiny. Short-term evaluations might be done quarterly to provide an early indication of program effectiveness or possible need for redirection. Many interventions produce initial effects that do not persist. Long-term evaluations are often conducted annually and are necessary to determine whether interventions produce lasting effects.

Evaluations should focus on the same types of information collected during the problem identification phase of the intervention, including information from employees about working conditions, levels of perceived stress, health problems, and satisfaction. Employee perceptions are usually the most sensitive measure of stressful working conditions and often provide the first indication of intervention effectiveness. Adding objective measures such as absenteeism and healthcare costs may also be useful. However, the effects of job stress interventions on such measures tend to be less clear-cut and can take a long time to appear. The job stress prevention process does not end with evaluation. Rather, job stress prevention should be seen as a continuous process that uses evaluation data to refine or redirect the intervention strategy.

Part Two

How Stress Affects the Body

Chapter 8

Alzheimer Disease

Chapter Contents

Section 8.1

What Is Alzheimer Disease?

This section includes text excerpted from "Alzheimer's Disease Fact Sheet," National Institute on Aging (NIA), National Institutes of Health (NIH), August 17, 2016.

Alzheimer disease (AD) is an irreversible, progressive brain disorder that slowly destroys memory and thinking skills, and eventually the ability to carry out the simplest tasks. In most people with Alzheimer, symptoms first appear in their mid-60s. Estimates vary, but experts suggest that more than 5 million Americans may have Alzheimer.

AD is ranked as the sixth leading cause of death in the United States, but estimates indicate that the disorder may rank third, just behind heart disease and cancer, as a cause of death for older people. Alzheimer is the most common cause of dementia among older adults. Dementia is the loss of cognitive functioning—thinking, remembering, and reasoning—and behavioral abilities to such an extent that it interferes with a person's daily life and activities. Dementia ranges in severity from the mildest stage, when it is just beginning to affect a person's functioning, to the most severe stage, when the person must depend completely on others for basic activities of daily living.

The causes of dementia can vary, depending on the types of brain changes that may be taking place. Other dementias include Lewy body dementia (LBD), frontotemporal disorders, and vascular dementia. It is common for people to have mixed dementia—a combination of two or more disorders, at least one of which is dementia. For example, some people have both AD and vascular dementia.

AD is named after Dr. Alois Alzheimer. In 1906, Dr. Alzheimer noticed changes in the brain tissue of a woman who had died of an unusual mental illness. Her symptoms included memory loss, language problems, and unpredictable behavior. After she died, he examined her brain and found many abnormal clumps (now called amyloid plaques) and tangled bundles of fibers (now called neurofibrillary, or tau, tangles).

These plaques and tangles in the brain are still considered some of the main features of AD. Another feature is the loss of connections between nerve cells (neurons) in the brain. Neurons transmit messages between different parts of the brain, and from the brain to muscles and organs in the body.

Changes in the Brain

Scientists continue to unravel the complex brain changes involved in the onset and progression of AD. It seems likely that damage to the brain starts a decade or more before memory and other cognitive problems appear. During this preclinical stage of AD, people seem to be symptom-free, but toxic changes are taking place in the brain. Abnormal deposits of proteins form amyloid plaques and tau tangles throughout the brain, and once-healthy neurons stop functioning, lose connections with other neurons, and die.

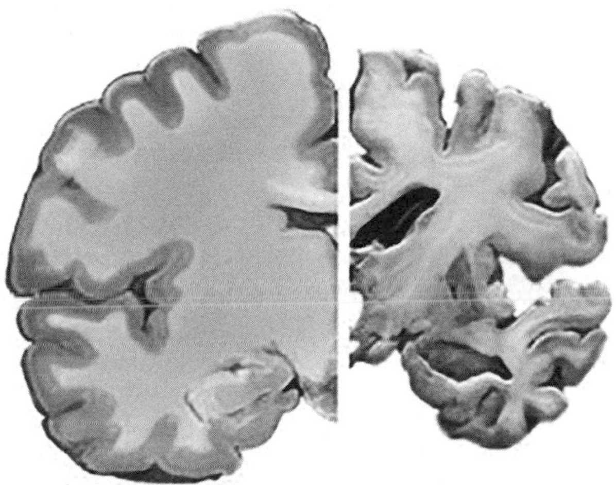

Figure 8.1. *Healthy Brain versus Severe Alzheimer*

The damage initially appears to take place in the hippocampus, the part of the brain essential in forming memories. As more neurons die, additional parts of the brain are affected, and they begin to shrink. By the final stage of Alzheimer, the damage is widespread, and brain tissue has shrunk significantly.

Signs and Symptoms of Alzheimer Disease (AD)

Memory problems are typically one of the first signs of cognitive impairment related to AD. Some people with memory problems have a condition called mild cognitive impairment (MCI). In MCI, people have more memory problems than normal for their age, but their symptoms do not interfere with their everyday lives. Movement difficulties and problems with the sense of smell have also been linked to MCI. Older people with MCI are at greater risk for developing

Alzheimer, but not all of them do. Some may even go back to normal cognition.

The first symptoms of Alzheimer vary from person to person. For many, the decline in nonmemory aspects of cognition, such as word-finding, vision/spatial issues, and impaired reasoning or judgment, may signal the very early stages of AD. Researchers are studying biomarkers (biological signs of disease found in brain images, cerebrospinal fluid, and blood) to see if they can detect early changes in the brains of people with MCI and in cognitively normal people who may be at greater risk for Alzheimer. Studies indicate that such early detection may be possible, but more research is needed before these techniques can be relied upon to diagnose Alzheimer disease in everyday medical practice.

Mild Alzheimer Disease (AD)

As AD progresses, people experience greater memory loss and other cognitive difficulties. Problems can include wandering and getting lost, trouble handling money and paying bills, repeating questions, taking longer to complete normal daily tasks, and personality and behavior changes. People are often diagnosed in this stage.

Moderate Alzheimer Disease (AD)

In this stage, damage occurs in areas of the brain that control language, reasoning, sensory processing, and conscious thought. Memory loss and confusion grow worse, and people begin to have problems recognizing family and friends. They may be unable to learn new things, carry out multistep tasks such as getting dressed, or cope with new situations. In addition, people at this stage may have hallucinations, delusions, and paranoia and may behave impulsively.

Severe Alzheimer Disease (AD)

Ultimately, plaques and tangles spread throughout the brain, and brain tissue shrinks significantly. People with severe Alzheimer cannot communicate and are completely dependent on others for their care. Near the end, the person may be in bed most or all of the time as the body shuts down.

Causes of Alzheimer Disease (AD)

Scientists don't yet fully understand what causes AD in most people. There is a genetic component to some cases of early-onset AD. Late-onset Alzheimer arises from a complex series of brain changes that occur over decades. The causes probably include a combination of genetic, environmental, and lifestyle factors. The importance of any one of these factors in increasing or decreasing the risk of developing Alzheimer may differ from person to person.

Diagnosis of Alzheimer Disease (AD)

Doctors use several methods and tools to help determine whether a person who is having memory problems has “possible Alzheimer dementia” (dementia may be due to another cause) or “probable Alzheimer dementia” (no other cause for dementia can be found).

To diagnose Alzheimer, doctors may:

- Ask the person and a family member or friend questions about overall health, past medical problems, ability to carry out daily activities, and changes in behavior and personality.
- Conduct tests of memory, problem-solving, attention, counting, and language.
- Carry out standard medical tests, such as blood and urine tests, to identify other possible causes of the problem.
- Perform brain scans, such as computed tomography (CT), magnetic resonance imaging (MRI), or positron emission tomography (PET), to rule out other possible causes for symptoms.
- These tests may be repeated to give doctors information about how the person’s memory and other cognitive functions are changing over time.

AD can be *definitely* diagnosed only after death, by linking clinical measures with an examination of brain tissue in an autopsy. People with memory and thinking concerns should talk to their doctor to find out whether their symptoms are due to Alzheimer or another cause, such as stroke, tumor, Parkinson disease (PD), sleep disturbances, side effects of medication, an infection, or a non-Alzheimer dementia. Some of these conditions may be treatable and possibly reversible.

If the diagnosis is Alzheimer, beginning treatment early in the disease process may help preserve daily functioning for some time, even though the underlying disease process cannot be stopped or reversed. An early diagnosis also helps families plan for the future. They can take care of financial and legal matters, address potential safety issues, learn about living arrangements, and develop support networks. In addition, an early diagnosis gives people greater opportunities to participate in clinical trials that are testing possible new treatments for AD or other research studies.

Treatment of Alzheimer Disease (AD)

AD is complex, and it is unlikely that any one drug or other intervention can successfully treat it. Current approaches focus on helping people maintain mental function, manage behavioral symptoms, and slow down certain problems, such as memory loss. Researchers hope to develop therapies targeting specific genetic, molecular, and cellular mechanisms so that the actual underlying cause of the disease can be stopped or prevented.

Maintaining Mental Function

Several medications are approved by the U.S. Food and Drug Administration (FDA) to treat symptoms of Alzheimer. Donepezil (Aricept®), rivastigmine (Exelon®), and galantamine (Razadyne®) are used to treat mild to moderate Alzheimer (donepezil can be used for severe Alzheimer as well). Memantine (Namenda®) is used to treat moderate to severe Alzheimer. These drugs work by regulating neurotransmitters, the chemicals that transmit messages between neurons. They may help reduce symptoms and help with certain behavioral problems. However, these drugs don't change the underlying disease process. They are effective for some but not all people, and may help only for a limited time. The FDA has also approved Aricept® and Namzaric®, a combination of Namenda® and Aricept®, for the treatment of moderate to severe AD.

Managing Behavior

Common behavioral symptoms of Alzheimer include sleeplessness, wandering, agitation, anxiety, and aggression. Scientists are learning why these symptoms occur and are studying new treatments—drug and nondrug—to manage them. Research has shown that treating behavioral symptoms can make people with Alzheimer more comfortable and makes things easier for caregivers.

Looking for New Treatments

AD research has developed to a point where scientists can look beyond treating symptoms to think about addressing underlying disease processes. In ongoing clinical trials, scientists are developing and testing several possible interventions, including immunization therapy, drug therapies, cognitive training, physical activity, and treatments used for cardiovascular disease and diabetes.

Support for Families and Caregivers

Caring for a person with AD can have high physical, emotional, and financial costs. The demands of day-to-day care, changes in family roles, and decisions about placement in a care facility can be difficult. There are several evidence-based approaches and programs that can help, and researchers are continuing to look for new and better ways to support caregivers.

Becoming well-informed about the disease is one important long-term strategy. Programs that teach families about the various stages of Alzheimer and about ways to deal with difficult behaviors and other caregiving challenges can help.

Good coping skills, a strong support network, and respite care are other ways that help caregivers handle the stress of caring for a loved one with AD. For example, staying physically active provides physical and emotional benefits. Some caregivers have found that joining a support group is a critical lifeline. These support groups allow caregivers to find respite, express concerns, share experiences, get tips, and receive emotional comfort. Many organizations sponsor in-person and online support groups, including groups for people with early-stage Alzheimer and their families.

Section 8.2

Alzheimer Disease and Stress

"Alzheimer Disease and Stress,"
© 2018 Omnigraphics. Reviewed June 2018.

Alzheimer disease affects nearly 4.5–5 million people in the United States and has steadily increased to 50 percent in the past 15 years. The Centers for Disease Control and Prevention (CDC) reported a new insight into the biomarkers that cause Alzheimer disease (AD). The Alzheimer Disease Neuroimaging Initiative (ADNI) revealed a high level of beta-amyloid that builds up in Alzheimer disease patients. Researchers believe that stressful events can cause inflammation in the brain, leading to Alzheimer disease and other related diseases. Disruption of neural circuits result in a loss of cognitive and motor function that cause Alzheimer disease. This disruption also reduces the ability to heal and develop a positive attitude toward life.

Frank LaFerla, a professor in neurobiology and behavior, and his group of researchers found that 13-month-old mice injected with dexamethasone showed an increase in beta-amyloid and tau protein levels, which led to the formation of plaque and tangles in the brain. They discovered that high levels of stress activate the hypothalamic-pituitary-adrenal (HPA) axis, which increases the level of corticosteroids that the body uses to respond to inflammation. Neurodegeneration is caused by the interruption of neural circuits that regulate behavioral and hormonal stress responses, causing neuropsychiatric complications.

Alzheimer disease is caused by a mix of genetic, lifestyle, and environmental causes. The corticotropin-releasing factor (CRF), a process by which the hormone is released by the brain during stress, increases the production of amyloid beta that causes Alzheimer disease. Increased activity of gamma secretase causes the production of Alzheimer disease-related proteins. Dealing with environmental factors that cause stress is the best known method for decreasing risk factors since research to intercept the CRF receptor from releasing Alzheimer disease-related proteins has not yet resolved the risks associated with this process.

The increase in cortisol levels is a biomarker that indicates the onset of Alzheimer disease. Reduced memory function is more pronounced in patients with higher levels of cortisol, a finding that appears to link an increase in the stress hormone to the development of Alzheimer disease. The hippocampus, a region of the brain responsible for memory function, has been linked to the production of cortisol, the stress hormone that causes degeneration of brain cells. Atrophy of the hippocampus causes a gradual decline in the working memory over a period of time.

Nonpharmacologic treatments such as therapeutic touch can reduce stress and anxiety levels in Alzheimer disease patients. Other studies have shown that stress relief reduces the progression of Alzheimer disease. Stress impacts our lives in many ways; therefore, the reduction of stress has health benefits and delays the onset of Alzheimer disease and progressions of diabetes, while improving cardiovascular health.

References

1. "Stress Significantly Hastens Progression of Alzheimer's Disease," ScienceDaily, August 30, 2006.
2. Glynn, Sarah. "Stress Can Lead to Alzheimer's Disease," *Medical News Today*, March 19, 2013.
3. Justice, Nicholas J. "The Relationship between Stress and Alzheimer's Disease," ScienceDirect, February 2018.
4. Merrillees, Louise. "Alzheimer's Disease Study Finds Potential Link between Stress Hormone and Speed of Decline," Australian Broadcasting Corporation, October 13, 2016.
5. "Some Evidence of Link between Stress, Alzheimer's Disease Discovered," ScienceDaily, September 16, 2015.

Chapter 9

Asthma

Chapter Contents

Section 9.1

What Is Asthma?

This section includes text excerpted from "Asthma," National Heart, Lung, and Blood Institute (NHLBI), May 1, 2018.

Asthma is a long-term (i.e., chronic) lung disease that inflames and narrows the airways. Asthma causes recurring periods of wheezing (a whistling sound when you breathe), chest tightness, shortness of breath, and coughing. The coughing often occurs at night or early in the morning.

Asthma affects people of all ages, but it most often starts during childhood. In the United States, more than 25 million people are known to have asthma. About 7 million of these people are children.

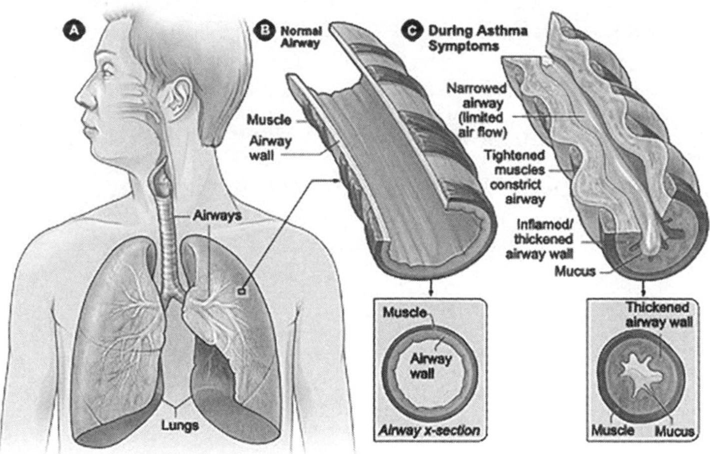

Figure 9.1. *Healthy Lungs versus Asthmatic*

Figure A shows the location of the lungs and airways in the body. Figure B shows a cross-section of a normal airway. Figure C shows a cross-section of an airway during asthma symptoms.

Sometimes asthma symptoms are mild and go away on their own or after minimal treatment with asthma medicine. Other times, symptoms continue to get worse.

When symptoms get more intense and/or more symptoms occur, you're having an asthma attack. Asthma attacks also are called flareups or exacerbations.

Treating symptoms when you first notice them is important. This will help prevent the symptoms from worsening and causing a severe asthma attack. Severe asthma attacks may require emergency care, and they can be fatal.

Causes

The exact cause of asthma isn't known. Researchers think some genetic and environmental factors interact to cause asthma, most often early in life. These factors include:

- An inherited tendency to develop allergies, called atopy
- Parents who have asthma
- Certain respiratory infections during childhood
- Contact with some airborne allergens or exposure to some viral infections in infancy or in early childhood when the immune system is developing

If asthma or atopy runs in your family, exposure to irritants (for example, tobacco smoke) may make your airways more reactive to substances in the air. Some factors may be more likely to cause asthma in some people than in others. Researchers continue to explore what causes asthma.

The "Hygiene Hypothesis"

One theory researchers have for what causes asthma is the "hygiene hypothesis." They believe that our Western lifestyle—with its emphasis on hygiene and sanitation—has resulted in changes in our living conditions and an overall decline in infections in early childhood.

Many young children no longer have the same types of environmental exposures and infections as children did in the past. This affects the way that young children's immune systems develop during very early childhood, and it may increase their risk for atopy and asthma. This is especially true for children who have close family members with one or both of these conditions.

Risk Factors

Asthma affects people of all ages, but it most often starts during childhood. In the United States, more than 22 million people are known to have asthma. Nearly 6 million of these people are children. Young children who often wheeze and have respiratory infections—as well as certain other risk factors—are at highest risk of developing asthma that continues beyond 6 years of age. The other risk factors include having allergies, eczema (an allergic skin condition), or parents who have asthma.

Among children, more boys have asthma than girls. But among adults, more women have the disease than men. It's not clear whether or how sex and sex hormones play a role in causing asthma. Most, but not all, people who have asthma have allergies. Some people develop asthma because of contact with certain chemical irritants or industrial dusts in the workplace. This type of asthma is called occupational asthma.

Screening and Prevention

You can't prevent asthma. However, you can take steps to control the disease and prevent its symptoms. For example:

- Learn about your asthma and ways to control it.
- Follow your written asthma action plan.
- Use medicines as your doctor prescribes.
- Identify and try to avoid things that make your asthma worse (asthma triggers). However, one trigger you should not avoid is physical activity. Physical activity is an important part of a healthy lifestyle. Talk with your doctor about medicines that can help you stay active.
- Keep track of your asthma symptoms and level of control.
- Get regular checkups for your asthma.

Signs, Symptoms, and Complications

Common signs and symptoms of asthma include:

- **Coughing.** Coughing from asthma often is worse at night or early in the morning, making it hard to sleep.
- **Wheezing.** Wheezing is a whistling or squeaky sound that occurs when you breathe.
- **Chest tightness.** This may feel like something is squeezing or sitting on your chest.
- **Shortness of breath.** Some people who have asthma say they can't catch their breath or they feel out of breath. You may feel like you can't get air out of your lungs.

Not all people who have asthma have these symptoms. Likewise, having these symptoms doesn't always mean that you have asthma. The best way to diagnose asthma for certain is to use a lung function test, a medical history (including type and frequency of symptoms), and a physical exam.

The types of asthma symptoms you have, how often they occur, and how severe they are may vary over time. Sometimes your symptoms may just annoy you. Other times, they may be troublesome enough to limit your daily routine. Severe symptoms can be fatal. It's important to treat symptoms when you first notice them so they don't become severe. With proper treatment, most people who have asthma can expect to have few, if any, symptoms either during the day or at night.

What Causes Asthma Symptoms to Occur?

Many things can trigger or worsen asthma symptoms. Your doctor will help you find out which things (sometimes called triggers) may cause your asthma to flare up if you come in contact with them. Triggers may include:

- Allergens from dust, animal fur, cockroaches, mold, and pollens from trees, grasses, and flowers
- Irritants such as cigarette smoke, air pollution, chemicals or dust in the workplace, compounds in home décor products, and sprays (such as hairspray)
- Medicines such as aspirin or other nonsteroidal anti-inflammatory drugs (NSAIDs) and nonselective beta-blockers
- Sulfites in foods and drinks
- Viral upper respiratory infections, such as colds
- Physical activity, including exercise

Other health conditions can make asthma harder to manage. Examples of these conditions include a runny nose, sinus infections, reflux disease, psychological stress, and sleep apnea. These conditions need treatment as part of an overall asthma care plan. Asthma is different for each person. Some of the triggers listed above may not affect you. Other triggers that do affect you may not be on the list. Talk with your doctor about the things that seem to make your asthma worse.

Diagnosis

Your primary care doctor will diagnose asthma based on your medical and family histories, a physical exam, and test results. Your doctor also will figure out the severity of your asthma—that is, whether it's intermittent, mild, moderate, or severe. The level of severity will determine what treatment you'll start on.

You may need to see an asthma specialist if:

- You need special tests to help diagnose asthma
- You've had a life-threatening asthma attack
- You need more than one kind of medicine or higher doses of medicine to control your asthma, or if you have overall problems getting your asthma well controlled
- You're thinking about getting allergy treatments

Medical and Family Histories

Your doctor may ask about your family history of asthma and allergies. He or she also may ask whether you have asthma symptoms and when and how often they occur. Let your doctor know whether your symptoms seem to happen only during certain times of the year or in certain places, or if they get worse at night.

Your doctor also may want to know what factors seem to trigger your symptoms or worsen them. Your doctor may ask you about related health conditions that can interfere with asthma management. These conditions include a runny nose, sinus infections, reflux disease, psychological stress, and sleep apnea.

Physical Exam

Your doctor will listen to your breathing and look for signs of asthma or allergies. These signs include wheezing, a runny nose or swollen nasal passages, and allergic skin conditions (such as eczema). Keep in mind that you can still have asthma even if you don't have these signs on the day that your doctor examines you.

Diagnostic Tests

Lung Function Test

Your doctor will use a test called spirometry to check how your lungs are working. This test measures how much air you can breathe in and out. It also measures how fast you can blow air out. Your doctor also may give you medicine and then test you again to see whether the results have improved. If the starting results are lower than normal and improve with the medicine, and if your medical history shows a pattern of asthma symptoms, your diagnosis will likely be asthma.

Other Tests

Your doctor may recommend other tests if he or she needs more information to make a diagnosis. Other tests may include:

- Allergy testing to find out which allergens affect you, if any
- A test to measure how sensitive your airways are. This is called a bronchoprovocation test. Using spirometry, this test repeatedly measures your lung function during physical activity or after you receive increasing doses of cold air or a special chemical to breathe in.
- A test to show whether you have another condition with the same symptoms as asthma, such as reflux disease, vocal cord dysfunction, or sleep apnea.
- A chest X-ray or an electrocardiogram (EKG). These tests will help find out whether a foreign object or any other disease may be causing your symptoms.

Diagnosing Asthma in Young Children

Most children who have asthma develop their first symptoms before 5 years of age. However, asthma in young children (aged 0–5 years) can be hard to diagnose.

Sometimes it's hard to tell whether a child has asthma or another childhood condition. This is because the symptoms of asthma also occur with other conditions.

Also, many young children who wheeze when they get colds or respiratory infections don't go on to have asthma after they're 6 years old.

A child may wheeze because he or she has small airways that become even narrower during colds or respiratory infections. The airways grow as the child grows older, so wheezing no longer occurs when the child gets colds.

A young child who has frequent wheezing with colds or respiratory infections is more likely to have asthma if:

- One or both parents have asthma

- The child has signs of allergies, including the allergic skin condition eczema
- The child has allergic reactions to pollens or other airborne allergens
- The child wheezes even when he or she doesn't have a cold or other infection

The most certain way to diagnose asthma is with a lung function test, a medical history, and a physical exam. However, it's hard to do lung function tests in children younger than 5 years. Thus, doctors must rely on children's medical histories, signs and symptoms, and physical exams to make a diagnosis. Doctors also may use a 4–6 week trial of asthma medicines to see how well a child responds.

Treatment

Asthma is a long-term disease that has no cure. The goal of asthma treatment is to control the disease. Good asthma control will:

- Prevent chronic and troublesome symptoms, such as coughing and shortness of breath
- Reduce your need for quick-relief medicines
- Help you maintain good lung function
- Let you maintain your normal activity level and sleep through the night
- Prevent asthma attacks that could result in an emergency room visit or hospital stay

To control asthma, partner with your doctor to manage your asthma or your child's asthma. Children aged 10 or older—and younger children who are able—should take an active role in their asthma care.

Taking an active role to control your asthma involves:

- Working with your doctor to treat other conditions that can interfere with asthma management
- Avoiding things that worsen your asthma (asthma triggers). However, one trigger you should not avoid is physical activity. Physical activity is an important part of a healthy lifestyle. Talk with your doctor about medicines that can help you stay active.

- Working with your doctor and other healthcare providers to create and follow an asthma action plan

An asthma action plan gives guidance on taking your medicines properly, avoiding asthma triggers (except physical activity), tracking your level of asthma control, responding to worsening symptoms, and seeking emergency care when needed. Asthma is treated with two types of medicines: long-term control and quick-relief medicines. Long-term control medicines help reduce airway inflammation and prevent asthma symptoms. Quick-relief, or "rescue," medicines relieve asthma symptoms that may flare up. Your initial treatment will depend on the severity of your asthma. Follow-up asthma treatment will depend on how well your asthma action plan is controlling your symptoms and preventing asthma attacks.

Your level of asthma control can vary over time and with changes in your home, school, or work environments. These changes can alter how often you're exposed to the factors that can worsen your asthma. Your doctor may need to increase your medicine if your asthma doesn't stay under control. On the other hand, if your asthma is well controlled for several months, your doctor may decrease your medicine. These adjustments to your medicine will help you maintain the best control possible with the least amount of medicine necessary. Asthma treatment for certain groups of people—such as children, pregnant women, or those for whom exercise brings on asthma symptoms—will be adjusted to meet their special needs.

Medicines

Your doctor will consider many things when deciding which asthma medicines are best for you. He or she will check to see how well a medicine works for you. Then, he or she will adjust the dose or medicine as needed. Asthma medicines can be taken in pill form, but most are taken using a device called an inhaler. An inhaler allows the medicine to go directly to your lungs. Not all inhalers are used the same way. Ask your doctor or another healthcare provider to show you the right way to use your inhaler. Review the way you use your inhaler at every medical visit.

Section 9.2

Managing Asthma Triggers: Stress

"Managing Asthma Triggers: Stress,"
© 2016 Omnigraphics. Reviewed June 2018.

Many people find that their asthma symptoms worsen when they are under stress. Countless everyday situations can contribute to stress, from work deadlines and money problems to school exams and peer pressure. Major life changes like getting married, starting a family, changing jobs, moving, or experiencing a death in the family can be tremendously stressful. For people with asthma, stress can trigger symptoms such as wheezing, coughing, and shortness of breath. As these symptoms grow worse, they can make people feel worried, anxious, frightened, and even panicked—thus increasing their stress levels further. This cyclical relationship makes it especially important for people with asthma to learn how to manage stress.

Stress and Asthma

Stress impacts the body in many ways, and some of these physical changes can trigger asthma. One common reaction to stressful situations is the "fight or flight" response. The body releases a surge of hormones that cause an increase in heart rate, muscle tension, and breathing rate. Although these changes prepare the body to face danger, they also increase the risk of asthma symptoms.

Some people react to stress in unhealthy ways, by drinking alcohol, smoking cigarettes, or overeating. Similarly, stress and anxiety can cause people to lose sleep, forego exercise, and stop taking their medication as directed. All of these behaviors can trigger asthma symptoms. Even some asthma treatments, such as oral steroids like prednisone, can affect mood and increase stress and anxiety.

Managing Stress

While it is impossible to avoid stress entirely, there are a number of proven methods that can help people manage it.

- **Recognize and avoid sources of stress.** Identifying major sources of stress—such as relationship issues, money problems, or work situations—is the first step in managing stress-related asthma. When people recognize the stressors that have the greatest impact on their lives, they can often be proactive, plan ahead, and cope with problems in a calmer manner. If the underlying causes of stress are hard to pinpoint, or if a certain situation seems overwhelming, it may be helpful to consult with a mental health professional.

- **Make a plan and get organized.** A large part of stress comes from feeling unprepared and worrying about what might happen. To regain a feeling of control over stressful situations, many people apply organization and time-management skills. It may be helpful to make a list of tasks that must be accomplished and prioritize them, so that the most important things can be done first. Checking tasks off the list can help alleviate stress.
- **Learn to delegate.** Many people feel stress because they try to handle too many responsibilities on their own. Delegating some tasks to other qualified people can help free up time and reduce stress. It is important to provide clear instructions and deadlines, yet also give others room to perform tasks in their own way, rather than looking over their shoulder and micromanaging.
- **Seek support when needed.** Acknowledging feelings of stress and seeking social support from family and friends is a valuable tool in managing tough situations. In addition to offering encouragement and emotional support, a trusted friend or relative can often provide a new perspective on a problem. Many people find that talking things over helps them feel better.
- **Maintain healthy habits.** To counteract the physical effects of stress, it is important to maintain healthy habits. Eating a healthy, well-balanced diet becomes even more vital during stressful times. It is particularly helpful to avoid eating processed foods that can cause extreme fluctuations in blood sugar levels, as well as to avoid drinking alcohol or smoking in response to stress. Daily exercise offers proven benefits in reducing stress, improving mood, and increasing overall health. Finally, getting plenty of sleep can help renew the physical energy and mental resources needed for coping with stress.
- **Make time to relax and have fun.** A wide variety of relaxation techniques are available to help people deal with stress, including yoga, meditation, deep breathing exercises, progressive muscle relaxation (PMR), and guided imagery. It is also important to step back from the stresses of daily life

periodically and reconnect with things that provide enjoyment and fulfillment. Taking a break and doing a fun activity or hobby can restore the positive energy needed to deal with stress.

References

1. "Stress and Anxiety," Asthma UK, March 2015.
2. "Stress and Asthma," WebMD Asthma Health Center, 2014.

Section 9.3

More Stress Means Worse Asthma in Inner-City Adults

This section includes text excerpted from "More Stress Means Worse Asthma in Inner-City Adults," Agency for Healthcare Research and Quality (AHRQ), U.S. Department of Health and Human Services (HHS), August 2010. Reviewed June 2018.

Living in the inner city brings with it a host of problems, such as crime, poor housing, lack of access to needed services, and unemployment. These and other factors create a lot of stress for residents in these areas. On top of this, asthma is a major medical problem in the inner city, where its prevalence, morbidity, and mortality are higher than other areas. A study has found a direct link between the level of stress and how much worse the asthma of inner-city adults is. Those who perceived higher stress levels were more likely to have increased asthma-related problems compared with persons with low-stress levels.

Juan P. Wisnivesky, M.D., Dr.P.H., of the Mount Sinai School of Medicine, and colleagues recruited adults with asthma being treated at two large urban internal medicine practices in Harlem, New York, and New Brunswick, New Jersey. All had moderate-to-severe asthma. Each patient was given a standardized questionnaire at the start of the study and then again at 1, 3, and 12 months after they enrolled. Items included questions about their asthma control, medication use, personal information, quality of life, and measurements of perceived stress.

The study's findings are based on 326 participants, the majority of whom were either black or Hispanic of low socioeconomic status. They also had various conditions in addition to asthma, such as hypertension (46.85%) and diabetes (24.6%). A participant's perceived stress level was associated with increased asthma problems and a poorer quality of life. Those with the highest stress levels displayed decreased adherence to their asthma medications.

According to the researchers, this resulting suboptimal self-management of asthma may partially explain the connection between increased stress and worse asthma outcomes. Given these findings, asthma programs aimed at inner-city populations should assess stress levels and consider management and coping techniques, as well as appropriate referrals, for some patients with poorly controlled asthma, suggest the study authors.

Chapter 10

Cancer and Stress

What Is Psychological Stress?

Psychological stress describes what people feel when they are under mental, physical, or emotional pressure. Although it is normal to experience some psychological stress from time to time, people who experience high levels of psychological stress or who experience it repeatedly over a long period of time may develop health problems (mental and/or physical).

Stress can be caused both by daily responsibilities and routine events, as well as by more unusual events, such as a trauma or illness in oneself or a close family member. When people feel that they are unable to manage or control changes caused by cancer or normal life activities, they are in distress. Distress has become increasingly recognized as a factor that can reduce the quality of life of cancer patients. There is even some evidence that extreme distress is associated with poorer clinical outcomes. Clinical guidelines are available to help doctors and nurses assess levels of distress and help patients manage it.

How Does the Body Respond during Stress?

The body responds to physical, mental, or emotional pressure by releasing stress hormones (such as epinephrine and norepinephrine) that increase blood pressure, speed heart rate, and raise blood sugar

---

This chapter includes text excerpted from "Psychological Stress and Cancer," National Cancer Institute (NCI), December 10, 2012. Reviewed June 2018.

levels. These changes help a person act with greater strength and speed to escape a perceived threat. Research has shown that people who experience intense and long-term (i.e., chronic) stress can have digestive problems, fertility problems, urinary problems, and a weakened immune system. People who experience chronic stress are also more prone to viral infections such as the flu or common cold and to have headaches, sleep trouble, depression, and anxiety.

Can Psychological Stress Cause Cancer?

Although stress can cause a number of physical health problems, the evidence that it can cause cancer is weak. Some studies have indicated a link between various psychological factors and an increased risk of developing cancer, but others have not. Apparent links between psychological stress and cancer could arise in several ways. For example, people under stress may develop certain behaviors, such as smoking, overeating, or drinking alcohol, which increase a person's risk for cancer. Or someone who has a relative with cancer may have a higher risk for cancer because of a shared inherited risk factor, not because of the stress induced by the family member's diagnosis.

How Does Psychological Stress Affect People Who Have Cancer?

People who have cancer may find the physical, emotional, and social effects of the disease to be stressful. Those who attempt to manage their stress with risky behaviors such as smoking or drinking alcohol or who become more sedentary may have a poorer quality of life after cancer treatment. In contrast, people who are able to use effective coping strategies to deal with stress, such as relaxation and stress management techniques, have been shown to have lower levels of depression, anxiety, and symptoms related to cancer and its treatment. However, there is no evidence that successful management of psychological stress improves cancer survival.

Evidence from experimental studies does suggest that psychological stress can affect a tumor's ability to grow and spread. For example, some studies have shown that when mice bearing human tumors were kept confined or isolated from other mice—conditions that increase stress—their tumors were more likely to grow and spread (metastasize). In one set of experiments, tumors transplanted into the mammary fat pads of mice had much higher rates of spread to the lungs and lymph nodes if the mice were chronically stressed than if the mice were not stressed. Studies in mice and in human cancer cells grown in the laboratory have found that the stress hormone norepinephrine, part of the body's fight-or-flight response system, may promote angiogenesis and metastasis.

In another study, women with triple-negative breast cancer who had been treated with neoadjuvant chemotherapy were asked about their use of beta-blockers, which are medications that interfere with certain stress hormones, before and during chemotherapy. Women who reported using beta-blockers had a better chance of surviving their cancer treatment without a relapse than women who did not report beta-blocker use. There was no difference between the groups, however, in terms of overall survival.

Although there is still no strong evidence that stress directly affects cancer outcomes, some data do suggest that patients can develop a sense of helplessness or hopelessness when stress becomes overwhelming. This response is associated with higher rates of death, although the mechanism for this outcome is unclear. It may be that people who feel helpless or hopeless do not seek treatment when they become ill, give up prematurely on or fail to adhere to potentially helpful therapy, engage in risky behaviors such as drug use, or do not maintain a healthy lifestyle, resulting in premature death.

How Can People Who Have Cancer Learn to Cope with Psychological Stress?

Emotional and social support can help patients learn to cope with psychological stress. Such support can reduce levels of depression, anxiety, and disease- and treatment-related symptoms among patients. Approaches can include the following:

- Training in relaxation, meditation, or stress management
- Counseling or talk therapy
- Cancer education sessions
- Social support in a group setting
- Medications for depression or anxiety
- Exercise

Some expert organizations recommend that all cancer patients be screened for distress early in the course of treatment. A number also recommend rescreening at critical points along the course of care.

Healthcare providers can use a variety of screening tools, such as a distress scale or questionnaire, to gauge whether cancer patients need help managing their emotions or with other practical concerns. Patients who show moderate to severe distress are typically referred to appropriate resources, such as a clinical health psychologist, social worker, chaplain, or psychiatrist.

Chapter 11

Diabetes and Stress

You can manage your diabetes and live a long and healthy life by taking care of yourself each day. Diabetes can affect almost every part of your body. Therefore, you will need to manage your blood glucose levels, also called blood sugar. Managing your blood glucose, as well as your blood pressure and cholesterol, can help prevent the health problems that can occur when you have diabetes. With the help of your healthcare team, you can create a diabetes self-care plan to manage your diabetes. Your self-care plan may include these steps:

- Manage your diabetes ABCs
- Follow your diabetes meal plan
- Make physical activity part of your routine
- Take your medicine
- Check your blood glucose levels
- Work with your healthcare team
- Cope with your diabetes in healthy ways

Manage Your Diabetes ABCs

Knowing your diabetes ABCs will help you manage your blood glucose, blood pressure, and cholesterol. Stopping smoking if you smoke will also help you manage your diabetes. Working toward your ABC

This chapter includes text excerpted from "Managing Diabetes," National Institute of Diabetes and Digestive and Kidney Diseases (NIDDK), November 2016.

goals can help lower your chances of having a heart attack, stroke, or other diabetes problems.

A for the A1C Test

The A1C test shows your average blood glucose level over the past 3 months. The A1C goal for many people with diabetes is below 7 percent. Ask your healthcare team what your goal should be.

B for Blood Pressure

The blood pressure goal for most people with diabetes is below 140/90 mm Hg. Ask what your goal should be.

C for Cholesterol

You have two kinds of cholesterol in your blood: Low-density lipoprotein (LDL) and high-density lipoprotein (HDL). LDL or "bad" cholesterol can build up and clog your blood vessels. Too much bad cholesterol can cause a heart attack or stroke. HDL or "good" cholesterol helps remove the "bad" cholesterol from your blood vessels.

Ask your healthcare team what your cholesterol numbers should be. If you are over 40 years of age, you may need to take a statin drug for heart health.

S for Stop Smoking

Not smoking is especially important for people with diabetes because both smoking and diabetes narrow blood vessels. Blood vessel narrowing makes your heart work harder. E-cigarettes aren't a safe option either.

If you quit smoking:

- You will lower your risk for heart attack, stroke, nerve disease, kidney disease, diabetic eye disease, and amputation
- Your cholesterol and blood pressure levels may improve
- Your blood circulation will improve
- You may have an easier time being physically active

If you smoke or use other tobacco products, stop. Ask for help so you don't have to do it alone. You can start by calling the national quitline at 800-QUITNOW or 800-784-8669. Keeping your A1C, blood pressure, and cholesterol levels close to your goals and stopping smoking may help prevent the long-term harmful effects of diabetes. These health problems include heart disease, stroke, kidney disease, nerve damage, and eye disease. You can keep track of your ABCs with a diabetes care record. Take it with you on your healthcare visits. Talk about your goals and how you are doing, and whether you need to make any changes in your diabetes care plan.

Follow Your Diabetes Meal Plan

Make a diabetes meal plan with help from your healthcare team. Following a meal plan will help you manage your blood glucose, blood pressure, and cholesterol.

Choose fruits and vegetables, beans, whole grains, chicken or turkey without the skin, fish, lean meats, and nonfat or low-fat milk and cheese. Drink water instead of sugar-sweetened beverages (SSBs). Choose foods that are lower in calories, saturated fat, trans fat, sugar, and salt.

Make Physical Activity Part of Your Daily Routine

Set a goal to be more physically active. Try to work up to 30 minutes or more of physical activity on most days of the week. Brisk walking and swimming are good ways to move more. If you are not active now, ask your healthcare team about the types and amounts of physical activity that are right for you. Swimming or water walking is a good way to move more. Following your meal plan and being more active can help you stay at or get to a healthy weight. If you are overweight or obese, work with your healthcare team to create a weight-loss plan that is right for you.

Take Your Medicine

Take your medicines for diabetes and any other health problems, even when you feel good or have reached your blood glucose, blood pressure, and cholesterol goals. These medicines help you manage your ABCs. Ask your doctor if you need to take aspirin to prevent a heart attack or stroke. Tell your healthcare professional if you cannot afford your medicines or if you have any side effects from your medicines.

Check Your Blood Glucose Levels

For many people with diabetes, checking their blood glucose level each day is an important way to manage their diabetes. Monitoring your blood glucose level is most important if you take insulin. The results of blood glucose monitoring can help you make decisions about food, physical activity, and medicines. Checking and recording your blood glucose level is an important part of managing diabetes.

The most common way to check your blood glucose level at home is with a blood glucose meter. You get a drop of blood by pricking the side of your fingertip with a lancet. Then you apply the blood to a test strip. The meter will show you how much glucose is in your blood at the moment. Ask your healthcare team how often you should check your blood glucose levels. Make sure to keep a record of your blood glucose self-checks. Take these records with you when you visit your healthcare team.

What Is Continuous Glucose Monitoring?

Continuous glucose monitoring (CGM) is another way to check your glucose levels. Most CGM systems use a tiny sensor that you insert under your skin. The sensor measures glucose levels in the fluids between your body's cells every few minutes and can show changes in your glucose level throughout the day and night. If the CGM system shows that your glucose is too high or too low, you should check your glucose with a blood glucose meter before making any changes to your eating plan, physical activity, or medicines. A CGM system is especially useful for people who use insulin and have problems with low blood glucose.

What Are the Recommended Targets for Blood Glucose Levels?

Many people with diabetes aim to keep their blood glucose at these normal levels:

- Before a meal: 80–130 mg/dL
- About 2 hours after a meal starts: less than 180 mg/dL

Talk with your healthcare team about the best target range for you. Be sure to tell your healthcare professional if your glucose levels often go above or below your target range.

What Happens If My Blood Glucose Level Becomes Too Low?

Sometimes blood glucose levels drop below where they should be, which is called hypoglycemia. For most people with diabetes, the blood glucose level is too low when it is below 70 mg/dL. Hypoglycemia can be life threatening and needs to be treated right away.

What Happens If My Blood Glucose Level Becomes Too High?

Doctors call high blood glucose hyperglycemia. Symptoms that your blood glucose levels may be too high include:

- Feeling thirsty
- Feeling tired or weak
- Headaches
- Urinating often
- Blurred vision

If you often have high blood glucose levels or symptoms of high blood glucose, talk with your healthcare team. You may need a change in your diabetes meal plan, physical activity plan, or medicines.

Work with Your Healthcare Team

Most people with diabetes get healthcare from a primary care professional. Primary care professionals include internists, family physicians, and pediatricians. Sometimes physician assistants and nurses with extra training, called nurse practitioners, provide primary care. You also will need to see other care professionals from time to time. A team of healthcare professionals can help you improve your diabetes self-care. Remember, you are the most important member of your healthcare team.

Besides a primary care professional, your healthcare team may include:

- An endocrinologist for more specialized diabetes care
- A registered dietitian, also called a nutritionist
- A nurse
- A certified diabetes educator
- A pharmacist
- A dentist
- An eye doctor
- A podiatrist, or foot doctor, for foot care

- A social worker, who can help you find financial aid for treatment and community resources
- A counselor or other mental healthcare professional

When you see members of your healthcare team, ask questions. Write a list of questions you have before your visit so you don't forget what you want to ask. Watch a video to help you get ready for your diabetes care visit. When you see your doctor, review your diabetes self-care plan and blood glucose chart. You should see your healthcare team at least twice a year, and more often if you are having problems or are having trouble reaching your blood glucose, blood pressure, or cholesterol goals. At each visit, be sure you have a blood pressure check, foot check, and weight check; and review your self-care plan. Talk with your healthcare team about your medicines and whether you need to adjust them. Routine healthcare will help you find and treat any health problems early, or may be able to help prevent them.

Talk with your doctor about what vaccines you should get to keep from getting sick, such as a flu shot and pneumonia shot. Preventing illness is an important part of taking care of your diabetes. Your blood glucose levels are more likely to go up when you're sick or have an infection.

Cope with Your Diabetes in Healthy Ways

Feeling stressed, sad, or angry is common when you live with diabetes. Stress can raise your blood glucose levels, but you can learn ways to lower your stress. Try deep breathing, gardening, taking a walk, doing yoga, meditating, doing a hobby, or listening to your favorite music. Consider taking part in a diabetes education program or support group that teaches you techniques for managing stress.

Depression is common among people with a long-term (i.e., chronic) illness. Depression can get in the way of your efforts to manage your diabetes. Ask for help if you feel down. A mental health counselor, support group, clergy member, friend, or family member who will listen to your feelings may help you feel better.

Try to get 7–8 hours of sleep each night. Getting enough sleep can help improve your mood and energy level. You can take steps to improve your sleep habits. If you often feel sleepy during the day, you may have obstructive sleep apnea, a condition in which your breathing briefly stops many times during the night. Sleep apnea is common in people who have diabetes. Talk with your healthcare team if you think you have a sleep problem. Remember, managing diabetes isn't easy, but it's worth it.

Chapter 12

Erectile Dysfunction

What Is Erectile Dysfunction (ED)?

Erectile dysfunction (ED) (also known as impotence) is the inability to get and keep an erection firm enough for sex. Having erection trouble from time to time isn't necessarily a cause for concern. But if ED is an ongoing problem, it may cause stress, cause relationship problems or affect your self-confidence. Even though it may seem awkward to talk with your doctor about ED, go in for an evaluation. Problems getting or keeping an erection can be a sign of a health condition that needs treatment, such as heart disease or poorly controlled diabetes. Treating an underlying problem may be enough to reverse your ED. If treating an underlying condition doesn't help your ED, medications or other direct treatments may work.

What Are the Causes of ED?

Male sexual arousal is a complex process that involves the brain, hormones, emotions, nerves, muscles, and blood vessels. ED can result from a problem with any of these. Likewise, stress and mental health problems can cause or worsen ED. Sometimes a combination of physical and psychological issues causes ED. For instance, a minor physical problem that slows your sexual response may cause anxiety about maintaining an erection. The resulting anxiety can lead to or worsen ED.

This chapter includes text excerpted from "Erectile Dysfunction (ED)," U.S. Department of Veterans Affairs (VA), July 2013. Reviewed June 2018.

Psychological Causes of ED

The brain plays a key role in triggering the series of physical events that cause an erection, starting with feelings of sexual excitement. A number of things can interfere with sexual feelings and cause or worsen ED. These include:

- Stress
- Depression, anxiety, or other mental health conditions
- Fatigue
- Relationship problems due to stress, poor communication, or other concerns

Physical Causes of ED

In most cases, ED is caused by something physical. Common causes include:

- Heart disease
- Clogged blood vessels (atherosclerosis)
- High blood pressure
- Diabetes
- Obesity
- Metabolic syndrome, a condition involving increased blood pressure, high insulin levels, body fat around the waist and high cholesterol
- Parkinson disease (PD)
- Multiple sclerosis (MS)
- Low testosterone (Low-T)
- Peyronie disease, development of scar tissue inside the penis
- Certain prescription medications
- Tobacco use
- Alcoholism and other forms of substance abuse
- Treatments for prostate cancer or enlarged prostate
- Surgeries or injuries that affect the pelvic area or spinal cord

What Are the Risk Factors for ED?

As you get older; erections may take longer to develop and may not be as firm. You may need more direct touch to your penis to get and keep an erection. This isn't a direct consequence of getting older. Usually, it's a result of underlying health problems or taking medications, which is more common as men age.

A variety of risk factors can contribute to ED. They include:

- Medical conditions, particularly diabetes or heart problems
- Using tobacco, which restricts blood flow to veins and arteries. Over time tobacco use can cause chronic health problems that lead to ED.
- Being overweight, especially if you're very overweight (obese)
- Certain medical treatments, such as prostate surgery or radiation treatment for cancer
- Injuries, particularly if they damage the nerves that control erections
- Medications, including antidepressants, antihistamines, and medications to treat high blood pressure, pain, or prostate cancer
- Psychological conditions, such as stress, anxiety, or depression
- Drug and alcohol use, especially, if you're a long-term drug user or heavy drinker
- Prolonged bicycling, which can compress nerves and affect blood flow to the penis—leading to temporary ED

What Are the Tests Used to Diagnose ED?

For many men, a physical exam and answering questions (medical history) are all that's needed before a doctor is ready to recommend a treatment. If your doctor suspects that underlying problems may be involved, or you have chronic health problems, you may need further tests, or you may need to see a specialist. Tests for underlying problems may include:

- **Physical exam.** This may include careful examination of your penis and testicles and checking your nerves for feeling.
- **Blood tests.** A sample of your blood may be sent to a lab to check for signs of heart disease, diabetes, low testosterone (low-T) levels, and other health problems.

- **Urine tests (urinalysis).** Like blood tests, urine tests are used to look for signs of diabetes and other underlying health conditions.
- **Ultrasound.** This test can check blood flow to your penis. It involves using a wand-like device (transducer) held over the blood vessels that supply the penis. It creates a video image to let your doctor see if you have blood flow problems. This test is sometimes done in combination with an injection of medications into the penis to determine if blood flow increases normally.
- **Overnight erection test.** Most men have erections during sleep without remembering them. This simple test involves wrapping special tape around your penis before you go to bed. If the tape is separated in the morning, your penis was erect at some time during the night. This indicates the cause of your ED is most likely psychological and not physical.

What Are the Treatments and Medications for ED?

A variety of options exist for treating ED. The cause and severity of your condition, and underlying health problems, are important factors in your doctor's recommending the best treatment or treatments for you. Your doctor can explain the risks and benefits of each treatment, and will consider your preferences. Your partner's preferences also may play a role in treatment choices.

Oral medications. Oral medications are a successful ED treatment for many men. They include:

- Sildenafil (Viagra)
- Tadalafil (Cialis)
- Vardenafil (Levitra)

All three medications work in much the same way. These drugs enhance the effects of nitric oxide, a natural chemical your body produces that relaxes muscles in the penis. This increases blood flow and allows you to get an erection in response to sexual stimulation. These medications vary in dosage, how long they work and their side effects. Your doctor will take into account your particular situation to determine which medication may work best. Don't expect these medications to fix your ED immediately. You may need to work with your doctor to find the right medication and dose for you. Before taking any prescription ED medication (including over-the-counter (OTC) supplements or herbal remedies), get your doctor's OK.

Although these medications can help many people, not all men should take them to treat ED. These medications may not work or may be dangerous for you if you:

- Take nitrate drugs for angina, such as nitroglycerin (Nitro-Bid, others), isosorbide mononitrate (Imdur), and isosorbide dinitrate (Isordil). Take a blood-thinning (anticoagulant) medication, alpha-blockers for enlarged prostate (benign prostatic hyperplasia (BPH)), or high blood pressure medications.
- Have heart disease or heart failure
- Have had a stroke
- Have very low blood pressure (hypotension) or uncontrolled high blood pressure (hypertension)
- Have uncontrolled diabetes

Other medications. Other medications for ED include:

- **Alprostadil self-injection.** With this method, you use a fine needle to inject alprostadil (Alprostadil, Caverject Impulse, Edex) into the base or side of your penis. In some cases, medications generally used for other conditions are used for penile injections on their own or in combination. Examples include papaverine, alprostadil, and phentolamine. Each injection generally produces an erection in 5–20 minutes that lasts about an hour. Because the needle used is very fine, pain from the injection site is usually minor. Side effects can include bleeding from the injection, prolonged erection, and formation of fibrous tissue at the injection site.
- **Alprostadil penis suppository.** Alprostadil intraurethral (MUSE) therapy involves placing a tiny alprostadil suppository inside your penis. You use a special applicator to insert the suppository about two inches down into your penis. Side effects can include pain, minor bleeding in the urethra, dizziness, and formation of fibrous tissue inside your penis.
- **Testosterone replacement.** Some men have ED caused by low levels of the hormone testosterone, and may need testosterone replacement therapy.

Penis pumps, surgery, and implants. Medications may not work or may not be a good choice for you. If this is the case, your doctor may recommend a different treatment.

Other treatments include:

- **Penis pumps.** A penis pump (vacuum constriction device) is a hollow tube with a hand-powered or battery-powered pump. The tube is placed over your penis, and then the pump is used to suck out the air inside the tube. This creates a vacuum that pulls blood into your penis. Once you get an erection, you slip a tension ring around the base of your penis to hold in the blood and keep it firm. You then remove the vacuum device. The erection typically lasts long enough for a couple to have sex. You remove the tension ring after intercourse.
- **Penile implants.** This treatment involves surgically placing devices into the two sides of the penis. These implants consist of either inflatable or semi-rigid rods made from silicone or polyurethane. The inflatable devices allow you to control when and how long you have an erection. The semirigid rods keep the penis firm but bendable. This treatment can be expensive and is usually not recommended until other methods have been tried first. As with any surgery, there is a risk of complications such as infection.
- **Blood vessel surgery.** In rare cases, a leaking blood vessel can cause ED and surgery is necessary to repair it.

Psychological counseling. If your ED is caused by stress, anxiety, or depression; your doctor may suggest that you, or you and your partner, visit a psychologist or counselor. Even if it is caused by something physical, ED can create stress and relationship tension.

What Are Some Things I Can Do about ED?

For many men, ED is caused or worsened by lifestyle choices. Here are some things you can do that may help:

- **Manage stress.** Learning how to manage stress can help prevent ED.
- **If you smoke, quit.** If you have trouble quitting, get help. Try nicotine replacement (such as gum or lozenges), available over-the-counter, or ask your doctor about prescription medication that can help you quit.
- **Lose weight.** Being overweight can cause—or worsen—ED.

- **Get regular exercise.** This can help with underlying problems that play a part in ED in a number of ways, including reducing stress, helping you lose weight and increasing blood flow.
- **Get treatment for alcohol or drug problems.** Drinking too much or taking certain illicit drugs can worsen ED directly or by causing long-term health problems.
- **Work through relationship issues.** Improve communication with your partner and consider couples or marriage counseling if you're having trouble working through problems on your own.

Chapter 13

Gastrointestinal Problems

Chapter Contents

Section 13.1

Irritable Bowel Syndrome

This section includes text excerpted from "Irritable Bowel Syndrome (IBS)," National Institute of Diabetes and Digestive and Kidney Diseases (NIDDK), November 2017.

What Is Irritable Bowel Syndrome (IBS)?

Irritable bowel syndrome (IBS) is a group of symptoms that occur together, including repeated pain in your abdomen and changes in your bowel movements, which may be diarrhea, constipation, or both. With IBS, you have these symptoms without any visible signs of damage or disease in your digestive tract. IBS is a functional gastrointestinal (GI) disorder. Functional GI disorders, which doctors now call disorders of gut-brain interactions, are related to problems with how your brain and your gut work together. These problems can cause your gut to be more sensitive and change how the muscles in your bowel contract. If your gut is more sensitive, you may feel more abdominal pain and bloating. Changes in how the muscles in your bowel contract lead to diarrhea, constipation, or both.

Who Is More Likely to Develop IBS?

Women are up to two times more likely than men to develop IBS. People younger than age 50 are more likely to develop IBS than people older than age 50.

Factors that can increase your chance of having IBS include:

- Having a family member with IBS
- A history of stressful, or difficult life events, such as abuse, in childhood
- Having a severe infection in your digestive tract

What Are the Symptoms of IBS?

The most common symptoms of IBS are pain in your abdomen, often related to your bowel movements, and changes in your bowel movements. These changes may be diarrhea, constipation, or both, depending on what type of IBS you have.

Other symptoms of IBS may include:

- Bloating
- The feeling that you haven't finished a bowel movement
- Whitish mucus in your stool

Women with IBS often have more symptoms during their periods. IBS can be painful but doesn't lead to other health problems or damage your digestive tract.

To diagnose IBS, your doctor will look for a certain pattern in your symptoms over time. IBS is a chronic disorder, meaning it lasts a long time, often years. However, the symptoms may come and go.

What Causes IBS?

Doctors aren't sure what causes IBS. Experts think that a combination of problems may lead to IBS. Different factors may cause IBS in different people.

Functional gastrointestinal (GI) disorders such as IBS are problems with brain-gut interaction—how your brain and gut work together. Experts think that problems with brain-gut interaction may affect how your body works and cause IBS symptoms. For example, in some people with IBS, food may move too slowly or too quickly through the digestive tract, causing changes in bowel movements. Some people with IBS may feel pain when a normal amount of gas or stool is in the gut.

Certain problems are more common in people with IBS. Experts think these problems may play a role in causing IBS. These problems include:

- Stressful or difficult early life events, such as physical or sexual abuse
- Certain mental disorders, such as depression, anxiety, and somatic symptom disorder
- Bacterial infections in your digestive tract
- Small intestinal bacterial overgrowth, an increase in the number, or a change in the type of bacteria in your small intestine
- Food intolerances, or sensitivities, in which certain foods cause digestive symptoms

Research suggests that genes may make some people more likely to develop IBS.

Diagnosis of IBS

How Do Doctors Diagnose IBS?

To diagnose IBS, doctors review your symptoms and medical and family history, and perform a physical exam. In some cases, doctors may order tests to rule out other health problems.

Review of Your Symptoms

Your doctor will ask about your symptoms and look for a certain pattern in your symptoms to diagnose IBS. Your doctor may diagnose IBS if you have pain in your abdomen along with two or more of the following symptoms:

- Your pain is related to your bowel movements. For example, your pain may improve or get worse after bowel movements.
- You notice a change in how often you have a bowel movement
- You notice a change in the way your stools look

Your doctor will ask how long you've had symptoms. Your doctor may diagnose IBS if:

- You've had symptoms at least once a week in the last 3 months and
- Your symptoms first started at least 6 months ago

Your doctor may diagnose IBS even if you've had symptoms for a shorter length of time. You should talk to your doctor if your symptoms are like the symptoms of IBS.

Your doctor will also ask about other symptoms. Certain symptoms may suggest that you have another health problem instead of IBS. These symptoms include:

- Anemia
- Bleeding from your rectum
- Bloody stools or stools that are black and tarry
- Weight loss

Medical and Family History

Your doctor will ask about:

- A family history of digestive diseases, such as celiac disease, colon cancer, or inflammatory bowel disease
- Medicines you take
- Recent infections
- Stressful events related to the start of your symptoms
- What you eat
- Your history of other health problems that are more common in people who have IBS

Physical Exam

During a physical exam, your doctor usually:

- Checks for abdominal bloating
- Listens to sounds within your abdomen using a stethoscope
- Taps on your abdomen checking for tenderness or pain

What Tests Do Doctors Use to Diagnose IBS?

In most cases, doctors don't use tests to diagnose IBS. Your doctor may order blood tests, stool tests, and other tests to check for other health problems.

Treatment for IBS

Doctors may treat IBS by recommending changes in what you eat and other lifestyle changes, medicines, probiotics, and mental health therapies. You may have to try a few treatments to see what works best for you. Your doctor can help you find the right treatment plan.

Changes to What You Eat and Other Lifestyle Changes

Changes in what you eat may help treat your symptoms. Your doctor may recommend trying one of the following changes:

- Eat more fiber
- Avoid gluten

- Follow a special eating plan called the low Fermentable Oligosaccharides, Disaccharides, Monosaccharides, and Polyols (FODMAP) diet.

Research suggests that other lifestyle changes may help IBS symptoms, including:

- Increasing your physical activity
- Reducing stressful life situations as much as possible
- Getting enough sleep

Medicines

Your doctor may recommend medicine to relieve your IBS symptoms. To treat IBS with diarrhea, your doctor may recommend:

- Loperamide
- Rifaximin (Xifaxan), an antibiotic
- Eluxadoline (Viberzi)
- Alosetron (Lotronex), which is prescribed only to women; is prescribed with special warnings and precautions.

To treat IBS with constipation, your doctor may recommend:

- Fiber supplements, when increasing fiber in your diet doesn't help
- Laxatives
- Lubiprostone (Amitiza)
- Linaclotide (Linzess)
- Plecanatide (Trulance)

Other medicines may help treat pain in your abdomen, including:

- Antispasmodics
- Antidepressants, such as low doses of tricyclic antidepressants (TCAs), and selective serotonin reuptake inhibitors (SSRIs)
- Coated peppermint oil capsules

Follow your doctor's instructions when you use medicine to treat IBS. Talk with your doctor about possible side effects and what to do if you have them.

Probiotics

Your doctor may also recommend probiotics. Probiotics are live microorganisms, most often bacteria, that are similar to microorganisms you normally have in your digestive tract. Researchers are still studying the use of probiotics to treat IBS. To be safe, talk with your doctor before using probiotics, or any other complementary, or alternative medicines, or practices. If your doctor recommends probiotics, talk with him or her about how much probiotics you should take and for how long.

Mental Health Therapies

Your doctor may recommend mental health therapies to help improve your IBS symptoms. Therapies used to treat IBS include:

- Cognitive behavioral therapy (CBT), which focuses on helping you change thought and behavior patterns to improve IBS symptoms
- Gut-directed hypnotherapy, in which a therapist uses hypnosis—a trance-like state in which you are relaxed or focused—to help improve your IBS symptoms
- Relaxation training, which can help you relax your muscles or reduce stress

Section 13.2

Peptic Ulcers

This section includes text excerpted from "Gateway to Health Communication and Social Marketing Practice—Ulcers," Centers for Disease Control and Prevention (CDC), September 15, 2017.

An ulcer is a sore or hole in the lining of the stomach or duodenum (the first part of the intestine). The most common ulcer symptom is gnawing or burning pain in the abdomen between the breastbone and the belly button. Ulcer pain often occurs when the stomach is empty, between meals, and in the early morning hours, but it can occur at any time. Less common symptoms include nausea, vomiting, or loss of appetite. Sometimes ulcers bleed. If bleeding continues for a long time, it may lead to anemia with weakness and fatigue. If bleeding is heavy, blood may appear in vomit or bowel movements, which may appear dark red or black.

What's the Problem?

Ninety percent of ulcers are caused by an infection with the bacterium *Helicobacter pylori* (*H. pylori*) and can be cured in about two weeks with appropriate antibiotic treatment. The other 10 percent of ulcers are caused by nonsteroidal anti-inflammatory drugs (NSAIDs) such as aspirin or ibuprofen. People who have an ulcer should be tested for *H. pylori* and if infected should be treated with appropriate antibiotics. *H. pylori* infection can be diagnosed by a blood test, a breath test or an endoscopy. During endoscopy, a small tube with a camera is inserted through the mouth and into the stomach to look for ulcers.

Who's at Risk?

Approximately 25 million Americans will have an ulcer at some point in their lifetime. People of any age can get an ulcer and women are affected just as often as men. There are approximately 500,000–850,000 new cases of ulcer disease each year and more than 1 million ulcer-related hospitalizations each year. Ulcer disease has a $6 billion annual impact on national healthcare budget. Curing an ulcer takes less time and costs substantially less than treating ulcer symptoms over a person's lifetime.

Can It Be Prevented?

To date, a vaccine for *H. pylori* is not yet available; scientists are still researching how the bacterium is transmitted. Most people still believe ulcers are caused by stress or spicy foods and are not aware that ulcers are caused by an infection that can be cured. It is possible that many chronic ulcer patients do not visit their doctors because they don't realize that their ulcers can be cured permanently with a 10–14 day course of antibiotic-based therapy. Many may, instead, continue to self-medicate with traditional ulcer treatment (H2 receptor antagonists) which became available as over-the-counter (OTC) medications in 1995. Primary care physicians still report treating more than 50 percent of first-time ulcer patients with acid-reducing medications and not antibiotic regimens.

Section 13.3

Stress Gastritis

This section includes text excerpted from "Gastritis," National Institute of Diabetes and Digestive and Kidney Diseases (NIDDK), July 2015.

What Is Gastritis?

Gastritis is a condition in which the stomach lining—known as the mucosa—is inflamed, or swollen. The stomach lining contains glands that produce stomach acid and an enzyme called pepsin. The stomach acid breaks down food and pepsin digests protein. A thick layer of mucus coats the stomach lining and helps prevent the acidic digestive juice from dissolving the stomach tissue. When the stomach lining is inflamed, it produces less acid and fewer enzymes. However, the stomach lining also produces less mucus and other substances that normally protect the stomach lining from acidic digestive juice.

Gastritis may be acute or chronic:

- Acute gastritis starts suddenly and lasts for a short time.
- Chronic gastritis is long lasting. If chronic gastritis is not treated, it may last for years or even a lifetime.

Gastritis can be erosive or nonerosive:

- Erosive gastritis can cause the stomach lining to wear away, causing erosions—shallow breaks in the stomach lining—or ulcers—deep sores in the stomach lining.
- Nonerosive gastritis causes inflammation in the stomach lining; however, erosions or ulcers do not accompany nonerosive gastritis.

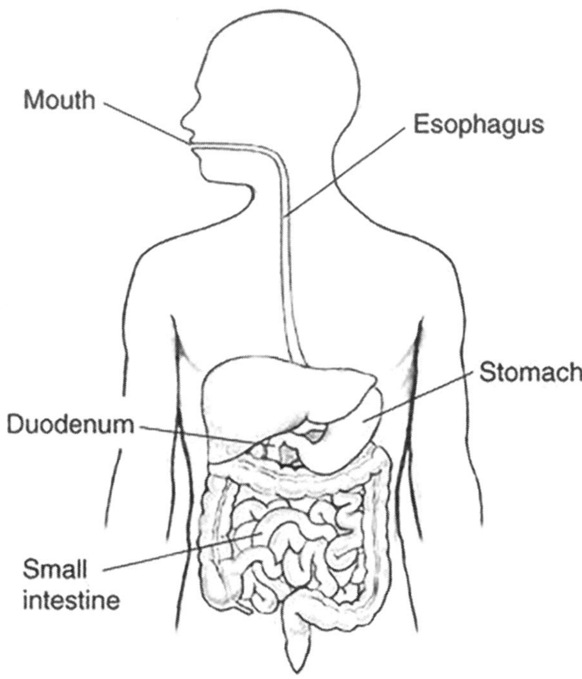

Figure 13.1. *Digestive System*

A healthcare provider may refer a person with gastritis to a gastroenterologist—a doctor who specializes in digestive diseases.

What Causes Gastritis?

Common causes of gastritis include:

- *Helicobacter pylori* (*H. pylori*) infection
- Damage to the stomach lining, which leads to reactive gastritis
- An autoimmune response

H. pylori is a type of bacteria—organisms that may cause an infection. *H. pylori* infection:

- Causes most cases of gastritis
- Typically causes nonerosive gastritis
- May cause acute or chronic gastritis

H. pylori infection is common, particularly in developing countries, and the infection often begins in childhood. Many people who are infected with *H. pylori* never have any symptoms. Adults are more likely to show symptoms when symptoms do occur. Researchers are not sure how the *H. pylori* infection spreads, although they think contaminated food, water, or eating utensils may transmit the bacteria. Some infected people have *H. pylori* in their saliva, which suggests that infection can spread through direct contact with saliva or other body fluids. Damage to the stomach lining, which leads to reactive gastritis. Some people who have damage to the stomach lining can develop reactive gastritis.

Reactive gastritis:

- May be acute or chronic
- May cause erosions
- May cause little or no inflammation

Reactive gastritis may also be called reactive gastropathy when it causes little or no inflammation. The causes of reactive gastritis may include:

- Nonsteroidal anti-inflammatory drugs (NSAIDs), a type of over-the-counter (OTC) medication. Aspirin and ibuprofen are common types of NSAIDs.
- Drinking alcohol
- Using cocaine
- Exposure to radiation or having radiation treatments
- Reflux of bile from the small intestine into the stomach. Bile reflux may occur in people who have had part of their stomach removed.
- A reaction to stress caused by traumatic injuries, critical illness, severe burns, and major surgery. This type of reactive gastritis is called stress gastritis.

In autoimmune gastritis, the immune system attacks healthy cells in the stomach lining. The immune system normally protects people from infection by identifying and destroying bacteria, viruses, and other potentially harmful foreign substances. Autoimmune gastritis is chronic and typically nonerosive.

Less common causes of gastritis may include:

- Crohn's disease, which causes inflammation and irritation of any part of the gastrointestinal (GI) tract.

- Sarcoidosis, a disease that causes inflammation that will not go away. The chronic inflammation causes tiny clumps of abnormal tissue to form in various organs in the body. The disease typically starts in the lungs, skin, and lymph nodes.
- Allergies to food, such as cow's milk and soy, especially in children.
- Infections with viruses, parasites, fungi, and bacteria other than *H. pylori*, typically in people with weakened immune systems.

What Are the Signs and Symptoms of Gastritis?

Some people who have gastritis have pain or discomfort in the upper part of the abdomen—the area between the chest and hips. However, many people with gastritis do not have any signs and symptoms. The relationship between gastritis and a person's symptoms is not clear. The term "gastritis" is sometimes mistakenly used to describe any symptoms of pain or discomfort in the upper abdomen. When symptoms are present, they may include:

- Upper abdominal discomfort or pain
- Nausea
- Vomiting

Seek Help for Symptoms of Bleeding in the Stomach

Erosive gastritis may cause ulcers or erosions in the stomach lining that can bleed. Signs and symptoms of bleeding in the stomach include:

- Shortness of breath
- Dizziness or feeling faint
- Red blood in vomit
- Black, tarry stools
- Red blood in the stool
- Weakness
- Paleness

A person with any signs or symptoms of bleeding in the stomach should call or see a healthcare provider right away.

What Are the Complications of Chronic and Acute Gastritis?

The complications of chronic gastritis may include:

- **Peptic ulcers.** Peptic ulcers are sores involving the lining of the stomach or duodenum, the first part of the small intestine. NSAID use and *H. pylori* gastritis increase the chance of developing peptic ulcers.
- **Atrophic gastritis.** Atrophic gastritis happens when chronic inflammation of the stomach lining causes the loss of the stomach lining and glands. Chronic gastritis can progress to atrophic gastritis.
- **Anemia.** Erosive gastritis can cause chronic bleeding in the stomach, and the blood loss can lead to anemia. Anemia is a condition in which red blood cells are fewer or smaller than normal, which prevents the body's cells from getting enough oxygen. Red blood cells contain hemoglobin, an iron-rich protein that gives blood its red color and enables the red blood cells to transport oxygen from the lungs to the tissues of the body. Research suggests that *H. pylori* gastritis and autoimmune atrophic gastritis can interfere with the body's ability to absorb iron from food, which may also cause anemia.
- **Vitamin B_{12} deficiency and pernicious anemia.** People with autoimmune atrophic gastritis do not produce enough intrinsic factor. Intrinsic factor is a protein made in the stomach and helps the intestines absorb vitamin B_{12}. The body needs vitamin B_{12} to make red blood cells and nerve cells. Poor absorption of vitamin B_{12} may lead to a type of anemia called pernicious anemia.
- **Growths in the stomach lining.** Chronic gastritis increases the chance of developing benign, or noncancerous, and malignant, or cancerous, growths in the stomach lining. Chronic *H. pylori* gastritis increases the chance of developing a type of cancer called gastric mucosa-associated lymphoid tissue (MALT) lymphoma.

In most cases, acute gastritis does not lead to complications. In rare cases, acute stress gastritis can cause severe bleeding that can be life threatening.

How Is Gastritis Diagnosed?

A healthcare provider diagnoses gastritis based on the following:

- Medical history
- Physical exam
- Upper GI endoscopy
- Other tests

Medical History

Taking a medical history may help the healthcare provider diagnose gastritis. He or she will ask the patient to provide a medical history. The history may include questions about chronic symptoms and travel to developing countries.

Physical Exam

A physical exam may help diagnose gastritis. During a physical exam, a healthcare provider usually:

- Examines a patient's body
- Uses a stethoscope to listen to sounds in the abdomen
- Taps on the abdomen checking for tenderness or pain

Upper Gastrointestinal Endoscopy

Upper GI endoscopy is a procedure that uses an endoscope—a small, flexible camera with a light—to see the upper GI tract. A healthcare provider performs the test at a hospital or an outpatient center. The healthcare provider carefully feeds the endoscope down the esophagus and into the stomach and duodenum. The small camera built into the endoscope transmits a video image to a monitor, allowing close examination of the GI lining. A healthcare provider may give a patient a liquid anesthetic to gargle or may spray anesthetic on the back of the patient's throat before inserting the endoscope. A healthcare provider will place an intravenous (IV) needle in a vein in the arm to administer sedation. Sedatives help patients stay relaxed and comfortable. The test may show signs of inflammation or erosions in the stomach lining.

The healthcare provider can use tiny tools passed through the endoscope to perform biopsies. A biopsy is a procedure that involves taking a piece of tissue for examination with a microscope by a pathologist—a doctor who specializes in examining tissues to diagnose diseases. A healthcare provider may use the biopsy to diagnose gastritis, find the cause of gastritis, and find out if chronic gastritis has progressed to atrophic gastritis.

Other Tests

A healthcare provider may have a patient complete other tests to identify the cause of gastritis or any complications. These tests may include the following:

- **Upper GI series.** It is an X-ray exam that provides a look at the shape of the upper GI tract. An X-ray technician performs this test at a hospital or an outpatient center, and a radiologist—a doctor who specializes in medical imaging—interprets the images. This test does not require anesthesia. A patient should not eat or drink before the procedure, as directed by the healthcare provider. Patients should check with their healthcare provider about what to do to prepare for an upper GI series. During the procedure, the patient will stand or sit in front of an X-ray machine and drink barium, a chalky liquid. Barium coats the esophagus, stomach, and small intestine so the radiologist and healthcare provider can see these organs' shapes more clearly on X-rays. A patient may experience bloating and nausea for a short time after the test. For several days afterward, barium liquid in the GI tract may cause white or light-colored stools. A healthcare provider will give the patient specific instructions about eating and drinking after the test.
- **Blood tests.** A healthcare provider may use blood tests to check for anemia or *H. pylori*. A healthcare provider draws a blood sample during an office visit or at a commercial facility and sends the sample to a lab for analysis.
- **Stool test.** A healthcare provider may use a stool test to check for blood in the stool, another sign of bleeding in the stomach, and for *H. pylori* infection. A stool test is an analysis of a sample of stool. The healthcare provider will give the patient a container for catching and storing the stool. The patient returns the sample to the healthcare provider or a commercial facility that will send the sample to a lab for analysis.
- **Urea breath test.** A healthcare provider may use a urea breath test to check for *H. pylori* infection. The patient swallows a

capsule, liquid, or pudding that contains urea—a waste product the body produces as it breaks down protein. The urea is "labeled" with a special carbon atom. If *H. pylori* are present, the bacteria will convert the urea into carbon dioxide. After a few minutes, the patient breathes into a container, exhaling carbon dioxide. A nurse or technician will perform this test at a healthcare provider's office or a commercial facility and send the samples to a lab. If the test detects the labeled carbon atoms in the exhaled breath, the healthcare provider will confirm an *H. pylori* infection in the GI tract.

How Is Gastritis Treated?

Healthcare providers treat gastritis with medications to:

- Reduce the amount of acid in the stomach
- Treat the underlying cause

Reduce the Amount of Acid in the Stomach

The stomach lining of a person with gastritis may have less protection from acidic digestive juice. Reducing acid can promote healing of the stomach lining. Medications that reduce acid include:

- Antacids, such as Alka-Seltzer, Maalox, Mylanta, Rolaids, and Riopan. Many brands use different combinations of three basic salts—magnesium, aluminum, and calcium—along with hydroxide or bicarbonate ions to neutralize stomach acid. Antacids, however, can have side effects. Magnesium salt can lead to diarrhea, and aluminum salt can cause constipation. Magnesium and aluminum salts are often combined in a single product to balance these effects. Calcium carbonate antacids, such as Tums, Titralac, and Alka-2, can cause constipation.
- H2 blockers, such as cimetidine (Tagamet HB), famotidine (Pepcid AC), nizatidine (Axid AR), and ranitidine (Zantac 75). H2 blockers decrease acid production. They are available in both over-the-counter and prescription strengths.
- Proton pump inhibitors (PPIs) include omeprazole (Prilosec, Zegerid), lansoprazole (Prevacid), dexlansoprazole (Dexilant), pantoprazole (Protonix), rabeprazole (AcipHex), and esomeprazole (Nexium). PPIs decrease acid production more effectively than H2 blockers. All of these medications are

available by prescription. Omeprazole and lansoprazole are also available in over-the-counter strength.

Treat the Underlying Cause

Depending on the cause of gastritis, a healthcare provider may recommend additional treatments.

- Treating *H. pylori* infection with antibiotics is important, even if a person does not have symptoms from the infection. Curing the infection often cures gastritis and decreases the chance of developing complications, such as peptic ulcer disease, MALT lymphoma, and gastric cancer.
- Avoiding the cause of reactive gastritis can provide some people with a cure. For example, if prolonged NSAID use is the cause of gastritis, a healthcare provider may advise the patient to stop taking the NSAIDs, reduce the dose, or change pain medications.
- Healthcare providers may prescribe medications to prevent or treat stress gastritis in a patient who is critically ill or injured. Medications to protect the stomach lining include sucralfate (Carafate), H2 blockers, and PPIs. Treating the underlying illness or injury most often cures stress gastritis.
- Healthcare providers may treat people with pernicious anemia due to autoimmune atrophic gastritis with vitamin B_{12} injections.

How Can Gastritis Be Prevented?

People may be able to reduce their chances of getting gastritis by preventing *H. pylori* infection. No one knows for sure how *H. pylori* infection spreads, so prevention is difficult. To help prevent infection, healthcare providers advise people to:

- Wash their hands with soap and water after using the bathroom and before eating
- Eat food that has been washed well and cooked properly
- Drink water from a clean, safe source

Chapter 14

Headache and Its Link to Stress

You're sitting at your desk, working on a difficult task, when it suddenly feels as if a belt or vice is being tightened around the top of your head. Or you have periodic headaches that occur with nausea and increased sensitivity to light or sound. Maybe you are involved in a routine, nonstressful task when you're struck by head or neck pain.

Sound familiar? If so, you've suffered one of the many types of headache that can occur on its own or as part of another disease or health condition.

Anyone can experience a headache. Nearly 2 out of 3 children will have a headache by age 15. More than 9 in 10 adults will experience a headache sometime in their life. Headache is our most common form of pain and a major reason cited for days missed at work or school as well as visits to the doctor. Without proper treatment, headaches can be severe and interfere with daily activities.

Certain types of headache run in families. Episodes of headache may ease or even disappear for a time and recur later in life. It is possible to have more than one type of headache at the same time.

Primary headaches occur independently and are not caused by another medical condition. It is uncertain what sets the process of a primary headache in motion. A cascade of events that affect blood

This chapter includes text excerpted from "Headache: Hope through Research," National Institute of Neurological Disorders and Stroke (NINDS), April 2016.

vessels and nerves inside and outside the head causes pain signals to be sent to the brain. Brain chemicals called neurotransmitters are involved in creating head pain, as are changes in nerve cell activity (called cortical spreading depression). Migraine, cluster, and tension-type headache (TTH) are the more familiar types of primary headache.

Secondary headaches are symptoms of another health disorder that causes pain-sensitive nerve endings to be pressed on or pulled or pushed out of place. They may result from underlying conditions including fever, infection, medication overuse, stress or emotional conflict, high blood pressure, psychiatric disorders, head injury or trauma, stroke, tumors, and nerve disorders (particularly trigeminal neuralgia, a chronic pain condition that typically affects a major nerve on one side of the jaw or cheek).

Headaches can range in frequency and severity of pain. Some individuals may experience headaches once or twice a year, while others may experience headaches more than 15 days a month. Some headaches may recur or last for weeks at a time. Pain can range from mild to disabling and may be accompanied by symptoms such as nausea or increased sensitivity to noise or light, depending on the type of headache.

Why Headaches Hurt

Information about touch, pain, temperature, and vibration in the head and neck is sent to the brain by the trigeminal nerve, one of 12 pairs of cranial nerves that start at the base of the brain.

The nerve has three branches that conduct sensations from the scalp, the blood vessels inside and outside of the skull, the lining around the brain (the meninges), and the face, mouth, neck, ears, eyes, and throat.

Brain tissue itself lacks pain-sensitive nerves and does not feel pain. Headaches occur when pain-sensitive nerve endings called nociceptors react to headache triggers (such as stress, certain foods or odors, or use of medicines) and send messages through the trigeminal nerve to the thalamus, the brain's "relay station" for pain sensation from all over the body. The thalamus controls the body's sensitivity to light and noise and sends messages to parts of the brain that manage awareness of pain and emotional response to it. Other parts of the brain may also be part of the process, causing nausea, vomiting, diarrhea, trouble concentrating, and other neurological symptoms.

When to See a Doctor

Not all headaches require a physician's attention. But headaches can signal a more serious disorder that requires prompt medical care. Immediately call or see a physician if you or someone you're with experience any of these symptoms:

- Sudden, severe headache that may be accompanied by a stiff neck
- Severe headache accompanied by fever, nausea, or vomiting that is not related to another illness
- "First" or "worst" headache, often accompanied by confusion, weakness, double vision, or loss of consciousness
- Headache that worsens over days or weeks or has changed in pattern or behavior
- Recurring headache in children
- Headache following a head injury
- Headache and a loss of sensation or weakness in any part of the body, which could be a sign of a stroke
- Headache associated with convulsions
- Headache associated with shortness of breath
- Two or more headaches a week
- Persistent headache in someone who has been previously headache-free, particularly in someone over age 50
- New headaches in someone with a history of cancer or human immunodeficiency virus (HIV) / acquired immunodeficiency syndrome (AIDS)

Diagnosing Your Headache

How and under what circumstances a person experiences a headache can be key to diagnosing its cause. Keeping a headache journal can help a physician better diagnose your type of headache and determine the best treatment. After each headache, note the time of day when it occurred; its intensity and duration; any sensitivity to light, odors, or sound; activity immediately prior to the headache; use of prescription and nonprescription medicines; amount of sleep the previous night; any stressful or emotional conditions; any influence from weather or daily activity; foods and fluids consumed in the past 24 hours; and any known health conditions at that time. Women should record the days of their menstrual cycles. Include notes about other family members who have a history of headache or other disorder. A pattern may emerge that can be helpful to reducing or preventing headaches.

Once your doctor has reviewed your medical and headache history and conducted a physical and neurological exam, lab screening and diagnostic tests may be ordered to either rule out or identify conditions that might be the cause of your headaches. Blood tests and urinalysis can help diagnose brain or spinal cord infections, blood vessel damage, and toxins that affect the nervous system. Testing a sample of the fluid that surrounds the brain and spinal cord can detect infections, bleeding in the brain (called a brain hemorrhage), and measure any buildup of pressure within the skull. Diagnostic imaging, such as with computed tomography (CT) and magnetic resonance imaging (MRI), can detect irregularities in blood vessels and bones, certain brain tumors and cysts, brain damage from head injury, brain hemorrhage, inflammation, infection, and other disorders. Neuroimaging also gives doctors a way to see what's happening in the brain during headache attacks. An electroencephalogram (EEG) measures brain wave activity and can help diagnose brain tumors, seizures, head injury, and inflammation that may lead to headaches.

Headache Types and Their Treatment

The International Classification of Headache Disorders (ICHD), published by the International Headache Society, is used to classify more than 150 types of primary and secondary headache disorders.

Primary headache disorders are divided into four main groups: migraine, TTH, trigeminal autonomic cephalgias (TAC) (a group of short-lasting but severe headaches), and a miscellaneous group.

Migraine

If you suffer from migraine headaches, you're not alone. About 12 percent of the U.S. population experience migraines. Migraine headaches are characterized by throbbing and pulsating pain caused by the activation of nerve fibers that reside within the wall of brain blood vessels traveling within the meninges.

Migraines headaches are recurrent attacks of moderate to severe pain that is throbbing or pulsing and often strikes one side of the head.

Untreated attacks last from 4–72 hours. Other common symptoms are increased sensitivity to light, noise, and odors; and nausea and vomiting. Routine physical activity, movement, or even coughing or sneezing can worsen the headache pain.

Migraines occur most frequently in the morning, especially upon waking. Some people have migraines at predictable times, such as before menstruation or on weekends following a stressful week of work. Many people feel exhausted or weak following a migraine but are usually symptom-free between attacks.

A number of different factors can increase your risk of having a migraine. These factors, which trigger the headache process, vary from person to person and include sudden changes in weather or environment, too much or not enough sleep, strong odors or fumes, emotion, stress, overexertion, loud or sudden noises, motion sickness, low blood sugar, skipped meals, tobacco, depression, anxiety, head trauma, hangover, some medications, hormonal changes, and bright or flashing lights. Medication overuse or missed doses may also cause headaches. In some 50 percent of migraine sufferers, foods or ingredients can trigger headaches. These include aspartame, caffeine (or caffeine withdrawal), wine and other types of alcohol, chocolate, aged cheeses, monosodium glutamate, some fruits and nuts, fermented or pickled goods, yeast, and cured or processed meats. Keeping a diet journal will help identify food triggers.

Migraine treatment is aimed at relieving symptoms and preventing additional attacks. Quick steps to ease symptoms may include napping or resting with eyes closed in a quiet, darkened room; placing a cool cloth or ice pack on the forehead, and drinking lots of fluid, particularly if the migraine is accompanied by vomiting. Small amounts of caffeine may help relieve symptoms during a migraine's early stages.

Drug therapy for migraine is divided into acute and preventive treatment. Acute or "abortive" medications are taken as soon as symptoms occur to relieve pain and restore function. Preventive treatment involves taking medicines daily to reduce the severity of future attacks or keep them from happening. The U.S. Food and Drug Administration (FDA) has approved a variety of drugs for these treatment methods. Headache drug use should be monitored by a physician, since some drugs may cause side effects.

Tension-Type Headache (TTH)

Tension-type headache (TTH), previously called muscle contraction headache, is the most common type of headache. Its name indicates the role of stress and mental or emotional conflict in triggering the pain and contracting muscles in the neck, face, scalp, and jaw. TTH may also be caused by jaw clenching, intense work, missed meals, depression, anxiety, or too little sleep. Sleep apnea may also cause TTH, especially in the morning. The pain is usually mild to moderate and feels as if constant pressure is being applied to the front of the face or to the head or neck. It also may feel as if a belt is being tightened around the head. Most often the pain is felt on both sides of the head. People who suffer TTH may also feel overly sensitive to light and sound but there is no preheadache aura as with migraine.

Typically, TTH usually disappears once the period of stress or related cause has ended. TTH affect women slightly more often than men. The headaches usually begin in adolescence and reach peak activity in the 30s. They have not been linked to hormones and do not have a strong hereditary connection.

There are two forms of TTH:

Episodic tension-type headaches occur between 10 and 15 days per month, with each attack lasting from 30 minutes to several days. Although the pain is not disabling, the severity of pain typically increases with the frequency of attacks.

Chronic tension-type attacks usually occur more than 15 days per month over a 3-month period. The pain, which can be constant over a period of days or months, strikes both sides of the head and is more severe and disabling than episodic headache pain. Chronic tension headaches can cause sore scalps—even combing your hair can be painful. Most individuals will have had some form of episodic TTH prior to the onset of chronic TTH.

The first step in caring for a TTH involves treating any specific disorder or disease that may be causing it. For example, arthritis of the neck is treated with anti-inflammatory medication and temporomandibular joint dysfunction may be helped by corrective devices for the mouth and jaw. A sleep study may be needed to detect sleep apnea and should be considered when there is a history of snoring, daytime sleepiness, or obesity.

A physician may suggest using analgesics, nonsteroidal anti-inflammatory drugs (NSAIDs), or antidepressants to treat a TTH that is not associated with a disease. Triptan drugs, barbiturates (drugs that have a relaxing or sedative effect), and ergot derivatives may provide relief to people who suffer from both migraine and TTH.

Alternative therapies for chronic TTH include biofeedback, relaxation training, meditation, and cognitive behavioral therapy (CBT) to reduce stress. A hot shower or moist heat applied to the back of the neck may ease symptoms of infrequent tension headaches. Physical therapy, massage, and gentle exercise of the neck may also be helpful.

Trigeminal Autonomic Cephalgias (TAC)

Some primary headaches are characterized by severe pain in or around the eye on one side of the face and autonomic (or involuntary) features on the same side, such as red and teary eye, drooping eyelid, and runny nose. These disorders, called TAC (cephalgia meaning head pain), differ in attack duration and frequency, and have episodic and chronic forms. Episodic attacks occur on a daily or near-daily basis for weeks or months with pain-free remissions. Chronic attacks occur on a daily or near-daily basis for a year or more with only brief remissions.

Cluster headache—the most severe form of primary headache—involves sudden, extremely painful headaches that occur in "clusters," usually at the same time of the day and night for several weeks. They strike one side of the head, often behind or around one eye, and may be preceded by a migraine-like aura and nausea. The pain usually peaks 5–10 minutes after onset and continues at that intensity for up to 3 hours. The nose and the eye on the affected side of the face may get red, swollen, and teary. Some people will experience restlessness and agitation, changes in heart rate and blood pressure, and sensitivity to light, sound, or smell. Cluster headaches often wake people from sleep.

Treatment options include noninvasive vagus nerve stimulation (approved by the FDA, using a hand-held device to provide electrical stimulation to the vagus nerve through the skin), triptan drugs, and oxygen therapy (in which pure oxygen is breathed through a mask to reduce blood flow to the brain). Certain antipsychotic drugs, calcium-channel blockers, and anticonvulsants can reduce pain severity and frequency of attacks. In extreme cases, electrical stimulation of the occipital nerve to prevent nerve signaling or surgical procedures that destroy or cut certain facial nerves may provide relief.

Paroxysmal hemicrania is a rare form of primary headache that usually begins in adulthood. Pain and related symptoms may be similar to those felt in cluster headaches, but with shorter duration. Attacks typically occur 5–40 times per day, with each attack lasting 2–45 minutes. Severe throbbing, claw-like, or piercing pain is felt on one side of the face-in, around, or behind the eye and occasionally reaching to the back of the neck. Other symptoms may include red and watery eyes, a drooping or swollen eyelid on the affected side of the face, and nasal congestion.

The NSAID indomethacin can quickly halt the pain and related symptoms of paroxysmal hemicrania, but symptoms recur once the drug treatment is stopped. Nonprescription analgesics and calcium-channel blockers can ease discomfort, particularly if taken when symptoms first appear.

SUNCT (Short-lasting, Unilateral, Neuralgiform headache attacks with Conjunctival injection and Tearing) is a very rare type of headache with bursts of moderate to severe burning, piercing, or throbbing pain that is usually felt in the forehead, eye, or temple on one side of the head. The pain usually peaks within seconds of onset and may follow a pattern of increasing and decreasing intensity. Attacks typically occur during the day and last from 5 seconds to 4 minutes per episode. Individuals generally have five to six attacks per hour and are pain-free between attacks. This primary headache is slightly more common in men than in women, with onset usually after age 50. SUNCT may be episodic, occurring once or twice annually with headaches that remit and recur, or chronic, lasting more than 1 year.

SUNCT is very difficult to treat. Anticonvulsants may relieve some of the symptoms, while anesthetics and corticosteroid drugs can treat some of the severe pain felt during these headaches. Surgery and glycerol injections to block nerve signaling along the trigeminal nerve have poor outcomes and provide only temporary relief in severe cases. Doctors are beginning to use deep brain stimulation (involving a surgically implanted battery-powered electrode that emits pulses of energy to surrounding brain tissue) to reduce the frequency of attacks in severely affected individuals.

Miscellaneous Primary Headaches

Other headaches that are not caused by other disorders include:

Chronic daily headache refers to a group of headache disorders that occur at least 15 days a month during a 3-month period. In addition to chronic tension-type headache (TTH), chronic migraine, and medication overuse headache, these headaches include hemicrania continua (HC) and new daily persistent headache. Individuals feel constant, mostly moderate pain throughout the day on the sides or top of the head. They may also experience other types of headache. Adolescents and adults may experience chronic daily headaches. In children, stress from school and family activities may contribute to these headaches.

- Hemicrania continua (HC) is marked by continuous, fluctuating pain that always occurs on the same side of the face and head. The headache may last from minutes to days and is associated with symptoms including tearing, red and irritated eyes, sweating, stuffy or runny nose, and swollen and drooping eyelids. The pain may get worse as the headache progresses. Migraine-like symptoms include nausea, vomiting, and sensitivity to light and sound. Physical exertion and alcohol use may increase headache severity. The disorder is more common in women than in men and its cause is unknown. HC has two forms: chronic, with daily headaches, and remitting or episodic, in which headaches may occur over a period of 6 months and are followed by a pain-free period of weeks to months before recurring. Most individuals have attacks of increased pain 3–5 times per 24-hour cycle. The NSAID indomethacin usually provides rapid relief from symptoms. Corticosteroids may also provide temporary relief from some symptoms.
- New daily persistent headache (NDPH), previously called chronic benign daily headache, is known for its constant daily pain that ranges from mild to severe. Individuals can often recount the exact date and time that the headache began. Daily headaches can occur for more than 3 months (and sometimes years) without lessening or ending. Symptoms include an abnormal sensitivity to light or sound, nausea, lightheadedness, and a pressing, throbbing, or tightening pain felt on both sides of the head. NDPH occurs more often in women than in men. Most sufferers do not have a prior history of headache. NDPH may occur spontaneously or following infection, medication use, trauma, high spinal fluid pressure, or other condition. The disorder has two forms: one that usually ends on its own within several months and does not require treatment, and a longer-lasting form that is difficult to treat. Muscle relaxants, antidepressants, and anticonvulsants may provide some relief.

Primary stabbing headache, also known as "ice pick" or "jabs and jolts" headache, is characterized by intense piercing pain that strikes without warning and generally lasts 1–10 seconds. The stabbing pain usually occurs around the eye but may be felt in multiple sites along the trigeminal nerve. Onset typically occurs between 45 and 50 years of age. Some individuals may have only one headache per year while others may have multiple headaches daily. Most attacks are spontaneous but headaches may be triggered by sudden movement, bright lights, or emotional stress. Primary stabbing headache occurs most often in people who have migraine, HC, tension-type, or cluster headaches. The disorder is hard to treat, because each attack is extremely short. Indomethacin and other headache preventive medications can relieve pain in people who have multiple episodes of primary stabbing headache.

Primary exertional headache may be brought on by fits of coughing or sneezing or intense physical activity such as running, basketball, lifting weights, or sexual activity. The headache begins at the onset of activity. Pain rarely lasts more than several minutes but can last up to 2 days. Symptoms may include nausea and vomiting. This type of headache is typically seen in individuals who have a family history of migraine. Warm-up exercises prior to the physical activity can help prevent the headache and indomethacin can relieve the headache pain.

Hypnic headache, previously called "alarm-clock" headache, awakens people mostly at night. Onset is usually after age 50. Hypnic headache may occur 15 or more times per month, with no known trigger. Bouts of mild to moderate throbbing pain usually last from 15 minutes to 3 hours after waking and are most often felt on both sides of the head. Other symptoms include nausea or increased sensitivity to sound or light. Hypnic headache may be a disorder of rapid eye movement (REM) sleep as the attacks occur most often during dreaming. Both men and women are affected by this disorder, which is usually treated with caffeine, indomethacin, or lithium.

If you've ever eaten or inhaled a cold substance very fast, you may have had what's called an ice cream headache (sometimes called "brain freeze"). This headache happens when cold materials such as cold drinks or ice cream hit the warm roof of your mouth. Local blood vessels constrict to reduce the loss of body heat and then relax and allow the blood flow to increase. The resulting burst of pain lasts for about 5 minutes. Ice cream headache is more common in individuals who have migraine. The pain stops once the body adapts to the temperature change.

Coping with Headache

Headache treatment is a partnership between you and your doctor, and honest communication is essential. Finding a quick fix to your headache may not be possible. It may take some time for your doctor or specialist to determine the best course of treatment. Avoid using OTC medicines more than twice a week, as they may actually worsen headache pain and the frequency of attacks. Visit a local headache support group meeting (if available) to learn how others with headache cope with their pain and discomfort. Relax whenever possible to ease stress and related symptoms, get enough sleep, regularly perform aerobic exercises, and eat a regularly scheduled and healthy diet that avoids food triggers. Gaining more control over your headache, stress, and emotions will make you feel better and let you embrace daily activities as much as possible.

Chapter 15

Heart and Cardiovascular Problems

Chapter Contents

Section 15.1

Stress and Heart Disease

This section includes text excerpted from "In Brief: Your Guide to Living Well with Heart Disease," National Heart, Lung, and Blood Institute (NHLBI), February 15, 2006. Reviewed June 2018.

If you have heart disease, or think you do, there's a lot you can do to protect your heart health. This section gives you the key steps to control the disease, including how to survive a heart attack and prevent serious damage to heart muscle. Caring for your heart is worth the effort. Use the information here to start today to take charge of your heart health.

What Is Heart Disease?

Coronary heart disease (CHD)—often simply called heart disease—occurs when the arteries that supply blood to the heart muscle become hardened and narrowed due to a buildup of plaque on the inner walls of the arteries. A heart attack occurs when the plaque bursts and a clot forms over the plaque, blocking flow through the artery and preventing oxygen and nutrients from getting to the heart. Heart disease is a lifelong condition. Even if you've had surgery or other procedures to help with blood flow in your heart, your arteries remain damaged. Their condition will worsen unless you make changes in your daily habits. There is much you can do to control heart disease, prevent a first or second heart attack, and increase your chances for a long and vital life.

Getting Tested

If you have been told that you have heart disease, you may have had one or more screening tests. Tests for blood pressure and cholesterol levels are often done as part of routine physicals. Additional tests that may indicate heart muscle damage or blood flow problems help doctors evaluate the severity of your condition. Most tests are done outside of the body and are painless.

Risk Factors

Risk factors are health conditions or habits that increase the chances of developing a disease or having it worsen. Because you already have heart disease, you'll need to work especially hard to control your risk factors. There are two types of heart disease risk factors—those that are beyond your control and those that can be changed. Those that can't be changed are a family history of early heart disease and age. For women, heart disease risk increases at age 55; for men, it's age 45.

The risk factors you can control are smoking, high blood pressure, high blood cholesterol, overweight/obesity, physical inactivity, and diabetes. While having even one risk factor is dangerous, having multiple risk factors is especially serious, because risk factors tend to "gang up" and worsen each other's effects.

Treatment

Heart disease and its risk factors can be treated in three ways: by making heart-healthy changes in your daily habits, by taking medication, and in some cases, by having a medical procedure.

Making lifestyle changes. Adopting new habits, such as not smoking, following a heart-healthy eating plan, maintaining a healthy weight, and becoming more physically active can go a long way in helping to reduce your risk for worsened heart disease. You may need to manage certain risk factors vigorously. For example, having heart disease means that if you have high levels of a type of cholesterol called low-density lipoprotein (LDL), the "bad" cholesterol, your goal should be to bring the level to below 100 mg/dL. With your doctor, go over your heart disease risk factors and discuss how to reduce or eliminate each one.

Taking medication. Sometimes, lifestyle changes alone aren't enough to control heart disease and its risk factors. Medications are often used to treat high blood cholesterol, high blood pressure, or heart disease itself. For instance, medicine may be used to relieve angina, the chest pain that often accompanies heart disease. If you do take medications, it is vital to also keep up your heart healthy lifestyle, because it can help to keep doses of some medications as low as possible. Be sure to take your medication exactly as your doctor advises. (This includes aspirin and other over-the-counter (OTC) medicines). If you have uncomfortable side effects, let your doctor know. You may be able to change the dosage or switch to another medication.

Special procedures. Advanced heart disease may require procedures to open an artery and improve blood flow. These procedures are usually done to ease severe chest pain or to clear blockages in blood vessels. Two common procedures are coronary angioplasty (or "balloon" angioplasty) and coronary artery bypass graft (CABG) (or bypass surgery).

Getting Help for a Heart Attack

If you have heart disease, you are at high risk for having a heart attack. But planning ahead so you know what to do if heart attack signs occur will help you get treatment fast—when it can save heart muscle and even your life.

Know the Warning Signs

The main warning signs for both men and women are:

- **Chest discomfort.** Most heart attacks involve discomfort in the center of the chest that lasts for more than a few minutes. It may feel like pressure, squeezing, fullness, or pain. The discomfort may be mild or severe, and it may come and go.
- **Discomfort in other areas of the upper body,** including one or both arms, the back, neck, jaw, or stomach.
- **Shortness of breath.** This may occur with or without chest discomfort.
- **Other signs** include nausea, light-headedness, or breaking out in a cold sweat.

Calling 9-1-1 Can Save Your Life

If you think you or someone else may be having a heart attack, calling 9-1-1 quickly can prevent disability or death. Emergency medical personnel can begin treatment even before you get to the hospital. They have the equipment and training to start your heart beating again if it stops. Wait no more than a few minutes—5 minutes at most—before calling 9-1-1.

Time is crucial because the clot-dissolving medicines and other treatments that can stop a heart attack work best when given within the first hour after a heart attack starts. Even if you're not sure if you're having a heart attack, call 9-1-1. If your symptoms stop completely in less than 5 minutes, you should still call your doctor.

When you get to the hospital, ask for tests that can show whether you are having a heart attack. Speak up. Don't let anyone tell you that you're overreacting. You have the right to be thoroughly examined for a possible heart attack.

Prepare a Heart Attack Survival Plan

Be sure your family, friends, and coworkers know the warning signs and what to do if you should have a heart attack. Write down medications you take, any medicines you are allergic to, and phone numbers for your doctor and a person to contact in an emergency. Give this information to family members and keep a copy at home and at work.

Recovering Well: The Importance of Cardiac Rehabilitation

Millions of people survive heart attacks or heart surgery and resume active, normal lives. The time it takes to recover from a heart attack or heart procedure will depend on many factors, including successful participation in a cardiac rehabilitation program. Cardiac rehabilitation programs include exercise training, education on heart healthy living, and counseling to reduce stress and help you return to an active life. Almost everyone with heart disease can benefit from some kind of cardiac rehabilitation. Women are helped by cardiac rehabilitation as much as men are. If your doctor does not talk to you about cardiac rehabilitation programs, speak up and find out about programs that might fit your needs.

Exercise training will help you learn to safely participate in physical activity to strengthen your heart and your muscles and improve your stamina. If you are still recovering from surgery, you may worry that exercise could be harmful. In fact, physical activity can help prevent future heart problems. Your cardiac rehabilitation team will plan a program for you that is safe and effective.

Cardiac rehabilitation programs will also help you learn new heart-healthy habits, control your risk factors, and offer support to cope with the challenges of adjusting to life following a heart attack or heart surgery. Depending on your needs, a program may help you quit smoking, manage conditions such as diabetes, follow a heart-healthy eating plan, lose weight, and manage stress.

Section 15.2

Stress and Coronary Heart Disease

This section includes text excerpted from "Coronary Heart Disease," National Heart, Lung, and Blood Institute (NHLBI), November 9, 2015.

What Is Coronary Heart Disease (CHD)?

Coronary heart disease (CHD) is a disease in which a waxy substance called plaque builds up inside the coronary arteries. These arteries supply oxygen-rich blood to your heart muscle.

When plaque builds up in the arteries, the condition is called atherosclerosis. The buildup of plaque occurs over many years.

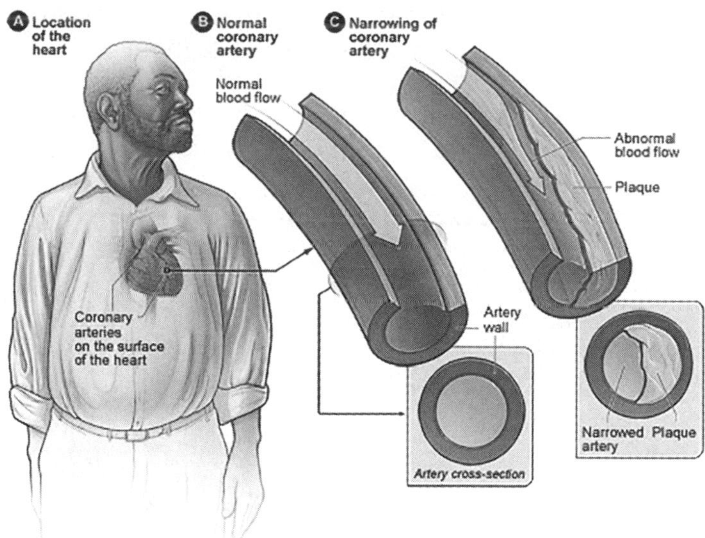

Figure 15.1. *Healthy Coronary Artery versus Damaged*

Figure A shows the location of the heart in the body. Figure B shows a normal coronary artery with normal blood flow. The inset image shows a cross-section of a normal coronary artery. Figure C shows a coronary artery narrowed by plaque. The buildup of plaque limits the flow of oxygen-rich blood through the artery. The inset image shows a cross-section of the plaque-narrowed artery.

If the flow of oxygen-rich blood to your heart muscle is reduced or blocked, angina or a heart attack can occur.

Angina is chest pain or discomfort. It may feel like pressure or squeezing in your chest. The pain also can occur in your shoulders, arms, neck, jaw, or back. Angina pain may even feel like indigestion.

A heart attack occurs if the flow of oxygen-rich blood to a section of heart muscle is cut off. If blood flow isn't restored quickly, the section of heart muscle begins to die. Without quick treatment, a heart attack can lead to serious health problems or death.

Over time, CHD can weaken the heart muscle and lead to heart failure and arrhythmias. Heart failure is a condition in which your heart can't pump enough blood to meet your body's needs. Arrhythmias are problems with the rate or rhythm of the heartbeat.

Other Names

- Atherosclerosis
- Coronary artery disease (CAD)
- Hardening of the arteries
- Heart disease
- Ischemic heart disease (IHD)
- Narrowing of the arteries

Causes

Research suggests that CHD starts when certain factors damage the inner layers of the coronary arteries. These factors include:

- Smoking
- High levels of certain fats and cholesterol in the blood
- High blood pressure
- High levels of sugar in the blood due to insulin resistance or diabetes
- Blood vessel inflammation

Plaque might begin to build up where the arteries are damaged. The buildup of plaque in the coronary arteries may start in childhood.

Over time, plaque can harden or rupture (break open). Hardened plaque narrows the coronary arteries and reduces the flow of oxygen-rich blood to the heart. This can cause angina (chest pain or discomfort).

If the plaque ruptures, blood cell fragments called platelets stick to the site of the injury. They may clump together to form blood clots.

Blood clots can further narrow the coronary arteries and worsen angina. If a clot becomes large enough, it can mostly or completely block a coronary artery and cause a heart attack.

Risk Factors

In the United States, CHD is a leading cause of death for both men and women. Each year, about 370,000 Americans die from CHD. Certain traits, conditions, or habits may raise your risk for CHD. The more risk factors you have, the more likely you are to develop the disease.

You can control many risk factors, which may help prevent or delay CHD.

Major Risk Factors

- **Unhealthy blood cholesterol levels.** This includes high LDL (low-density lipoprotein) cholesterol (sometimes called "bad" cholesterol) and low HDL (high-density lipoprotein) cholesterol (sometimes called "good" cholesterol).
- **High blood pressure.** Blood pressure is considered high if it stays at or above 140/90 mmHg over time. If you have diabetes or chronic kidney disease, high blood pressure is defined as 130/80 mmHg or higher. (The mmHg is millimeters of mercury—the units used to measure blood pressure.)
- **Smoking.** Smoking can damage and tighten blood vessels, lead to unhealthy cholesterol levels, and raise blood pressure. Smoking also can limit how much oxygen reaches the body's tissues.
- **Insulin resistance.** This condition occurs if the body can't use its own insulin properly. Insulin is a hormone that helps move blood sugar into cells where it's used for energy. Insulin resistance may lead to diabetes.
- **Diabetes.** With this disease, the body's blood sugar level is too high because the body doesn't make enough insulin or doesn't use its insulin properly.

- **Overweight or obesity.** The terms "overweight" and "obesity" refer to body weight that's greater than what is considered healthy for a certain height.
- **Metabolic syndrome.** Metabolic syndrome is the name for a group of risk factors that raises your risk for CHD and other health problems, such as diabetes and stroke.
- **Lack of physical activity.** Being physically inactive can worsen other risk factors for CHD, such as unhealthy blood cholesterol levels, high blood pressure, diabetes, and overweight or obesity.
- **Unhealthy diet.** An unhealthy diet can raise your risk for CHD. Foods that are high in saturated and trans fats, cholesterol, sodium, and sugar can worsen other risk factors for CHD.
- **Older age.** Genetic or lifestyle factors cause plaque to build up in your arteries as you age. In men, the risk for CHD increases starting at age 45. In women, the risk for CHD increases starting at age 55.
- A **family history** of early CHD is a risk factor for developing coronary heart disease, specifically if a father or brother is diagnosed before age 55, or a mother or sister is diagnosed before age 65.

Although older age and a family history of early heart disease are risk factors, it doesn't mean that you'll develop CHD if you have one or both. Controlling other risk factors often can lessen genetic influences and help prevent CHD, even in older adults.

Emerging Risk Factors

Researchers continue to study other possible risk factors for CHD. High levels of a protein called C-reactive protein (CRP) in the blood may raise the risk of CHD and heart attack. High levels of CRP are a sign of inflammation in the body. Inflammation is the body's response to injury or infection. Damage to the arteries' inner walls may trigger inflammation and help plaque grow. Research is underway to find out whether reducing inflammation and lowering CRP levels also can reduce the risk of CHD and heart attack. High levels of triglycerides in the blood also may raise the risk of CHD, especially in women. Triglycerides are a type of fat.

Other Risks Related to CHD

Other conditions and factors also may contribute to CHD, including:

- **Sleep apnea.** Sleep apnea is a common disorder in which you have one or more pauses in breathing or shallow breaths while you sleep. Untreated sleep apnea can increase your risk for high blood pressure, diabetes, and even a heart attack or stroke.
- **Stress.** Research shows that the most commonly reported "trigger" for a heart attack is an emotionally upsetting event, especially one involving anger.
- **Alcohol.** Heavy drinking can damage the heart muscle and worsen other CHD risk factors. Men should have no more than two drinks containing alcohol a day. Women should have no more than one drink containing alcohol a day.
- **Preeclampsia.** This condition can occur during pregnancy. The two main signs of preeclampsia are a rise in blood pressure and excess protein in the urine. Preeclampsia is linked to an increased lifetime risk of heart disease, including CHD, heart attack, heart failure, and high blood pressure.

Screening and Prevention

You can prevent and control coronary heart disease (CHD) by taking action to control your risk factors with heart-healthy lifestyle changes and medicines. Examples of risk factors you can control include high blood cholesterol, high blood pressure, and overweight and obesity. Only a few risk factors—such as age, gender, and family history—can't be controlled.

Your risk for CHD increases with the number of risk factors you have. To reduce your risk of CHD and heart attack, try to control each risk factor you have by adopting the following heart-healthy lifestyles:

- Heart-healthy eating
- Maintaining a healthy weight
- Managing stress
- Physical activity
- Quitting smoking

Know your family history of health problems related to CHD. If you or someone in your family has CHD, be sure to tell your doctor. If lifestyle changes aren't enough, you also may need medicines to control your CHD risk factors.

Signs, Symptoms, and Complications

A common symptom of coronary heart disease (CHD) is angina. Angina is chest pain or discomfort that occurs if an area of your heart muscle doesn't get enough oxygen-rich blood. Angina may feel like pressure or squeezing in your chest. You also may feel it in your shoulders, arms, neck, jaw, or back. Angina pain may even feel like indigestion. The pain tends to get worse with activity and go away with rest. Emotional stress also can trigger the pain.

Another common symptom of CHD is shortness of breath. This symptom occurs if CHD causes heart failure. When you have heart failure, your heart can't pump enough blood to meet your body's needs. Fluid builds up in your lungs, making it hard to breathe.

The severity of these symptoms varies. They may get more severe as the buildup of plaque continues to narrow the coronary arteries.

Signs and Symptoms of Heart Problems Related to CHD

Some people who have CHD have no signs or symptoms—a condition called silent CHD. The disease might not be diagnosed until a person has signs or symptoms of a heart attack, heart failure, or an arrhythmia (an irregular heartbeat).

Heart Attack

A heart attack occurs if the flow of oxygen-rich blood to a section of heart muscle is cut off. This can happen if an area of plaque in a coronary artery ruptures (breaks open).

Blood cell fragments called platelets stick to the site of the injury and may clump together to form blood clots. If a clot becomes large enough, it can mostly or completely block blood flow through a coronary artery.

If the blockage isn't treated quickly, the portion of heart muscle fed by the artery begins to die. Healthy heart tissue is replaced with scar tissue. This heart damage may not be obvious, or it may cause severe or long-lasting problems.

Heart with Muscle Damage and a Blocked Artery

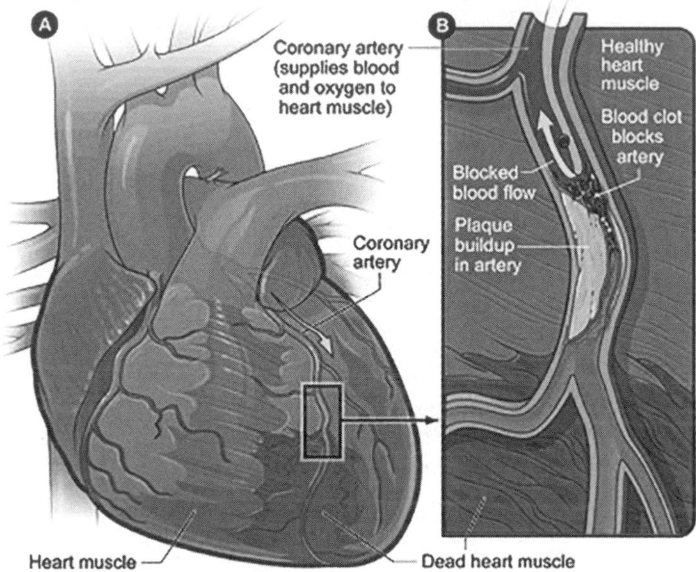

Figure 15.2. *Heart with Muscle Damage and a Blocked Artery*

Figure A is an overview of a heart and coronary artery showing damage (dead heart muscle) caused by a heart attack. Figure B is a cross-section of the coronary artery with plaque buildup and a blood clot.

The most common heart attack symptom is chest pain or discomfort. Most heart attacks involve discomfort in the center or left side of the chest that often lasts for more than a few minutes or goes away and comes back.

The discomfort can feel like uncomfortable pressure, squeezing, fullness, or pain. The feeling can be mild or severe. Heart attack pain sometimes feels like indigestion or heartburn.

The symptoms of angina can be similar to the symptoms of a heart attack. Angina pain usually lasts for only a few minutes and goes away with rest.

Chest pain or discomfort that doesn't go away or changes from its usual pattern (for example, occurs more often or while you're resting) might be a sign of a heart attack. If you don't know whether your chest pain is angina or a heart attack, call 9-1-1. All chest pain should be checked by a doctor.

Other common signs and symptoms of a heart attack include:

- Upper body discomfort in one or both arms, the back, neck, jaw, or upper part of the stomach

- Shortness of breath, which may occur with or before chest discomfort
- Nausea (feeling sick to your stomach), vomiting, light-headedness or fainting, or breaking out in a cold sweat
- Sleep problems, fatigue (tiredness), or lack of energy

Heart Failure

Heart failure is a condition in which your heart can't pump enough blood to meet your body's needs. Heart failure doesn't mean that your heart has stopped or is about to stop working.

The most common signs and symptoms of heart failure are shortness of breath or trouble breathing; fatigue; and swelling in the ankles, feet, legs, stomach, and veins in the neck.

All of these symptoms are the result of fluid buildup in your body. When symptoms start, you may feel tired and short of breath after routine physical effort, like climbing stairs.

Arrhythmia

An arrhythmia is a problem with the rate or rhythm of the heartbeat. When you have an arrhythmia, you may notice that your heart is skipping beats or beating too fast.

Some people describe arrhythmias as a fluttering feeling in the chest. These feelings are called palpitations.

Some arrhythmias can cause your heart to suddenly stop beating. This condition is called sudden cardiac arrest (SCA). SCA usually causes death if it's not treated within minutes.

Diagnosis

Your doctor will diagnose coronary heart disease (CHD) based on your medical and family histories, your risk factors for CHD, a physical exam, and the results from tests and procedures. No single test can diagnose CHD. If your doctor thinks you have CHD, he or she may recommend one or more of the following tests.

Electrocardiogram (EKG)

An EKG is a simple, painless test that detects and records the heart's electrical activity. The test shows how fast the heart is beating and its rhythm (steady or irregular). An EKG also records the strength and timing of electrical signals as they pass through the heart.

An EKG can show signs of heart damage due to CHD and signs of a previous or current heart attack.

Stress Testing

During stress testing, you exercise to make your heart work hard and beat fast while heart tests are done. If you can't exercise, you may be given medicine to raise your heart rate. When your heart is working hard and beating fast, it needs more blood and oxygen. Plaque-narrowed arteries can't supply enough oxygen-rich blood to meet your heart's needs. A stress test can show possible signs and symptoms of CHD, such as:

- Abnormal changes in your heart rate or blood pressure
- Shortness of breath or chest pain
- Abnormal changes in your heart rhythm or your heart's electrical activity

If you can't exercise for as long as what is considered normal for someone your age, your heart may not be getting enough oxygen-rich blood. However, other factors also can prevent you from exercising long enough (for example, lung diseases, anemia, or poor general fitness). As part of some stress tests, pictures are taken of your heart while you exercise and while you rest. These imaging stress tests can show how well blood is flowing in your heart and how well your heart pumps blood when it beats.

Echocardiography

Echocardiography (echo) uses sound waves to create a moving picture of your heart. The picture shows the size and shape of your heart and how well your heart chambers and valves are working. Echo also can show areas of poor blood flow to the heart, areas of heart muscle that aren't contracting normally, and previous injury to the heart muscle caused by poor blood flow.

Chest X-Ray

A chest X-ray takes pictures of the organs and structures inside your chest, such as your heart, lungs, and blood vessels. A chest X-ray can reveal signs of heart failure, as well as lung disorders and other causes of symptoms not related to CHD.

Blood Tests

Blood tests check the levels of certain fats, cholesterol, sugar, and proteins in your blood. Abnormal levels might be a sign that you're at risk for CHD.

Coronary Angiography and Cardiac Catheterization

Your doctor may recommend coronary angiography if other tests or factors show that you're likely to have CHD. This test uses dye and special X-rays to show the insides of your coronary arteries. To get the dye into your coronary arteries, your doctor will use a procedure called cardiac catheterization. A thin, flexible tube called a catheter is put into a blood vessel in your arm, groin (upper thigh), or neck. The tube is threaded into your coronary arteries, and the dye is released into your bloodstream.

Special X-rays are taken while the dye is flowing through your coronary arteries. The dye lets your doctor study the flow of blood through your heart and blood vessels.

Cardiac catheterization usually is done in a hospital. You're awake during the procedure. It usually causes little or no pain, although you may feel some soreness in the blood vessel where your doctor inserts the catheter.

Treatment

Treatments for coronary heart disease (CHD) include heart-healthy lifestyle changes, medicines, medical procedures and surgery, and cardiac rehabilitation. Treatment goals may include:

- Lowering the risk of blood clots forming (blood clots can cause a heart attack)
- Preventing complications of coronary heart disease
- Reducing risk factors in an effort to slow, stop, or reverse the buildup of plaque
- Relieving symptoms
- Widening or bypassing clogged arteries

Heart-Healthy Lifestyle Changes

Your doctor may recommend heart-healthy lifestyle changes if you have CHD. Heart-healthy lifestyle changes include:

- Managing stress
- Heart-healthy eating
- Maintaining a healthy weight
- Physical activity
- Quitting smoking

Managing Stress

Research shows that the most commonly reported "trigger" for a heart attack is an emotionally upsetting event—particularly one involving anger. Also, some of the ways people cope with stress—such as drinking, smoking, or overeating—aren't healthy. Learning how to manage stress, relax, and cope with problems can improve your emotional and physical health. Consider healthy stress-reducing activities, such as:

- A stress management program
- Meditation
- Physical activity
- Relaxation therapy
- Talking things out with friends or family

Heart-Healthy Eating

Your doctor may recommend heart-healthy eating, which should include:

- Fat-free or low-fat dairy products, such as fat-free milk
- Fish high in omega-3 fatty acids, such as salmon, tuna, and trout, about twice a week
- Fruits, such as apples, bananas, oranges, pears, and prunes
- Legumes, such as kidney beans, lentils, chickpeas, black-eyed peas, and lima beans
- Vegetables, such as broccoli, cabbage, and carrots

- Whole grains, such as oatmeal, brown rice, and corn tortillas

When following a heart-healthy diet, you should avoid eating:

- A lot of red meat
- Palm and coconut oils
- Sugary foods and beverages

Dietary Approaches to Stop Hypertension

Your doctor may recommend the Dietary Approaches to Stop Hypertension (DASH) eating plan if you have high blood pressure. The DASH eating plan focuses on fruits, vegetables, whole grains, and other foods that are heart healthy and low in fat, cholesterol, and sodium and salt.

The DASH eating plan is a good heart-healthy eating plan, even for those who don't have high blood pressure.

Alcohol

Try to limit alcohol intake. Too much alcohol can raise your blood pressure and triglyceride levels, a type of fat found in the blood. Alcohol also adds extra calories, which may cause weight gain. Men should have no more than two drinks containing alcohol a day. Women should have no more than one drink containing alcohol a day. One drink is:

- 12 ounces of beer
- 5 ounces of wine
- 1½ ounces of liquor

Maintaining a Healthy Weight

Maintaining a healthy weight is important for overall health and can lower your risk for coronary heart disease. Aim for a Healthy Weight by following a heart-healthy eating plan and keeping physically active. Knowing your body mass index (BMI) helps you find out if you're a healthy weight in relation to your height and gives an estimate of your total body fat. To figure out your BMI, check out the National Heart, Lung, and Blood Institute's (NHLBI) online BMI calculator (www.nhlbi.nih.gov/health/educational/lose_wt/BMI/bmicalc.htm) or talk to your doctor.

A BMI:

- Below 18.5 is a sign that you are underweight

- Between 18.5 and 24.9 is in the normal range
- Between 25 and 29.9 is considered overweight
- Of 30 or more is considered obese

A general goal to aim for is a BMI of less than 25. Your doctor or healthcare provider can help you set an appropriate BMI goal. Measuring waist circumference helps screen for possible health risks. If most of your fat is around your waist rather than at your hips, you're at a higher risk for heart disease and type 2 diabetes. This risk may be high with a waist size that is greater than 35 inches for women or greater than 40 inches for men. If you're overweight or obese, try to lose weight. A loss of just 3–5 percent of your current weight can lower your triglycerides, blood glucose, and the risk of developing type 2 diabetes. Greater amounts of weight loss can improve blood pressure readings, lower LDL cholesterol, and increase HDL cholesterol.

Physical Activity

Routine physical activity can lower many CHD risk factors, including LDL ("bad") cholesterol, high blood pressure, and excess weight. Physical activity also can lower your risk for diabetes and raise your HDL cholesterol level. HDL is the "good" cholesterol that helps prevent coronary heart disease.

Everyone should try to participate in moderate-intensity aerobic exercise at least 2 hours and 30 minutes per week, or vigorous aerobic exercise for 1 hour and 15 minutes per week. Aerobic exercise, such as brisk walking, is any exercise in which your heart beats faster and you use more oxygen than usual. The more active you are, the more you will benefit. Participate in aerobic exercise for at least 10 minutes at a time spread throughout the week.

Talk with your doctor before you start a new exercise plan. Ask your doctor how much and what kinds of physical activity are safe for you.

Quitting Smoking

If you smoke, quit. Smoking can raise your risk for CHD and heart attack and worsen other CHD risk factors. Talk with your doctor about programs and products that can help you quit smoking. Also, try to avoid secondhand smoke. If you have trouble quitting smoking on your own, consider joining a support group. Many hospitals, workplaces, and community groups offer classes to help people quit smoking.

Medicines

Sometimes lifestyle changes aren't enough to control your blood cholesterol levels. For example, you may need statin medications to control or lower your cholesterol. By lowering your cholesterol level, you can decrease your chance of having a heart attack or stroke. Doctors usually prescribe statins for people who have:

- CHD, peripheral artery disease (PAD), or had a stroke
- Diabetes
- High LDL cholesterol levels

Doctors may discuss beginning statin treatment with those who have an elevated risk for developing heart disease or having a stroke.

Your doctor also may prescribe other medications to:

- Decrease your chance of having a heart attack or dying suddenly
- Lower your blood pressure
- Prevent blood clots, which can lead to heart attack or stroke
- Prevent or delay the need for a stent or percutaneous coronary intervention (PCI) or surgery, such as coronary artery bypass grafting (CABG)
- Reduce your heart's workload and relieve CHD symptoms

Take all medicines regularly, as your doctor prescribes. Don't change the amount of your medicine or skip a dose unless your doctor tells you to. You should still follow a heart-healthy lifestyle, even if you take medicines to treat your CHD.

Living With

Coronary heart disease (CHD) can cause serious complications. However, if you follow your doctor's advice and adopt healthy lifestyle habits, you can prevent or reduce the risk of:

- Dying suddenly from heart problems
- Having a heart attack and damaging your heart muscle
- Damaging your heart because of reduced oxygen supply
- Having arrhythmias (irregular heartbeats)

Ongoing Care

Lifestyle changes and medicines can help control CHD. Lifestyle changes include following a healthy diet, being physically active, maintaining a healthy weight, quitting smoking, and managing stress. Work closely with your doctor to control your blood pressure and manage your blood cholesterol and blood sugar levels.

A blood test called a lipoprotein panel will measure your cholesterol and triglyceride levels. A fasting blood glucose test will check your blood sugar level and show whether you're at risk for or have diabetes. These tests show whether your risk factors are controlled, or whether your doctor needs to adjust your treatment for better results. Talk with your doctor about how often you should schedule office visits or blood tests. Between those visits, call your doctor if you have any new symptoms or if your symptoms worsen.

Heart Attack Warning Signs

CHD raises your risk for a heart attack. Learn the signs and symptoms of a heart attack, and call 9-1-1 if you have any of these symptoms:

- Chest pain or discomfort. This involves uncomfortable pressure, squeezing, fullness, or pain in the center or left side of the chest that can be mild or strong. This pain or discomfort often lasts more than a few minutes or goes away and comes back.
- Upper body discomfort in one or both arms, the back, neck, jaw, or upper part of the stomach
- Shortness of breath, which may occur with or before chest discomfort
- Nausea (feeling sick to your stomach), vomiting, lightheadedness or fainting, or breaking out in a cold sweat

Symptoms also may include sleep problems, fatigue (tiredness), and lack of energy. The symptoms of angina can be similar to the symptoms of a heart attack. Angina pain usually lasts for only a few minutes and goes away with rest. Chest pain or discomfort that doesn't go away or changes from its usual pattern (for example, occurs more often or while you're resting) can be a sign of a heart attack. If you don't know whether your chest pain is angina or a heart attack, call 9-1-1. Let the people you see regularly know you're at risk for a heart attack. They can seek emergency care for you if you suddenly faint, collapse, or have other severe symptoms.

Emotional Issues and Support

Living with CHD may cause fear, anxiety, depression, and stress. You may worry about heart problems or making lifestyle changes that are necessary for your health.

Talk about how you feel with your healthcare team. Talking to a professional counselor also can help. If you're very depressed, your doctor may recommend medicines or other treatments that can improve your quality of life. Joining a patient support group may help you adjust to living with CHD. You can see how other people who have the same symptoms have coped with them. Talk with your doctor about local support groups or check with an area medical center. Support from family and friends also can help relieve stress and anxiety. Let your loved ones know how you feel and what they can do to help you.

Section 15.3

Stress and Broken Heart Syndrome

This section includes text excerpted from "Broken Heart Syndrome," National Heart, Lung, and Blood Institute (NHLBI), August 11, 2014. Reviewed June 2018.

What Is Broken Heart Syndrome?

Broken heart syndrome is a condition in which extreme stress can lead to heart muscle failure. The failure is severe, but often short term. Most people who experience broken heart syndrome think they may be having a heart attack, a more common medical emergency caused by a blocked coronary (heart) artery. The two conditions have similar symptoms, including chest pain and shortness of breath. However, there's no evidence of blocked coronary arteries in broken heart syndrome, and most people have a full and quick recovery.

Broken heart syndrome is a recently recognized heart problem. It was originally reported in the Asian population in 1990 and named takotsubo cardiomyopathy. In this condition, the heart is so weak that it assumes a bulging shape ("tako tsubo" is the term for an octopus trap, whose shape resembles the bulging appearance of the heart during this condition). Cases have since been reported worldwide, and the first reports of broken heart syndrome in the United States appeared in 1998. The condition also is commonly called stress-induced cardiomyopathy.

The cause of broken heart syndrome is not fully known. In most cases, symptoms are triggered by extreme emotional or physical stress, such as intense grief, anger, or surprise. Researchers think that the stress releases hormones that "stun" the heart and affect its ability to pump blood to the body. (The term "stunned" is often used to indicate that the injury to the heart muscle is only temporary.)

People who have broken heart syndrome often have sudden intense chest pain and shortness of breath. These symptoms begin just a few minutes to hours after exposure to the unexpected stress. Many seek emergency care, concerned they are having a heart attack. Often, patients who have broken heart syndrome have previously been healthy. Women are more likely than men to have broken heart syndrome. Researchers are just starting to explore what causes this disorder and how to diagnose and treat it.

Broken Heart Syndrome versus Heart Attack

Symptoms of broken heart syndrome can look like those of a heart attack.

Most heart attacks are caused by blockages and blood clots forming in the coronary arteries, which supply the heart with blood. If these clots cut off the blood supply to the heart for a long enough period of time, heart muscle cells can die, leaving the heart with permanent damage. Heart attacks most often occur as a result of coronary heart disease (CHD), also called coronary artery disease (CAD).

Broken heart syndrome is quite different. Most people who experience broken heart syndrome have fairly normal coronary arteries, without severe blockages or clots. The heart cells are "stunned" by stress hormones but not killed. The "stunning" effects reverse quickly, often within just a few days or weeks. In most cases, there is no lasting damage to the heart.

Because symptoms are similar to a heart attack, it is important to seek help right away. You, and sometimes emergency care providers, may not be able to tell that you have broken heart syndrome until you have some tests.

All chest pain should be checked by a doctor. If you think you or someone else may be having heart attack symptoms or a heart attack, don't ignore it or feel embarrassed to call for help. Call 9-1-1 for emergency medical care. In the case of a heart attack, acting fast at the first sign of symptoms can save your life and limit damage to your heart.

Other Names

- Apical ballooning syndrome (ABS)
- Stress cardiomyopathy
- Stress-induced cardiomyopathy
- Takotsubo cardiomyopathy (TCM)
- Transient left ventricular apical ballooning syndrome (TLVABS)

Causes

The cause of broken heart syndrome isn't fully known. However, extreme emotional or physical stress is believed to play a role in causing the temporary disorder. Although symptoms are similar to those of a heart attack, what is happening to the heart is quite different. Most heart attacks are caused by near or complete blockage of a coronary artery. In broken heart syndrome, the coronary arteries are not blocked, although blood flow may be reduced.

Potential Triggers

In most cases, broken heart syndrome occurs after an intense and upsetting emotional or physical event. Some potential triggers of broken heart syndrome are:

- Emotional stressors—extreme grief, fear, or anger, for example as a result of the unexpected death of a loved one, financial or legal trouble, intense fear, domestic abuse, confrontational argument, car accident, public speaking, or even a surprise party.
- Physical stressors—an asthma attack, serious illness or surgery, or exhausting physical effort.

Potential Causes

Researchers think that sudden stress releases hormones that overwhelm or "stun" the heart. (The term "stunned" is often used to indicate that the injury to the heart muscle is only temporary.) This can trigger changes in heart muscle cells or coronary blood vessels, or both. The heart becomes so weak that its left ventricle (which is the chamber that pumps blood from your heart to your body) bulges and cannot pump well, while the other parts of the heart work normally or with even more forceful contractions. As a result, the heart is unable to pump properly. Researchers are trying to identify the precise way in which the stress hormones affect the heart. Broken heart syndrome may result from a hormone surge, coronary artery spasm, or microvascular dysfunction.

Hormone Surge

Intense stress causes large amounts of the “fight or flight” hormones, such as adrenaline and noradrenaline, to be released into your bloodstream. The hormones are meant to help you cope with the stress. Researchers think that the sudden surge of hormones overwhelms and stuns the heart muscle, producing symptoms similar to those of a heart attack.

Coronary Artery Spasm

Some research suggests that the extreme stress causes a temporary, sudden narrowing of one of the coronary arteries as a result of a spasm. The spasm slows or stops blood flow through the artery and starves a part of the heart of oxygen-rich blood.

Microvascular Dysfunction

Another theory that is gaining traction is that the very small coronary arteries (called microvascular arteries) do not function well due to low hormone levels occurring before or after menopause. The microvascular arteries fail to provide enough oxygen-rich blood to the heart muscle.

Risk Factors

Broken heart syndrome affects women more often than men. Often, people who experience broken heart syndrome have previously been healthy. Research shows that the traditional risk factors for heart disease may not apply to broken heart syndrome. People who might be at increased risk for broken heart syndrome include:

- Women who have gone through menopause, particularly women in their sixties and seventies

- People who often have no previous history of heart disease
- Asian and White populations

Although these are the characteristics for most cases of broken heart syndrome, the condition can occur in anyone. Research is ongoing to learn more about broken heart syndrome and its causes.

Screening and Prevention

Researchers are still learning about broken heart syndrome, and no treatments have been shown to prevent it. For people who have experienced the condition, the risk of recurrence is low. An emotionally upsetting or serious physical event can trigger broken heart syndrome. Learning how to manage stress, relax, and cope with problems can improve your emotional and physical health.

Having supportive people in your life with whom you can share your feelings or concerns can help relieve stress. Physical activity, medicine, and relaxation therapy also can help relieve stress. You may want to consider taking part in a stress management program. Also, some of the ways people cope with stress—such as drinking, smoking, or overeating—aren't healthy. Learning to manage stress includes adopting healthy habits that will keep your stress levels low and make it easier to deal with stress when it does happen. A healthy lifestyle includes following a healthy diet, being physically active, maintaining a healthy weight, and quitting smoking.

Signs, Symptoms, and Complications

All chest pain should be checked by a doctor. Because symptoms of broken heart syndrome are similar to those of a heart attack, it is important to seek help right away. Your doctor may not be able to diagnose broken heart syndrome until you have some tests.

Common Signs and Symptoms

The most common symptoms of broken heart syndrome are sudden, sharp chest pain and shortness of breath. Typically these symptoms begin just minutes to hours after experiencing a severe, and usually unexpected, stress.

Because the syndrome involves severe heart muscle weakness, some people also may experience signs and symptoms such as fainting, arrhythmias (fast or irregular heartbeats), cardiogenic shock (when the heart can't pump enough blood to meet the body's needs), low blood pressure, and heart failure.

Differences from a Heart Attack

Some of the signs and symptoms of broken heart syndrome differ from those of a heart attack. For example, in people who have broken heart syndrome:

- Symptoms (chest pain and shortness of breath) occur suddenly after having extreme emotional or physical stress
- Electrocardiogram (EKG) results don't look the same as the results for a person having a heart attack. (An EKG is a test that records the heart's electrical activity.)
- Blood tests show no signs or mild signs of heart damage.
- Tests show enlarged and unusual movement of the lower left heart chamber (the left ventricle).
- Tests show no signs of blockages in the coronary arteries.
- Recovery time is quick, usually within days or weeks (compared with the recovery time of a month or more for a heart attack).

Complications

Broken heart syndrome can be life threatening in some cases. It can lead to serious heart problems such as:

- Heart failure, a condition in which the heart can't pump enough blood to meet the body's needs
- Heart rhythm problems that cause the heart to beat much faster or slower than normal
- Heart valve problems

The good news is that most people who have broken heart syndrome make a full recovery within weeks. With medical care, even the most critically ill tend to make a quick and complete recovery.

Diagnosis

Because the symptoms are similar, at first your doctor may not be able to tell whether you are experiencing broken heart syndrome or having a heart attack. Therefore, the doctor's immediate goals will be:

- To determine what's causing your symptoms
- To determine whether you're having or about to have a heart attack

Your doctor will diagnose broken heart syndrome based on your signs and symptoms, your medical and family histories, and the results from tests and procedures.

Specialists Involved

Your doctor may refer you to a cardiologist. A cardiologist is a doctor who specializes in diagnosing and treating heart diseases and conditions.

Physical Exam and Medical History

Your doctor will do a physical exam and ask you to describe your symptoms. He or she may ask questions such as when your symptoms began, where you are feeling pain or discomfort and what it feels like, and whether the pain is constant or varies. To learn about your medical history, your doctor may ask about your overall health, risk factors for coronary heart disease (CHD) and other heart diseases, and family history. Your doctor will ask whether you've recently experienced any major stresses.

Diagnostic Tests and Procedures

No single test can diagnose broken heart syndrome. The tests and procedures for broken heart syndrome are similar to those used to diagnose CHD or heart attack. The diagnosis is made based on the results of the following standards tests to rule out heart attack and imaging studies to help establish broken heart syndrome.

Standard Tests and Procedures

Electrocardiogram (EKG)

An EKG is a simple, painless test that detects and records the heart's electrical activity. The test shows how fast your heart is beating and whether its rhythm is steady or irregular. An EKG also records the strength and timing of electrical signals as they pass through each part of the heart. The EKG may show abnormalities in your heartbeat, a sign of broken heart syndrome as well as heart damage due to CHD.

Blood Tests

Blood tests check the levels of certain substances in your blood, such as fats, cholesterol, sugar, and proteins. Blood tests help greatly in diagnosing broken heart syndrome, because certain enzymes (proteins in the blood) may be present in the blood to indicate the condition.

Imaging Procedures

Echocardiography

Echocardiography (echo) uses sound waves to create a moving picture of your heart. The test provides information about the size and shape of your heart and how well your heart chambers and valves are working. Echo also can show areas of heart muscle that aren't contracting well because of poor blood flow or previous injury.

The echo may show slowed blood flow in the left chamber of the heart.

Chest X-Ray

A chest X-ray is a painless test that creates pictures of the structures in your chest, such as your heart, lungs, and blood vessels. Your doctor will need a chest X-ray to analyze whether your heart has the enlarged shape that is a sign of broken heart syndrome.

A chest X-ray can reveal signs of heart failure, as well as lung disorders and other causes of symptoms not related to broken heart syndrome.

Cardiac Magnetic Resonance Imaging (MRI)

Cardiac magnetic resonance imaging (MRI) is a common test that uses radio waves, magnets, and a computer to make both still and moving pictures of your heart and major blood vessels. Doctors use cardiac MRI to get pictures of the beating heart and to look at its structure and function. These pictures can help them decide the best way to treat people who have heart problems.

Coronary Angiography and Cardiac Catheterization

Your doctor may recommend coronary angiography if other tests or factors suggest you have CHD. This test uses dye and special X-rays to look inside your coronary arteries.

To get the dye into your coronary arteries, your doctor will use a procedure called cardiac catheterization. A thin, flexible tube called a catheter is put into a blood vessel in your arm, groin (upper thigh), or neck. The tube is threaded into your coronary arteries, and the dye is released into your bloodstream.

Special X-rays are taken while the dye is flowing through your coronary arteries. The dye lets your doctor study the flow of blood through your heart and blood vessels.

Ventriculogram

Ventriculogram is another test that can be done during a cardiac catheterization that examines the left ventricle, which is the heart's main pumping chamber. During this test, a dye is injected into the inside of the heart and X-ray pictures are taken. The test can show the ventricle's size and how well it pumps blood. It also shows how well the blood flows through the aortic and mitral values.

Treatment

Even though broken heart syndrome may feel like a heart attack, it's a very different problem that needs a different type of treatment. The good news is that broken heart syndrome is usually treatable, and most people make a full recovery. Most people who experience broken heart syndrome stay in the hospital for a few days to a week. Initial treatment is aimed at improving blood flow to the heart, and may be similar to that for a heart attack until the diagnosis is clear. Further treatment can include medicines and lifestyle changes.

Medicines

Doctors may prescribe medicines to relieve fluid buildup, treat blood pressure problems, prevent blood clots, and manage stress hormones. Medicines are often discontinued once heart function has returned to normal.

Your doctor may prescribe the following medicines:

- ACE inhibitors (or angiotensin-converting enzyme inhibitors), to lower blood pressure and reduce strain on your heart
- Beta-blockers, to slow your heart rate and lower your blood pressure to decrease your heart's workload
- Diuretics (water or fluid pills), to help reduce fluid buildup in your lungs and swelling in your feet and ankles

- Antianxiety medicines, to help manage stress hormones

Take all of your medicines as prescribed. If you have side effects or other problems related to your medicines, tell your doctor. He or she may be able to provide other options.

Treatment of Complications

Broken heart syndrome can be life threatening in some cases. Because the syndrome involves severe heart muscle weakness, patients can experience shock, heart failure, low blood pressure, and potentially life-threatening heart rhythm abnormalities. The good news is that this condition improves very quickly, so with proper diagnosis and management, even the most critically ill tend to make a quick and complete recovery.

Lifestyle Changes

To stay healthy, it's important to find ways to reduce stress and cope with particularly upsetting situations. Learning how to manage stress, relax, and cope with problems can improve your emotional and physical health. Having supportive people in your life with whom you can share your feelings or concerns can help relieve stress. Physical activity, medicine, and relaxation therapy also can help relieve stress. You may want to consider taking part in a stress management program.

Treatments Not Helpful for Broken Heart Syndrome

Several procedures used to treat a heart attack are not helpful in treating broken heart syndrome. These procedures—percutaneous coronary intervention (PCI) (sometimes referred to as angioplasty), stent placement, and surgery—treat blocked arteries, which is not the cause of broken heart syndrome.

Living With

Most people who have broken heart syndrome make a full recovery within weeks. The risk is low for a repeat episode of this disorder.

Ongoing medical care and adopting a healthy lifestyle can help speed recovery and contribute to a long, healthy life.

Medicines

Some doctors recommend long-term treatment with beta-blockers or similar medicines to block the effects of stress hormones on the heart.

Regular Checkups

To check your heart health, your doctor may recommend echocardiography about a month after you're diagnosed with broken heart syndrome. Talk with your doctor about how often you should schedule follow-up visits.

Managing Stress

Learning how to manage stress, relax, and cope with problems can improve your emotional and physical health. Having supportive people in your life with whom you can share your feelings or concerns can help relieve stress. Physical activity, medicine, and relaxation therapy also can help relieve stress. You may want to consider taking part in a stress management program.

Section 15.4

Stress and Cholesterol Levels

This section includes text excerpted from "Cholesterol Levels: What You Need to Know," MedlinePlus, National Institutes of Health (NIH), December 4, 2017.

What Is Cholesterol?

Cholesterol is a waxy, fat-like substance that's found in all the cells in your body. Your liver makes cholesterol, and it is also in some foods, such as meat and dairy products. Your body needs some cholesterol to work properly. But if you have too much cholesterol in your blood, you have a higher risk of coronary artery disease.

How Do You Measure Cholesterol Levels?

A blood test called a lipoprotein panel can measure your cholesterol levels. Before the test, you'll need to fast (not eat or drink anything but water) for 9–12 hours. The test gives you information about your:

- **Total cholesterol**—a measure of the total amount of cholesterol in your blood. It includes the two types—low-density lipoprotein (LDL) cholesterol and high-density lipoprotein (HDL) cholesterol.
- **LDL (bad) cholesterol**—the main source of cholesterol buildup and blockage in the arteries
- **HDL (good) cholesterol**—HDL helps remove cholesterol from your arteries
- **Non-HDL**—this number is your total cholesterol minus your HDL. Your non-HDL includes LDL and other types of cholesterol such as VLDL (very-low-density lipoprotein)
- **Triglycerides**—another form of fat in your blood that can raise your risk for heart disease, especially in women

What Do My Cholesterol Numbers Mean?

Cholesterol numbers are measured in milligrams per deciliter (mg/dL). Here are the healthy levels of cholesterol, based on your age and gender:

Table 15.1. Anyone Age 19 or Younger

Type of Cholesterol	Healthy Level
Total Cholesterol	Less than 170mg/dL
Non-HDL	Less than 120mg/dL
LDL	Less than 100mg/dL
HDL	More than 45mg/dL

Table 15.2. Men Age 20 or Older

Type of Cholesterol	Healthy Level
Total Cholesterol	125–200mg/dL
Non-HDL	Less than 130mg/dL
LDL	Less than 100mg/dL
HDL	40mg/dL or higher

Table 15.3. Women Age 20 or Older

Type of Cholesterol	Healthy Level
Total Cholesterol	125–200mg/dL
Non-HDL	Less than 130mg/dL
LDL	Less than 100mg/dL
HDL	50mg/dL or higher

Triglycerides are not a type of cholesterol, but they are part of a lipoprotein panel (the test that measures cholesterol levels). A normal triglyceride level is below 150 mg/dL. You might need treatment if you have triglyceride levels that are borderline high (150–199 mg/dL) or high (200 mg/dL or more).

How Often Should I Get a Cholesterol Test?

When and how often you should get a cholesterol test depends on your age, risk factors, and family history. The general recommendations are:

For people who are age 19 or younger:

- The first test should be between ages 9–11
- Children should have the test again every 5 years
- Some children may have this test starting at age 2 if there is a family history of high blood cholesterol, heart attack, or stroke

For people who are age 20 or older:

- Younger adults should have the test every 5 years
- Men ages 45–65 and women ages 55–65 should have it every 1–2 years

What Affects My Cholesterol Levels?

A variety of things can affect cholesterol levels. These are some things you can do to lower your cholesterol levels:

- **Diet.** Saturated fat and cholesterol in the food you eat make your blood cholesterol level rise. Saturated fat is the main problem, but cholesterol in foods also matters. Reducing the amount of saturated fat in your diet helps lower your blood cholesterol level. Foods that have high levels of saturated fats include some meats, dairy products, chocolate, baked goods, and deep-fried and processed foods.

- **Weight.** Being overweight is a risk factor for heart disease. It also tends to increase your cholesterol. Losing weight can help lower your LDL (bad) cholesterol, total cholesterol, and triglyceride levels. It also raises your HDL (good) cholesterol level.
- **Physical activity.** Not being physically active is a risk factor for heart disease. Regular physical activity can help lower LDL (bad) cholesterol and raise HDL (good) cholesterol levels. It also helps you lose weight. You should try to be physically active for 30 minutes on most, if not all, days.
- **Smoking.** Cigarette smoking lowers your HDL (good) cholesterol. HDL helps to remove bad cholesterol from your arteries. So a lower HDL can contribute to a higher level of bad cholesterol.

Things outside of your control that can also affect cholesterol levels include:

- **Age and gender.** As women and men get older, their cholesterol levels rise. Before the age of menopause, women have lower total cholesterol levels than men of the same age. After the age of menopause, women's LDL (bad) cholesterol levels tend to rise.
- **Heredity.** Your genes partly determine how much cholesterol your body makes. High blood cholesterol can run in families.
- **Race.** Certain races may have an increased risk of high blood cholesterol. For example, African Americans typically have higher HDL and LDL cholesterol levels than whites.

How Can I Lower My Cholesterol?

There are two main ways to lower your cholesterol:

- Heart-healthy lifestyle changes, which include:
    - **Heart-healthy eating.** A heart-healthy eating plan limits the amount of saturated and trans fats that you eat. Examples include the therapeutic lifestyle changes diet and the Dietary Approaches to Stop Hypertension (DASH) eating plan.
    - **Weight management.** If you are overweight, losing weight can help lower your LDL (bad) cholesterol.

- **Physical activity.** Everyone should get regular physical activity (30 minutes on most, if not all, days).
- **Managing stress.** Research has shown that chronic stress can sometimes raise your LDL cholesterol and lower your HDL cholesterol.
- **Quitting smoking.** Quitting smoking can raise your HDL cholesterol. Since HDL helps to remove LDL cholesterol from your arteries, having more HDL can help to lower your LDL cholesterol.

- **Drug treatment.** If lifestyle changes alone do not lower your cholesterol enough, you may also need to take medicines. There are several types of cholesterol medicines available, including statins. The medicines work in different ways and can have different side effects. Talk to your healthcare provider about which one is right for you. While you are taking medicines to lower your cholesterol, you should continue with the lifestyle changes.

Chapter 16

Infertility and Stress

What Is Infertility?

In general, infertility is defined as not being able to get pregnant (conceive) after one year (or longer) of unprotected sex. Because fertility in women is known to decline steadily with age, some providers evaluate and treat women aged 35 years or older after 6 months of unprotected sex. Women with infertility should consider making an appointment with a reproductive endocrinologist—a doctor who specializes in managing infertility. Reproductive endocrinologists may also be able to help women with recurrent pregnancy loss, defined as having two or more spontaneous miscarriages.

Pregnancy is the result of a process that has many steps.
To get pregnant:

- A woman's body must release an egg from one of her ovaries (ovulation).

This chapter contains text excerpted from the following sources: Text beginning with the heading "What Is Infertility?" is excerpted from "Reproductive Health—Infertility FAQs," Centers for Disease Control and Prevention (CDC), April 18, 2018; Text under the heading "Fertility and Infertility and the Environment" is excerpted from "Reproductive and Birth Outcomes," Centers for Disease Control and Prevention (CDC), January 10, 2017; Text under the heading "Stress May Delay Women Getting Pregnant" is excerpted from "NIH Study Indicates Stress May Delay Women Getting Pregnant," National Institutes of Health (NIH), August 11, 2010. Reviewed June 2018.

- A man's sperm must join with the egg along the way (fertilize).
- The fertilized egg must go through a fallopian tube toward the uterus (womb).
- The fertilized egg must attach to the inside of the uterus (implantation).

Infertility may result from a problem with any or several of these steps. Impaired fecundity is a condition related to infertility and refers to women who have difficulty getting pregnant or carrying a pregnancy to term.

Is Infertility a Common Problem?

Yes. About 6 percent of married women aged 15–44 years in the United States are unable to get pregnant after one year of trying (infertility). Also, about 12 percent of women aged 15–44 years in the United States have difficulty getting pregnant or carrying a pregnancy to term, regardless of marital status (impaired fecundity).

Is Infertility Just a Woman's Problem?

No, infertility is not always a woman's problem. Both men and women can contribute to infertility.

Many couples struggle with infertility and seek help to become pregnant, but it is often thought of as only a woman's condition. However, in about 35 percent of couples with infertility, a male factor is identified along with a female factor. In about 8 percent of couples with infertility, a male factor is the only identifiable cause.

Almost 9 percent of men aged 25–44 years in the United States reported that they or their partner saw a doctor for advice, testing, or treatment for infertility during their lifetime.

What Causes Infertility in Men?

Infertility in men can be caused by different factors and is typically evaluated by a semen analysis. When a semen analysis is performed, the number of sperm (concentration), motility (movement), and morphology (shape) are assessed by a specialist. A slightly abnormal semen analysis does not mean that a man is necessarily infertile. Instead, a semen analysis helps determine if and how male factors are contributing to infertility.

Disruption of Testicular or Ejaculatory Function

- Varicoceles, a condition in which the veins on a man's testicles are large and cause them to overheat. The heat may affect the number or shape of the sperm.
- Trauma to the testes may affect sperm production and result in lower number of sperm.
- Unhealthy habits such as heavy alcohol use, smoking, anabolic steroid use, and illicit drug use.
- Use of certain medications and supplements.
- Cancer treatment involving the use of certain types of chemotherapy, radiation, or surgery to remove one or both testicles.
- Medical conditions such as diabetes, cystic fibrosis, certain types of autoimmune disorders, and certain types of infections may cause testicular failure.

Hormonal Disorders

- Improper function of the hypothalamus or pituitary glands. The hypothalamus and pituitary glands in the brain produce hormones that maintain normal testicular function. Production of too much prolactin, a hormone made by the pituitary gland (often due to the presence of a benign pituitary gland tumor), or other conditions that damage or impair the function of the hypothalamus or the pituitary gland may result in low or no sperm production.
- These conditions may include benign and malignant (cancerous) pituitary tumors, congenital adrenal hyperplasia (CAH), exposure to too much estrogen, exposure to too much testosterone, Cushing syndrome, and chronic use of medications called glucocorticoids.

Genetic Disorders

- Genetic conditions such as a Klinefelter syndrome (KS), Y-chromosome microdeletion (YCM), myotonic dystrophy (DM), and other, less common genetic disorders may cause no sperm to be produced, or low numbers of sperm to be produced.

What Increases a Man's Risk of Infertility?

- Age. Although advanced age plays a much more important role in predicting female infertility, couples in which the male partner is 40 years old or older are more likely to report difficulty conceiving.
- Being overweight or obese
- Smoking
- Excessive alcohol use
- Use of marijuana
- Exposure to testosterone. This may occur when a doctor prescribes testosterone injections, implants, or topical gel for low testosterone, or when a man takes testosterone or similar medications illicitly for the purposes of increasing their muscle mass.
- Exposure to radiation.
- Frequent exposure of the testes to high temperatures, such as that which may occur in men confined to a wheelchair, or through frequent sauna or hot tub use.
- Exposure to certain medications such as flutamide, cyproterone, bicalutamide, spironolactone, ketoconazole, or cimetidine.
- Exposure to environmental toxins including exposure to pesticides, lead, cadmium, or mercury.

What Causes Infertility in Women?

Women need functioning ovaries, fallopian tubes, and a uterus to get pregnant. Conditions affecting any one of these organs can contribute to female infertility. Some of these conditions are listed below and can be evaluated using a number of different tests.

Disruption of Ovarian Function (Presence or Absence of Ovulation (Anovulation) and Effects of Ovarian "Age")

A woman's menstrual cycle is, on average, 28 days long. Day 1 is defined as the first day of "full flow." Regular predictable periods that occur every 24–32 days likely reflect ovulation. A woman with irregular periods is likely not ovulating.

Ovulation can be predicted by using an ovulation predictor kit and can be confirmed by a blood test to check the woman's progesterone level on day 21 of her menstrual cycle. Although several tests exist to evaluate a woman's ovarian function, no single test is a perfect predictor of fertility. The most commonly used markers of ovarian function include follicle stimulating hormone (FSH) value on day 3–5 of the menstrual cycle, antimüllerian hormone value (AMH), and antral follicle count (AFC) using a transvaginal ultrasound.

Disruptions in ovarian function may be caused by several conditions and warrants an evaluation by a doctor.

When a woman doesn't ovulate during a menstrual cycle, it's called anovulation. Potential causes of anovulation include the following:

- **Polycystic ovary syndrome (PCOS).** PCOS is a condition that causes women to not ovulate, or to ovulate irregularly. Some women with PCOS have elevated levels of testosterone, which can cause acne and excess hair growth. PCOS is the most common cause of female infertility.
- **Diminished ovarian reserve (DOR).** Women are born with all of the eggs that they will ever have, and a woman's egg count decreases over time. Diminished ovarian reserve is a condition in which there are fewer eggs remaining in the ovaries than normal. The number of eggs a woman has declines naturally as a woman ages. It may also occur due to congenital, medical, surgical, or unexplained causes. Women with diminished ovarian reserve may be able to conceive naturally, but will produce fewer eggs in response to fertility treatments.
- **Functional hypothalamic amenorrhea (FHA).** FHA is a condition caused by excessive exercise, stress, or low body weight. It is sometimes associated with eating disorders such as anorexia.
- **Improper function of the hypothalamus and pituitary glands.** The hypothalamus and pituitary glands in the brain produce hormones that maintain normal ovarian function. Production of too much of the hormone prolactin by the pituitary gland (often as the result of a benign pituitary gland tumor), or improper function of the hypothalamus or pituitary gland, may cause a woman not to ovulate.
- **Premature ovarian insufficiency (POI).** POI, sometimes referred to as premature menopause, occurs when a woman's

ovaries fail before she is 40 years of age. Although certain exposures, such as chemotherapy or pelvic radiation therapy, and certain medical conditions may cause POI, the cause is often unexplained. About 5–10 percent of women with POI conceive naturally and have a normal pregnancy.

- **Menopause.** Menopause is an age-appropriate decline in ovarian function that usually occurs around age 50. By definition, a woman in menopause has not had a period in one year. She may experience hot flashes, mood changes, difficulty sleeping, and other symptoms as well.

Fallopian Tube Obstruction (Whether Fallopian Tubes Are Open, Blocked, or Swollen)

Risk factors for blocked fallopian tubes (tubal occlusion) can include a history of pelvic infection, history of ruptured appendicitis, history of gonorrhea or chlamydia, known endometriosis, or a history of abdominal surgery.

Tubal evaluation may be performed using an X-ray that is called a hysterosalpingogram (HSG), or by chromopertubation (CP) in the operating room at time of laparoscopy, a surgical procedure in which a small incision is made and a viewing tube called a laparoscope is inserted.

- Hysterosalpingogram (HSG) is an X-ray of the uterus and fallopian tubes. A radiologist injects dye into the uterus through the cervix and simultaneously takes X-ray pictures to see if the dye moves freely through fallopian tubes. This helps evaluate tubal caliber (diameter) and patency.
- Chromopertubation (CP) is similar to an HSG but is done in the operating room at the time of a laparoscopy. Blue-colored dye is passed through the cervix into the uterus and spillage and tubal caliber (shape) is evaluated.

Abnormal Uterine Contour (Physical Characteristics of the Uterus)

Depending on a woman's symptoms, the uterus may be evaluated by transvaginal ultrasound to look for fibroids or other anatomic abnormalities. If suspicion exists that the fibroids may be entering the endometrial cavity, a sonohysterogram (SHG) or hysteroscopy (HSC) may be performed to further evaluate the uterine environment.

What Increases a Woman's Risk of Infertility?

Female fertility is known to decline with:

- Age. More women are waiting until their 30s and 40s to have children. In fact, about 20 percent of women in the United States now have their first child after age 35. About one-third of couples in which the woman is older than 35 years have fertility problems. Aging not only decreases a woman's chances of having a baby, but also increases her chances of miscarriage and of having a child with a genetic abnormality.
- Aging decreases a woman's chances of having a baby in the following ways:
  - She has a smaller number of eggs left.
  - Her eggs are not as healthy.
  - She is more likely to have health conditions that can cause fertility problems.
  - She is more likely to have a miscarriage.
- Smoking
- Excessive alcohol use
- Extreme weight gain or loss
- Excessive physical or emotional stress that results in amenorrhea (absent periods)

Fertility and Infertility and the Environment

According to data from the National Survey of Family Growth (NSFG), 11 percent of U.S. couples had impaired fertility from 2006–2010. Waiting to have a child until later in life and existing medical conditions are not the only causes of male and female infertility. It is believed that environmental contaminants may cause infertility by creating other health conditions. For example, some research suggests that environmental contaminants can affect a woman's menstruation and ovulation. Low-level exposures to compounds such as phthalates, polychlorinated biphenyls (PCBs), dioxin, and pesticides are suspected risk factors. Much more research needs to be done to find out how environmental contaminants may be affecting human fertility.

Exposure and Risk

For many people who want to start a family, the dream of having a child is not easily realized. About 6 percent of women in the United States ages 15–44 years have difficulty getting pregnant or staying pregnant. Infertility is a problem that can affect both men and women. It can be caused by many factors which may include the following:

- Stress
- Age
- Poor diet
- Genetics
- Nutrition
- Behavior
- Some medicines
- Athletic training
- Being overweight or underweight
- Tobacco use
- Alcohol consumption
- Sexually transmitted diseases (STDs)
- Health problems that cause hormonal changes

The amount and quality of a man's sperm can be affected by:

- Alcohol
- Illegal drugs
- Environmental toxins
- Tobacco use
- Some medicines
- Radiation treatment or chemotherapy for cancer
- Age

Prevention

Most healthy women younger than 30 years of age should not worry about infertility unless they have been trying to conceive for at least a year. At this point, women and their partners should talk with their doctors about a fertility evaluation. A woman's chances of conceiving decreases quickly every year after the age of 30. Women in this age group who have been trying to conceive for six months should also talk with their doctors about having a complete and timely fertility evaluation.

Some health issues increase a woman's chances of having fertility problems. Women with the following issues should consult their doctors:

- Irregular or no menstrual periods
- Very painful periods
- Endometriosis
- Pelvic inflammatory disease (PID)
- More than one miscarriage

No matter what age, a woman should always talk to her doctor before trying to get pregnant. Doctors can help women prepare their body for a healthy baby. They can also answer questions on fertility and give advice on conceiving.

Stress May Delay Women Getting Pregnant

A study by researchers at the National Institutes of Health (NIH) and the University of Oxford supports the widespread belief that stress may reduce a woman's chance of becoming pregnant. The study is the first of its kind to document, among women without a history of fertility problems, an association between high levels of a substance indicative of stress and a reduced chance of becoming pregnant.

The researchers showed that women who had higher levels of a substance called alpha-amylase were less likely to get pregnant than were women with lower levels of the substance. Alpha-amylase is secreted into saliva by the parotid gland, the largest of the salivary glands. Although alpha-amylase digests starch, in recent years many researchers have used it as a barometer of the body's response to physical or psychological stress. The substance is secreted when the nervous system produces catecholamines, compounds that initiate a type of stress response.

In addition to researchers at the NIH's *Eunice Kennedy Shriver* National Institute of Child Health and Human Development (NICHD) and the University of Oxford, England, the study also includes an author from The Ohio State University College of Medicine (OSU-COM), Columbus.

"The study results suggest that finding safe ways to alleviate stress may play a role in helping couples become pregnant," said Alan E. Guttmacher, M.D., director of the NICHD. The study was published online in *Fertility and Sterility*. To conduct the study, the researchers charted the ovulation cycles of 274 English women aged 18–40 years who were trying to conceive, and who participated in the Oxford Conception Study (OCS) led by Cecilia Pyper, MB.BS. This clinical study sought to determine whether daily information from a fertility-monitoring device would increase the conception rate in women wishing to achieve pregnancy. The women were given at-home fertility test kits to track the phases of their monthly cycles.

"This is the first study to show an association between a biomarker of stress and a reduction in women's chances of conceiving throughout the fertile window—underscoring the importance of considering stress when attempting to identify the determinants of conception," Dr. Pyper said.

On the sixth day of her cycle, each woman collected a sample of her saliva, which was subsequently tested for alpha-amylase. The women's saliva samples were also analyzed for cortisol, another hormone produced by the adrenal glands in response to stress. Each woman took part in the study until she became pregnant, or at the end of six menstrual cycles.

The researchers found that, all other factors being equal, women with high alpha-amylase levels were less likely to conceive than were women with low levels, during the fertile window—the six days when conception is most likely to occur. The researchers did not find a correlation between cortisol levels and the chances of conception.

"Overall, the 25 percent of women in the study who had the highest alpha-amylase levels had roughly an estimated 12 percent reduction in getting pregnant each cycle in comparison to women with the lowest concentrations," said the study's first author, Germaine Buck Louis, Ph.D., M.S., director of the NICHD's Division of Epidemiology, Statistics, and Prevention Research (DESPR).

Dr. Buck Louis added that she and her colleagues are currently conducting a study with a larger group of women to confirm the findings. Similarly, they also hope to learn whether stress is associated with infertility.

"It has been suggested that stress may increase with the disappointment of several failed attempts at getting pregnant, setting off a cycle in which pregnancy becomes even more difficult to achieve," she said.

The current findings also suggest the need for finding appropriate ways to help women alleviate stress while trying to conceive.

"The question is, 'what do you do to help women to relax?' People often turn to alcohol or tobacco to relieve stress, but these substances also reduce the likelihood of pregnancy," Dr. Buck Louis said. She added that additional research may be needed to determine whether relaxation techniques such as meditation, biofeedback, yoga, or increasing social support can assist women having difficulty conceiving.

Chapter 17

Multiple Sclerosis and Stress

Depression in multiple sclerosis (MS) may be a consequence of the multiple challenges associated with managing a chronic illness. In addition to neurological deficits, MS is frequently associated with losses in vocational status, social roles, sense of control, and participation abilities. The nature of MS is unpredictable and potentially unrelenting. Perceptions regarding the uncertainty in disease, intrusiveness in daily activities, and lack of hope have been associated with depression. Life stress and coping abilities may also mediate psychosocial outcomes.

Physical and Cognitive Impairment

Global physical impairment has been associated with higher levels of depression in some studies but not others. At first glance, the relationship between impairment and depression appears to be mixed. However, a clearer relationship between depression and impairment appears when studies use more focused measures of physical impairment. For example, Minden et al. found no link between depression and disease severity at a global level; however, depressive episodes were likely to occur within 1 month of a steroid-treated exacerbation of MS. Similarly, another study found increased prevalence of depression during times of MS exacerbations and increased physical impairment.

This chapter includes text excerpted from "Depression and Multiple Sclerosis: Review of a Lethal Combination," U.S. Department of Veterans Affairs (VA), February 2006. Reviewed June 2018.

In addition to temporal variation, certain types of physical disability may be differentially related to depression. For example, a study of veterans found that perceived mobility and bladder impairment were not associated with increased risk of depression but reports of perceived bowel impairment and "at least occasional" falls were associated with elevated risk of depression. A possible explanation for these findings comes from Devins et al. who found that the relationship between physical disability and depression is indirect: disability affects psychosocial outcome to the degree that impairment is intrusive and personal control is threatened.

Physical and cognitive impairments are differentially related to functional outcomes, which highlights the need for separate consideration of these areas. Persons with high levels of cognitive impairment are less likely to work outside the home, more likely to require assistance with activities of daily living, and more likely to have limited social support. Some studies have indicated that patients with MS-related cognitive impairment report higher levels of depression than patients without cognitive impairment. Other studies do not support this relationship. Some evidence exists that the specific type of cognitive impairment may be differentially related to depression. For example, Kenealy et al. found that MS patients with impaired autobiographical memory were less likely to be depressed than those with intact autobiographical memory. The link between cognitive impairment and depression is further complicated by possible bidirectional influence. Not only may cognitive impairment precipitate depression, but depression in a patient with MS may also result in reduced attention and working memory capacity. In sum, depression and cognition are clearly related independent of physical disability, but more research is required for a better understanding of this link.

Vocational Changes

In the general population, increased risk of depression is associated with unemployment, disability, "homemaker" status, and living at or near the poverty level. A recent population-based study found that persons with disabilities were 5.0 times more likely than persons without disabilities to lose their jobs. The rates of depression were higher among persons with disabilities than persons without disabilities; unemployment status explained nearly 30 percent of the elevated depression found in the group with disabilities. The authors argue that the effects of unemployment and disability on depression are independent and additive.

In the MS literature, the links between unemployment and depression are mixed. Given that a majority of patients with MS lose their jobs and about one-third experience a decrease in standard of living, vocational and financial losses may mediate the relationship between MS and depression. Unemployment among patients with MS is associated with a lower quality of life (QOL). Williams et al. reported that unemployment was the strongest predictor of a major depressive episode in persons with MS and that the odds of depression were 3.2 times higher among those who were unemployed. This contrasts with a large community-based sample of patients with MS in which unemployment was not associated with depression. Further research will clarify the relationship between vocation and depression in patients with MS.

Social Changes

Studies have generally found that lower levels of perceived social support are associated with depression in MS. A significant portion of patients with MS report qualitative changes in social networks and personal relationships as a result of their disease, including the loss of professional colleagues, diminished contact with social groups, and loss of social independence. Concurrently, many patients with MS become increasingly reliant on care providers and core family members, which often increases caregiver burden. Marital status appears to remain relatively constant after MS diagnosis, and many married patients with MS report that they obtain most support from their spouse. However, patients with the highest levels of MS disability perceive less overall support, and those with longer duration of illness perceive less effective and affirmation support than those with shorter duration of illness. A number of studies have found that woman and unmarried persons with MS are at particular risk for diminished social support during their illness. Moreover, unsupportive relationships are significantly and independently correlated with depression and a lower sense of purpose. Future studies of social support should address the influence of both supportive and unsupportive behaviors.

Coping

Most research on coping in MS has relied heavily on Lazarus and Folkman's model that describes coping as "constantly changing cognitive and behavioral efforts to manage specific external and/or internal demands that are appraised as taxing or exceeding the resources of the person." This model (and subsequent modifications) suggests that most coping strategies available to an individual experiencing a stressor fall into two global yet distinct categories: emotion-focused coping and problem-focused coping. Emotion-focused coping most often represents the individual's reactive efforts to reduce distress caused by the stressor (e.g., avoidance, wishful thinking). Problem-focused coping represents the individual's active efforts to change a stressful situation through modifications of the environment, his- or herself, or the actual stressor (e.g., information gathering, goal setting).

Several studies have identified a link between emotion-focused coping and poor adjustment in MS; depression was the most common outcome reported. In cross-sectional surveys, emotion-focused coping has been related to lower self-esteem, global distress, and depression. Similar results were found in studies that examined the relationship between coping styles and depression over time. One common interpretation of these findings is that emotion-focused coping is ineffective and leads to poorer adjustment. However, others have argued that in a progressive degenerative disease with often limited opportunities for actively reducing disability or symptoms, emotion-focused coping may be useful and be a substantial portion of a patient's available coping efforts. Furthermore, seemingly passive strategies such as acceptance may have important benefits.

The relationship between problem-focused coping and adjustment in MS is less well established. Problem-focused coping has been linked to higher self-esteem, global distress, and depression, but other studies have failed to find a correlation. Longitudinal studies have sometimes found associations between problem-focused coping and depression. This link, however, is often observed only at one of several time points and not when emotion-focused coping is examined simultaneously. Despite limited data, problem-focused coping is viewed as particularly promising because it has been associated with well-being in general population samples and because problem-focused strategies are the foundation of many psychosocial interventions. Certain problem-focused coping strategies are also argued to be more helpful than others or only appropriate in particular circumstances. These important nuances may be lost in studies that measure coping with global scales.

Chapter 18

Weight Loss, Cortisol, and Your Brain

Americans everywhere are struggling to lose weight—and to keep from putting those lost pounds right back on. For many, it's discouraging to have their best efforts fail while those of other dieters succeed.

Researchers at the Agricultural Research Service's (ARS) Western Human Nutrition Research Center (WHNRC) in Davis, California, are conducting studies that may provide new insights into the underlying causes of this disparity in dieting success.

Given America's obesity epidemic, such research is timely and relevant. The Centers for Disease Control and Prevention (CDC) estimates that 35 percent of U.S. adults and 18 percent of kids and adolescents age 6 through 19 are overweight or obese. Both conditions are associated with increased risk of type 2 diabetes, cardiovascular disease, and other chronic disorders.

Chemist Nancy L. Keim, nutrition scientist Kevin D. Laugero, and their colleagues have looked at several factors that may affect weight-management success. Their analysis included assessing volunteers' patterns of decisionmaking and evaluating changes in their levels of cortisol—a stress-associated hormone.

This chapter includes text excerpted from "Weight Loss, Cortisol, and Your Brain," Agricultural Research Service (ARS), U.S. Department of Agriculture (USDA), March 2013. Reviewed June 2018.

The study volunteers, 29 obese but otherwise healthy women age 20–45, were asked to eat all their meals at the nutrition center, where their food was prepared for them.

The research began with a 3-week baseline phase, during which the intent was to stabilize the volunteers' weight. That was followed by a 12-week reduced-calorie regimen intended to help the volunteers shed pounds. During this weight-loss phase, meals provided 500 fewer daily calories than the total each volunteer would have needed if the goal had been to maintain her weight.

Two exceptions to this outline were built into the study: During each of the two study phases, volunteers had an "all you can eat" evening meal. These buffet dinners were provided for each volunteer to eat privately, to help rule out the effect that social pressure might have on what, and how much, the volunteer chose to eat.

Weight Loss Differs

For many people, dieting "involves an ongoing series of decisions," Keim notes. "We wanted to get a snapshot of volunteers' patterns of decisionmaking."

To do this, the researchers selected the Iowa Gambling Task, or IGT, a test that is widely used to evaluate what's known as "executive function." This umbrella term encompasses decisionmaking, differentiating good from bad, being cognizant of the potential future consequences of current actions, and resisting the temptation of short-term, immediate rewards in favor of longer-term benefits.

These functions are thought to be handled in a region of the brain known as the "prefrontal cortex."

During the IGT test, volunteers had a limited amount of time to choose cards from among four decks displayed face down on their computer screen. Each card offers, in "play" money, a monetary penalty and a monetary reward. As the test progresses, players can learn to distinguish a "good" from a "bad" deck in terms of the risks and rewards offered, and they can modify their future choices accordingly—or not.

"We found that the volunteers who lost the most weight had the highest IGT scores," Keim says. "To the best of our knowledge, this study is the first controlled-feeding weight-loss trial to report an association between diet-induced weight loss and performance on the IGT.

"The application of the IGT is really in its infancy in terms of decisionmaking about food—and eating in general. We intend to continue to use this test in studies that are designed to delve into how people make decisions about what they eat."

Dieting and Decision-Making

To learn more about volunteers' cortisol levels, the scientists collected saliva samples throughout the day on two test dates, one near the beginning of the weight-loss regimen and one near the end.

"Increases in cortisol concentration have long been regarded as a reliable indicator of psychological stress, even though those increases can also be caused by other factors," says Laugero. "Stress is considered to be a contributing factor to dieters' relapsing back to old eating habits and regaining weight.

"We found that our volunteers' cortisol concentrations generally increased from the beginning to the end of the reducing-diet phase of the study. Dieting may have been stressful for them. They were experiencing an element of outside control over what they ate, in that we asked them to eat only the foods that we offered them. Also, each dieter had to exercise restraint for 12 weeks, except perhaps during the buffet meal. That's a relatively long time.

"In addition to its association with stress, cortisol is thought to affect our eating habits and how our bodies metabolize fat," Laugero points out. "Some animal studies suggest that cortisol contributes to obesity, but the association remains unclear and controversial."

Cortisol Levels Compared to Iowa Gambling Task (IGT) Scores

In another analysis of the cortisol data, the scientists found that volunteers whose cortisol levels had increased the most were those with the lowest IGT scores.

"The IGT has been used in earlier research concerning eating disorders and obesity," Laugero says, "but our study is apparently the first weight-loss trial of its kind to report an association between cortisol concentrations and IGT scores." Says Laugero, stress is "already known to have a degrading effect on regions of the brain, including the prefrontal cortex, that are involved in decisionmaking."

Perhaps most interesting of all, the prefrontal cortex is also involved in releasing cortisol. "Some cross-talk that we don't fully understand may be taking place," says Laugero. "A better understanding of that communication may lead to successful, science-based strategies for reaching and maintaining a healthy weight."

Everyone, not just dieters, might benefit. Obesity adds an estimated $190 billion to the nation's annual healthcare costs.

Keim and Laugero, who are with the ARS Obesity and Metabolism Research Unit, collaborated in the study with unit physiologists Sean H. Adams and Marta D. Van Loan and postdoctoral researcher Megan G. Witbracht of the University of California-Davis Department of Nutrition.

The study was part of a larger investigation headed by Van Loan. A peer-reviewed article in Physiology and Behavior documents the investigation.

Chapter 19

Chronic Pain and Stress-Related Disorders

What Is Chronic Pain?

Chronic pain is when a person suffers from pain in a particular area of the body (for example, in the back or the neck) for at least 3–6 months. It may be as bad as, or even worse than, short-term pain, but it can feel like more of a problem because it lasts a longer time. Chronic pain lasts beyond the normal amount of time that an injury takes to heal.

Chronic pain can come from many things. Some people get chronic pain from normal wear and tear of the body or from aging. Others have chronic pain from various types of cancer, or other chronic medical illnesses. In some cases, the chronic pain may be from an injury that happened during an accident or an assault. Some chronic pain has no explanation.

How Common Is Chronic Pain?

Approximately one in three Americans suffer from some kind of chronic pain in their lifetimes, and about one-quarter of them are not able to do day to day activities because of their chronic pain. Between

---

This chapter includes text excerpted from "Chronic Pain and PTSD: A Guide for Patients," U.S. Department of Veterans Affairs (VA), August 13, 2015.

80 percent and 90 percent of Americans experience chronic problems in the neck or lower back.

How Do Healthcare Providers Evaluate Pain?

Care providers generally assess chronic pain during a physical exam, but how much pain someone is in is hard to determine. Every person is different and perceives and experiences pain in different ways. There is often very little consistency when different doctors try to measure a patient's pain. Sometimes the care provider may not believe the patient, or might minimize the amount of pain. All of these things can be frustrating for the person in pain. Additionally, this kind of experience often makes patients feel helpless and hopeless, which in turn increases tension and pain and makes the person more upset. Conversation between the doctor and patient is important, including sharing information about treatment options. If no progress is made, get a second opinion.

What Is the Experience of Chronic Pain Like Physically?

There are many forms of chronic pain, including pain felt in: the low back (most common); the neck; the mouth, face, and jaw (TMJ); the pelvis; or the head (e.g., tension and migraine headaches). Of course, each type of condition results in different experiences of pain. People with chronic pain are less able to function well in daily life than those who do not suffer from chronic pain. They may have trouble with things such as walking, standing, sitting, lifting light objects, doing paperwork, standing in line at a grocery store, going shopping, or working. Many patients with chronic pain cannot work because of their pain or physical limitations.

What Is the Experience of Chronic Pain Like Psychologically?

Research has shown that many patients who experience chronic pain (up to 100% of these patients) tend to also be diagnosed with depression. Because the pain and disability are always there and that may even become worse over time, many of them think suicide is the only way to end their pain and frustration. They think they have no control over their life. This frustration may also lead the person to use drugs or have unneeded surgery.

Chronic Pain and Posttraumatic Stress Disorder (PTSD)

Some people's chronic pain stems from a traumatic event, such as a physical or sexual assault, a motor vehicle accident, or some type of disaster. Under these circumstances, the person may experience both chronic pain and posttraumatic stress disorder (PTSD). The person in pain may not even realize the connection between their pain and a traumatic event. Approximately 15–35 percent of patients with chronic pain also have PTSD. Only 2 percent of people who do not have chronic pain have PTSD. One study found that 51 percent of patients with chronic low back pain had PTSD symptoms. For people with chronic pain, the pain may actually serve as a reminder of the traumatic event, which will tend to make the PTSD even worse. Survivors of physical, psychological, or sexual abuse tend to be more at risk for developing certain types of chronic pain later in their lives.

Chapter 20

Pregnancy and Stress

It is normal to feel some stress during pregnancy. Your body is going through many changes, and as your hormones change, so do your moods. Too much stress can cause you to have trouble sleeping, headaches, loss of appetite, or a tendency to overeat—all of which can be harmful to you and your developing baby. High levels of stress can also cause high blood pressure, which increases your chance of having preterm labor or a low-birth-weight infant. You should talk about stress with your healthcare provider and loved ones. If you are feeling stress because of uncertainty or fear about becoming a mother, experiencing work-related stress, or worrying about miscarriage, talk to your healthcare provider during your prenatal visits.

Posttraumatic Stress Disorder (PTSD) and Pregnancy

Posttraumatic stress disorder (PTSD) is a more serious type of stress that can negatively affect your baby. PTSD occurs when you have problems after seeing or going through a painful event, such as rape, abuse, a natural disaster, or the death of a loved one. You may experience:

This chapter contains text excerpted from the following sources: Text in this chapter begins with excerpts from "Will Stress during Pregnancy Affect My Baby?" *Eunice Kennedy Shriver* National Institute of Child Health and Human Development (NICHD), January 31, 2017; Text under the heading "Stress during Pregnancy" is excerpted from "Child Health USA 2013," Health Resources and Services Administration (HRSA), October 2, 2015.

- Anxiety
- Flashbacks and upsetting memories
- Nightmares
- Strong physical reactions to situations, people, or things that remind you of the event
- Avoidance of places, activities, and people you once enjoyed
- Feeling more aware of things
- Guilt

PTSD occurs in as many as 8 percent of women during pregnancy, increasing their infant's risk of preterm birth or low birth weight. PTSD also increases the risk for behaviors such as smoking and drinking, which contribute to other problems. Reducing stress is important for preventing problems during your pregnancy and for reducing your risk for health problems that may affect your developing child. Identify the source of your stress and take steps to remove it or lessen it. Make sure you get enough exercise (under a doctor's supervision), eat healthy foods, and get lots of sleep. Some women experience extreme sadness and/or anxiety during pregnancy and after giving birth. Talk to your healthcare provider if you feel overwhelmed, sad, or anxious. Treatment and counseling can help.

Stress during Pregnancy

The health and emotional well-being of a woman, both before and during her pregnancy, can impact the future health of her child. Experiencing stressful events or environmental hardships, such as financial instability, the death of a loved one, or divorce, while pregnancy can place an additional strain on a woman and increase her likelihood of adverse birth outcomes, including preterm birth and low birthweight. Pregnant women are encouraged to utilize their support networks to help manage stress and to speak with their provider if they experience depression.

In 2009–2010, nearly three-fourths of recent mothers in a 30-state area reported that they had experienced at least one stressful event in the 12 months prior to delivery of their child. The most commonly reported stressful events were moving to a new address (33.7%), arguing with husband or partner more than usual (24.7%), serious illness and hospitalization of a family member (22.9%), and inability to pay lots of bills (22.7%).

The proportion of mothers reporting that they had experienced at least one stressful event ranged from 80.1 percent among non-Hispanic American Indian/Alaska Native women to 56.4 percent among non-Hispanic Asian women. Experiencing six or more stressful events was most common among non-Hispanic American Indian/Alaska Native mothers (13.6%), and least common among non-Hispanic Asian mothers (1.0%).

*Stressful Events Experienced during the 12 Months Prior to Delivery, 2009–2010**

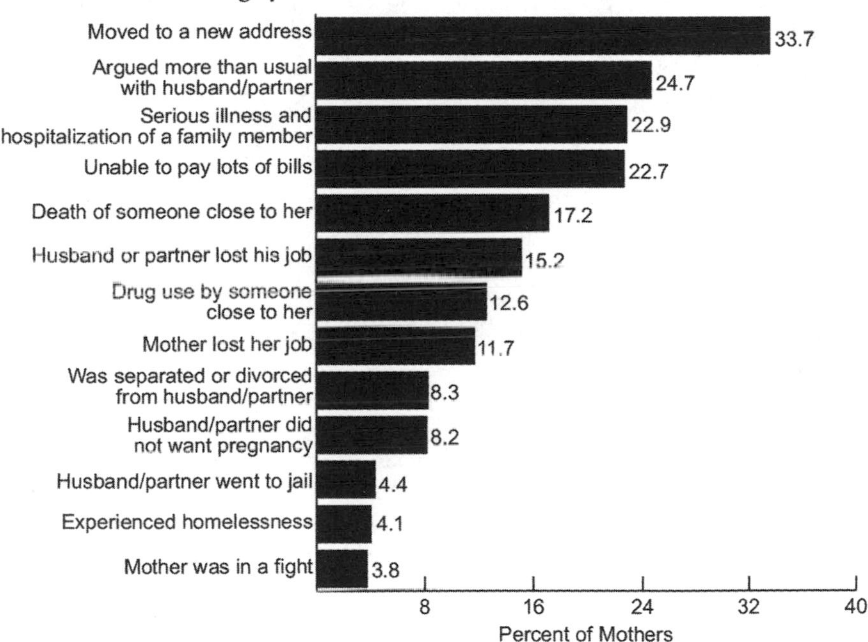

Figure 20.1. *Stressful Events Experienced during Pregnancy* (Source: Centers for Disease Control and Prevention (CDC), Pregnancy Risk Assessment Monitoring System (PRAMS).)

**Includes data from a total of 30 states and New York City; 25 states contributed both years. Mothers completed surveys between 2 and 9 months postpartum.*

Mothers Experiencing Stressful Events during the 12 Months Prior to Delivery, by Number of Events and Race/ Ethnicity, 2009–2010***

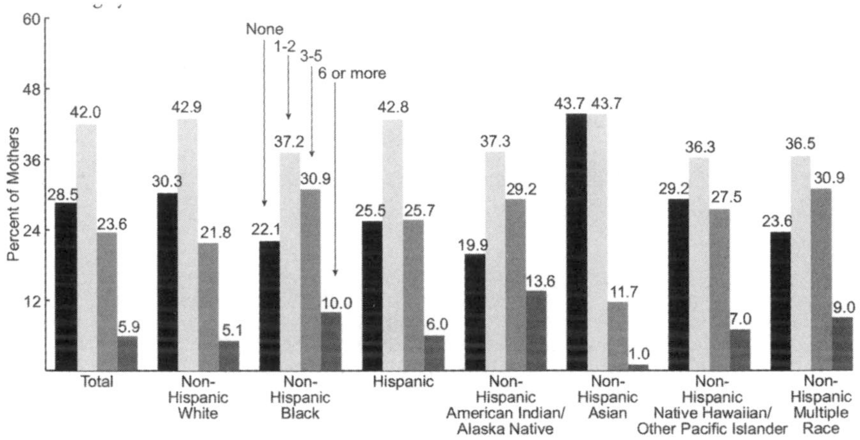

Figure 20.2. *Mothers Experiencing Stressful Events* during Pregnancy, by Number of Events and Race/Ethnicity* (Source: Centers for Disease Control and Prevention (CDC), Pregnancy Risk Assessment Monitoring System (PRAMS).)

**Total number of stressful events experienced by the mother from the following: moved to a new address, argued more than usual with husband/partner, serious illness and hospitalization of a family member, unable to pay lots of bills, death of someone close to her, husband/partner lost job, drug use by someone close to her, lost job, was divorced or separated, husband/partner did not want job, experience homeless, husband/partner went to jail, was in a fight.*

***Includes data from a total of 30 states and New York City; 25 states contributed both years. Mothers completed surveys between 2 and 9 months postpartum.*

Chapter 21

Skin Problems

Chapter Contents

Section 21.1

What Is Psoriasis?

This section includes text excerpted from "Psoriasis," National Institute of Arthritis and Musculoskeletal and Skin Diseases (NIAMS), March 30, 2017.

What Is It?

Psoriasis is a skin disease that causes red, scaly skin that may feel painful, swollen, or hot. If you have psoriasis, you are more likely to get some other conditions, including:

- Psoriatic arthritis, a condition that causes joint pain and swelling
- Cardiovascular problems, which affect the heart and blood circulation system
- Obesity
- High blood pressure
- Diabetes

Some treatments for psoriasis can have serious side effects, so be sure to talk about them with your doctor and keep all your appointments.

Who Gets Psoriasis?

Anyone can get psoriasis, but it is more common in adults. Certain genes have been linked to psoriasis, so you are more likely to get it if someone else in your family has it.

What Are the Types?

There are several different types of psoriasis. Here are a few examples:

- Plaque psoriasis, which causes patches of skin that are red at the base and covered by silvery scales
- Guttate psoriasis, which causes small, drop-shaped lesions on your trunk, limbs, and scalp. This type of psoriasis is most often triggered by upper respiratory infections, such as strep throat.

- Pustular psoriasis, which causes pus-filled blisters. Attacks or flares can be caused by medications, infections, stress, or certain chemicals.
- Inverse psoriasis, which causes smooth, red patches in folds of skin near the genitals, under the breasts or in the armpits. Rubbing and sweating can make this type of psoriasis worse.
- Erythrodermic psoriasis, which causes red and scaly skin over much of your body. This can be a reaction to a bad sunburn or taking certain medications, such as corticosteroids. It can also happen if you have a different type of psoriasis that is not well controlled. This type of psoriasis can be very serious, so if you have it, you should see a doctor immediately.

What Are the Symptoms?

Psoriasis usually causes patches of thick, red skin with silvery scales that itch or feel sore. These patches can show up anywhere on your body, but they usually occur on the elbows, knees, legs, scalp, lower back, face, palms, and soles of feet. They can also show up on your fingernails and toenails, genitals, and inside your mouth. You may find that your skin gets worse for a while, which is called a flare, and then improves.

What Causes Psoriasis?

Psoriasis is an autoimmune disease, which means that your body's immune system—which protects you from diseases—starts overacting and causing problems. If you have psoriasis, a type of white blood cells called the T cells become so active that they trigger other immune system responses, including swelling and fast turnover of skin cells.

Your skin cells grow deep in the skin and rise slowly to the surface. This is called cell turnover, and it usually takes about a month. If you have psoriasis, though, cell turnover can take only a few days. Your skin cells rise too fast and pile up on the surface, causing your skin to look red and scaly. Some things may cause a flare, meaning your psoriasis becomes worse for a while, including:

- Infections
- Stress
- Changes in the weather that dry out your skin

- Certain medicines
- Cuts, scratches, or sunburns

Certain genes have been linked to psoriasis, meaning it runs in families.

Is There a Test?

Psoriasis can be hard to diagnose because it can look like other skin diseases. Your doctor may look at a small sample of your skin under a microscope to help them figure out if psoriasis is causing your skin condition.

How Is Psoriasis Treated?

There are several different types of treatment for psoriasis. Your doctor may recommend that you try one of these or a combination of them:

- Topical treatment, which means putting creams on your skin
- Light therapy, which involves a doctor shining an ultraviolet light on your skin or getting more sunlight. It's important that a doctor controls the amount of light you are getting from this therapy, because too much ultraviolet light may make your psoriasis worse.
- Systemic treatment, which can include taking prescription medicines or getting shots of medicine

Who Treats Psoriasis?

Several types of healthcare professionals may treat you, including:

- Dermatologists, who treat skin problems
- Internists, who diagnose and treat adults

Living with Psoriasis

Psoriasis is a chronic disease, which means it lasts a long time. You can take an active role in treating your psoriasis. Besides going to your doctor regularly, here are some things you can try to help manage your symptoms:

- Keeping your skin well moisturized

- Staying healthy overall
- Joining support groups or counseling to help you realize you are not alone in dealing with psoriasis and to share ideas for coping with the disease

Section 21.2

The Psoriasis–Stress Link

This section includes text excerpted from "Spotlight on Psoriasis," *NIH News in Health*, National Institutes of Health (NIH), August 2016.

You may have heard of psoriasis, but do you know what it is? Psoriasis is a long-term (i.e., chronic), skin disorder that affects more than 6.7 million U.S. adults. Symptoms can vary, but it's usually recognized by itchy or sore patches of thick, red skin with silvery scales. There's currently no cure, but treatment often helps.

Psoriasis occurs when skin cells quickly rise to the surface of the skin and build up into thick patches, or plaques. Ordinarily, skin cells mature as they rise from their origins below the surface of the skin. In psoriasis, these cells pile up before they've had a chance to properly mature.

Psoriasis actually begins in the immune system, which normally protects the body against infection and disease. In psoriasis, the immune system becomes misdirected and overactive. This can cause redness and swelling (inflammation) and lead to the rapid buildup of skin cells.

Plaques are most often found on the elbows, knees, or scalp. But they can also affect the face, fingernails, toenails, soft tissues of the genitals, or any skin-covered region. "Patients can have a lot of symptoms like itching, cracking, and bleeding that can disrupt their sleep and their social relationships," says Dr. Joel Gelfand, a skin specialist (dermatologist) at the University of Pennsylvania. People with moderate to severe psoriasis may feel self-conscious or have a poor self-image, which can lead to depression or social isolation.

Some people with psoriasis also experience joint inflammation that produces arthritis-like pain. This condition is called psoriatic arthritis.

Gelfand and other National Institutes of Health (NIH)-supported researchers have found that psoriasis—especially severe psoriasis—is linked to certain other disorders as well, such as heart conditions, obesity, high blood pressure, and diabetes.

Psoriasis can occur at any age, but it typically first appears in young adulthood. Many people with psoriasis have a family history of the disorder. Researchers have been able to identify certain genes linked to the disease, but they still don't fully understand the disease process. They do know that it isn't contagious. You can't "catch" psoriasis by touching someone who has it.

Psoriasis can be hard to diagnose, because it can look like other skin diseases. Your doctor might need to look at a small skin sample under a microscope. It's often best to make an appointment with a primary care doctor or a dermatologist to get an accurate diagnosis.

There are many approaches for treating psoriasis. Safe and proven treatment options include creams, light therapy, and medications given as pills or a shot.

"Treatment decisions in psoriasis need to be highly individualized and tailored toward the patient's clinical condition and underlying health status, as well as their preferences and goals," Gelfand says. Be sure to ask your doctor about the best treatment options for you.

Psoriasis symptoms may briefly worsen, or flare. These flares can arise when people are stressed or experience a traumatic event like the death of a family member or friend. Smoking, heavy alcohol use, and being overweight can also aggravate psoriasis.

Gelfand and other NIH-funded researchers have been working to develop better therapies. "It's a great time to be hopeful and optimistic about this disease," Gelfand says. "Most of the therapies coming out now seem to be well-tolerated and have impressive effectiveness."

Avoid Psoriasis Triggers

Factors that may trigger psoriasis or make it worse include:

- Physical and emotional stress
- Injury to the skin such as cuts or burns
- Infections, especially strep throat
- Cold weather
- Smoking or heavy alcohol use

Section 21.3

Is Acne Linked to Stress?

This section includes text excerpted from "Understanding Acne," *NIH News in Health*, National Institutes of Health (NIH), January 2010. Reviewed June 2018.

There are many myths about what causes acne. Some people blame foods for their outbreaks. Some think that dirty skin causes it. But there's little evidence that either has much effect on most people's acne.

People of all races and ages get acne. About 4 of every 5 people between the ages of 11 and 30 have outbreaks at some point. It's most common in adolescents and young adults. Although acne is usually not a serious health threat, it can be upsetting, and severe acne can lead to permanent scarring. Fortunately, for most people, acne tends to go away by the time they reach their 30s.

Acne begins in the skin's oil glands. The oils travel up a canal called a follicle, which also contains a hair. The oils empty onto the skin surface through the follicle's opening, or pore.

The hair, oil, and cells that line the narrow follicle can form a plug and block the pore, preventing oil from reaching the skin's surface. This mix of oil and cells allows bacteria that normally live on the skin to grow in plugged follicles. Your body's defense system then moves to attack the bacteria and the area gets inflamed.

If the plugged follicle stays beneath the skin, you get a white bump called a whitehead. If it reaches the surface of the skin and opens up, you get a blackhead. It's not because of dirt; the oil becomes black on the skin's surface when it's exposed to air. Both whiteheads and blackheads may stay in the skin for a long time. Eventually, the wall of the plugged follicle can break down, leading to pimples, or zits.

One important factor in acne is an increase in certain hormones during puberty. These hormones cause the oil glands to enlarge and make more oil. Hormone changes related to pregnancy or starting or stopping birth control pills can also cause acne.

Studies suggest that you can inherit a tendency to develop acne from your parents, so genes likely play some role. Stress doesn't cause acne, but research has found that for people who have acne, stress can make it worse.

Certain drugs are also known to cause acne. Greasy cosmetics, for example, can alter the cells of the follicles and make them stick together, producing a plug. If you have acne, try oil-free cosmetics.

Choose products labeled noncomedogenic (meaning they don't promote the formation of closed pores).

If you have acne, don't rub or touch your pimples. Squeezing, pinching or picking at them can lead to scars or dark blotches. Gently wash your face with a mild cleanser twice a day—and after heavy exercise. Don't use strong soaps or rough scrub pads; they may make the problem worse. It's also important to shampoo your hair regularly. If you have oily hair, you may want to wash it every day.

Several over-the-counter (OTC) medicines can treat mild acne. It may take up to 8 weeks before you notice an improvement. For more severe acne, talk to your doctor about the options. Researchers continue to work on developing new drugs to treat acne. They're also trying to better understand the causes of acne so they can explore new remedies. In the meantime, there are several available treatments that may help.

Acne Flare-Ups

The exact cause of acne is unknown, but certain factors can cause it to flare. They include:

- Stress
- Squeezing or picking at blemishes
- Hard scrubbing of the skin
- Changing hormone levels in adolescent girls—and adult women 2–7 days before their menstrual period starts
- Oil from skin products (moisturizers or cosmetics) or grease in the work environment (for example, a kitchen with fry vats)
- Pressure from sports helmets, or equipment, backpacks, tight collars, or tight sports uniforms
- Skin irritants, such as pollution, and high humidity

Chapter 22

Sleep

Chapter Contents

Section 22.1

Stress and Sleep

This section contains text excerpted from the following sources: Text in this section begins with excerpts from "Get Enough Sleep," Office of Disease Prevention and Health Promotion (ODPHP), U.S. Department of Health and Human Services (HHS), March 20, 2018; Text under the heading "Getting a Good Night's Sleep" is excerpted from "5 Reasons to Get a Good Night's Sleep," Smokefree.gov, U.S. Department of Health and Human Services (HHS), November 29, 2012. Reviewed June 2018.

It's important to get enough sleep. Sleep helps keep your mind and body healthy.

How Much Sleep Do I Need?

Most adults need 7–8 hours of good quality sleep on a regular schedule each night. Make changes to your routine if you can't find enough time to sleep.

Getting enough sleep isn't only about total hours of sleep. It's also important to get good quality sleep on a regular schedule so you feel rested when you wake up.

If you often have trouble sleeping—or if you often still feel tired after sleeping—talk with your doctor.

How Much Sleep Do Children Need?

Kids need even more sleep than adults.

- Teens need 8–10 hours of sleep each night.
- School-aged children need 9–12 hours of sleep each night.
- Preschoolers need to sleep between 10 and 13 hours a day (including naps).
- Toddlers need to sleep between 11 and 14 hours a day (including naps).
- Babies need to sleep between 12 and 16 hours a day (including naps).

Why Is Getting Enough Sleep Important?

Getting enough sleep has many benefits. It can help you:

- Get sick less often
- Stay at a healthy weight
- Lower your risk for serious health problems, like diabetes and heart disease
- Reduce stress and improve your mood
- Think more clearly and do better in school and at work
- Get along better with people
- Make good decisions and avoid injuries—for example, sleepy drivers cause thousands of car accidents every year

Does It Matter When I Sleep?

Yes. Your body sets your "biological clock" according to the pattern of daylight where you live. This helps you naturally get sleepy at night and stay alert during the day.

If you have to work at night and sleep during the day, you may have trouble getting enough sleep. It can also be hard to sleep when you travel to a different time zone.

Why Can't I Fall Asleep?

Many things can make it harder for you to sleep, including:

- Stress or anxiety
- Pain
- Certain health conditions, like heartburn or asthma
- Some medicines
- Caffeine (usually from coffee, tea, and soda)
- Alcohol and other drugs
- Untreated sleep disorders, like sleep apnea or insomnia

If you are having trouble sleeping, try making changes to your routine to get the sleep you need. You may want to:

- Change what you do during the day—for example, exercise in the morning instead of at night.
- Create a comfortable sleep environment—and make sure your bedroom is dark and quiet.
- Set a bedtime routine—and go to bed at the same time every night.

How Can I Tell If I Have a Sleep Disorder?

Sleep disorders can cause many different problems. Keep in mind that it's normal to have trouble sleeping every now and then. People with sleep disorders generally experience these problems on a regular basis.

Common signs of sleep disorders include:

- Trouble falling or staying asleep
- Still feeling tired after a good night's sleep
- Sleepiness during the day that makes it difficult to do everyday activities, like driving a car or concentrating at work
- Frequent loud snoring
- Pauses in breathing or gasping while sleeping
- Itchy feelings in your legs or arms at night that feel better when you move or massage the area
- Trouble moving your arms and legs when you wake up

If you have any of these signs, talk to a doctor or nurse. You may need to be tested or treated for a sleep disorder.

Take Action!

Making small changes to your daily routine can help you get the sleep you need. Change what you do during the day.

- Try to spend some time outdoors every day.
- Plan your physical activity for earlier in the day, not right before you go to bed.
- Stay away from caffeine (including coffee, tea, and soda) late in the day.
- If you have trouble sleeping at night, limit daytime naps to 20 minutes or less.

- If you drink alcohol, drink only in moderation. This means no more than 1 drink a day for women and no more than 2 drinks a day for men. Alcohol can keep you from sleeping well.
- Don't eat a big meal close to bedtime.
- Quit smoking. The nicotine in cigarettes can make it harder for you to sleep.

Create a good sleep environment.

- Make sure your bedroom is dark. If there are street lights near your window, try putting up light-blocking curtains.
- Keep your bedroom quiet.
- Consider keeping electronic devices—like TVs, computers, and smartphones—out of the bedroom.

Set a bedtime routine.

- Go to bed at the same time every night.
- Get the same amount of sleep each night.
- Avoid eating, talking on the phone, or reading in bed.
- Avoid using computers or smartphones, watching TV, or playing video games at bedtime.
- If you find yourself up at night worrying about things, use these tips to help manage stress.

If you are still awake after staying in bed for more than 20 minutes, get up. Do something relaxing, like reading or meditating, until you feel sleepy.

If you are concerned about your sleep, see a doctor.

Talk with a doctor or nurse if you have any of the following signs of a sleep disorder:

- Frequent, loud snoring
- Pauses in breathing during sleep
- Trouble waking up in the morning
- Pain or itchy feelings in your legs or arms at night that feel better when you move or massage the area
- Trouble staying awake during the day

Even if you aren't aware of problems like these, talk with a doctor if you feel like you often have trouble sleeping.

Getting a Good Night's Sleep

A good night's sleep makes you feel better and gives you the energy you need to face the world, while lack of sleep can make you moody, impatient, and unable to concentrate.

There are many benefits to getting a good night's sleep:

1. **Improves your emotional health**

   Getting a good night's sleep will help you better cope with stress without cigarettes, mindless munching, alcohol, or other drugs.

2. **Improves your physical health and mental sharpness**

   Getting the recommended 7–9 hours of sleep can help prevent chronic diseases such as diabetes and heart disease and strengthens your immune system. Sleep also improves your ability to think clearly and make good decisions.

3. **Improves hormone and energy regulation**

   Ever notice how much more tempting those chocolate chip cookies are when you are sleep-deprived? Getting a good night's sleep may help to control weight gain by keeping hormones and metabolism in check.

4. **Helps you to avoid injuries and accidents**

   When we're tired, we're mentally and physically fatigued, slowing down our reaction times. This can make us more prone to accidents like tripping or making bad decisions behind the wheel.

5. **Slows the aging process**

   When you sleep, your body has a chance to rest and restore which is important for feeling and looking younger.

Sleep recommendations vary across a person's lifetime. Most adults should aim for 7–9 hours of sleep each night. If you are meeting the sleep recommendations on a regular basis, keep up the good sleep habits!

Section 22.2

Insomnia

This section includes text excerpted from "Insomnia," National Heart, Lung, and Blood Institute (NHLBI), November 9, 2011. Reviewed June 2018.

Insomnia is a common sleep disorder. People who have insomnia have trouble falling asleep, staying asleep, or both. As a result, they may get too little sleep or have poor-quality sleep. They may not feel refreshed when they wake up.

Causes

Primary Insomnia

Primary insomnia isn't a symptom or side effect of another medical condition. It is its own distinct disorder, and its cause isn't well understood. Primary insomnia usually lasts for at least 1 month. Many life changes can trigger primary insomnia. It may be due to major or long-lasting stress or emotional upset. Travel or other factors, such as work schedules that disrupt your sleep routine, also may trigger primary insomnia. Even if these issues are resolved, the insomnia may not go away. Trouble sleeping can persist because of habits formed to deal with the lack of sleep. These habits might include taking naps, worrying about sleep, and going to bed early. Researchers continue to try to find out whether some people are born with an increased risk for primary insomnia.

Secondary Insomnia

Secondary insomnia is the symptom or side effect of another problem. This type of insomnia often is a symptom of an emotional, neurological, or other medical or sleep disorder. Emotional disorders that can cause insomnia include depression, anxiety, and posttraumatic stress disorder (PTSD). Alzheimer disease (AD) and Parkinson disease (PD) are examples of neurological disorders that can cause insomnia. Many other disorders or factors also can cause insomnia, such as:

- Conditions that cause chronic (ongoing) pain, such as arthritis and headache disorders
- Conditions that make it hard to breathe, such as asthma and heart failure

- An overactive thyroid
- Gastrointestinal disorders, such as heartburn
- Stroke
- Sleep disorders, such as restless legs syndrome and sleep-related breathing problems
- Menopause and hot flashes

Secondary insomnia also can be a side effect of some medicines. For example, certain asthma medicines, such as theophylline, and some allergy and cold medicines can cause insomnia. Beta-blockers also can cause the condition. These medicines are used to treat heart conditions. Commonly used substances also can cause insomnia. Examples include caffeine and other stimulants, tobacco and other nicotine products, and alcohol and other sedatives.

Risk Factors

Insomnia is a common disorder. It affects women more often than men. The disorder can occur at any age. However, older adults are more likely to have insomnia than younger people.

People who might be at increased risk for insomnia include those who:

- Have a lot of stress
- Are depressed or have other emotional distress, such as divorce or death of a spouse
- Have lower incomes
- Work at night or have frequent major shifts in their work hours
- Travel long distances with time changes
- Have certain medical conditions or sleep disorders that can disrupt sleep
- Have an inactive lifestyle

Young and middle-aged African Americans also might be at increased risk for insomnia. Research shows that, compared with Caucasian Americans, it takes African Americans longer to fall asleep. They also have lighter sleep, don't sleep as well, and take more naps. Sleep-related breathing problems also are more common among African Americans.

Signs, Symptoms, and Complications

The main symptom of insomnia is trouble falling or staying asleep, which leads to lack of sleep. If you have insomnia, you may:

- Lie awake for a long time before you fall asleep
- Sleep for only short periods
- Be awake for much of the night
- Feel as if you haven't slept at all
- Wake up too early

The lack of sleep can cause other symptoms. You may wake up feeling tired or not well-rested, and you may feel tired during the day. You also may have trouble focusing on tasks. Insomnia can cause you to feel anxious, depressed, or irritable. Insomnia also can affect your daily activities and cause serious problems. For example, you may feel drowsy while driving. Driver sleepiness (not related to alcohol) is responsible for almost 20 percent of all serious car crash injuries. Research also shows that insomnia raises older women's risk of falling. If insomnia is affecting your daily activities, talk with your doctor. Treatment may help you avoid symptoms and problems related to the disorder. Also, poor sleep may be a sign of other health problems. Finding and treating those problems could improve your overall health and sleep.

Diagnosis

Your doctor will likely diagnose insomnia based on your medical and sleep histories and a physical exam. He or she also may recommend a sleep study. For example, you may have a sleep study if the cause of your insomnia is unclear.

Medical History

To find out what's causing your insomnia, your doctor may ask whether you:

- Have any new or ongoing health problems
- Have painful injuries or health conditions, such as arthritis
- Take any medicines, either over-the-counter (OTC) or prescription

- Have symptoms or a history of depression, anxiety, or psychosis
- Are coping with highly stressful life events, such as divorce or death

Your doctor also may ask questions about your work and leisure habits. For example, he or she may ask about your work and exercise routines; your use of caffeine, tobacco, and alcohol; and your long-distance travel history. Your answers can give clues about what's causing your insomnia.

Your doctor also may ask whether you have any new, or ongoing work, or personal problems, or other stresses in your life. Also, he or she may ask whether you have other family members who have sleep problems.

Sleep History

To get a better sense of your sleep problem, your doctor will ask you for details about your sleep habits. Before your visit, think about how to describe your problems, including:

- How often you have trouble sleeping and how long you've had the problem
- When you go to bed and get up on workdays and days off
- How long it takes you to fall asleep, how often you wake up at night, and how long it takes to fall back asleep
- Whether you snore loudly and often or wake up gasping or feeling out of breath
- How refreshed you feel when you wake up, and how tired you feel during the day
- How often you doze off or have trouble staying awake during routine tasks, especially driving

To find out what's causing or worsening your insomnia, your doctor also may ask you:

- Whether you worry about falling asleep, staying asleep, or getting enough sleep
- What you eat or drink, and whether you take medicines before going to bed
- What routine you follow before going to bed
- What the noise level, lighting, and temperature are like where you sleep

- What distractions, such as a TV or computer, are in your bedroom

To help your doctor, consider keeping a sleep diary for 1 or 2 weeks. Write down when you go to sleep, wake up, and take naps. For example, you might note: Went to bed at 10 a.m.; woke up at 3 a.m. and couldn't fall back asleep; napped after work for 2 hours. Also write down how much you sleep each night, as well as how sleepy you feel throughout the day.

Physical Exam

Your doctor will do a physical exam to rule out other medical problems that might cause insomnia. You also may need blood tests to check for thyroid problems or other conditions that can cause sleep problems.

Sleep Study

Your doctor may recommend a sleep study called a polysomnogram (PSG) if he or she thinks an underlying sleep disorder is causing your insomnia. You'll likely stay overnight at a sleep center for this study. The PSG records brain activity, eye movements, heart rate, and blood pressure. A PSG also records the amount of oxygen in your blood, how much air is moving through your nose while you breathe, snoring, and chest movements. The chest movements show whether you're making an effort to breathe.

Treatment

Lifestyle changes often can help relieve short-term (i.e., acute) insomnia. These changes might make it easier to fall asleep and stay asleep. A type of counseling called cognitive behavioral therapy (CBT) can help relieve the anxiety linked to chronic (ongoing) insomnia. Anxiety tends to prolong insomnia. Several medicines also can help relieve insomnia and re-establish a regular sleep schedule. However, if your insomnia is the symptom or side effect of another problem, it's important to treat the underlying cause (if possible).

Lifestyle Changes

If you have insomnia, avoid substances that make it worse, such as:

- Caffeine, tobacco, and other stimulants. The effects of these substances can last as long as 8 hours.

- Certain OTC and prescription medicines that can disrupt sleep (for example, some cold and allergy medicines). Talk with your doctor about which medicines won't disrupt your sleep.
- Alcohol. An alcoholic drink before bedtime might make it easier for you to fall asleep. However, alcohol triggers sleep that tends to be lighter than normal. This makes it more likely that you will wake up during the night.

Try to adopt bedtime habits that make it easier to fall asleep and stay asleep. Follow a routine that helps you wind down and relax before bed. For example, read a book, listen to soothing music, or take a hot bath. Try to schedule your daily exercise at least 5–6 hours before going to bed. Don't eat heavy meals or drink a lot before bedtime. Make your bedroom sleep-friendly. Avoid bright lighting while winding down. Try to limit possible distractions, such as a TV, computer, or pet. Make sure the temperature of your bedroom is cool and comfortable. Your bedroom also should be dark and quiet. Go to sleep around the same time each night and wake up around the same time each morning, even on weekends. If you can, avoid night shifts, alternating schedules, or other things that may disrupt your sleep schedule.

Cognitive Behavioral Therapy (CBT)

CBT for insomnia targets the thoughts and actions that can disrupt sleep. This therapy encourages good sleep habits and uses several methods to relieve sleep anxiety. For example, relaxation techniques and biofeedback are used to reduce anxiety. These strategies help you better control your breathing, heart rate, muscles, and mood.

CBT also aims to replace sleep anxiety with more positive thinking that links being in bed with being asleep. This method also teaches you what to do if you're unable to fall asleep within a reasonable time. CBT also may involve talking with a therapist one-on-one or in group sessions to help you consider your thoughts and feelings about sleep. This method may encourage you to describe thoughts racing through your mind in terms of how they look, feel, and sound. The goal is for your mind to settle down and stop racing. CBT also focuses on limiting the time you spend in bed while awake. This method involves setting a sleep schedule. At first, you will limit your total time in bed to the typical short length of time you're usually asleep.

This schedule might make you even more tired because some of the allotted time in bed will be taken up by problems falling asleep.

However, the resulting tiredness is intended to help you get to sleep more quickly. Over time, the length of time spent in bed is increased until you get a full night of sleep. For success with CBT, you may need to see a therapist who is skilled in this approach weekly over 2–3 months. CBT works as well as prescription medicine for many people who have chronic insomnia. It also may provide better long-term relief than medicine alone. For people who have insomnia and major depressive disorder, CBT combined with antidepression medicines has shown promise in relieving both conditions.

Medicines

Many prescription medicines are used to treat insomnia. Some are meant for short-term use, while others are meant for longer use. Talk to your doctor about the benefits and side effects of insomnia medicines. For example, insomnia medicines can help you fall asleep, but you may feel groggy in the morning after taking them.

Rare side effects of these medicines include sleep eating, sleep walking, or driving while asleep. If you have side effects from an insomnia medicine, or if it doesn't work well, tell your doctor. He or she might prescribe a different medicine. Some insomnia medicines can be habit forming. Ask your doctor about the benefits and risks of insomnia medicines.

Over-the-Counter (OTC) Products

Some over-the-counter (OTC) products claim to treat insomnia. These products include melatonin, L-tryptophan supplements, and valerian teas or extracts.

The U.S. Food and Drug Administration (FDA) doesn't regulate "natural" products and some food supplements. Thus, the dose and purity of these substances can vary. How well these products work and how safe they are isn't well understood.

Chapter 23

Teeth Grinding (Bruxism) and Stress

Bruxism is a disorder characterized by grinding, gnashing, and clenching of the teeth. Although it can have many different causes, it is often related to stress. Bruxism is widely prevalent, affecting an estimated 30–40 million people in the United States. People with bruxism may unconsciously clench their jaws during the day or grind their teeth while they are asleep at night. In most cases, bruxism is treatable with proper care and attention.

Symptoms and Diagnosis

Bruxism is usually diagnosed through a visit to a dentist. During a regular dental checkup, a dentist will look for and inquire about the following symptoms:

- Damaged teeth
- Unusual teeth sensitivity
- Swelling and pain in the jaw or facial muscles around the mouth
- Tongue indentations
- Headaches or earaches
- Frequent awakening or poor quality of sleep

"Bruxism," © 2015 Omnigraphics. Reviewed June 2018.

If the patient shows signs of bruxism, the dentist may prescribe a splint or mouthguard to prevent the teeth from grinding together. If the problem seems to be stress-related, the patient may be referred to a therapist or a counselor who will suggest methods for modifying the patient's behavior and sleep patterns.

Causes

Although various factors may contribute to bruxism, it is often related to the patient's emotional and psychological state. Nearly 70 percent of cases of bruxism can be traced to stress and anxiety. For children, the stress may be due to such causes as school exams, bullying by classmates, scolding from parents, or moving to a new neighborhood. Some small children may grind their teeth as part of the teething process or due to frequent earaches. Among children, bruxism often appears between the ages of three and ten years and then disappears on its own at puberty.

For adults, common sources of stress may include workplace tensions, family problems, relationship issues, or anxiety about health conditions. Certain personality types tend to be more vulnerable to stress-related bruxism, including those who are highly aggressive, competitive, or hyperactive. Certain lifestyle factors can increase the risk of developing bruxism, such as smoking, alcohol consumption, and drug use. Some dental disorders can also aggravate bruxism, such as improper teeth alignment or jaw movement. Bruxism may also develop as a side effect of certain medications, or as a symptom of neurological disorders like Huntington disease (HD) and Parkinson disease (PD). Finally, bruxism is often related to sleep disorders, such as excessive snoring, pauses in breathing, or obstructive sleep apnea (OSA).

Treatments

Treatments for bruxism should be selected to best fit the individual patient and the underlying cause of the disorder. When a dental problem is determined to be the cause of bruxism, a dental appliance such as a splint or mouthguard might alleviate the condition. These devices help prevent the teeth from grinding together and also help protect the tooth enamel from further damage. Various dental procedures can also be performed to correct misalignment of the teeth and jaw or address damage to the teeth from clenching and grinding.

Behavioral therapy can also help patients deal with improper mouth and jaw alignment. Correcting the position and placement of the tongue, teeth, and lips can bring about a significant improvement in the condition. Biofeedback is another treatment method used to assess and alter the movement of the muscles around the mouth and jaw. The doctor may use monitoring equipment to help guide the patient toward overcoming the habit of clenching the jaw or grinding the teeth.

If the primary cause of bruxism is determined to be psychological in nature, a number of behavioral and related therapies may help alleviate the condition. Stress management is the foremost issue to be addressed in people with bruxism. Counseling sessions with experts can help patients develop coping strategies. Other popular means of reducing stress include meditation, relaxation, exercise, and music. Hypnosis is a proven method of treatment for people who tend to grind their teeth at night. Most people with bruxism respond well with the proper treatment.

References

1. "Causes of Bruxism," Bruxism Association, n.d.
2. "Bruxism," Nemours Foundation, 2015.

Part Three

How Stress Affects Mental Health

Chapter 24

Depression

Chapter Contents

Section 24.1

What Is Depression?

This section includes text excerpted from "Depression: What You Need to Know," National Institute of Mental Health (NIMH), December 13, 2015.

Depression Is a Real Illness

Sadness is something we all experience. It is a normal reaction to difficult times in life and usually passes with a little time. When a person has depression, it interferes with daily life and normal functioning. It can cause pain for both the person with depression and those who care about him or her. Doctors call this condition "depressive disorder," or "clinical depression." It is a real illness. It is not a sign of a person's weakness or a character flaw. You can't "snap out of" clinical depression. Most people who experience depression need treatment to get better.

Signs and Symptoms

Sadness is only a small part of depression. Some people with depression may not feel sadness at all. Depression has many other symptoms, including physical ones. If you have been experiencing any of the following signs and symptoms for at least 2 weeks, you may be suffering from depression:

- Persistent sad, anxious, or "empty" mood
- Feelings of hopelessness, pessimism
- Feelings of guilt, worthlessness, helplessness
- Loss of interest or pleasure in hobbies and activities
- Decreased energy, fatigue, being "slowed down"
- Difficulty concentrating, remembering, making decisions
- Difficulty sleeping, early-morning awakening, or oversleeping
- Appetite and/or weight changes
- Thoughts of death or suicide, suicide attempts
- Restlessness, irritability
- Persistent physical symptoms

Factors That Play a Role in Depression

Many factors may play a role in depression, including genetics, brain biology and chemistry, and life events such as trauma, loss of a loved one, a difficult relationship, an early childhood experience, or any stressful situation.

Depression can happen at any age, but often begins in the teens or early 20s or 30s. Most chronic mood and anxiety disorders in adults begin as high levels of anxiety in children. In fact, high levels of anxiety as a child could mean a higher risk of depression as an adult.

Depression can co-occur with other serious medical illnesses such as diabetes, cancer, heart disease, and Parkinson disease. Depression can make these conditions worse and vice versa. Sometimes medications taken for these illnesses may cause side effects that contribute to depression. A doctor experienced in treating these complicated illnesses can help work out the best treatment strategy.

Research on depression is ongoing, and one day these discoveries may lead to better diagnosis and treatment.

Depression Affects People in Different Ways

Not everyone who is depressed experiences every symptom. Some people experience only a few symptoms. Some people have many. The severity and frequency of symptoms, and how long they last, will vary depending on the individual, and his or her particular illness. Symptoms may also vary depending on the stage of the illness.

Women

Women with depression do not all experience the same symptoms. However, women with depression typically have symptoms of sadness, worthlessness, and guilt. Depression is more common among women than among men. Biological, life cycle, hormonal, and psychosocial factors that are unique to women may be linked to their higher depression rate. For example, women are especially vulnerable to developing postpartum depression after giving birth, when hormonal and physical changes and the new responsibility of caring for a newborn can be overwhelming.

Men

Men often experience depression differently than women. While women with depression are more likely to have feelings of sadness, worthlessness, and excessive guilt, men are more likely to be very tired, irritable, lose interest in once-pleasurable activities, and have difficulty sleeping.

Men may turn to alcohol or drugs when they are depressed. They also may become frustrated, discouraged, irritable, angry, and sometimes abusive. Some men may throw themselves into their work to avoid talking about their depression with family or friends, or behave recklessly. And although more women attempt suicide, many men die by suicide in the United States.

Children

Before puberty, girls and boys are equally likely to develop depression. A child with depression may pretend to be sick, refuse to go to school, cling to a parent, or worry that a parent may die. Because normal behaviors vary from one childhood stage to another, it can be difficult to tell whether a child is just going through a temporary "phase" or is suffering from depression. Sometimes the parents become worried about how the child's behavior has changed, or a teacher mentions that "your child doesn't seem to be himself." In such a case, if a visit to the child's pediatrician rules out physical symptoms, the doctor will probably suggest that the child be evaluated, preferably by a mental health professional who specializes in the treatment of children. Most chronic mood disorders, such as depression, begin as high levels of anxiety in children.

Teens

The teen years can be tough. Teens are forming an identity apart from their parents, grappling with gender issues and emerging sexuality, and making independent decisions for the first time in their lives. Occasional bad moods are to be expected, but depression is different.

Older children and teens with depression may sulk, get into trouble at school, be negative and irritable, and feel misunderstood. If you're unsure if an adolescent in your life is depressed or just "being a teenager," consider how long the symptoms have been present, how severe they are, and how different the teen is acting from his or her usual self. Teens with depression may also have other disorders such as anxiety, eating disorders, or substance abuse. They may also be at higher risk for suicide.

Children and teenagers usually rely on parents, teachers, or other caregivers to recognize their suffering and get them the treatment they need. Many teens don't know where to go for mental health treatment or believe that treatment won't help. Others don't get help because they think depression symptoms may be just part of the typical stress of school or being a teen. Some teens worry what other people will think if they seek mental healthcare.

Depression often persists, recurs, and continues into adulthood, especially if left untreated. If you suspect a child or teenager in your life is suffering from depression, speak up right away.

Older People

Having depression for a long period of time is not a normal part of growing older. Most older adults feel satisfied with their lives, despite having more illnesses or physical problems. But depression in older adults may be difficult to recognize because they may show different, less obvious symptoms.

Sometimes older people who are depressed appear to feel tired, have trouble sleeping, or seem grumpy and irritable. Confusion or attention problems caused by depression can sometimes look like Alzheimer disease or other brain disorders. Older adults also may have more medical conditions such as heart disease, stroke, or cancer, which may cause depressive symptoms. Or they may be taking medications with side effects that contribute to depression.

Some older adults may experience what doctors call vascular depression, also called arteriosclerotic depression or subcortical ischemic depression. Vascular depression may result when blood vessels become less flexible and harden over time, becoming constricted. The hardening of vessels prevents normal blood flow to the body's organs, including the brain. Those with vascular depression may have or be at risk for heart disease or stroke.

Sometimes it can be difficult to distinguish grief from major depression. Grief after loss of a loved one is a normal reaction and generally does not require professional mental health treatment. However, grief that is complicated and lasts for a very long-time following a loss may require treatment.

Older adults who had depression when they were younger are more at risk for developing depression in late life than those who did not have the illness earlier in life.

Depression Is Treatable

Depression, even the most severe cases, can be treated. The earlier treatment begins, the more effective it is. Most adults see an improvement in their symptoms when treated with antidepressant drugs, talk therapy (psychotherapy), or a combination of both.

If you think you may have depression, start by making an appointment to see your doctor or healthcare provider. This could be your primary doctor or a health provider who specializes in diagnosing and treating mental health conditions (psychologist or psychiatrist).

Certain medications, and some medical conditions, such as viruses or a thyroid disorder, can cause the same symptoms as depression. A doctor can rule out these possibilities by doing a physical exam, interview, and lab tests. If the doctor can find no medical condition that may be causing the depression, the next step is a psychological evaluation.

Talking to Your Doctor

How well you and your doctor talk to each other is one of the most important parts of getting good healthcare. But talking to your doctor isn't always easy. It takes time and effort on your part as well as your doctor's.

To prepare for your appointment, make a list of:

- Any symptoms you've had, including any that may seem unrelated to the reason for your appointment:
  - When did your symptoms start?
  - How severe are your symptoms?
  - Have the symptoms occurred before?
  - If the symptoms have occurred before, how were they treated?
- Key personal information, including any major stresses or recent life changes
- All medications, vitamins, or other supplements that you're taking, including how much and how often
- Questions to ask your health provider

If you don't have a primary doctor or are not at ease with the one you currently see, now may be the time to find a new doctor. Whether you just moved to a new city, changed insurance providers, or had a bad experience with your doctor or medical staff, it is worthwhile to spend time finding a doctor you can trust.

Tests and Diagnosis

Your doctor or healthcare provider will examine you and talk to you at the appointment. Your doctor may do a physical exam and ask questions about your health and symptoms. There are no lab tests that can specifically diagnose depression, but your doctor may also order some lab tests to rule out other conditions.

Ask questions if the doctor's explanations or instructions are unclear, bring up problems even if the doctor doesn't ask, and let the doctor know if you have concerns about a particular treatment or change in your daily life.

Your doctor may refer you to a mental health professional, such as a psychiatrist, psychologist, social worker, or mental health counselor, who should discuss with you any family history of depression or other mental disorder, and get a complete history of your symptoms. The mental health professional may also ask if you are using alcohol or drugs, and if you are thinking about death or suicide.

If your doctor does not refer you to a mental health professional or you feel your concerns were not adequately addressed, call or visit the website for your health insurance provider, Medicare, or Medicaid. You can also try searching in the Substance Abuse and Mental Health Services Administration's (SAMHSA) Behavioral Health Treatment Services Locator.

Need Help Now?

Call the 24-hour, toll-free confidential National Suicide Prevention Lifeline (NSPL) at 800-273-TALK (800-273-8255).

Treatment

Depression is treated with medicines, talk therapy (where a person talks with a trained professional about his or her thoughts and feelings; sometimes called "psychotherapy"), or a combination of the two.

Remember: No two people are affected the same way by depression. There is no "one-size-fits-all" for treatment. It may take some trial and error to find the treatment that works best for you.

Medications

Because information about medications is always changing, the following section may not list all the types of medications available to treat depression. Check the U.S. Food and Drug Administration

(FDA) website for the latest news and information on warnings, patient medication guides, or newly approved medications.

Antidepressants are medicines that treat depression. They may help improve the way your brain uses certain chemicals that control mood or stress.

There are several types of antidepressants:

- Selective serotonin reuptake inhibitors (SSRIs)
- Serotonin and norepinephrine reuptake inhibitors (SNRIs)
- Tricyclic antidepressants (TCAs)
- Monoamine oxidase inhibitors (MAOIs)

There are other antidepressants that don't fall into any of these categories and are considered unique, such as Mirtazapine and Bupropion.

Although all antidepressants can cause side effects, some are more likely to cause certain side effects than others. You may need to try several different antidepressant medicines before finding the one that improves your symptoms and has side effects that you can manage.

Most antidepressants are generally safe, but the U.S. Food and Drug Administration (FDA) requires that all antidepressants carry black box warnings, the strictest warnings for prescriptions. In some cases, children, teenagers, and young adults under age 25 may experience an increase in suicidal thoughts or behavior when taking antidepressants, especially in the first few weeks after starting or when the dose is changed.

The warning also says that patients of all ages taking antidepressants should be watched closely, especially during the first few weeks of treatment.

Common side effects listed by the FDA for antidepressants are:

- Nausea and vomiting
- Weight gain
- Diarrhea
- Sleepiness
- Sexual problems

Other more serious but much less common side effects listed by the FDA for antidepressant medicines can include seizures, heart problems, and an imbalance of salt in your blood, liver damage, suicidal thoughts, or serotonin syndrome (a life-threatening reaction where your body makes too much serotonin). Serotonin syndrome can cause shivering, diarrhea, fever, seizures, and stiff or rigid muscles.

Your doctor may have you see a talk therapist in addition to taking medicine. Ask your doctor about the benefits and risks of adding talk therapy to your treatment. Sometimes talk therapy alone may be the best treatment for you.

If you are having suicidal thoughts or other serious side effects like seizures or heart problems while taking antidepressant medicines, contact your doctor immediately.

Talk Therapy ("Psychotherapy")

Several types of psychotherapy—or "talk therapy"—can help people with depression. There are several types of psychotherapies that may be effective in treating depression. Examples include cognitive-behavioral therapy, interpersonal therapy, and problem-solving therapy.

Cognitive Behavioral Therapy (CBT)

CBT can help an individual with depression change negative thinking. It can help you interpret your environment and interactions in a positive, realistic way. It may also help you recognize things that may be contributing to the depression and help you change behaviors that may be making the depression worse.

Interpersonal Therapy (IPT)

IPT is designed to help an individual understand and work through troubled relationships that may cause the depression or make it worse. When a behavior is causing problems, IPT may help you change the behavior. In IPT, you explore major issues that may add to your depression, such as grief, or times of upheaval, or transition.

Problem-Solving Therapy (PST)

PST can improve an individual's ability to cope with stressful life experiences. It is an effective treatment option, particularly for older adults with depression. Using a step-by-step process, you identify problems and come up with realistic solutions. It is a short-term therapy and may be conducted in an individual or group format.

For mild to moderate depression, psychotherapy may be the best option. However, for severe depression or for certain people, psychotherapy may not be enough. For teens, a combination of medication and psychotherapy may be the most effective approach to treating major depression and reducing the chances of it coming back. Another study looking at depression treatment among older adults found that people who responded to initial treatment of medication and IPT were less likely to have recurring depression if they continued their combination treatment for at least 2 years.

Section 24.2

Depression, Trauma, and PTSD

This section includes text excerpted from "Depression, Trauma, and PTSD," U.S. Department of Veterans Affairs (VA), August 13, 2015.

Depression is a common problem that can occur following trauma. It involves feelings of sadness or low mood that last more than just a few days. Unlike a blue mood that comes and goes, depression is longer lasting. Depression can get in the way of daily life and make it hard to function. It can affect your eating and sleeping, how you think, and how you feel about yourself.

How Common Is Depression Following Trauma?

In any given year, almost 1 in 10 adult Americans has some type of depression. Depression often occurs after trauma. For example, a survey of survivors from the Oklahoma City bombing showed that 23 percent had depression after the bombing. This was compared to 13 percent who had depression before the bombing. Posttraumatic stress disorder (PTSD) and depression are often seen together. Results from a large national survey showed that depression is nearly 3–5 times more likely in those with PTSD than those without PTSD.

What Are the Symptoms of Depression?

Depression is more than just feeling sad. Most people with depression feel down or sad more days than not for at least 2 weeks. Or they find they no longer enjoy or have interest in things anymore. If you have depression, you may notice that you're sleeping and eating a lot more or less than you used to. You may find it hard to stay focused. You may feel down on yourself or hopeless. With more severe depression, you may think about hurting or killing yourself.

How Are Depression and Trauma Related?

Depression can sometimes seem to come from out of the blue. It can also be caused by a stressful event such as a divorce or a trauma. Trouble coping with painful experiences or losses often leads to depression. For example, Veterans returning from a war zone may have painful memories and feelings of guilt or regret about their war experiences. They may have been injured or lost friends. Disaster survivors may have lost a loved one, a home, or have been injured. Survivors of violence or abuse may feel like they can no longer trust other people. These kinds of experiences can lead to both depression and PTSD.

Many symptoms of depression overlap with the symptoms of PTSD. For example, with both depression and PTSD, you may have trouble sleeping or keeping your mind focused. You may not feel pleasure or interest in things you used to enjoy. You may not want to be with other people as much. Both PTSD and depression may involve greater irritability. It is quite possible to have both depression and PTSD at the same time.

How Is Depression Treated?

There are many treatment options for depression. You should be assessed by a healthcare professional who can decide which type of treatment is best for you. In many cases, milder forms of depression are treated by counseling or therapy. More severe depression is treated with medicines or with both therapy and medicine.

Research has shown that certain types of therapy and medicine are effective for both depression and PTSD. Since the symptoms of PTSD and depression can overlap, treatment that helps with PTSD may also result in improvement of depression. Cognitive behavioral therapy (CBT) is a type of therapy that is proven effective for both problems. CBT can help patients change negative styles of thinking and acting that can lead to both depression and PTSD. A type of medicine that is effective for both depression and PTSD is a selective serotonin reuptake inhibitor (SSRI).

What Can I Do about Feelings of Depression?

Depression can make you feel worn out, worthless, helpless, hopeless, and sad. These feelings can make you feel as though you are never going to feel better. You may even think that you should just give up. Some symptoms of depression, such as being tired or not having the desire to do anything, can also get in the way of your seeking treatment.

It is very important for you to know that these negative thoughts and feelings are part of depression. If you think you might be depressed, you should seek help in spite of these feelings. You can expect them to change as treatment begins working. In the meantime, here is a list of things you can do that may improve your mood:

- Talk with your doctor or healthcare provider.
- Talk with family and friends.
- Spend more time with others and get support from them. Don't close yourself off.
- Take part in activities that might make you feel better. Do the things you used to enjoy before you began feeling depressed. Even if you don't feel like it, try doing some of these things. Chances are you will feel better after you do.
- Engage in mild exercise.
- Set realistic goals for yourself.
- Break up goals and tasks into smaller ones that you can manage.

Depression is common in those who have PTSD. The symptoms of depression can make it hard to function, and may also get in the way of your getting treatment. Be aware that there are effective treatments for both depression and PTSD. If you think you may be depressed, talk to your doctor or see Where to Get Help (www.ptsd.va.gov/public/where-to-get-help.asp) for more mental health resources.

Section 24.3

Stress Indicators Detected in Depression-Prone Women's Sweat

This section includes text excerpted from "Errant Stress/ Immune Indicators Detected in Depression-Prone Women's Sweat," National Institute of Mental Health (NIMH), July 29, 2008. Reviewed June 2018.

An experimental skin patch test detected abnormal levels of markers for immune function and stress in the sweat of women with histories of depression, National Institute of Mental Health (NIMH) researchers say. If confirmed, the noninvasive technique could become an easier alternative to a blood test for predicting risk for inflammatory disorders, such as metabolic syndrome, cardiovascular disease, osteoporosis, and diabetes, which often occur with depression.

"Even though most of them had few symptoms, women with a history of depression showed biomarkers in sweat and blood consistent with a 'fight or flight' stress response," explained Esther Sternberg, M.D., chief of NIMH's Section on Neuroendocrine Immunology and Behavior (SNIB). Inflammation-related immune messenger chemicals soared as much as five-fold and a nerve chemical that normally acts as a brake on the stress response plummeted, while an adrenalin-like nerve chemical was elevated.

Although similar abnormalities in stress and immune indicators had previously been linked to depression, the new study is the first to demonstrate the feasibility of accurately measuring them in sweat.

In the study, 19 women, most in remission from depression, and 17 healthy controls wore abdominal sweat patches for a day. Variations in marker levels in their sweat correlated strongly with levels in their blood—and also with severity of depression and anxiety symptoms. These changes predispose patients to metabolic syndrome and other inflammatory illnesses, Sternberg said.

In the women with histories of depression, five immune system chemical messengers called cytokines were elevated several-fold, as were three stress-related brain chemicals called neuropeptides. Cytokines regulate neuropeptides and other brain chemicals that control pain, mood and other behaviors altered in depression. A four-fold drop in levels of a neuropeptide called vasoactive intestinal peptide (VIP) coupled with a rise in an adrenalin-like neuropeptide called Neuropeptide Y (NPY) signaled a runaway stress response.

Unlike a blood test, which provides a brief snapshot of marker levels at one point in time, the sweat patch test provides a window into these levels over the course of a day. It may also be a more practical way to monitor the patterns in people on-the-go. However, larger studies, with patients both on-and-off antidepressant medications, will be required to confirm the results, and determine whether the method can be applied to other conditions, Sternberg added.

Working with Sternberg on the study were Drs. Giovanni Cizza of the National Institutes of Health (NIH), National Institute of Diabetes and Digestive and Kidney Diseases (NIDDK), Terry Phillips of National Institute of Biomedical Imaging and Bioengineering (NIBIB), Andrea Marques of National Institute of Mental Health (NIMH), and other members of the Premenopausal, Osteoporosis Women, Alendronate, Depression (P.O.W.E.R.) Study Group.

Patients may someday receive a sweat patch in the mail, wear it for a day, and then give it to their doctor for analysis of their risk for inflammatory illness. Levels of IL-1, an immune system chemical messenger known to affect brain function, were five times higher in sweat of mostly asymptomatic women with a history of major depressive disorder (MDD) compared with healthy controls (HC). Levels of the chemical, one of several such cytokines tested, were comparable in sweat and blood, suggesting that the skin patch is a reliable measure of these indicators, which increase the risk for metabolic and inflammatory illness.

In response to stress, immune system cells secrete chemical messengers called cytokines, which travel to the brain and regulate mood, pain and other behaviors altered in depression. Cytokine levels were significantly elevated in sweat from women with a history of depression—even though most had only mild symptoms. High levels of the chemicals are associated with increased risk for inflammation-related illness.

Section 24.4

Stress, Depression, and the Role of Unhealthy Behaviors among Minority Older Adults

This section includes text excerpted from "Stress, Depression, and the Role of Unhealthy Behaviors among Minority Older Adults," National Institutes of Health (NIH), August 16, 2016.

We have all experienced stress at some point in time. For brief periods of stress, we may figure out a temporary way to cope which would limit the impact of the stressor on our health. However, stress that is brought on by taxing life events that accumulate over time (i.e., chronic stress) can have a significant influence on the mental health of older adults.

Depression among older adults can lead to fatal consequences through a number of pathways such as illness or disease; decreased physical, cognitive, and/or social functioning; increased self-neglect; and higher risk of suicide. Some researchers hypothesize that stress from inequalities in social, economic, and environmental opportunities may cause worse mental health among racial/ethnic minorities such as African Americans.

The relationship between chronic stress and depression may differ for Latinos.

However, the relationship between chronic stress and depression may differ for Latinos. The prevalence of major depression is higher among Latinos (7.9–8.6%) than African Americans (4.2–5.6%) or Whites (3.9–5.3%). This higher prevalence may partially be the result of a differential effect that chronic stress and unhealthy behaviors have on depression for Latinos. Unhealthy behaviors such as cigarette smoking, obesity, and excessive alcohol drinking differ by race/ethnicity and several biological mechanisms have been identified to explain the use of unhealthy behaviors to cope with chronic stress. These same mechanisms may help explain the role of unhealthy behaviors in the relationship between chronic stress and depression.

Prevalence of major depression is higher among Latinos than African Americans and Whites.

Past research has observed that among African Americans adults, as chronic stress increased, those who engage in unhealthy behaviors were able to prevent a future episode of clinical depression to some degree. Dr. Erik J. Rodriquez and his colleagues at the University of California, San Francisco (UCSF) decided to investigate whether unhealthy behaviors modified the effect of chronic stress on subsequent depression among Latinos as well as African Americans and Whites.

They hypothesized that engaging in one or more unhealthy behaviors would strengthen the relationship between chronic stress and depressive symptoms for Latinos and weaken this relationship among African Americans. Funding for their research was supported in part by the UCSF Clinical and Translational Science Institute (CTSI), the National Institute on Aging (NIA), and the National Cancer Institute (NCI).

Dr. Rodriquez analyzed longitudinal, nationally representative data from the 2006–2008 Health and Retirement Study (HRS) to assess the role of unhealthy behaviors in the relationship between chronic stress and significant depressive symptoms. Unhealthy behaviors included current smoking, excessive/binge drinking, and obesity. Chronic stress was defined by nine previously used factors.

Depressive symptoms were measured by the eight-item Center for Epidemiologic Studies Depression (CESD) scale, with ≥4 symptoms having defined significant. Multivariable logistic regression assessed the effects of chronic stress and unhealthy behaviors in 2006 on significant depressive symptoms in 2008 among Latinos, African Americans, and Whites. An interaction term between the number of unhealthy behaviors and the number of chronic stressors was constructed and tested for each racial/ethnic group.

As chronic stress increased, Latinos who engaged in unhealthy behaviors more likely to report significant depressive symptoms.

Their results showed that higher levels of chronic stress in 2006 increased the risk of depressive symptoms in 2008 among Latinos by 54 percent, African Americans by 78 percent, and Whites by 40 percent. Unhealthy behaviors modified this relationship among Latinos. More specifically, as chronic stress increased, Latinos who engaged in one or more unhealthy behaviors were more likely to report significant depressive symptoms in the future. Unhealthy behaviors did not change the relationship between chronic stress and significant depressive symptoms for either African Americans or Whites.

These findings revealed that unhealthy behaviors were not an effective coping mechanism for chronic stress in terms of preventing significant depressive symptoms. Some researchers have hypothesized that the relatively low prevalence of depression observed among African Americans may be the result of effective, yet unhealthy, behaviors that alleviate the symptoms of chronic stress. Some hypothesized that this form of coping works through the same biological mechanisms that contribute to some mental disorders. However, the results of Dr. Rodriquez and colleagues did not confirm this hypothesis.

While there is debate as to whether unhealthy behaviors are coping mechanisms for chronic stress among African Americans, limited published research has been able to either support or refute the relationships between chronic stress, unhealthy behaviors, and depression. Findings from their research add to some previous research that failed to confirm the association of coping with chronic stress through unhealthy behaviors using longitudinal, nationally representative data and clinical diagnoses of major depression. They concluded that unhealthy behaviors, cumulatively, may strengthen the relationship between chronic stress and depression among certain racial/ethnic groups such as Latinos.

The results of Dr. Rodriquez and colleagues add to the understanding of the role of unhealthy behaviors in the relationship between chronic stress and significant depressive symptoms as well as expand the knowledge from past research to another racial/ethnic group: Latinos. Their findings may also be used to inform the decisions of clinicians to screen and provide recommendations for stress and unhealthy behaviors among older-aged Latinos who report symptoms of depression.

Chapter 25

Anxiety Disorders

Anxiety disorders are mental disorders that can occur at any age. Everyone feels worried and fearful at times. People with anxiety disorders worry a lot and are fearful and nervous. These feelings cause distress and impair daily life. The person may avoid situations such as work, school, and social activities.

There are several types of anxiety disorders. This chapter focuses on generalized anxiety disorder (GAD), panic disorder, and social anxiety disorder (SAD).

Signs and Symptoms

Generalized Anxiety Disorder (GAD)

A person with generalized anxiety disorder (GAD) has excessive feelings, thoughts, emotions, and actions. He or she has anxiety or worrying most of the time for at least six months. The worry may be related to job performance, money, health, and other activities. Sometimes the worry shifts from one focus to another. An adult with GAD has several of the following symptoms; a child may have just one symptom:

- Restlessness, or feeling wound up or on edge
- Being easily tired

This chapter includes text excerpted from "Anxiety Disorders," Substance Abuse and Mental Health Services Administration (SAMHSA), April 5, 2017.

- Trouble concentrating, or feeling that their "mind goes blank"
- Irritability
- Muscle tension, aching, or soreness
- Sleep problems, such as trouble falling asleep or staying asleep, restlessness at night, or unsatisfying sleep
- A person with GAD also may have a change in appetite and frequent sweating, nausea, or diarrhea

Panic Disorder

A person with panic disorder has unexpected or expected panic attacks. Panic attacks arc sudden periods of intense fear, anxiety, or discomfort. The attack reaches a peak within minutes. It may cause an urge to escape or flee. During a panic attack, a person has several of the following symptoms:

- Pounding heart or fast heart rate
- Sweating
- Trembling or shaking
- Shortness of breath
- Feelings of choking
- Chest pain or discomfort
- Nausea or abdominal distress
- Dizziness or feeling lightheaded
- Chills or feeling overheated
- Numbness or tingling
- Feelings of unreality or being unconnected to oneself
- Fear of going crazy or losing control
- Fear of dying

After one or more panic attacks, he or she usually has one or both of:

- Worry that another panic attack might occur, and irrational fear that this will lead to loss of control of thoughts and feelings, a heart attack, or dying
- Trying to avoid panic attacks, such as by avoiding certain situations or places, or by stopping exercise or other activities

Social Anxiety Disorder (SAD)

Social anxiety disorder (SAD) is sometimes called "social phobia." The person fears being embarrassed or negatively judged by others in a social setting. This worry often causes him or her to withdraw or avoid certain situations. This causes problems at work, at school, or in relationships.

A person with SAD often has the following symptoms for more than six months:

- Being afraid of or worrying about social situations, such as meeting new people or eating in front of others
- Feeling very self-conscious in front of others and worrying about offending others or being humiliated, embarrassed, or rejected
- Avoiding social situations that cause fear and anxiety, feeling dread or doom leading up to a feared situation, or being very uncomfortable if able to stay in the situation
- Feeling fear or worry about a situation greater than the actual threat and beyond what most people would feel
- Having problems at work, school, or in relationships due to the symptoms
- Changing the daily routine in response to the symptoms

A person with SAD sometimes feels nauseous. They may blush, tremble, sweat, or say their mind "goes blank" in feared situations.

A small subgroup of people with SAD fear having to perform, present, or talk in front of a group.

Risk Factors

There is no single cause of anxiety disorders. Genetics, brain structure and function, and environmental factors all seem to be involved.

General Anxiety Disorder (GAD)

About 3 percent of adults and 1 percent of adolescents have GAD. Females are much more likely than males to have GAD. Most people with GAD develop symptoms between childhood and middle age.

Panic Disorder

About 3 percent of adults and adolescents have panic disorder. Females are more likely than males to have panic disorder. Most people develop panic disorder between ages 20–24. It can occur much earlier, but rarely starts after age 45.

About 25–50 percent of people with panic disorder also have agoraphobia. They start avoiding places such as crowded areas, buses, and elevators. Agoraphobia can occur without panic disorder.

Risk factors for panic disorder include having stressors in the months before the first panic attack. Stressors can include marriage problems, health problems, use of illicit drugs, misuse of medications, or death of a close family member.

Social Anxiety Disorder (SAD)

About 7 percent of adults have SAD in a given year. Children may have social anxiety symptoms. The rate of SAD decreases with age. It is more common in women than in men.

All Anxiety Disorders

Genetics and biological factors. Anxiety disorders tend to run in families. A person who has a close relative with an anxiety disorder or depression is more likely to develop an anxiety disorder. It is unclear whether one or more genes are involved. In some people, an overactive thyroid can contribute to anxiety disorders. A person who tends to feel distressed and withdraw from unfamiliar situations, people, and places may be more likely to develop an anxiety disorder.

Brain structure and function. Certain brain structures seem to play a role in anxiety disorders. The amygdala, the part of the brain that controls emotion, may be involved.

Environment factors. Environmental factors that may lead to anxiety disorders include:

- Smoking or using tobacco products, and nicotine withdrawal
- Having a parent with anxiety, depression, or bipolar disorder
- Having breathing problems, such as asthma, and fearing suffocation
- Withdrawal from alcohol or a medication such as a benzodiazepine

- Exposure to stressful life events in childhood and/or adulthood
- Physical or mental abuse, death of a loved one, desertion, divorce, or isolation
- Caffeine, prescription medications, and over-the-counter (OTC) medicines such as diet pills and allergy medications that contain pseudoephedrine

Evidence-Based Treatments

Anxiety disorders do not go away on their own, but they are among the most treatable mental disorders. If untreated, anxiety disorders can become chronic. Anxiety disorders can be treated with a combination of psychotherapy, sometimes called "talk therapy," and medication. The treatment plan should consider each person's needs and choices. A person should consult a healthcare professional when choosing the right treatment and consider their own gender, race, ethnicity, language, and culture.

Psychotherapy

Cognitive behavioral therapy (CBT) can help people with anxiety disorders. It teaches a person new ways of thinking, acting, and reacting to situations that cause anxiety. It can also help people learn social skills, which is vital for treating SAD. CBT may be done one-on-one or with a group of people who have similar problems. Two helpful approaches are cognitive therapy and exposure therapy. Cognitive therapy focuses on challenging unhelpful thoughts related to anxiety. Exposure therapy focuses on confronting fears so people no longer feel they must avoid certain activities.

Family therapy helps family members improve communication and resolve conflicts. Family therapy is usually short term. It is sometimes used if a person's family may be contributing to their anxiety. The family members learn to avoid doing so.

Acceptance and commitment therapy (ACT) is helpful for people with anxiety disorders. Unlike cognitive behavioral therapy (which aims to reduce problematic thoughts and actions), ACT focuses on acceptance. The person gains insight into patterns of thinking, patterns of avoidance, and the presence or absence of action that is in line with chosen life values. The goal is to reduce the struggle to control or do away with these things, and to increase involvement in meaningful activities. ACT is especially helpful for people with GAD, and maybe a good fit for older adults.

Medications

Medications are helpful in treating anxiety disorders. Medications do not cure anxiety disorders but often relieve symptoms. Medication and psychotherapy can be used separately or in combination. Medication may be used if psychotherapy alone is not effective, or if a person does not have access to psychotherapy.

The most common medications for anxiety disorders are antidepressants, benzodiazepines, and beta-blockers.

Antidepressants can be helpful for treating anxiety disorders. A doctor should closely monitor anyone who recently started taking an antidepressant. In some cases, children, teenagers, and young adults (under age 25) may have more suicidal thoughts or actions when taking antidepressants. This is more likely in the first few weeks after starting a medication, or when the dose is changed. Women who are pregnant, planning to become pregnant, or breastfeeding should talk to their prescriber about possible health risks to herself, the fetus, or her nursing child. It is important to consult with a healthcare prescriber before stopping an antidepressant. Stopping these medications abruptly can cause serious health problems.

Benzodiazepines are often prescribed to people with anxiety disorders to help reduce worrying, panic attacks, or extreme fear. Benzodiazepines should be monitored by the prescriber. They can lead to physical dependency.

Beta-blockers are helpful in treating the physical symptoms of anxiety, especially social anxiety. Physicians prescribe them to control rapid heartbeat, shaking, trembling, and blushing.

Complementary Therapies and Activities

Complementary therapies and activities can help people with mental disorders improve their well-being and are meant to be used along with evidence-based treatments.

Stress-management techniques, mindfulness, and meditation can help people with anxiety disorders learn to calm their thoughts and may enhance the effects of therapy.

Progressive muscle relaxation management includes forms of meditation and exercises that help reduce muscle tension and anxiety. These guided exercises help break the cycle of muscle tensions tied to anxiety.

Daily exercise, healthy nutrition, and adequate sleep improve a person's motivation and ability to participate in treatment and reduce stress levels.

Chamomile capsules may have some benefits for some people with mild to moderate GAD.

Recovery and Social Support Services and Activities

Recovery is a process of change through which people improve their health and wellness, live self-directed lives, and strive to reach their full potential. This includes:

- Overcoming or managing one's condition(s) or symptoms
- Having a stable and safe place to live
- Conducting meaningful daily activities, such as a job, school, volunteerism, and family caretaking
- Having relationships and social networks that provide support, friendship, love, and hope

Recovery helps a person develop resilience, increasing the ability to cope with adversity and adapt to challenges or change.

Self-help and support groups can provide people with the knowledge and support to make treatment decisions that work for them. Organizations and websites provide self-help information and help people find local support groups. Peer and family support services can help foster hope and promote outreach and engagement for those with behavioral health conditions. This includes both peer-to-peer and family-to-family supports provided by a certified peer or family support specialist who can promote hope, foster recovery, and build resilience skills.

Future Directions in Research and Treatment

Researchers are exploring the role of genes in anxiety disorders. Some research has found that a subgroup of people with panic disorder have a common gene. It is unclear whether there are distinct genetic forms of panic disorder, or one set of genes that make a person more likely to have panic disorder or anxiety disorders generally.

Research is also studying new treatments. Certain types of treatments might work better for certain groups such as military veterans, children, and adolescents. Use of computers, cell phone, tablets, and mobile applications to treat anxiety disorders is a growing area of interest.

Chapter 26

Bipolar Disorder

Bipolar disorder (previously called "manic-depressive disorder") is characterized by extremes in mood and related changes in behavior and thoughts. In this condition, an individual experiences both highs (mania or its milder form, hypomania), and lows (depression), or a mixture of these symptoms at the same time. Unlike depression, the symptoms of bipolar may not be distressing to individuals with bipolar disorder, and may go unnoticed by them. The symptoms of bipolar disorder may wax and wane, but the condition itself is chronic and requires ongoing management. However, with good treatment and self-management skills, individuals with bipolar disorder can lead productive and fulfilling lives. Approximately one in every hundred people (1%) develop bipolar disorder.

Symptoms

- **Mania (highs):** It may include feelings of euphoria, increased energy, and a heightened sense of optimism. Often times, those diagnosed with Bipolar disorder have a high degree of energy, have little need for sleep, and cannot turn off the racing

This chapter contains text excerpted from the following sources: Text in this chapter begins with the excerpts from "Bipolar," U.S. Department of Veterans Affairs (VA), December 9, 2015; Text beginning with the heading "Evidence-Based Treatments" is excerpted from "Bipolar Disorders," Substance Abuse and Mental Health Services Administration (SAMHSA), May 12, 2017.

thoughts in their mind. Many also report having periods of increased energy and drive along with irritability. Milder forms of mania are called hypomania.

- **Depression (lows):** It consists of sad or blue moods, sometimes with a sense that things will never get better. Often people stop feeling pleasure in usual activities and become overly pessimistic, hopeless, guilty, or even think about ending their lives. Sometimes there are physical changes as well, such as sleeping too little or too much and eating too little or too much.
- **Other symptoms:** It may at times accompany bipolar disorder. Specifically, common co-occurring conditions include posttraumatic stress disorder (PTSD) and substance use disorders (SUD). Occasionally individuals diagnosed with bipolar disorder may experience hallucinations (seeing or hearing things that are not there) or delusions (strange, fixed beliefs) when severely manic or depressed. These additional symptoms require treatment as well.

Causes

There is no single identifiable cause of bipolar disorder. Rather, it is believed that a variety of individual characteristics and outside factors contribute to the onset of bipolar symptoms, usually during early adulthood.

- **Genetics:** There is some indication that genetics plays a role in predisposing an individual to bipolar disorder, but researchers have been unable to identify any specific genetic cause. It is more likely that the disorder is caused by a combination of genetic factors and environmental triggers.
- **Biological factors:** Research has linked bipolar disorder to problems with certain brain chemicals called neurotransmitters (for example, norepinephrine, serotonin, and dopamine). These neurotransmitters let brain cells communicate with one another, and research indicates that problems in this communication can contribute to bipolar disorder.
- **Life stressors:** Research suggests that both physical stressors (like change in seasons or use of drugs) and social stressors (like family stress or job stress) can affect the onset and course of bipolar disorder symptoms.

Evidence-Based Treatments

Treatment for those with bipolar disorder focuses on helping the person better control their mood swings and other bipolar symptoms. The treatment plan should consider each person's needs and choices. A person should consult a healthcare professional when choosing the right treatment and consider his or her own gender, race, ethnicity, language, and culture.

A person-centered effective treatment plan usually includes using both medication and psychotherapy, ensuring that the person has a support system, and helping the person engage in meaningful activities.

A long-term relationship with a qualified physician is important for effective treatment. Bipolar disorder is a lifelong illness, with repeated episodes of mania and depression. Between episodes, many people with bipolar disorder are free of mood changes, but some people have lingering symptoms. Long-term, continuous treatment helps to control these symptoms. Effective treatment can help a person achieve their recovery goals.

Psychotherapy

In combination with medication, psychotherapy—sometimes called "talk therapy"—can be an effective treatment for bipolar disorder. It can provide support, education, and guidance to people with bipolar disorder and their families.

Psychotherapies used as part of a treatment plan for a person with bipolar disorder include:

Cognitive behavioral therapy (CBT) focuses on a person's thoughts and beliefs, and how they influence mood and actions. It aims to change a person's thinking to be more adaptive and healthy.

Family psychoeducation and skill building includes family members in therapy sessions to learn about the disorder and its treatment. This can improve communication and problem solving for managing symptoms.

Interpersonal and social rhythm therapy focuses on improving relationships, sleep, and daily routines and activities.

Psychoeducation provides training about health disorders and how to manage symptoms.

Medications

Different types of medications can help control symptoms of bipolar disorder. A person may need to try several medications to find ones that work best. Medications that are generally used to treat bipolar disorder include:

- Lithium
- Mood stabilizers
- Second generation antipsychotics
- Antidepressants

People with bipolar disorder may have trouble sleeping. Sometimes the medication they take for bipolar symptoms causes sleep problems. If sleeplessness does not improve, a doctor may suggest a change in medications, or prescribe sedatives or a sleep medication.

Other Treatment Options

Electroconvulsive therapy (ECT) can provide relief for people with severe bipolar disorder not helped by standard psychotherapies or medications. Sometimes ECT is used for bipolar symptoms when other illnesses or pregnancy make taking medications too risky. ECT may cause short-term side effects, including confusion, disorientation, and memory loss.

Safety planning involves developing strategies to limit the risks of danger to self and others. Safety planning may include a crisis plan or removal of dangerous items or weapons from places where the person can access them.

Behavior Health Advance Directive

A person with bipolar disorder is encouraged to create a behavioral health advance directive, stating:

- Where they wish to receive care
- What treatments they want
- Who can make legal healthcare decisions for them, if they cannot do so due to their illness

Advance directive laws vary across states.

Complementary Therapies and Activities

Complementary therapies and activities can help people improve their well-being, and are meant to be used along with evidence-based treatments.

Maintaining a life/mood chart provides a record of daily mood symptoms, treatments, sleep patterns, and life events. This can help people and their healthcare professionals track and treat bipolar disorder symptoms more effectively. A regular routine for sleep, physical activity, meals, and engagement in school, work, and volunteerism can be helpful in managing symptoms.

Folate, vitamin B, and omega-3 supplements may be helpful for people with depression or bipolar disorder when used with standard care.

Exercise and aerobic activity is often recommended to help with symptoms of bipolar disorder, especially during periods of depression.

Self-education or learning more about bipolar disorder through books, videos, and online resources can be helpful. Bibliotherapy is increasingly used in mental healthcare. It encourages a person to think about how their life relates to the content of books, poetry, and other written materials. This can help a person learn new coping strategies, change behaviors, and reduce distress.

Apps for health improvement and personal support are available for smartphones and tablets.

Chapter 27

Disordered Eating and Stress

Chapter Contents

Section 27.1

Emotional Eating

"Emotional Eating," © 2017 Omnigraphics.
Reviewed June 2018.

Emotional eating is a term used to describe the use of food to deal with feelings or, as some experts put it, eating in response to an emotional "trigger." This trigger could be stress, sadness, anxiety, loneliness, anger, or boredom. People who engage in emotional eating often gain weight, because even though food might make them feel better temporarily, the relief doesn't last long, and the underlying emotions remain, compounded by guilt, which causes them to eat more in attempt to feel better again. Surprisingly, emotional eating can even be the result of positive feelings. Many people reward themselves with food after a significant accomplishment or use holidays as an excuse to eat compulsively. Emotional eating is something that most of us do occasionally, such as when cramming for an important test, getting over a breakup, or indulging in a rich dessert on a special occasion, but when it becomes a regular pattern it can be a danger to your health.

Signs of Emotional Eating

There are significant differences between emotional eating and eating to satisfy hunger. Some signs of emotional eating include:

- **Suddenness.** Physical hunger tends to come on gradually as the length of time since your last meal increases. But emotional hunger is more sudden, the craving feels urgent, and it's hard to control.
- **Lack of satisfaction.** Normal hunger lessens when you're full, but with emotional eating you tend to eat to the point where you're uncomfortably stuffed.
- **Craving specific foods.** Many types of food can satisfy physical hunger, but emotional eating is characterized by a desire for specific food items, often sweet or fatty things like chips, candy, pizza, or fast-food burgers.
- **Lack of awareness.** Normally, there's a mindfulness to eating. You're aware of the amount of food on your plate, how fast you're eating it, and what's going on around you. With emotional

eating, you might be surprised to find that you at an entire bag of chocolate chip cookies without realizing it.

- **Guilt.** When eating to satisfy hunger, you don't have any particular bad feelings about the meal. But emotional eating—especially binging on junk food—can lead to feelings of guilt, regret, or shame.

A number of experts recommend the "broccoli test" to determine if you're really hungry or emotionally hungry. Ask yourself if you'd eat raw broccoli or some other healthy food, such as fruit. If the answer is yes, then you're actually hungry; if not, then you have an emotional craving.

Causes of Emotional Eating

There are numerous causes of emotional eating, but some of the most common contributing factors include:

- **Stress.** Stress—especially long-term stress—causes the brain to release a hormone called cortisol, which not only increases appetite, but also can reduce impulse control, making it hard to curb the urge to eat. In addition, studies show that cortisol increases cravings for foods that are high in fat, sugar, or both.
- **Negative emotions.** Many people turn to food as a means of coping with feelings like fear, anger, sadness, anxiety, loneliness, and resentment. The food serves as a distraction and a source of comfort, at least temporarily, allowing them to escape feeling bad for a while.
- **Food as a reward.** Say you've aced a test, so you treat yourself with a chocolate sundae. That's a fairly common way that people reward themselves with food. But there are those who do this habitually, using food as a replacement for other positive experiences that are missing from their lives. Some of these habits go back to childhood, when their parents rewarded them with treats for good behavior.
- **Body image.** People with poor body image often compensate for these feelings by eating. Most often, the negative feelings about their bodies stem from being overweight, so frequent binge eating—especially on junk food—is one of the least healthy ways to overcome these feelings.

- **Social influences.** Cultures all over the world celebrate with food. It's normal to get together with family or friends for a meal and conversation. But some families and some groups of friends tend to put pressure on their members to overindulge on a regular basis. And if one of the members is particularly susceptible to emotional eating, that can create a problem.

Solutions to Emotional Eating

Managing emotional eating means finding healthier ways to process emotions than by indulging in compulsive eating. But that's easier said than done. In practice, controlling ingrained emotional eating habits can be a difficult process, sometimes requiring specialized help. Some ways to break the unhealthy eating cycle include:

- **Relieve stress.** For some people, this can be as simple as calling a friend to chat or playing with a pet, rather than eating during stressful times. Others manage stress through yoga, meditation, music, exercise, massage, or dancing. In some cases, anti-anxiety medication, prescribed by a doctor, may be necessary.
- **Accept emotions.** Bad feelings are part of life, and eating won't change that. Some experts recommend letting yourself experience difficult feelings in order to normalize them. This may not be easy without assistance, so it might be a good idea to work with a therapist, psychologist, or other trained professional.
- **Alternative rewards.** Rather than treating yourself with junk food, find other ways to reward yourself for accomplishments. This might include going to a movie or concert, a weekend trip, a new haircut, new clothes, or a visit to a museum.
- **Be aware.** It's important to be mindful of what you're eating each day. It may be tedious, but one way to do this is to keep a food journal, noting what you ate and why you ate it. Another idea is always to put a controlled amount of food on a plate, and don't go back for seconds. Never eat out of an entire bag of snacks or tub of ice cream. Limiting portions like this can help keep you aware of the amount you're consuming.
- **Don't get overly hungry.** Eat when you're just beginning to get hungry. Being overly hungry is a common way of triggering

emotional eating. The best advice is to eat a number of small meals per day, rather than one or two large ones.

- **Get help.** There are therapists who specialize in working with people with eating disorders. They can help you rethink your approach to food, assist with body-image issues, and suggest strategies for coping with emotions. In addition, there are likely a number of support groups in your area where you can get advice and a sympathetic ear as you cope with emotional eating.

A good first step in controlling emotional eating is to speak with your doctor. He or she may run some simple tests, have useful advice, and can put you in touch with other professionals who can help.

References

1. "Emotional Eating," Waldencenter.org, 2015.
2. "Emotional Eating vs. Mindful Eating: How to Stop Stress Eating and Satisfy Your Needs with Mindfulness," Helpguide.org, February, 2016.
3. Gavin, Mary L., MD. "Emotional Eating," KidsHealth.org, September, 2014.
4. Goldberg, Joseph, MD. "How to Stop Emotional Eating," WebMD.com, May 19, 2016.
5. Kromberg, Jennifer, PsyD. "Emotional Eating? 5 Reasons You Can't Stop," Psychology Today, September 18, 2013.
6. Nguyen-Rodriguez, Selena T., PhD, MPH. "Psychological Determinants of Emotional Eating in Adolescence," Journal of Treatment & Prevention, April 23, 2009.
7. "Why Stress Causes People to Overeat," Harvard Mental Health Letter, February, 2012.

Section 27.2

Eating Disorders Linked to Feelings of Extreme Distress

This section includes text excerpted from "Eating Disorders," National Institute of Mental Health (NIMH), February 2016.

There is a commonly held view that eating disorders are a lifestyle choice. Eating disorders are actually serious and often fatal illnesses that cause severe disturbances to a person's eating behaviors. Obsessions with food, body weight, and shape may also signal an eating disorder. Common eating disorders include anorexia nervosa, bulimia nervosa, and binge-eating disorder.

Signs and Symptoms

Anorexia Nervosa

People with anorexia nervosa may see themselves as overweight, even when they are dangerously underweight. People with anorexia nervosa typically weigh themselves repeatedly, severely restrict the amount of food they eat, and eat very small quantities of only certain foods. Anorexia nervosa has the highest mortality rate of any mental disorder. While many young women and men with this disorder die from complications associated with starvation, others die of suicide. In women, suicide is much more common in those with anorexia than with most other mental disorders.

Symptoms include:

- Extremely restricted eating
- Extreme thinness (emaciation)
- A relentless pursuit of thinness, and unwillingness to maintain a normal, or healthy weight
- Intense fear of gaining weight
- Distorted body image, a self-esteem that is heavily influenced by perceptions of body weight and shape, or a denial of the seriousness of low body weight

Other symptoms may develop over time, including:

- Thinning of the bones (osteopenia or osteoporosis)

- Mild anemia, and muscle wasting, and weakness
- Brittle hair and nails
- Dry and yellowish skin
- Growth of fine hair all over the body (lanugo)
- Severe constipation
- Low blood pressure, slowed breathing, and pulse
- Damage to the structure, and function of the heart
- Brain damage
- Multiorgan failure
- Drop in internal body temperature, causing a person to feel cold all the time
- Lethargy, sluggishness, or feeling tired all the time
- Infertility

Bulimia Nervosa

People with bulimia nervosa have recurrent and frequent episodes of eating unusually large amounts of food and feeling a lack of control over these episodes. This binge-eating is followed by behavior that compensates for the overeating such as forced vomiting, excessive use of laxatives, or diuretics, fasting, excessive exercise, or a combination of these behaviors. Unlike anorexia nervosa, people with bulimia nervosa usually maintain what is considered a healthy or relatively normal weight.

Symptoms include:

- Chronically inflamed and sore throat
- Swollen salivary glands in the neck and jaw area
- Worn tooth enamel, and increasingly sensitive, and decaying teeth as a result of exposure to stomach acid
- Acid reflux disorder and other gastrointestinal problems
- Intestinal distress and irritation from laxative abuse
- Severe dehydration from purging of fluids
- Electrolyte imbalance (too low or too high levels of sodium, calcium, potassium, and other minerals) which can lead to stroke, or heart attack

Binge Eating Disorder (BED)

People with binge eating disorder (BED) lose control over his or her eating. Unlike bulimia nervosa, periods of binge eating are not followed by purging, excessive, or fasting. As a result, people with BED often are overweight or obese. BED is the most common eating disorder in the United States.

Symptoms include:

- Eating unusually large amounts of food in a specific amount of time
- Eating even when you're full or not hungry
- Eating fast during binge episodes
- Eating until you're uncomfortably full
- Eating alone or in secret to avoid embarrassment
- Feeling distressed, ashamed, or guilty about your eating
- Frequently dieting, possibly without weight loss

Risk Factors

Eating disorders frequently appear during the teen years or young adulthood but may also develop during childhood or later in life. These disorders affect both genders, although rates among women are higher than among men. Like women who have eating disorders, men also have a distorted sense of body image. For example, men may have muscle dysmorphia, a type of disorder marked by an extreme concern with becoming more muscular.

Researchers are finding that eating disorders are caused by a complex interaction of genetic, biological, behavioral, psychological, and social factors. Researchers are using the latest technology and science to better understand eating disorders.

One approach involves the study of human genes. Eating disorders run in families. Researchers are working to identify deoxyribonucleic acid (DNA) variations that are linked to the increased risk of developing eating disorders.

Brain imaging studies are also providing a better understanding of eating disorders. For example, researchers have found differences in patterns of brain activity in women with eating disorders in comparison with healthy women. This kind of research can help guide the development of new means of diagnosis and treatment of eating disorders.

Treatments and Therapies

Adequate nutrition, reducing excessive exercise, and stopping purging behaviors are the foundations of treatment. Treatment plans are tailored to individual needs and may include one or more of the following:

- Individual, group, and/or family psychotherapy
- Medical care and monitoring
- Nutritional counseling
- Medications

Psychotherapies

Psychotherapies such as a family-based therapy called the Maudsley approach, where parents of adolescents with anorexia nervosa assume responsibility for feeding their child, appear to be very effective in helping people gain weight and improve eating habits and moods.

To reduce or eliminate binge-eating and purging behaviors, people may undergo cognitive behavioral therapy (CBT), which is another type of psychotherapy that helps a person learn how to identify distorted, or unhelpful thinking patterns, and recognize, and change inaccurate beliefs.

Medications

Evidence also suggests that medications such as antidepressants, antipsychotics, or mood stabilizers approved by the U.S. Food and Drug Administration (FDA) may also be helpful for treating eating disorders and other co-occurring illnesses such as anxiety or depression.

Section 27.3

Nocturnal Sleep-Related Eating Disorder

"Nocturnal Sleep-Related Eating Disorder,"
© 2018 Omnigraphics. Reviewed June 2018.

About 1–3 percent of the general population appears to be affected by sleep-related eating disorder (SRED). Both men and women can have this disorder, but it is more common among women. Sleep eating is also known to run in the family. The onset of this disease is typically between the ages 20 and 40. SRED can also be triggered by other sleep disorders or medical conditions.

What Is Nocturnal Sleep-Related Eating Disorder (NSRED)?

Sleep eating is a disorder in which the patient is hungry and eats at night. Patients diet during the day and are vulnerable to eating at night, but have no memory of doing so. In most cases, people with sleep-related eating disorder (SRED) have a history of alcoholism, drug abuse, and other sleep disorders. They often eat different types of food at odd hours, and may even eat inedible substances. They lose their appetite for food, which often results in anxiety, stress, or depression.

More than 50 percent of these individual's gain weight from consuming food during sleeping hours. They also feel drowsy and experience extreme emotions. Sometimes, low blood sugar (hypoglycemia) can also cause SRED. Dyssomnia is a conscious behavior, while parasomnia is an unconscious behavior. People with SRED usually:

- Become ill from inadequately cooked food or ingesting toxic substances
- Develop metabolic conditions (Type 2 diabetes or elevated cholesterol)
- Develop cavities or tooth decay from eating sugary foods
- Have unrefreshing sleep and feel sleepy or tired during the day
- Injure themselves preparing food (lacerations, burns)
- Gain weight

Sleep eating is an arousal disorder in which:

- The patient indulges in abnormal behavior during arousal from slow-wave sleep
- The patient indulges in repetitive and automatic motor activity
- The patient is unaware of the entire episode as it is occurring
- The patient finds it difficult to wake up despite vigorous attempts

Symptoms

People with sleep-related eating disorders often eat toxic substances and often in strange combinations. Continuous episodes of binge eating only occur when the patients are partially awake. The following conditions are seen in people with sleep-related eating disorder:

- Do something dangerous while getting or cooking food
- Continuous episodes of binge eating and drinking during the time when they sleep
- Have eating episodes that disturb their sleep and cause insomnia, resulting in unrefreshing sleep
- Decline in health from eating foods that are high in calories
- Have a loss of appetite in the morning

If something else is causing the problem, it may be one of the following reasons:

- A mental health disorder
- A medical condition
- Another sleep disorder
- Substance abuse
- Medication use

Risk Factors

About 65–80 percent of SRED patients are females between the ages of 22 and 29. SRED can also occur from the use of certain medicines that are used to treat depression and other sleep problems. Sleep disorder is an ongoing problem and most people with SRED were sleepwalkers as children. Sleep-related disorders include the following:

- Restless legs syndrome (RLS)
- Periodic limb movement disorder (PLMD)
- Obstructive sleep apnea (OSA)
- Irregular sleep-wake rhythm
- Sleep-related dissociative disorders

SRED symptoms typically include the following:

- Dieting during the day
- Daytime eating disorders
- Ending the abuse of alcohol or drugs
- Use of certain medications
- Quitting smoking

SRED may result in:

- Encephalitis (brain swelling)
- Hepatitis (liver infection)
- Narcolepsy
- Stress

Diagnosis

It is important for patients to inform their doctor when this eating disorder begins. Keep your doctor informed about your complete medical history. Make sure to inform the doctor of any medication that you have been taking. Maintain a sleep diary to help the doctor understand your sleeping patterns. The doctor will do an overnight sleep study called a "polysomnogram." The polysomnogram will chart your brain waves, heartbeat, and breathing as you sleep. The unusual behaviors that occur during the night will be recorded on a video, which will help your doctor determine the patterns of your sleep eating disorder.

Treatment

Treatment for sleep-related disorders involves stress management classes, counseling, clinical interview, and limited intake or avoidance of alcohol and caffeine. The physician may change some of your medicines to make it easier for you to treat SRED. Plenty of sleep is required on a daily basis. It is important to consult a sleep specialist to check for signs of sleep disorders.

Consulting a psychotherapist may help reduce stress and anxiety. The physician may recommend medicines such as benzodiazepine to treat your sleep-related disorder. Mirapex and Sinemet are effective dopaminergic agents for sleep eaters.

References

1. "Sleep-Related Eating Disorders," National Center for Biotechnology Information (NCBI), U.S. National Library of Medicine (NLM), November 2006.
2. "Sleep-Related Eating Disorders," The Cleveland Clinic Foundation. April 22, 2017.
3. "Sleep Eating Disorder—Overview and Facts," American Academy of Sleep Medicine (AASM), n.d.

Chapter 28

Obsessive-Compulsive Disorder

Obsessive-compulsive disorder (OCD) is a common mental disorder. It affects children, adolescents, and adults. A person with OCD has unwanted and upsetting thoughts, images, or urges—obsessions—or repetitive actions or mental acts—compulsions. There are many treatment options to manage OCD.

Signs and Symptoms

People with OCD have obsessions, compulsions, or both. The obsessions and compulsions are time-consuming, cause distress, and impair daily life.

Obsessions are repeated and unwanted thoughts, urges, or mental images. These cause anxiety, distress, guilt, or shame. The person tries to ignore or stop the obsessions. Examples of obsessions include:

- Fears about safety and uncertainty, such as forgetting to turn off the stove or lock the door
- Unwanted thoughts and doubts about having harmed others, such as running over someone in your car or hurting a loved one

---

This chapter includes text excerpted from "Obsessive-Compulsive Disorder (OCD)," Substance Abuse and Mental Health Services Administration (SAMHSA), May 12, 2017.

- Unwanted or taboo thoughts about things such as sex (such as inappropriate sexual relations), religion (such as blasphemous thoughts), and harming others (such as stabbing others)
- Fear of germs or contamination
- Concerns or urges about having things balanced, in perfect order, or just right

Compulsions are excessive repetitive actions or mental acts that a person with OCD feels the urge to do in response to an obsession. The aim is to reduce distress or prevent a feared event or situation. Compulsions provide short-term relief from distress caused by obsessions, but make OCD symptoms worse over time. Compulsions are extreme or not based in reality.

Examples of compulsions include:

- Repeatedly checking things such as assignments, or seeing if the door is locked or the stove is off
- Mental rituals such as excessive counting or repeatedly reviewing past events conversations
- Excessively asking for reassurance, "confessing" and apologizing for intrusive thoughts
- Actions to make things perfect, such as excessive rewriting and arranging things
- Extreme religious or moral rituals such as repetitive prayer, confessing, and following rules rigidly outside of typical faith practice
- Excessive cleaning or hand washing
- Avoiding people, places, objects, or situations that bring on obsessions or compulsions

Most people with OCD also have another mental disorder. This might be depression, anxiety, substance use or an eating problem.

Some people with OCD also have a tic disorder. Motor tics are sudden, brief, repetitive movements. Tics may involve eye blinking and other eye movements, grimacing, shoulder shrugging, and head or shoulder jerking. Common vocal tics include repetitive throat clearing, sniffing, or grunting sounds.

Risk Factors

OCD affects about 2–3 percent of the population. OCD affects men and women equally. Symptoms start in childhood or the early 20s. Often, symptoms are not diagnosed for many years. The causes of OCD are unknown. Risk factors include genetics, brain structure and function, environmental factors, and issues related to thoughts and actions.

Genetics

OCD tends to run in families. Twin and family studies show that a person with a close relative with OCD—such as a parent, sibling, or child—is at a higher risk for OCD. Genetic factors play a role, but no specific genetic cause is known.

Brain Structure and Function

Imaging studies have shown differences in brain structures and brain functioning in people with OCD. How this is related to OCD is unknown. Some research suggests that imbalances of chemicals in the brain may cause OCD.

Environmental Factors

Environmental stressors may trigger OCD in some people. Stressors may include abuse, trauma, illness, death in the family, conflict with loved ones, pregnancy and childbirth, or major life changes. These events may also worsen OCD symptoms. Rarely, illnesses such as infection, brain injury, or stroke can lead to OCD symptoms.

Cognitive and Behavioral Factors

A person's thinking patterns, temperament, or ways of interacting with the world may increase the risk of OCD.

Evidence-Based Treatments

OCD is treatable. Without proper treatment, symptoms usually get worse. But people often do not get proper diagnosis and treatment until years after symptoms start.

Effective treatments for OCD include cognitive behavior therapy (CBT), medication, and combinations of both. The treatment plan should consider each person's needs and choices. A person should consult a healthcare professional when choosing the right treatment and consider his or her own gender, race, ethnicity, language, and culture.

Psychotherapy

There are many forms of psychotherapy, sometimes called "talk therapy," that are effective for OCD.

CBT is the most effective treatment for OCD. CBT often involves working one-to-one with a therapist. Families are often involved with children and teens with OCD. CBT may be offered in group and family-based formats. Treatment often involves 12–20 weekly sessions, but some people need longer or more frequent therapy. Medication to reduce anxiety about starting treatment may help a person start and succeed with psychotherapy.

Exposure and response prevention is a type of CBT that reduces obsessions, compulsions, and anxiety in OCD. In this therapy, people with OCD gradually face their fears while avoiding compulsions. Facing fears (exposure) while resisting rituals (response prevention) reduces OCD symptoms over time. Exposure and response prevention helps people manage OCD through reduced anxiety and accepting uncertainty. Eventually, the obsession causes little or no anxiety. Most people improve after treatment.

Medications

The most commonly used medications for OCD symptoms are selective serotonin reuptake inhibitors (SSRIs). These medications may take several weeks to start working, but some people improve faster. If symptoms do not improve, the treatment plan may include trying other medications. Not all medications have been thoroughly tested in children with OCD, so this requires caution. People who do not respond to medication alone may benefit from exposure and response prevention instead of medication or combined with medication.

Other Treatment Options

Most people with OCD respond to treatment in an office setting. Some people need more intensive treatment, such as intensive outpatient programs, day programs, residential care, and inpatient care.

Complementary Therapies and Activities

Complementary therapies and activities can help people improve their well-being, and are meant to be used along with evidence-based treatments (EBT).

Cognitive therapy is a form of CBT that reduces OCD symptoms. The person learns to change their thinking about obsessive thoughts. Often, the person keeps a record of obsessions to identify and correct negative ideas. Cognitive therapy may be helpful when used with exposure and response prevention.

Motivational interviewing can help a person accept the need for treatment and overcome the difficult aspects of treatment. Motivational interviewing may help people with OCD be willing to start exposure and response prevention.

Family therapy may help families when stress and tension may be making a person's OCD symptoms worse. Also, it may help families cope with the symptoms.

Acceptance and commitment therapy is sometimes combined with exposure and response prevention. This approach helps a person prepare for life's difficulties and be more flexible in thoughts and actions. It helps people to think about their problems, and to not overreact or avoid them.

Regular aerobic exercise can help reduce OCD-related stress and anxiety. Also, staying connected with family and friends, getting enough sleep, getting good nutrition, and using relaxation techniques can help a person engage in treatment and manage OCD symptoms.

Recovery and Social Support Services and Activities

Recovery is a process of change through which people improve their health and wellness, live self-directed lives, and strive to reach their full potential. This includes:

- Overcoming or managing one's condition(s) or symptoms
- Having a stable and safe place to live
- Conducting meaningful daily activities, such as a job, school, volunteerism, and family caretaking
- Having relationships and social networks that provide support, friendship, love, and hope

Recovery helps a person develop resilience, increasing the ability to cope with adversity, and adapt to challenges or change.

Self-help and support groups can provide people with the knowledge and support to make treatment decisions that work for them. Organizations and websites provide self-help information and help people find local and online support groups. Peer and family support services can help foster hope and promote outreach and engagement for those with behavioral health conditions. This includes both peer-to-peer and family-to-family supports provided by a certified peer or family support specialist who can promote hope, foster recovery, and build resiliency skills.

Future Directions in Research and Treatment

The National Institute of Mental Health (NIMH) funds research into new treatments for people whose OCD does not respond well to usual therapies. These new approaches include finding genetics and biological causes, new therapy approaches, and other medical techniques.

Chapter 29

Substance Abuse, Addiction, and Stress

Chapter Contents

Section 29.1

Tobacco and Stress

This section includes text excerpted from the following sources: Text under the heading "Stress and Smoking" is excerpted from "Reduce Your Stress," Centers for Disease Control and Prevention (CDC), March 21, 2018; Text under the heading "Risk and Protective Factors" is excerpted from "Adolescents and Tobacco: Risk and Protective Factors," U.S. Department of Health and Human Services (HHS), July 27, 2016.

Stress and Smoking

Some people smoke when they feel stressed. They use smoking as a way to cope. There are many problems with using cigarettes as a way to cope with stress or other unpleasant feelings.

- Smoking isn't a long-term stress reliever. In the time it takes to smoke a cigarette, you could do something else that's more effective—like take a short walk or try a relaxation exercise.
- Smoking doesn't solve the problem that's giving you stress. Your stress will return.
- Nicotine addiction causes stress. Cravings for nicotine feel stressful because your body begins to go through withdrawal.

Smoking isn't a solution for stress. Try other ways to deal, like talking it out or exercising.

Some smokers find it hard to give up cigarettes as a way to cope with stress. It's important to find healthy ways to handle stress and take care of yourself without smoking. There are many other ways to cope with stress that don't involve smoking.

Risk and Protective Factors of Smoking

Approximately 5.6 million adolescents who are currently under the age of 18 will die prematurely due to a smoking-related illness. There are several characteristics and risks associated with tobacco use and with difficulty quitting—many of these factors are applicable not only to adolescents but to all individuals, regardless of age.

Factors Associated with Likelihood to Smoke or Use Tobacco

Numerous factors influence adolescents' decisions to start smoking or to use other tobacco products. These factors include some individual characteristics, such as stress, and low self-esteem, but also social characteristics, such as having parents, siblings, or friends who smoke. Exposure and susceptibility to tobacco advertising can also affect smoking initiation among adolescents.

Certain characteristics increase the likelihood that an adolescent will smoke:

- **Older age.** Rates of regular cigarette smoking and other tobacco use are higher among older adolescents than they are among younger adolescents (although the rate of smoking initiation is higher among younger adolescents).
- **Being male.** Females tend to smoke fewer cigarettes a day, use cigarettes with lower nicotine content, and inhale cigarette smoke less deeply, than do males. Males are also more likely than females to use e-cigarettes.
- **Being white, multi-ethnic, American Indian, or Alaska Native.** White adolescents are more likely to smoke cigarettes than black or Hispanic adolescents (though black adolescents are more likely to smoke cigars). However, adolescents who are multi-ethnic, as well as American Indian and Alaska Natives, are more likely than any other race or ethnic group to use tobacco.
- **Lacking college plans.** Adolescents who plan to attend four years of college are much more likely to be nonsmokers than are their peers who lack such plans.
- **Having parents who are not college educated.** Adolescents whose parents had little or no college education are much more likely to smoke than those whose parents have a college education or more.
- **Experiencing highly stressful events.** Having experienced numerous highly stressful events in childhood is linked with a greater risk of starting smoking by age and with ever smoking. Among these stressors are being a witness or victim of abuse, experiencing a parental separation, or growing up

in a household in which a family member is mentally ill or incarcerated.

- **Perception of risk.** The percentage of adolescents who see smoking as posing a "great risk" to them has steadily increased since the peak of tobacco cigarette use in the 1990's. This has helped contribute to the decline in use seen over the past two decades. Conversely, a low percentage perceive a "great risk" in using e-cigarettes regularly; in fact, about 20 percent of adolescents see a "great risk" in regular e-cigarette use. This is one of the lowest levels of perceived risk measured across all substance categories.

Factors Making It Difficult to Stop Smoking

Research points to multiple factors that lead to tobacco addiction in adolescence, from genetic patterns, to influences of parents and peers, to difficult life circumstances. First and foremost, nicotine is a highly addictive drug that affects individuals on a cellular level, meaning addiction is difficult to overcome for adolescents, as well as adults. Factors that make it difficult to stop smoking include:

- **Physical effects.** The effects of nicotine, including the "reward" feeling, quickly wear off, motivating the user to keep using tobacco to recapture that feeling and to prevent withdrawal symptoms. Those withdrawal symptoms are unpleasant and include irritability, craving, attention problems, disturbed sleep, and increased appetite.
- **Behavioral factors.** In addition to the physical factors that make it harder for adolescents to quit smoking, behavioral factors also come into play: adolescents frequently associate smoking, its smell and feel, with a number of behaviors, including using alcohol and hanging out with friends who smoke. The influence of peers on adolescents' smoking behavior seems to decline with age, but is an important factor in whether adolescents begin smoking, and whether their smoking escalates to daily use.
- **Smoking early in adolescence.** Research shows that the earlier adolescents begin smoking cigarettes, the more likely they are to become addicted to nicotine. According to results from a nationally representative health survey, nearly 90 percent of adults who smoke became regular smokers during adolescence or earlier.

- **Concerns about weight gain.** For some adolescents, concerns about weight gain may be associated with the decision to begin smoking or with a reluctance to quit. Females are less likely to try to quit smoking and are more likely to relapse if they do quit.
- **Genetics.** A half-dozen genes, among the thousands that a person inherits, can affect how the brain reacts to nicotine, including the likelihood of becoming addicted.

Section 29.2

Alcohol and Stress

This section includes text excerpted from "Alcohol Alert Number 85—The Link between Stress and Alcohol," National Institute on Alcohol Abuse and Alcoholism (NIAAA), May 16, 2013. Reviewed June 2018.

At present, more and more servicemen and women are leaving active duty and returning to civilian life. That transition can be difficult. The stresses associated with military service are not easily shed. But dealing with stress is not limited to recent Veterans. A new job, a death in the family, moving across the country, a breakup, or getting married—all are situations that can result in psychological and physical symptoms collectively known as "stress."

One way that people may choose to cope with stress is by turning to alcohol. Drinking may lead to positive feelings and relaxation, at least in the short term. Problems arise, however, when stress is ongoing and people continue to try and deal with its effects by drinking alcohol. Instead of "calming your nerves," long-term, heavy drinking can actually work against you, leading to a host of medical and psychological problems and increasing the risk for alcohol dependence.

This Alert explores the relationship between alcohol and stress, including identifying some common sources of stress, examining how the body responds to stressful situations, and the role that alcohol plays—both in alleviating and perpetuating stress.

Alcohol's Role in Stress

To better understand how alcohol interacts with stress, researchers looked at the number of stressors occurring in the past year in a group of men and women in the general population and how those stressors related to alcohol use. They found that both men and women who reported higher levels of stress tended to drink more. Moreover, men tended to turn to alcohol as a means for dealing with stress more often than did women. For example, for those who reported at least six stressful incidents, the percentage of men binge drinking was about 1.5 times that of women, and alcohol use disorders (AUDs) among men were 2.5 times higher than women.

Veterans who have been in active combat are especially likely to turn to alcohol as a means of relieving stress. Posttraumatic stress disorder (PTSD), which has been found in 14–22 percent of Veterans returning from wars in Afghanistan and Iraq, has been linked to increased risk for alcohol abuse and dependence.

Stress and Alcoholism Recovery

The impact of stress does not cease once a patient stops drinking. Newly sober patients often relapse to drinking to alleviate the symptoms of withdrawal, such as alcohol craving, feelings of anxiety, and difficulty sleeping. Many of these symptoms of withdrawal can be traced to the hypothalamic-pituitary-adrenal (HPA) axis, the system at the core of the stress response.

Long-term, heavy drinking can actually alter the brain's chemistry, resetting what is "normal." It causes the release of higher amounts of cortisol and adrenocorticotropic hormone. When this hormonal balance is shifted, it impacts the way the body perceives stress and how it responds to it. For example, a long-term heavy drinker may experience higher levels of anxiety when faced with a stressful situation than someone who never drank or who drank only moderately.

In addition to being associated with negative or unpleasant feelings, cortisol also interacts with the brain's reward or "pleasure" systems. Researchers believe this may contribute to alcohol's reinforcing effects, motivating the drinker to consume higher levels of alcohol in an effort to achieve the same effects.

Cortisol also has a role in cognition, including learning and memory. In particular, it has been found to promote habit-based learning, which fosters the development of habitual drinking and increases the risk of relapse. Cortisol also has been linked to the development of psychiatric disorders (such as depression) and metabolic disorders.

These findings have significant implications for clinical practice. By identifying those patients most at risk of alcohol relapse during early recovery from alcoholism, clinicians can help patients to better address how stress affects their motivation to drink.

Early screening also is vital. For example, Veterans who turn to alcohol to deal with military stress and who have a history of drinking prior to service are especially at risk for developing problems. Screening for a history of alcohol misuse before military personnel are exposed to military trauma may help identify those at risk for developing increasingly severe PTSD symptoms.

Interventions then can be designed to target both the symptoms of PTSD and alcohol dependence. Such interventions include cognitive–behavioral therapies, such as exposure-based therapies, in which the patient confronts the cues that cause feelings of stress but without the risk of danger. Patients then can learn to recognize those cues and to manage the resulting stress. Researchers recommend treating PTSD and AUDs simultaneously rather than waiting until after patients have been abstinent from alcohol or drugs for a sustained period (e.g., 3 months).

Medications also are currently being investigated for alcoholism that works to stabilize the body's response to stress. Some scientists believe that restoring balance to the stress-response system may help alleviate the problems associated with withdrawal and, in turn, aid in recovery. More work is needed to determine the effectiveness of these medications.

Section 29.3

Substance Abuse, Stress, and Trauma

This section contains text excerpted from the following sources: Text in this section begins with excerpts from "The Influence of Stress on the Transition from Drug Use to Addiction," National Institute on Alcohol Abuse and Alcoholism (NIAAA), 2008. Reviewed June 2018; Text beginning with the heading "Traumatic Stress and Substance Abuse" is excerpted from "PTSD: National Center for PTSD—PTSD and Substance Abuse in Veterans," U.S. Department of Veterans Affairs (VA), August 13, 2015; Text beginning with the heading "Stressful Experiences Affect Likelihood of Remission of Drug Dependence, Continued Drug Use, and Relapse" is excerpted from "Stressful Experiences Affect Likelihood of Remission of Drug Dependence, Continued Drug Use, and Relapse," National Institute on Drug Abuse (NIDA), February 2, 2018.

Stress—that is, any type of stimulus that challenges the organism's normal internal balance—induces a physiologic response involving a variety of hormones and other signaling molecules that act on, among other organs, the brain. This stress response also can influence the progression of alcohol and other drug (AOD) addiction through various stages. For example, AODs can directly activate the stress response. In turn, certain stress hormones (i.e., glucocorticoids and corticotrophin-releasing factor) also act on the brain system that mediates the rewarding experiences associated with AOD use (i.e., the mesocorticolimbic dopamine system). Moreover, elevated glucocorticoid levels and stress increase AOD self-administration in certain animal models. During a later stage of the addiction process, in contrast, excessive and/or prolonged stress may impair the reward system, inducing heavier AOD use to maintain the rewarding experience. During the final stage of addiction, when the addicted person experiences withdrawal symptoms if no drug is consumed, chronic AOD use results in gross impairment of the normal stress response and other signaling mechanisms in the brain, resulting in a state of anxiety and internal stress. At this stage, people continue to use AODs mainly to relieve this negative-affect state.

Addiction to alcohol and other drugs (AODs) is a complex phenomenon influenced by genetic and environmental determinants. For example, in both animals (i.e., rodents and nonhuman primates) and humans, various forms of stress play a role in escalating AOD use as the individual progresses from episodic exposure to addiction. Studies in specific rodent models have shown that stress and certain hormones released in response to stress (i.e., glucocorticoids) increase AOD self-administration during the earliest stage of addiction development (i.e., the acquisition phase). Once rodents are addicted to AODs, high levels of glucocorticoids and other stress-related molecules (i.e., stress peptides) produced by the addicted animal create an internal form of stress that is characterized by anxiety-like behaviors.

Traumatic Stress and Substance Abuse

Some people try to cope with their posttraumatic stress disorder (PTSD) symptoms by drinking heavily, using drugs, or smoking too much. People with PTSD have more problems with drugs and alcohol both before and after getting PTSD. Also, even if someone does not have a problem with alcohol before a traumatic event, getting PTSD increases the risk that he or she will develop a drinking or drug problem.

Eventually, the overuse of these substances can develop into substance use disorder (SUD), and treatment should be given for both PTSD and SUD to lead to successful recovery. The good news is that treatment of co-occurring (happening at the same time) PTSD and SUD works.

How Common Is Co-Occurring PTSD and SUD in Veterans?

Studies show that there is a strong relationship between PTSD and SUD, in both civilian and military populations, as well as for both men and women.

Specific to Veterans:

- More than 2 of 10 Veterans with PTSD also have SUD.
- War Veterans with PTSD and alcohol problems tend to be binge drinkers. Binges may be in response to bad memories of combat trauma.
- Almost 1 out of every 3 Veterans seeking treatment for SUD also has PTSD.
- The number of Veterans who smoke (nicotine) is almost double for those with PTSD (about 6 of 10) versus those without a PTSD diagnosis (3 of 10).

- In the wars in Iraq and Afghanistan, about 1 in 10 returning soldiers seen in U.S. Department of Veterans Affairs (VA) have a problem with alcohol or other drugs.

How Can Co-Occurring PTSD and SUD Create Problems?

If someone has both PTSD and SUD, it is likely that he or she also has other health problems (such as physical pain), relationship problems (with family and/or friends), or problems in functioning (like keeping a job or staying in school). Using drugs and/or alcohol can make PTSD symptoms worse.

For example:

- PTSD may create sleep problems (trouble falling asleep or waking up during the night). You might "medicate" yourself with alcohol or drugs because you think it helps your sleep, but drugs and alcohol change the quality of your sleep and make you feel less refreshed.
- PTSD makes you feel "numb," like being cut off from others, angry and irritable, or depressed. PTSD also makes you feel like you are always "on guard." All of these feelings can get worse when you use drugs and alcohol.
- Drug and alcohol use allows you to continue the cycle of "avoidance" found in PTSD. Avoiding bad memories and dreams or people and places can actually make PTSD last longer. You cannot make as much progress in treatment if you avoid your problems.
- You may drink or use drugs because it distracts you from your problems for a short time, but drugs and alcohol make it harder to concentrate, be productive, and enjoy all parts of your life.

What Treatments Are Offered for Co-Occurring PTSD and SUD?

Evidence shows that in general people have improved PTSD and SUD symptoms when they are provided treatment that addresses both conditions. This can involve any of the following (alone or together):

- Individual or group cognitive behavioral treatments (CBT)
- Specific psychological treatments for PTSD, such as cognitive processing therapy (CPT) or prolonged exposure (PE)

Stressful Experiences Affect Likelihood of Remission of Drug Dependence, Continued Drug Use, and Relapse

Researchers at the University of Michigan's Center for the Study of Drugs, Alcohol, Smoking, and Health (DASH) examined associations between stressful life events and drug use in the responses of 921 adults to the National Epidemiologic Survey on Alcohol and Related Conditions (NESARC). All these respondents reported that at some time prior to the past year, they had symptoms that met the criteria for a diagnosis of drug dependence. At the time of the interview, 560 (60.5%) were no longer dependent and had been abstinent for at least a full year. The remaining 361 had used drugs during the past year.

The researchers compared the respondents' drug histories during the past year with their reports of stressful life events during that time. The stressful events considered included:

- Death of a family member or close friend
- Serious illness/injury of a family member or close friend
- Move or new member of the household
- Fired or laid off from a job
- Unemployed and looking for a job for more than 1 month
- Trouble with a boss or coworker
- Change of job, job responsibilities, or work hours
- Divorce, separation, or end of a steady relationship
- Serious problem with a neighbor, friend, or relative
- Major financial crisis, bankruptcy, or inability to pay bills on time more than once
- Trouble with the police, arrest, or incarceration (respondent or a family member)
- Victim of a crime (respondent or family member)

The researchers found that, consistent with their hypothesis, the respondents who had reported stressful experiences had about 20 percent higher odds of being among those who had used drugs during that year.

Moreover, the number of reported stressful life events correlated with the severity of drug use. Those who had remained abstinent all year reported an average of 2.7 stressful events, and those who were dependent on drugs reported an average of 4.7 stressful events. Those who used drugs but were not dependent and those in partial remission reported 3.9 and 4.0 stressful events, respectively.

These relationships between stressful experiences and drug use were independent of demographic factors that increased the likelihood of past-year drug use: being a man, being 18–24 years old, being unmarried or divorced, and having low personal income.

Impact Persists but Weakens over Time

Three years after their interviews, 758 of the respondents responded to follow-ups. Their rate of past-year abstinence was 69 percent, with only 7 percent drug dependent. The stressful events reported in the earlier interview predicted the severity of drug involvement reported in the follow-up interview. Thus, respondents who reported a whole year of abstinence at the follow-up interview had reported an average of 3.0 stressful events before their first interview, compared with 4.4 among those who were dependent at the follow-up.

Researchers comment, "Our results suggest a strong association between stressful events and remission from drug use over a relatively long, 3-year timescale. Programs that target stress exposure, as well as stress reactivity and resilience, could be a helpful component of a comprehensive plan for chronic-care disease management and relapse prevention."

The relationship between stress and drug remission is complex. Stressful life events can trigger relapse; at the same time, drug use also can create stressful life consequences for individuals and families. The researchers propose that untangling the causal dynamics between the two will be challenging, but could benefit treatment still further."In future studies, ecological momentary assessments and intensive longitudinal methods could be used to study stress and relapse with greater temporal resolution," they say. "Emerging technological innovations involving tools like smartphones or wearable sensors could help us understand the temporal relationships between stress and remission and identify which interventions are most effective for which people under which circumstances."

Chapter 30

Bereavement, Mourning, and Grief

People cope with the loss of a loved one in different ways. Most people who experience grief will cope well. Others will have severe grief and may need treatment. There are many things that can affect the grief process of someone who has lost a loved one to cancer. They include:

- The personality of the person who is grieving
- The relationship with the person who died
- The loved one's cancer experience and the way the disease progressed
- The grieving person's coping skills and mental health history
- The amount of support the grieving person has
- The grieving person's cultural and religious background
- The grieving person's social and financial position

This chapter defines grief and bereavement and describes the different types of grief reactions, treatments for grief, important issues for grieving children, and cultural responses to grief and loss.

This chapter includes text excerpted from "Grief, Bereavement, and Coping with Loss (PDQ®)—Patient Version," National Cancer Institute (NCI), March 6, 2013. Reviewed June 2018.

Bereavement and Grief

Bereavement is the period of sadness after losing a loved one through death. Grief and mourning occur during the period of bereavement. Grief and mourning are closely related. Mourning is the way we show grief in public. The way people mourn is affected by beliefs, religious practices, and cultural customs. People who are grieving are sometimes described as bereaved.

Grief is the normal process of reacting to the loss. It is the emotional response to the loss of a loved one. Common grief reactions include the following:

- Feeling emotionally numb
- Feeling unable to believe the loss occurred
- Feeling anxiety from the distress of being separated from the loved one
- Mourning along with depression
- A feeling of acceptance

Types of Grief Reactions

Anticipatory Grief

Anticipatory grief occurs when a death is expected, but before it happens. It may be felt by the families of people who are dying and by the person dying. Anticipatory grief helps family members get ready emotionally for the loss. It can be a time to take care of unfinished business with the dying person, such as saying "I love you" or "I forgive you."

Like grief that occurs after the death of a loved one, anticipatory grief involves mental, emotional, cultural, and social responses. However, anticipatory grief is different from grief that occurs after the death. Symptoms of anticipatory grief include the following:

- Depression
- Feeling a greater than usual concern for the dying person
- Imagining what the loved one's death will be like
- Getting ready emotionally for what will happen after the death

Anticipatory grief helps family members cope with what is to come. For the patient who is dying, anticipatory grief may be too much to handle and may cause him or her to withdraw from others.

Some researchers report that anticipatory grief is rare. Studies showed that periods of acceptance and recovery usually seen during grief are not common before the patient's actual death. The bereaved may feel that trying to accept the loss of a loved one before death occurs may make it seem that the dying patient has been abandoned. Also, grief felt before the death will not decrease the grief felt afterward or make it last a shorter time.

Normal Grief

During normal grief, the bereaved person moves toward accepting the loss and is able to continue normal day-to-day life even though it is hard to do. Common grief reactions include:

- Emotional numbness, shock, disbelief, or denial. These often occur right after the death, especially if the death was not expected.
- Anxiety over being separated from the loved one. The bereaved may wish to bring the person back and become lost in thoughts of the deceased. Images of death may occur often in the person's everyday thoughts.
- Distress that leads to crying; sighing; having dreams, illusions, and hallucinations of the deceased; and looking for places or things that were shared with the deceased.
- Anger
- Periods of sadness, loss of sleep, loss of appetite, extreme tiredness, guilt, and loss of interest in life. Day-to-day living may be affected.

In normal grief, symptoms will occur less often and will feel less severe as time passes. Recovery does not happen in a set period of time. For most bereaved people having normal grief, symptoms lessen between 6 months and 2 years after the loss.

Grief bursts or pangs are short periods (20–30 minutes) of very intense distress. Sometimes these bursts are caused by reminders of the deceased person. At other times they seem to happen for no reason.

There are several theories about how the normal grief process works. Experts have described different types and numbers of stages that people go through as they cope with a loss. At this time, there is not enough information to prove that one of these theories is more correct than the others.

Although many bereaved people have similar responses as they cope with their losses, there is no typical grief response. The grief process is personal.

Complicated Grief

There is no right or wrong way to grieve, but studies have shown that there are patterns of grief that are different from the most common. This has been called complicated grief.

Complicated grief reactions that have been seen in studies include:

- **Minimal grief reaction:** A grief pattern in which the person has no, or only a few, signs of distress or problems that occur with other types of grief.
- **Chronic grief:** A grief pattern in which the symptoms of common grief last for a much longer time than usual. These symptoms are a lot like ones that occur with major depression, anxiety, or posttraumatic stress.

Factors That Affect Complicated Grief

Studies have looked at how the following factors affect the grief response:

- **Whether the death is expected or unexpected.** It may seem that any sudden, unexpected loss might lead to more difficult grief. However, studies have found that bereaved people with high self-esteem and/or a feeling that they have control over life are likely to have a normal grief reaction even after an unexpected loss. Bereaved people with low self-esteem and/or a sense that life cannot be controlled are more likely to have complicated grief after an unexpected loss. This includes more depression and physical problems.
- **The personality of the bereaved.** Studies have found that people with certain personality traits are more likely to have long-lasting depression after a loss. These include people who are very dependent on the loved one (such as a spouse), and people who deal with distress by thinking about it all the time.
- **The religious beliefs of the bereaved.** Some studies have shown that religion helps people cope better with grief. Other studies have shown it does not help or causes more distress. Religion seems to help people who go to church often. The

positive effect on grief may be because church-goers have more social support.

- **Whether the bereaved is male or female.** In general, men have more problems than women do after a spouse's death. Men tend to have worse depression and more health problems than women do after the loss. Some researchers think this may be because men have less social support after a loss.
- **The age of the bereaved.** In general, younger bereaved people have more problems after a loss than older bereaved people do. They have more severe health problems, grief symptoms, and other mental and physical symptoms. Younger bereaved people, however, may recover more quickly than older bereaved people do, because they have more resources and social support.
- **The amount of social support the bereaved has.** Lack of social support increases the chance of having problems coping with a loss. Social support includes the person's family, friends, neighbors, and community members who can give psychological, physical, and financial help. After the death of a close family member, many people have a number of related losses. The death of a spouse, for example, may cause a loss of income and changes in lifestyle and day-to-day living. These are all related to social support.

Treatment of Grief

Normal grief may not need to be treated. Most bereaved people work through grief and recover within the first 6 months to 2 years. Researchers are studying whether bereaved people experiencing normal grief would be helped by formal treatment. They are also studying whether treatment might prevent complicated grief in people who are likely to have it. For people who have serious grief reactions or symptoms of distress, treatment may be helpful.

Complicated grief may be treated with different types of psychotherapy (talk therapy). Researchers are studying the treatment of mental, emotional, social, and behavioral symptoms of grief. Treatment methods include discussion, listening, and counseling.

Complicated grief treatment (CGT) is a type of grief therapy that was helpful in a clinical trial. It has three phases:

- The first phase includes talking about the loss and setting goals toward recovery. The bereaved are taught to work on these two things.

- The second phase includes coping with the loss by retelling the story of the death. This helps bereaved people who try not to think about their loss.
- The last phase looks at progress that has been made toward recovery and helps the bereaved make future plans. The bereaved's feelings about ending the sessions are also discussed.

In a clinical trial of patients with complicated grief, CGT was compared to interpersonal psychotherapy (IPT). IPT is a type of psychotherapy that focuses on the person's relationships with others and is helpful in treating depression. In patients with complicated grief, the CGT was more helpful than IPT.

Cognitive behavioral therapy (CBT) for complicated grief was helpful in a clinical trial. It works with the way a person's thoughts and behaviors are connected. CBT helps the patient learn skills that change attitudes and behaviors by replacing negative thoughts and changing the rewards of certain behaviors.

A clinical trial compared CBT to counseling for complicated grief. Results showed that patients treated with CBT had more improvement in symptoms and general mental distress than those in the counseling group.

Depression related to grief is sometimes treated with drugs. There is no standard drug therapy for depression that occurs with grief. Some healthcare professionals think depression is a normal part of grief and doesn't need to be treated. Whether to treat grief-related depression with drugs is up to the patient and the healthcare professional to decide.

Clinical trials of antidepressants for depression related to grief have found that the drugs can help relieve depression. However, they give less relief and take longer to work than they do when used for depression that is not related to grief.

Children and Grief

A child's grief process is different from an adult's. Children do not react to loss in the same ways as adults. These are some of the ways children's grief is different:

- Children may seem to show grief only once in a while and for short times. This may be because a child is not able to feel strong emotions for long periods of time. A grieving child may be sad one minute and playful the next. Often families think the child doesn't really understand the loss or has gotten over it quickly. Usually, neither is true. Children's minds protect them from what is too much for them to handle emotionally.

- Mourning is a process that continues over years in children. Feelings of loss may occur again and again as the child gets older. This is common at important times, such as going to camp, graduating from school, getting married, or having children.
- Grieving children may not show their feelings as openly as adults. Grieving children may throw themselves into activities instead of withdrawing or showing grief.
- Children cannot think through their thoughts and feelings like adults. Children have trouble putting their feelings about grief into words. Strong feelings of anger and fears of death or being left alone may show up in the behavior of grieving children. Children often play death games as a way of working out their feelings and worries. These games give children a safe way to express their feelings.
- Grieving adults may withdraw and not talk to other people about the loss. Children, however, often talk to the people around them (even strangers) to see how they react and to get clues for how they should respond to the loss.
- Children may ask confusing questions. For example, a child may ask, "I know grandpa died, but when will he come home?" This is a way of testing reality and making sure the story of the death has not changed.

Several factors can affect how a child will cope with grief. Although grief is different for each child, several factors can affect the grief process of a child:

- The child's age and stage of development
- The child's personality
- The child's previous experiences with death
- The child's relationship with the deceased
- The cause of death
- The way the child acts and communicates within the family
- How stable the family life is after the loss

- How the child continues to be cared for
- Whether the child is given the chance to share and express feelings and memories
- How the parents cope with stress
- Whether the child has ongoing relationships with other adults

Children at different stages of development have different understandings of death and the events near death

Infants

Infants do not recognize death, but feelings of loss and separation are part of developing an awareness of death. Children who have been separated from their mother may be sluggish and quiet, may not respond to a smile or a coo, may have physical symptoms (such as weight loss), and may sleep less.

Age 2–3 Years

Children at this age often confuse death with sleep and may feel anxiety as early as age 3. They may stop talking and appear to feel overall distress.

Age 3–6 Years

At this age children see death as a kind of sleep; the person is alive, but only in a limited way. The child cannot fully separate death from life. Children may think that the person is still living, even though he or she might have been buried. The child may ask questions about the deceased (for example, how does the deceased eat, go to the toilet, breathe, or play?). Young children know that death is physical, but think it is not final.

The child's understanding of death may involve "magical thinking." For example, the child may think that his or her thoughts can cause another person to become sick or die. Grieving children under 5 may have trouble eating, sleeping, and controlling the bladder and bowel.

Age 6–9 Years

Children at this age are often very curious about death, and may ask questions about what happens to the body when it dies. Death is thought of as a person or spirit separate from the person who was alive, such as a skeleton, ghost, angel, or bogeyman. They may see death as final and scary but as something that happens mostly to old people (and not to themselves).

Grieving children can become afraid of school, have learning problems, show antisocial or aggressive behavior, or become overly worried about their own health and complain of imaginary symptoms. Children this age may either withdraw from others or become too attached and clingy.

Boys often become more aggressive and destructive (for example, acting out in school), instead of showing their sadness openly.

When one parent dies, children may feel abandoned by both the deceased parent and the living parent, whose grief may make him or her unable to emotionally support the child.

Age 9 and Older

Children aged 9 and older know that death cannot be avoided and do not see it as a punishment. By the time a child is 12 years old, death is seen as final and something that happens to everyone.

Table 30.1. Grief and Developmental Stages

Age	Understanding of Death	Expressions of Grief
Infancy to 2 years	Is not yet able to understand death.	Quietness, crankiness, decreased activity, poor sleep, and weight loss.
	Separation from mother causes changes.	
2–6 years	Death is like sleeping.	Asks many questions (How does she go to the bathroom? How does she eat?).
		Problems in eating, sleeping, and bladder and bowel control.
		Fear of being abandoned.
		Tantrums.
	Dead person continues to live and function in some ways.	"Magical thinking" (Did I think or do something that caused the death? Like when I said I hate you and I wish you would die?).
	Death is not final.	
	Dead person can come back to life.	

Table 30.1. Continued

Age	Understanding of Death	Expressions of Grief
6–9 years	Death is thought of as a person or spirit (skeleton, ghost, bogeyman).	Curious about death.
		Asks specific questions.
		May have fears about school.
	Death is final and scary.	May have aggressive behavior (especially boys).
		Worries about imaginary illnesses.
	Death happens to others, it won't happen to me.	May feel abandoned.
9 and older	Everyone will die.	Strong emotions, guilt, anger, shame.
		Increased anxiety over own death.
		Mood swings.
	Death is final.	Fear of rejection; not wanting to be different from peers.
	Even I will die.	Changes in eating habits.
		Sleeping problems.
		Regressive behavior (loss of interest in outside activities).
		Impulsive behavior.
		Feels guilty about being alive (especially related to death of a brother, sister, or peer).

Most children who have had a loss have three common worries about death. Children coping with a loss often have these three questions:

Did I Make the Death Happen?

Children often think that they have "magical powers." If a mother is irritated and says, "You'll be the death of me" and later dies, her child may wonder if he or she actually caused the mother's death. Also, when children argue, one may say (or think), "I wish you were dead." If that child dies, the surviving child may think that those thoughts caused the death.

Is It Going to Happen to Me?

The death of another child may be very hard for a child. If the child thinks that the death may have been prevented (by either a parent or a doctor) the child may fear that he or she could also die.

Who Is Going to Take Care of Me?

Since children depend on parents and other adults to take care of them, a grieving child may wonder who will care for him or her after the death of an important person.

Talking honestly about the death and including the child in rituals may help the grieving child.

Explain the Death and Answer Questions

Talking about death helps children learn to cope with a loss. When talking about death with children, describe it simply. Each child should be told the truth using as much detail as he or she is able to understand. Answer questions in language the child can understand. Children often worry that they will also die, or that their surviving parent will go away. They need to be told that they will be safe and taken care of.

Use the Correct Language

When talking with the child about death, include the correct words, such as "cancer," "died," and "death." Using other words or phrases (for example, "he passed away," "he is sleeping," or "we lost him") can confuse children and cause them to misunderstand.

Include the Child in Planning and Attending Memorial Ceremonies

When a death occurs, children may feel better if they are included in planning and attending memorial ceremonies. These events help children remember the loved one. Children should not be forced to be involved in these ceremonies, but encourage them to take part when they feel comfortable doing so. Before a child attends a funeral, wake, or memorial service, give the child a full explanation of what to expect. A familiar adult or family member may help with this if the surviving parent's grief makes him or her unable to.

Cultural Responses to Grief and Loss

Cultures have different ways of coping with death. Grief felt for the loss of loved ones occurs in people of all ages and cultures. Different cultures, however, have different myths and mysteries about death that affect the attitudes, beliefs, and practices of the bereaved.

Individual, personal experiences of grief are similar in different cultures. The ways in which people of all cultures feel grief personally are similar. This has been found to be true even though different cultures have different mourning ceremonies and traditions to express grief.

Cultural issues that affect people who are dealing with the loss of a loved one include rituals, beliefs, and roles. Helping family members cope with the death of a loved one includes showing respect for the family's culture and the ways they honor the death. The following questions may help caregivers learn what is needed by the person's culture:

- What are the cultural rituals for coping with dying, the deceased person's body, and honoring the death?
- What are the family's beliefs about what happens after death?
- What does the family feel is a normal expression of grief and the acceptance of the loss?
- What does the family consider to be the roles of each family member in handling the death?
- Are certain types of death less acceptable (for example, suicide), or are certain types of death especially hard for that culture (for example, the death of a child)?

Death, grief, and mourning are normal life events. All cultures have practices that best meet their needs for dealing with death. Caregivers who understand the ways different cultures respond to death can help patients of these cultures work through their own normal grieving process.

Chapter 31

Common Reactions after Trauma

After going through a trauma, survivors often say that their first feeling is a relief to be alive. This may be followed by stress, fear, and anger. Trauma survivors may also find they are unable to stop thinking about what happened. Many survivors will show a high level of arousal, which causes them to react strongly to sounds and sights around them.

Most people have some kind of stress reaction after a trauma. Having such a reaction has nothing to do with personal weakness. Stress reactions may last for several days or even a few weeks. For most people, if symptoms occur, they will slowly decrease over time.

What Are Common Reactions to Trauma?

All kinds of trauma survivors commonly experience stress reactions. This is true for veterans, children, and disaster rescue or relief workers. If you understand what is happening when you or someone you know reacts to a traumatic event, you may be less fearful and better able to handle things.

Reactions to a trauma may include:

- Feeling hopeless about the future
- Feeling detached or unconcerned about others

This chapter includes text excerpted from "Common Reactions after Trauma," U.S. Department of Veteran Affairs (VA), August 13, 2015.

- Having trouble concentrating or making decisions
- Feeling jumpy and getting startled easily at sudden noises
- Feeling on guard and constantly alert
- Having disturbing dreams and memories or flashbacks
- Having work or school problems

You may also experience more physical reactions such as:

- Stomach upset and trouble eating
- Trouble sleeping and feeling very tired
- Pounding heart, rapid breathing, feeling edgy
- Sweating
- Severe headache if thinking of the event
- Failure to engage in exercise, diet, safe sex, regular healthcare
- Excess smoking, alcohol, drugs, food
- Having your ongoing medical problems get worse

You may have more emotional troubles such as:

- Feeling nervous, helpless, fearful, sad
- Feeling shocked, numb, and not able to feel love or joy
- Avoiding people, places, and things related to the event
- Being irritable or having outbursts of anger
- Becoming easily upset or agitated
- Blaming yourself or having negative views of oneself or the world
- Distrust of others, getting into conflicts, being over-controlling
- Being withdrawn, feeling rejected, or abandoned
- Loss of intimacy or feeling detached

Recovery from Stress Reactions

Turn to your family and friends when you are ready to talk. They are your personal support system. Recovery is an ongoing gradual process. It doesn't happen through suddenly being "cured" and it doesn't mean that you will forget what happened. Most people will recover from trauma naturally. If your stress reactions are getting in the way of your relationships, work, or other important activities, you may want to talk to a counselor or your doctor. Good treatments are available.

Common Problems That Can Occur after a Trauma

- **Posttraumatic stress disorder (PTSD).** PTSD is a condition that can develop after you have gone through a life-threatening event. If you have PTSD, you may have trouble keeping yourself from thinking over and over about what happened to you. You may try to avoid people and places that remind you of the trauma. You may feel numb. Lastly, if you have PTSD, you might find that you have trouble relaxing. You may startle easily and you may feel on guard most of the time.
- **Depression.** Depression involves feeling down or sad more days than not. If you are depressed, you may lose interest in activities that used to be enjoyable or fun. You may feel low in energy and be overly tired. You may feel hopeless or in despair, and you may think that things will never get better. Depression is more likely when you have had losses such as the death of close friends. If you are depressed, at times you might think about hurting or killing yourself. For this reason, getting help for depression is very important.
- **Self-blame, guilt, and shame.** Sometimes in trying to make sense of a traumatic event, you may blame yourself in some way. You may think you are responsible for bad things that happened, or for surviving when others didn't. You may feel guilty for what you did or did not do. Remember, we all tend to be our own worst critics. Most of the time, that guilt, shame, or self-blame is not justified.
- **Suicidal thoughts.** Trauma and personal loss can lead a depressed person to think about hurting or killing themselves. If you think someone you know may be feeling suicidal, you should directly ask them. You will not put the idea in their head. If someone is thinking about killing themselves, call the Suicide Prevention Lifeline 800-273-TALK (800-273-8255) (www.suicidepreventionlifeline.org). You can also call a counselor, doctor, or 911.

- **Anger or aggressive behavior.** Trauma can be connected with anger in many ways. After a trauma, you might think that what happened to you was unfair or unjust. You might not understand why the event happened and why it happened to you. These thoughts can result in intense anger. Although anger is a natural and healthy emotion, intense feelings of anger and aggressive behavior can cause problems with family, friends, or coworkers. If you become violent when angry, you just make the situation worse. Violence can lead to people being injured, and there may be legal consequences.
- **Alcohol/drug abuse.** Drinking or "self-medicating" with drugs is a common, and unhealthy, way of coping with upsetting events. You may drink too much or use drugs to numb yourself and to try to deal with difficult thoughts, feelings, and memories related to the trauma. While using alcohol or drugs may offer a quick solution, it can actually lead to more problems. If someone close begins to lose control of drinking or drug use, you should try to get them to see a healthcare provider about managing their drinking or drug use.

Summing It All Up

Right after a trauma, almost every survivor will find himself or herself unable to stop thinking about what happened. Stress reactions, such as increased fear, nervousness, jumpiness, upsetting memories, and efforts to avoid reminders, will gradually decrease over time for most people.

Use your personal support systems, family and friends, when you are ready to talk. Recovery is an ongoing gradual process. It doesn't happen through suddenly being "cured" and it doesn't mean that you will forget what happened. Most people will recover from trauma naturally over time. If your emotional reactions are getting in the way of your relationships, work, or other important activities, you may want to talk to a counselor.

Chapter 32

Types of Stress-Related Disorders That Develop after Trauma

Chapter Contents

Section 32.1

Dissociative Disorders

"Dissociative Disorders,"
© 2015 Omnigraphics. Reviewed June 2018.

Dissociation is a psychological state that involves feeling disconnected from reality. A dissociative disorder is a mental health condition in which the affected person experiences a disconnection from their thoughts, feelings, memories, perceptions, consciousness, or identity.

For many people, dissociation is used as a defense mechanism to block out the memory of extremely stressful or traumatic life experiences, particularly from childhood. Dissociative disorders are often found in individuals who were exposed to physical, emotional, or sexual abuse as children, for instance, and in those who endured such traumatic events as natural disasters, wars, accidents, violent crimes, or the tragic loss of a loved one. Dissociative disorders often manifest themselves during stressful situations in adulthood, which can make it difficult for people affected to deal with the challenges of everyday life.

Research suggests that around 2–3 percent of people are affected by dissociative disorders. Some of the common symptoms include episodes of memory or sensory loss, feelings of emotional detachment, or a sense of watching oneself from the outside. Dissociative disorders often coincide with other mental health issues, such as mood swings, attention deficits, drug and alcohol dependence, anxiety, panic attacks, and suicidal tendencies.

According to the American Psychiatric Association's (APA) *Diagnostic and Statistical Manual (DSM)*, dissociative disorders take three main forms: depersonalization/derealization disorder; dissociative amnesia; and dissociative identity disorder.

Depersonalization/Derealization Disorder

Depersonalization is a profound sense of detachment or alienation from one's own body, mind, or identity. People with depersonalization disorder may experience an "out of body" sensation, or feel as if they are looking at their own life from an external perspective, like watching a movie. Some people affected by this condition may not recognize their own face in a mirror.

Derealization is the sense that the world does not seem real. People with derealization disorder may report that their surroundings appear hazy, foggy, phony, or far away. Familiar places may seem unfamiliar, and close friends may seem like strangers. In some cases, situations take on a dreamlike quality, and the affected person may feel disoriented and have difficulty determining what is real and what is not.

Dissociative Amnesia

Dissociative amnesia is the inability to remember people, events, or personal information. This memory loss is too substantial to be considered normal forgetfulness, and it is not related to aging, disease, or a head injury. In most cases, people with dissociative amnesia forget a traumatic incident or an extremely stressful period of time. They may also experience smaller lapses in which they forget the content of a conversation or a talent or skill that they have learned.

Dissociative amnesia may be localized, selective, or generalized. In localized amnesia, the memory lapse is concerned with a particular event or span of time. In selective amnesia, the affected person forgets certain parts of a traumatic incident but may remember others. In generalized amnesia, the affected person is unable to remember anything about their own identity or life history. In rare cases dissociative amnesia may take the form of fugue, in which a person travels for hours or days without a sense of their own identity, then suddenly regains awareness and wonders how they got there.

Dissociative Identity Disorder

Dissociative identity disorder, formerly known as multiple personality disorder, is characterized by a deep uncertainty or confusion about one's identity. People affected by this disorder may feel the presence of other people or alternate identities (known as "alters") within themselves. Each of these alters may have their own name, history, voice, mannerisms, and worldview.

A child who has suffered a severe psychological trauma is more likely to develop a dissociative identity disorder. Since the child's mind lacks the coping mechanisms to process the stressful experience, the still-developing personality may find it easier to dissociate and pretend that it was happening to someone else.

Treatment for Dissociative Disorders

Before diagnosing a dissociative disorder, a doctor may perform tests to rule out physical conditions that may cause similar symptoms, such as a head injury, brain tumor, sleep deprivation, or drug addiction. If no physical cause is found, the patient may be referred to a mental health professional for further evaluation. The mental health specialist will likely inquire about childhood trauma and screen the patient for trauma-related conditions, such as anxiety, depression, posttraumatic stress disorder, and substance abuse. Although there is no medication to treat dissociation, antidepressants and antianxiety drugs may provide some relief from the symptoms of associated conditions.

Psychiatrists often treat dissociative disorders with counseling designed to help the patient cope with the underlying trauma. They view dissociation as a normal defense mechanism that the brain may use to adapt to a difficult situation in early life. Dissociation only becomes dysfunctional when it persists into adulthood and governs an individual's response to everyday challenges. In these cases, the patient may benefit from a course of psychotherapy to help them understand and process the traumatic event.

Eye movement desensitization and reprocessing (EMDR) is another technique that can help alleviate symptoms related to psychological trauma. In EMDR, the patient makes side-to-side eye motions, usually by following the movement of the therapist's finger, while recalling the traumatic incident. Although doctors are not sure how EMDR works, it appears to help the brain process distressing memories so that they have less impact on the patient's daily life.

References

1. "Dissociative Disorders," National Alliance on Mental Illness (NAMI), n.d.
2. "Dissociative Disorders," NHS Choices, Gov.UK, 2014.
3. "Dissociation FAQs," International Society for the Study of Trauma and Dissociation (ISSTD), 2014.

Section 32.2

Acute Stress Disorder

This section contains text excerpted from "Acute Stress Disorder," U.S. Department of Veterans Affairs (VA), May 4, 2018.

What Is Acute Stress Disorder (ASD)?

Acute stress disorder, or ASD, was introduced into the *Diagnostic and Statistical Manual of Mental Disorders (DSM-IV)* in 1994. In DSM-5 (2013), ASD was reclassified in the Trauma- and Stressor-Related Disorders. A diagnosis of ASD has been integral in helping facilitate access to healthcare after trauma exposure. Debate continues regarding ASD as a predictor of posttraumatic stress disorder (PTSD).

- The diagnosis of ASD can only be considered from 3 days to one month following a traumatic event (commonly referred to as the acute phase). If posttraumatic symptoms persist beyond a month, the clinician would assess for the presence of PTSD. The ASD diagnosis would no longer apply.
- ASD requires meeting criteria for at least 9 of the 14 symptoms.

How Do PTSD and ASD Differ?

ASD and PTSD share the same requirement for exposure to a traumatic event (Criterion A). Many of the ASD symptoms are similar to those for PTSD. Yet, ASD and PTSD differ in several important ways:

- PTSD diagnosis requires meeting a certain number of symptoms within established clusters. For ASD, symptoms are not classified within clusters; therefore, an individual meets diagnosis based upon expression of symptoms in total.
- PTSD includes nonfear based symptoms (i.e., risky or destructive behavior, overly negative thoughts and assumptions about oneself or the world, exaggerated blame of self or others for causing the trauma, negative affect, decreased interest in activities, feeling isolated), whereas ASD does not.
- PTSD includes a dissociative subtype, whereas in ASD, depersonalization and derealization are included as symptoms under the dissociative heading.

Is ASD Predictive of PTSD?

ASD is a risk factor for developing subsequent PTSD. However, not all individuals who meet criteria for ASD will go onto develop PTSD, and many individuals who develop PTSD do not first have an ASD diagnosis. Regardless of whether an individual goes on to develop PTSD, a diagnosis of ASD is important so that individuals experiencing early significant distress in response to a trauma can be identified and treated.

How Common Is ASD Following Trauma Exposure?

ASD is a risk factor for developing subsequent PTSD. However, not all individuals who meet criteria for ASD will go onto develop PTSD, and many individuals who develop PTSD do not first have an ASD diagnosis. Regardless of whether an individual goes on to develop PTSD, a diagnosis of ASD is important so that individuals experiencing early significant distress in response to a trauma can be identified and treated.

ASD prevalence rates vary in trauma-exposed populations across studies and across different trauma types, with an average of 19 percent. Some trauma types are associated with higher rates of ASD than others. For example, prevalence estimates of ASD range from 13–21 percent following motor vehicle accidents and 14 percent after brain injury; to 24 percent following assault and 59 percent following rape. Of note, these rates are based on DSM-IV ASD criteria. Currently, there are no prevalence estimates of ASD in adults using DSM-5 criteria.

Who Is at Risk for ASD?

While many studies have examined factors that place individuals at risk for developing PTSD, only a handful of studies have examined risk factors for the development of ASD. Factors that elevate the risk of developing ASD are past psychiatric disorders, prior trauma, greater trauma severity, avoidant coping, high neuroticism, and being female. Trauma as a result of an assault is associated with a higher risk for developing ASD than other types of trauma.

How Is ASD Diagnosed?

There are few well-established and empirically-validated measures to assess ASD. The tools with the strongest psychometric properties are described below:

- The Acute Stress Disorder Structured Interview–5 (ASDI-5). The original ASDI was developed and validated for the DSM-IV diagnostic criteria of ASD. The psychometric properties of the ASDI-5 which was updated for DSM-5, have not yet been studied.
- The Acute Stress Disorder Scale (ASDS) is a 14-item self-report measure of ASD symptoms. It has been updated to be consistent with ASD in DSM-5, and psychometric studies of the ASDS for DSM-5 are not available to date.

What Are Effective Treatments for ASD?

Cognitive Behavioral Interventions (CBT)

Clinical practice guidelines recommend trauma-focused CBT as a first-line treatment of ASD. Bryant and colleagues have conducted the only studies that specifically assessed and treated ASD. They have shown that a brief trauma-focused cognitive behavioral treatment may not only ameliorate ASD, but it may also prevent the subsequent development of PTSD.

Other research that assesses traumatic stress symptoms following acute trauma support this finding, showing that PTSD symptom severity is significantly lower at follow-up (3–6 months) after brief trauma-focused cognitive behavioral interventions.

There are a number of potential barriers to entering treatment in the early aftermath of traumatic stress. For instance, in postdisaster or military deployment environments, the basic needs and priorities of those exposed to trauma may preclude the time and energy to engage in treatment, and individuals may not be ready to identify themselves as someone in need of traditional mental health services.

While a number of studies have reported multiple barriers to entry into early CBT treatment for PTSD, the investigators strongly endorse that early clinical intervention should be offered, as it yields success in those who complete treatment, and results in markedly greater overall population impact. For instance, in one study, Shalev and colleagues reported that while about a third of those with initial PTSD recovered by 5 months, delaying treatment prolonged the duration of symptoms.

Psychological First Aid (PFA)

A number of psychological first aid (PFA) models have been developed to meet the needs in the early aftermath of disasters and traumatic stress. PFA focuses on addressing initial needs and concerns by providing support and resources, and differs from traditional mental health services in that it is strengths based, flexible, and has a supportive, psychoeducational—rather than psychotherapeutic—focus.

While PFA models have not received controlled empirical support to date, they are generally considered evidence-informed, and are the strategies most appropriate and least likely to do harm as posttrauma early intervention. Studies suggest that PFA is well-received by both providers and recipients. For instance, recipients of PFA in one study reported a heightened ability to be calm and to help themselves and others, a greater sense of emotional control, improved functioning, and strengthened family relationships.

Psychological Debriefing (PD)

Psychological debriefing (PD) is not recommended after trauma exposure. PD is a structured group intervention for early implementation after potentially traumatic events, and it has been widely implemented in police, fire, emergency medicine, and military settings since its introduction. As a programmed group intervention, PD assumes that all individuals who have experienced the same traumatic stressor have similar needs.

Additionally, because it does not include an assessment component, it cannot be tailored for each person's immediate status and context. Finally, those who implement PD often assume that a single session of help occurring over a few hours is sufficient, without either mandated follow-up or mechanisms for assessing who needs greater help.

Several reviews of studies of the efficacy of PD have failed to find evidence that it prevents long-term negative outcomes and two randomized controlled trials of PD have reported a higher incidence of negative outcomes in those who received PD compared with those who did not receive any intervention.

Section 32.3

Posttraumatic Stress Disorder (PTSD)

This section contains text excerpted from "Posttraumatic Stress Disorder," National Institute of Mental Health (NIMH), February 2016.

Posttraumatic stress disorder (PTSD) is a disorder that develops in some people who have experienced a shocking, scary, or dangerous event. It is natural to feel afraid during and after a traumatic situation. Fear triggers many split-second changes in the body to help defend against danger or to avoid it. This "fight-or-flight" response is a typical reaction meant to protect a person from harm.

Nearly everyone will experience a range of reactions after trauma, yet most people recover from initial symptoms naturally. Those who continue to experience problems may be diagnosed with PTSD. People who have PTSD may feel stressed or frightened even when they are not in danger.

Signs and Symptoms

Not every traumatized person develops long-term (i.e., chronic) or even short-term (i.e., acute) PTSD. Not everyone with PTSD has been through a dangerous event. Some experiences, like the sudden, unexpected death of a loved one, can also cause PTSD. Symptoms usually begin early, within 3 months of the traumatic incident, but sometimes they begin years afterward. Symptoms must last more than a month and be severe enough to interfere with relationships or work to be considered PTSD.

The course of the illness varies. Some people recover within 6 months, while others have symptoms that last much longer. In some people, the condition becomes chronic.

A doctor who has experience helping people with mental illnesses, such as a psychiatrist or psychologist, can diagnose PTSD.

To be diagnosed with PTSD, an adult must have all of the following for at least 1 month:

- At least one re-experiencing symptom
- At least one avoidance symptom
- At least two arousal and reactivity symptoms
- At least two cognition and mood symptoms

Re-experiencing symptoms include:

- Flashbacks—reliving the trauma over and over, including physical symptoms like a racing heart or sweating
- Bad dreams
- Frightening thoughts

Re-experiencing symptoms may cause problems in a person's everyday routine. The symptoms can start from the person's own thoughts and feelings. Words, objects, or situations that are reminders of the event can also trigger re-experiencing symptoms.

Avoidance symptoms include:

- Staying away from places, events, or objects that are reminders of the traumatic experience
- Avoiding thoughts or feelings related to the traumatic event

Things that remind a person of the traumatic event can trigger avoidance symptoms. These symptoms may cause a person to change his or her personal routine. For example, after a bad car accident, a person who usually drives may avoid driving or riding in a car.

Arousal and reactivity symptoms include:

- Being easily startled
- Feeling tense or "on edge"
- Having difficulty sleeping
- Having angry outbursts

Arousal symptoms are usually constant, instead of being triggered by things that remind one of the traumatic events. These symptoms can make the person feel stressed and angry. They may make it hard to do daily tasks, such as sleeping, eating, or concentrating.

Cognition and mood symptoms include:

- Trouble remembering key features of the traumatic event
- Negative thoughts about oneself or the world
- Distorted feelings like guilt or blame
- Loss of interest in enjoyable activities

Cognition and mood symptoms can begin or worsen after the traumatic event, but are not due to injury or substance use. These symptoms can make the person feel alienated or detached from friends or family members.

It is natural to have some of these symptoms after a dangerous event. Sometimes people have very serious symptoms that go away after a few weeks. This is called acute stress disorder, or ASD. When the symptoms last more than a month, seriously affect one's ability to function, and are not due to substance use, medical illness, or anything except the event itself, they might be PTSD. Some people with PTSD don't show any symptoms for weeks or months. PTSD is often accompanied by depression, substance abuse, or one or more of the other anxiety disorders.

Do Children React Differently than Adults?

Children and teens can have extreme reactions to trauma, but their symptoms may not be the same as adults. In very young children (less than 6 years of age), these symptoms can include:

- Wetting the bed after having learned to use the toilet
- Forgetting how to or being unable to talk
- Acting out the scary event during playtime
- Being unusually clingy with a parent or other adult

Older children and teens are more likely to show symptoms similar to those seen in adults. They may also develop disruptive, disrespectful, or destructive behaviors. Older children and teens may feel guilty for not preventing injury or deaths. They may also have thoughts of revenge. The National Institute of Mental Health (NIMH) offers free print materials in English and Spanish. These can be read online, downloaded, or delivered to you in the mail.

Risk Factors

Anyone can develop PTSD at any age. This includes war veterans, children, and people who have been through a physical or sexual assault, abuse, accident, disaster, or many other serious events. According to the National Center for PTSD, about 7 or 8 out of every 100 people will experience PTSD at some point in their lives. Women are more likely to develop PTSD than men, and genes may make some people more likely to develop PTSD than others.

Not everyone with PTSD has been through a dangerous event. Some people develop PTSD after a friend or family member experiences danger or harm. The sudden, unexpected death of a loved one can also lead to PTSD.

Why Do Some People Develop PTSD and Other People Do Not?

It is important to remember that not everyone who lives through a dangerous event develops PTSD. In fact, most people will not develop the disorder.

Many factors play a part in whether a person will develop PTSD. Some examples are listed below. Risk factors make a person more likely to develop PTSD. Other factors, called resilience factors, can help reduce the risk of the disorder.

Risk Factors and Resilience Factors for PTSD

Some factors that increase risk for PTSD include:

- Living through dangerous events and traumas
- Getting hurt
- Seeing another person hurt, or seeing a dead body
- Childhood trauma
- Feeling horror, helplessness, or extreme fear
- Having little or no social support after the event
- Dealing with extra stress after the event, such as loss of a loved one, pain and injury, or loss of a job or home
- Having a history of mental illness or substance abuse

Some resilience factors that may reduce the risk of PTSD include:

- Seeking out support from other people, such as friends and family
- Finding a support group after a traumatic event
- Learning to feel good about one's own actions in the face of danger
- Having a positive coping strategy, or a way of getting through the bad event and learning from it
- Being able to act and respond effectively despite feeling fear

Researchers are studying the importance of these and other risk and resilience factors, including genetics and neurobiology. With more research, someday it may be possible to predict who is likely to develop PTSD and to prevent it.

Treatments and Therapies

The main treatments for people with PTSD are medications, psychotherapy ("talk" therapy), or both. Everyone is different, and PTSD affects people differently so a treatment that works for one person may not work for another. It is important for anyone with PTSD to be treated by a mental health provider who is experienced with PTSD. Some people with PTSD need to try different treatments to find out what works for their symptoms.

If someone with PTSD is going through an ongoing trauma, such as being in an abusive relationship, both of the problems need to be addressed. Other ongoing problems can include panic disorder, depression, substance abuse, and feeling suicidal.

Medications

The most studied medications for treating PTSD include antidepressants, which may help control PTSD symptoms such as sadness, worry, anger, and feeling numb inside. Antidepressants and other medications may be prescribed along with psychotherapy. Other medications may be helpful for specific PTSD symptoms. For example, although it is not currently U.S. Food and Drug Administration (FDA) approved, research has shown that Prazosin may be helpful with sleep problems, particularly nightmares, commonly experienced by people with PTSD.

Doctors and patients can work together to find the best medication or medication combination, as well as the right dose. Check the FDA website (www.fda.gov) for the information on patient medication guides, warnings, or newly approved medications.

Psychotherapy

Psychotherapy (sometimes called "talk therapy") involves talking with a mental health professional to treat a mental illness. Psychotherapy can occur one-on-one or in a group. Talk therapy treatment for PTSD usually lasts 6–12 weeks, but it can last longer. Research shows that support from family and friends can be an important part of recovery.

Many types of psychotherapy can help people with PTSD. Some types target the symptoms of PTSD directly. Other therapies focus on social, family, or job-related problems. The doctor or therapist may combine different therapies depending on each person's needs.

Effective psychotherapies tend to emphasize a few key components, including education about symptoms, teaching skills to help identify the triggers of symptoms, and skills to manage the symptoms. One helpful form of therapy is called cognitive behavioral therapy, or CBT. CBT can include:

- **Exposure therapy.** This helps people face and control their fear. It gradually exposes them to the trauma they experienced in a safe way. It uses imagining, writing, or visiting the place where the event happened. The therapist uses these tools to help people with PTSD cope with their feelings.
- **Cognitive restructuring.** This helps people make sense of the bad memories. Sometimes people remember the event differently than how it happened. They may feel guilt or shame about something that is not their fault. The therapist helps people with PTSD look at what happened in a realistic way.

There are other types of treatment that can help as well. People with PTSD should talk about all treatment options with a therapist. Treatment should equip individuals with the skills to manage their symptoms and help them participate in activities that they enjoyed before developing PTSD.

How Talk Therapies Help People Overcome PTSD

Talk therapies teach people helpful ways to react to the frightening events that trigger their PTSD symptoms. Based on this general goal, different types of therapy may:

- Teach about trauma and its effects
- Use relaxation and anger-control skills
- Provide tips for better sleep, diet, and exercise habits
- Help people identify and deal with guilt, shame, and other feelings about the event
- Focus on changing how people react to their PTSD symptoms. For example, therapy helps people face reminders of the trauma.

Beyond Treatment: How Can I Help Myself?

It may be very hard to take that first step to help yourself. It is important to realize that although it may take some time, with treatment, you can get better. If you are unsure where to go for help, ask your family doctor. You can also check the National Institute of Mental Health's (NIMH) Help for Mental Illnesses page (www.nimh.nih.gov/health/find-help/index.shtml) or search online for "mental health providers," "social services," "hotlines," or "physicians" for phone numbers and addresses. An emergency room doctor can also provide temporary help and can tell you where and how to get further help.

To help yourself while in treatment:

- Talk with your doctor about treatment options.
- Engage in mild physical activity or exercise to help reduce stress.
- Set realistic goals for yourself.
- Break up large tasks into small ones, set some priorities, and do what you can as you can.
- Try to spend time with other people, and confide in a trusted friend or relative. Tell others about things that may trigger symptoms.
- Expect your symptoms to improve gradually, not immediately.
- Identify and seek out comforting situations, places, and people.

Caring for yourself and others is especially important when large numbers of people are exposed to traumatic events (such as natural disasters, accidents, and violent acts).

Next Steps for PTSD Research

In the last decade, progress in research on the mental and biological foundations of PTSD has lead scientists to focus on better understanding the underlying causes of why people experience a range of reactions to trauma.

- NIMH-funded researchers are exploring trauma patients in acute care settings to better understand the changes that occur in individuals whose symptoms improve naturally. Other research is looking at how fear memories are affected by learning, changes in the body, or even sleep.

- Research on preventing the development of PTSD soon after trauma exposure is also underway.
- Still other research is attempting to identify what factors determine whether someone with PTSD will respond well to one type of intervention or another, aiming to develop more personalized, effective, and efficient treatments.
- As gene research and brain imaging technologies continue to improve, scientists are more likely to be able to pinpoint when and where in the brain PTSD begins. This understanding may then lead to better-targeted treatments to suit each person's own needs or even prevent the disorder before it causes harm.

Chapter 33

Relationships and Traumatic Stress

How Does Trauma Affect Relationships?

Trauma survivors with posttraumatic stress disorder (PTSD) may have trouble with their close family relationships or friendships. The symptoms of PTSD can cause problems with trust, closeness, communication, and problem solving. These problems may affect the way the survivor acts with others. In turn, the way a loved one responds to him or her affects the trauma survivor. A circular pattern can develop that may sometimes harm relationships.

How Might Trauma Survivors React?

In the first weeks and months following a trauma, survivors may feel angry, detached, tense or worried in their relationships. In time, most are able to resume their prior level of closeness in relationships. Yet the 5–10 percent of survivors who develop PTSD may have lasting relationship problems.

Survivors with PTSD may feel distant from others and feel numb. They may have less interest in social or sexual activities. Because survivors feel irritable, on guard, jumpy, worried, or nervous, they may not

---

This chapter includes text excerpted from "Relationships and PTSD," U.S. Department of Veteran Affairs (VA), August 13, 2015.

be able to relax or be intimate. They may also feel an increased need to protect their loved ones. They may come across as tense or demanding.

The trauma survivor may often have trauma memories or flashbacks. He or she might go to great lengths to avoid such memories. Survivors may avoid any activity that could trigger a memory. If the survivor has trouble sleeping or has nightmares, both the survivor and partner may not be able to get enough rest. This may make sleeping together harder.

Survivors often struggle with intense anger and impulses. In order to suppress angry feelings and actions, they may avoid closeness. They may push away or find fault with loved ones and friends. Also, drinking and drug problems, which can be an attempt to cope with PTSD, can destroy intimacy and friendships. Verbal or physical violence can occur.

In other cases, survivors may depend too much on their partners, family members, and friends. This could also include support persons such as healthcare providers or therapists.

Dealing with these symptoms can take up a lot of the survivor's attention. He or she may not be able to focus on the partner. It may be hard to listen carefully and make decisions together with someone else. Partners may come to feel that talking together and working as a team are not possible.

How Might Loved Ones React?

Partners, friends, or family members may feel hurt, cut off, or down because the survivor has not been able to get over the trauma. Loved ones may become angry or distant toward the survivor. They may feel pressured, tense, and controlled. The survivor's symptoms can make a loved one feel like he or she is living in a war zone or in constant threat of danger. Living with someone who has PTSD can sometimes lead the partner to have some of the same feelings of having been through trauma.

In sum, a person who goes through a trauma may have certain common reactions. These reactions affect the people around the survivor. Family, friends, and others then react to how the survivor is behaving. This, in turn, comes back to affect the person who went through the trauma.

Trauma Types and Relationships

Certain types of "human-made" traumas can have a more severe effect on relationships. These traumas include:

- Childhood sexual and physical abuse
- Rape

- Domestic violence
- Combat
- Terrorism
- Genocide
- Torture
- Kidnapping
- Prisoner of war

Survivors of human-made traumas often feel a lasting sense of terror, horror, endangerment, and betrayal. These feelings affect how they relate to others. They may feel like they are letting down their guard if they get close to someone else and trust them. This is not to say a survivor never feels a strong bond of love or friendship. However, a close relationship can also feel scary or dangerous to a trauma survivor.

Do All Trauma Survivors Have Relationship Problems?

Many trauma survivors do not develop PTSD. Also, many people with PTSD do not have relationship problems. People with PTSD can create and maintain good relationships by:

- Building a personal support network to help cope with PTSD while working on family and friend relationships
- Sharing feelings honestly and openly, with respect and compassion
- Building skills at problem solving and connecting with others
- Including ways to play, be creative, relax, and enjoy others

What Can Be Done to Help Someone Who Has PTSD?

Relations with others are very important for trauma survivors. Social support is one of the best things to protect against getting PTSD. Relationships can offset feelings of being alone.

Relationships may also help the survivor's self-esteem. This may help reduce depression and guilt. A relationship can also give the survivor a way to help someone else. Helping others can reduce feelings of failure or feeling cut off from others. Lastly, relationships are a source of support when coping with stress.

If you need to seek professional help, try to find a therapist who has skills in treating PTSD as well as working with couples or families.

Many treatment approaches may be helpful for dealing with relationship issues. Options include:

- One-to-one and group therapy
- Anger and stress management
- Assertiveness training
- Couples counseling
- Family education classes
- Family therapy

Chapter 34

Traumatic Stress in Children and Teens

This chapter provides information regarding what events cause posttraumatic stress disorder (PTSD) in children, how many children develop PTSD, risk factors associated with PTSD, what PTSD looks like in children, other effects of trauma on children, and treatments for PTSD.

What Events Cause PTSD in Children?

Any life-threatening event or event that threatens physical harm can cause PTSD. These events may include:

- Sexual abuse or violence (does not require threat of harm)
- Physical abuse
- Natural or human-made disasters, such as fires, hurricanes, or floods
- Violent crimes such as kidnapping or school shootings
- Motor vehicle accidents such as automobile and plane crashes

---

This chapter includes text excerpted from "PTSD in Children and Adolescents," U.S. Department of Veterans Affairs (VA), February 23, 2016.

PTSD can also occur after witnessing violence. These events may include exposure to:

- Community violence
- Domestic violence
- War

Finally, in some cases learning about these events happening to someone close to you can cause PTSD.

How Many Children and Adolescents Experience Traumatic Events?

The best information on very young children comes from annual statistics from the U.S. Department of Health and Human Services (HHS) on child abuse. These rates underestimate traumatic exposure given that they address abuse only and not other types of traumatic events. Also, they underestimate abuse because not all abuse is reported.

In 2011, child protective services in the United States received 3.4 million referrals, representing 6.2 million children. Of those cases referred, about 19 percent were substantiated and occurred in the following frequencies.

- More than 75 percent (78.5%) suffered neglect
- More than 15 percent (17.6%) suffered physical abuse
- Less than 10 percent (9.1%) suffered sexual abuse

In older children, there have been several national studies. The National Survey of Children's Exposure to Violence (NatSCEV) reports on 1 year and lifetime prevalence of childhood victimization in a nationally representative sample of 4549 children aged 0–17. More than half (60.6%) of the sample experienced or witnessed victimization in the past year. Specifically in the past year:

- Almost half (46.3%) experienced physical assault
- 1 in 10 (10.2%) experienced child maltreatment
- Fewer than 1 in 10 (6.1%) had experienced sexual victimization
- More than 1 in 4 (25.3%) had witnessed domestic or community

As children age there is more opportunity for exposure, thus lifetime exposure was one third to one half higher than past year exposure.

As an example, among 14–17-year-old girls, 18.7 have experienced a completed or attempted sexual assault in their lifetime and more than a third had witnessed parental assault.

A second national study asked 4,023 adolescents aged 12–17 if they had ever experienced sexual or physical assault or witnessed violence. Almost half (47%) had experienced one of these types of traumas. Specifically in their lifetime:

- 8 percent experienced sexual assault
- 22 percent experienced physical assault
- 39 percent witnessed violence

How Many Children Develop PTSD?

The National Comorbidity Survey Replication Adolescent Supplement (NCS-A) is a nationally representative sample of over 10,000 adolescents aged 13–18. Results indicate that 5 percent of adolescents have met criteria for PTSD in their lifetime. Prevalence is higher for girls than boys (8.0% versus 2.3%) and increase with age. Current rates (in the past month) are 3.9 percent overall. There are no definitive studies on prevalence rates of PTSD in younger children in the general population.

What Are the Risk Factors for PTSD?

Both the type of event and the intensity of exposure impact the degree to which an event results in PTSD. For example, in one study of a fatal sniper attack that occurred at an elementary school proximity to the shooting was directly related to the percentage of children who developed PTSD. Of those children who directly witnessed the shooting on the playground, 77 percent had moderate to severe PTSD symptoms, whereas 67 percent of those in the school building at the time and only 26 percent of the children who had gone home for the day had moderate or severe symptoms.

In addition to exposure variables, other risk factors include:

- Female gender
- Previous trauma exposure
- Preexisting psychiatric disorders
- Parental psychopathology
- Low social support

Parents have been shown to have protective factors (practice parameters). Both parental support and lower levels of parental PTSD have been found to predict lower levels of PTSD in children.

There is less clarity in the findings connecting PTSD with ethnicity and age.

While some studies find that minorities report higher levels of PTSD symptoms, researchers have shown that this is due to other factors such as differences in levels of exposure. It is not clear how a child's age at the time of exposure to a traumatic event affects the occurrence or severity of PTSD. While some studies find a relationship, others do not.

Differences that do occur may be due to differences in the way PTSD is expressed in children and adolescents of different ages or developmental levels.

What Does PTSD Look Like in Children?

As in adults, PTSD in children and adolescence requires the presence of re-experiencing, avoidance and numbing, and arousal symptoms. However, researchers and clinicians are beginning to recognize that PTSD may not present itself in children the same way it does in adults. Criteria for PTSD include age-specific features for some symptoms.

Elementary School-Aged Children

Clinical reports suggest that elementary school-aged children may not experience visual flashbacks or amnesia for aspects of the trauma. However, they do experience "time skew" and "omen formation," which are not typically seen in adults.

Time skew refers to a child mis-sequencing trauma-related events when recalling the memory. Omen formation is a belief that there were warning signs that predicted the trauma. As a result, children often believe that if they are alert enough, they will recognize warning signs and avoid future traumas.

School-aged children also reportedly exhibit posttraumatic play or reenactment of the trauma in play, drawings, or verbalizations. Posttraumatic play is different from reenactment in that posttraumatic play is a literal representation of the trauma, involves compulsively repeating some aspect of the trauma, and does not tend to relieve anxiety.

An example of posttraumatic play is an increase in shooting games after exposure to a school shooting. Posttraumatic reenactment, on the other hand, is more flexible and involves behaviorally recreating aspects of the trauma (e.g., carrying a weapon after exposure to violence).

Adolescents and Teens

PTSD in adolescents may begin to more closely resemble PTSD in adults. However, there are a few features that have been shown to differ. As discussed above, children may engage in traumatic play following a trauma. Adolescents are more likely to engage in traumatic reenactment, in which they incorporate aspects of the trauma into their daily lives. In addition, adolescents are more likely than younger children or adults to exhibit impulsive and aggressive behaviors.

Besides PTSD, What Are the Other Effects of Trauma on Children?

Besides PTSD, children and adolescents who have experienced traumatic events often exhibit other types of problems. Perhaps the best information available on the effects of traumas on children comes from a review of the literature on the effects of child sexual abuse.

In this review, it was shown that sexually abused children often have problems with fear, anxiety, depression, anger and hostility, aggression, sexually inappropriate behavior, self-destructive behavior, feelings of isolation and stigma, poor self-esteem, difficulty in trusting others, substance abuse, and sexual maladjustment.

These problems are often seen in children and adolescents who have experienced other types of traumas as well. Children who have experienced traumas also often have relationship problems with peers and family members, problems with acting out, and problems with school performance.

Along with associated symptoms, there are a number of psychiatric disorders that are commonly found in children and adolescents who have been traumatized. One commonly co-occurring disorder is major depression. Other disorders include substance abuse; anxiety disorders such as separation anxiety, panic disorder, and generalized anxiety disorder (GAD); and externalizing disorders such as attention deficit hyperactivity disorder (ADHD), oppositional defiant disorder (ODD), and conduct disorder (CD).

How Is PTSD Treated in Children and Adolescents?

Although some children show a natural remission in PTSD symptoms over a period of a few months, a significant number of children continue to exhibit symptoms for years if untreated. Trauma-Focused psychotherapies have the most empirical support for children and adolescents.

Cognitive Behavioral Therapy (CBT)

Research studies show that CBT is the most effective approach for treating children. The treatment with the best empirical evidence is Trauma-Focused CBT (TF-CBT). TF-CBT generally includes the child directly discussing the traumatic event (exposure), anxiety management techniques such as relaxation and assertiveness training, and correction of inaccurate or distorted trauma-related thoughts.

Although there is some controversy regarding exposing children to the events that scare them, exposure-based treatments seem to be most relevant when memories or reminders of the trauma distress the child. Children can be exposed gradually and taught relaxation so that they can learn to relax while recalling their experiences. Through this procedure, they learn that they do not have to be afraid of their memories.

CBT also involves challenging children's false beliefs such as, "the world is totally unsafe." The majority of studies have found that it is safe and effective to use CBT for children with PTSD.

CBT is often accompanied by psycho-education and parental involvement. Psycho-education is education about PTSD symptoms and their effects.

It is as important for parents and caregivers to understand the effects of PTSD as it is for children. Research shows that the better parents cope with the trauma, and the more they support their children, the better their children will function. Therefore, it is important for parents to seek treatment for themselves in order to develop the necessary coping skills that will help their children.

Play Therapy

Play therapy can be used to treat young children with PTSD who are not able to deal with the trauma more directly. The therapist uses games, drawings, and other techniques to help the children process their traumatic memories.

Psychological First Aid (PFA)

Psychological first aid (PFA) has been used for school-aged children and adolescents exposed to disasters and community violence and can be used in schools and traditional settings. PFA involves providing comfort and support, normalizing the children's reactions, helping caregivers deal with changes in the child's emotions and behavior, teaching calming and problem-solving skills, and referring the most symptomatic children for additional treatment.

Eye Movement Desensitization and Reprocessing (EMDR)

Another therapy, EMDR, combines cognitive therapy with directed eye movements. While EMDR has been shown to be effective in treating adults, research with children is not as strong. Studies indicate that it is the cognitive component rather than the eye movements that accounts for the change.

Medications

Selective serotonin reuptake inhibitors (SSRIs) are approved for use in adults with PTSD. SSRIs are approved for use in children and adolescents with depression and OCD. Preliminary evidence suggests SSRIs may be effective in treating PTSD, however, there may also be risks such as irritability, poor sleep, and inattention. At this time, there is insufficient evidence to support the use of SSRIs.

Specialized Interventions

Specialized interventions may be necessary for children exhibiting particularly problematic symptoms or behaviors, such as inappropriate sexual behaviors, extreme behavioral problems, or substance abuse.

Chapter 35

Returning from the War Zone: PTSD in Military Personnel

Posttraumatic Stress Disorder (PTSD)[1]

PTSD can occur after you have been through a traumatic event. Professionals do not know why it occurs in some and not others. But PTSD is treatable.

Symptoms of PTSD

- **Re-experiencing.** Re-experiencing bad memories of a traumatic event can come back at any time. You may feel the same terror and horror you did when the event took place. Sometimes there's a trigger: a sound, sight, or smell that causes you to relive the event.

This chapter includes text excerpted from documents published by two public domain sources. Text under headings marked 1 are excerpted from "Returning from the War Zone—A Guide for Military Personnel," U.S. Department of Veterans Affairs (VA), January 2014. Reviewed June 2018; Text under headings marked 2 are excerpted from "How Common Is PTSD?" U.S. Department of Veterans Affairs (VA), October 3, 2016.

- **Avoidance.** People with PTSD often go to great lengths to avoid things that might remind them of the traumatic event they endured.
- **Negative changes in beliefs and feelings.** The way you think about yourself and others changes because of the trauma. You may have trouble experiencing your emotions, think no one can be trusted, or feel guilt or shame.
- **Hypervigilance or increased arousal.** Those suffering from PTSD may operate on "high-alert" at all times, often have very short fuses, and tend to startle easily.

How Likely Are You to Get PTSD?

It depends on many factors, such as:

- How severe the trauma was
- If you were injured
- The intensity of your reaction to the trauma
- Whether someone you were close to died or was injured
- How much your own life was in danger
- How much you felt you could not control things
- How much help and support you got following the event

Steps to solving the problem and getting help:

PTSD is a treatable condition. If you think you have PTSD, or just some of its reactions or symptoms (such as nightmares or racing thoughts), it's important to let your doctor or even a chaplain know. These people can help you set up other appointments as needed.

There are several steps to addressing PTSD:

- Assessment: Having a professional evaluate you with a full interview.
- Educating yourself and your family about PTSD, its symptoms, and how it can affect your life.
- Some antidepressants can relieve symptoms of PTSD. These medications do not treat the underlying cause, yet do provide some symptom relief.
- Cognitive behavioral therapy (CBT) generally seeks to balance your thinking and help you express and cope with your emotions about the traumatic experience.

There are different types of therapy but in most you will learn:

- How the problem affects you and others
- Goal setting about ways to improve your life
- New coping skills
- How to accept your thoughts and feelings, and strategies to deal with them

Meet with several therapists before choosing one. Finding a therapist involves learning:

- What kinds of treatment each therapist offers
- What you can expect from the treatment and the therapist
- What the therapist expects of you

How Common Is Posttraumatic Stress Disorder (PTSD)?[2]

Posttraumatic stress disorder (PTSD) can occur after you have been through a trauma. A trauma is a shocking and dangerous event that you see or that happens to you. During this type of event, you think that your life or others' lives are in danger.

Going through trauma is not rare. About 6 of every 10 men (or 60%) and 5 of every 10 women (or 50%) experience at least one trauma in their lives. Women are more likely to experience sexual assault and child sexual abuse. Men are more likely to experience accidents, physical assault, combat, disaster, or to witness death or injury.

PTSD can happen to anyone. It is not a sign of weakness. A number of factors can increase the chance that someone will develop PTSD, many of which are not under that person's control. For example, if you were directly exposed to the trauma or injured, you are more likely to develop PTSD.

Here are some facts (based on the United States population):

- About 7 or 8 out of every 100 people (or 7–8% of the population) will have PTSD at some point in their lives.
- About 8 million adults have PTSD during a given year. This is only a small portion of those who have gone through a trauma.
- About 10 of every 100 women (or 10%) develop PTSD sometime in their lives compared with about 4 of every 100 men (or 4%).

PTSD and the Military[2]

When you are in the military, you may see combat. You may have been on missions that exposed you to horrible and life-threatening experiences. These types of events can lead to PTSD.

The number of Veterans with PTSD varies by service era:

- **Operations Iraqi Freedom (OIF) and Enduring Freedom (OEF):** About 11–20 out of every 100 Veterans (or between 11–20%) who served in OIF or OEF have PTSD in a given year.
- **Gulf War (Desert Storm):** About 12 out of every 100 Gulf War Veterans (or 12%) have PTSD in a given year.
- **Vietnam War:** About 15 out of every 100 Vietnam Veterans (or 15%) were currently diagnosed with PTSD at the time of the most recent study in the late 1980s, the National Vietnam Veterans Readjustment Study (NVVRS). It is estimated that about 30 out of every 100 (or 30%) of Vietnam Veterans have had PTSD in their lifetime.

Other factors in a combat situation can add more stress to an already stressful situation. This may contribute to PTSD and other mental health problems. These factors include what you do in the war, the politics around the war, where the war is fought, and the type of enemy you face.

Another cause of PTSD in the military can be military sexual trauma (MST). This is any sexual harassment or sexual assault that occurs while you are in the military. MST can happen to both men and women and can occur during peacetime, training, or war.

Among Veterans who use VA healthcare, about:

- 23 out of 100 women (or 23%) reported sexual assault when in the military.
- 55 out of 100 women (or 55%) and 38 out of 100 men (or 38%) have experienced sexual harassment when in the military.

There are many more male Veterans than there are female Veterans. So, even though military sexual trauma is more common in women Veterans, over half of all Veterans with military sexual trauma are men.

Common Reactions to Trauma[1]

Almost all service members will have reactions after returning from a war zone. These behaviors are normal, especially during the first weeks at home. Most service members will successfully readjust with few major problems. It may take a few months, but you will feel better again.

You, your family, and friends need to be prepared for some common stress reactions. Such predictable reactions do not, by themselves, mean that you have a problem, such as posttraumatic stress disorder (PTSD), which requires professional help. Below are lists of common physical, mental/emotional, and behavioral reactions that you should expect.

Common Physical Reactions

- Trouble sleeping, overly tired
- Stomach upset, trouble eating
- Headaches and sweating when thinking of the war
- Rapid heartbeat or breathing
- Existing health problems become worse
- Experiencing shock, being numb, unable to feel happy

Common Mental and Emotional Reactions

- Bad dreams, nightmares
- Flashbacks or frequent unwanted memories
- Anger
- Feeling nervous, helpless, or fearful
- Feeling guilty, self-blame, shame
- Feeling sad, rejected, or abandoned
- Agitated, easily upset, irritated, or annoyed
- Feeling hopeless about the future

Insomnia can occur, and when you do sleep, you may have nightmares. Or you may have no trouble sleeping, but wake up feeling overly tired.

If any of your comrades died during the war, you may be thinking a lot about them. You may feel anger, resentment, or even guilt related to their deaths. Or, you might be in a state of shock, feeling emotionally numb or dazed.

During this time, you may find common family issues more irritating. You may feel anxious or "keyed up." Anger and aggression are common war zone stress reactions, but they may scare your partner, children, and you as well. Minor incidents can lead to severe over-reactions, such as yelling at your partner, kids, or others.

Common Behavioral Reactions

- Trouble concentrating
- Edgy, jumpy and easily startled
- Being on guard, always alert, concerned too much about safety and security
- Avoiding people or places related to the trauma
- Too much drinking, smoking, or drug use
- Lack of exercise, poor diet, or healthcare
- Problems doing regular tasks at work or school
- Aggressive driving habits

Some avoidance is normal. But if you are constantly avoiding everything that reminds you of your war zone experiences, this can create major difficulties at home. For instance, you may avoid seeing other people for fear that they might ask you about the war. If you are doing this, you can become isolated and withdrawn. Your family and friends will not be able to provide the social support you need, even if you don't know it.

Aggressive driving is also extremely common among service members returning from conflicts in the Middle East. Although you want to drive when you get back, you need to use extra caution. This is particularly true if you're feeling edgy or upset.

Back Home with Family[1]

There is usually a "honeymoon" phase shortly after demobilization, but honeymoons come to an end. You and members of your family have had unique experiences and have changed. You'll need to get to know each other again and appreciate what each other went through. Very likely, you'll need to renegotiate some of your roles. You will need time to rebuild intimacy and learn how to rely on one another again for support.

In addition, your interests may have changed. You may need to re-examine future plans, dreams, and expectations. You and your family will also need to re-examine common goals. When you return to life at home, you may:

- Feel pressured by requests for time and attention from family, friends, and others.
- Be expected to perform home, work, and school responsibilities, or care for children before you are ready.
- Find that your parents are trying to be too involved or treat you like a child again.
- Face different relationships with children who now have new needs and behaviors.
- Be confronted by the needs of partners who have had their own problems.

Financial Concerns

You may have financial issues to handle when you return home.

- Be careful not to spend impulsively.
- Seek assistance if making ends meet is hard due to changes in income.

Work Challenges

Readjusting to work can take time.

- You may feel bored, or that you find no meaning in your former work.
- You may have trouble finding a job.

If You Have Children

Children react differently to deployment depending on their age. They can cry, act out, be clingy, withdraw or rebel. To help you can:

- Provide extra attention, care, and physical closeness.
- Understand that they may be angry and perhaps rightly so.
- Discuss things. Let kids know they can talk about how they feel. Accept how they feel and don't tell them they should not feel that way.

- Tell kids their feelings are normal. Be prepared to tell them many times.
- Maintain routines and plan for upcoming events.

Common Reactions You May Have That Will Affect Family-and-Friend Relationships[1]

At first, many service members feel disconnected or detached from their partner and/or family. You may be unable to tell your family about what happened. You may not want to scare them by speaking about the war. Or maybe you think that no one will understand.

You also may find it's hard to express positive feelings. This can make loved ones feel like they did something wrong or are not wanted anymore. Sexual closeness may also be awkward for a while. Remember, it takes time to feel close again.

When reunited with family, you may also feel:

- **Mistrusting:** During your deployment, you trusted only those closest to you, in your unit. It can be difficult to begin to confide in your family and friends again.
- **Over-controlling or overprotective:** You might find that you're constantly telling the kids "Don't do that!" or "Be careful, it's not safe!" Rigid discipline may be necessary during wartime, but families need to discuss rules and share in decisions.
- **Short tempered:** More conflicts with others may be due to poor communication and/or unreasonable expectations.

Resilience Training (Formerly, Battlemind)[1]

Service members are well trained to go to war, but in the past, they were not well prepared to come home. In the past few years, the military has made a greater effort to prepare troops for re-entry to civilian life. One way to prepare is to make troops aware that the same mindset that helps them survive in a combat zone can backfire when used in the "home zone." Postdeployment resilience training helps service members understand how a military mindset is useful at war but not at home. For example:

- Discipline, which is essential in the military, can cause problems if applied too strictly with family. Your 13-year-old daughter might not obey orders in the same way you are used to!

- While deployed, buddies are the only ones you talk with, but at home this can lead you to withdraw from family and friends. Take time to reconnect with loved ones.

Each branch of the military has their own training on how to build resilience.

Healthy Coping for Common Reactions to Trauma[1]

With homecoming, you may need to re-learn how to feel safe, comfortable, and trusting with your family. You must get to know one another again. Good communication with your partner, children, parents, siblings, friends, coworkers, and others is the key. Give each other the chance to understand what you have been through. When talking as a family, be careful to listen to one another. Families work best when there is respect for one another, and a willingness to be open and consider alternatives.

Tips for Feeling Better

It's fine for you to spend some time alone. But, if you spend too much time alone or avoid social gatherings, you will be isolated from family and friends. You need the support of these people for a healthy adjustment. You can help yourself to feel better by:

- Getting back to regular patterns of sleep and exercise
- Pursuing hobbies and creative activities
- Planning sufficient R and R and intimate time
- Trying relaxation techniques (meditation, breathing exercises) to reduce stress
- Learning problems to watch out for and how to cope with them
- Striking a balance between staying connected with former war buddies and spending individual time with your partner, kids, other family members, and friends
- Communicating more than the "need-to-know" bare facts
- Talking about your war zone experiences at a time and pace that feels right to you
- Not drinking to excess, or when you're feeling depressed or to avoid disturbing memories. Drink responsibly, or don't drink
- Creating realistic workloads for home, school, and work

Steps to Assuming Normal Routines

Soon after your return, plan to have an open and honest discussion with your family about responsibilities. You all need to decide how they should be split up now that you're home. It's usually best to take on a few tasks at first and then more as you grow accustomed to being home. Be willing to compromise so that both you and your family members feel your needs are understood and respected.

Try to re-establish a normal sleep routine as quickly as possible. Go to bed and get up at the same time every day. Do not drink to help yourself sleep. You might try learning some relaxation techniques, such as deep breathing, yoga, or meditation.

Steps to Controlling Anger

Recognize and try to control your angry feelings. Returning service members don't always realize how angry they are. In fact, you may only recognize your emotion when someone close to you points it out. You can help control your anger by:

- Counting to 10 or 20 before reacting
- Figuring out the cues or situations that trigger your anger so you can be better prepared
- Learning relaxation techniques (breathing, yoga, meditation)
- Learning ways to deal with irritation and frustration and how not to be provoked into aggressive behavior
- Walking away
- Thinking about the ultimate consequences of your responses
- Writing things down
- Learn tips to controlling anger

Red Flags[1]

You now know the reactions that are normal following deployment to war. But sometimes the behaviors that kept you alive in the war zone get on the wrong track. You may not be able to shut them down after you've returned home safely.

Some problems may need outside assistance to solve. Even serious postdeployment psychological problems can be treated successfully and cured.

Admitting you have a problem can be tough:

- You might think you should cope on your own.
- You think others can't help you.
- You believe the problem(s) will go away on their own.
- You are embarrassed to talk to someone about it.

Confront Mental Health "Stigma"

Mental health problems are not a sign of weakness. The reality is that injuries, including psychological injuries, affect the strong and the brave just like everyone else. Some of the most successful officers and enlisted personnel have experienced these problems.

But stigma about mental health issues can be a huge barrier for people who need help. Finding the solution to your problem is a sign of strength and maturity. Getting assistance from others is sometimes the only way to solve something. For example, if you cannot scale a wall on your own and need a comrade to do so, you use them! Knowing when and how to get help is actually part of military training.

If your reactions are causing significant distress or interfering with how you function, you will need outside assistance. Things to watch for include:

- Relationship troubles—frequent and intense conflicts, poor communication, inability to meet responsibilities
- Work, school, or other community functioning—frequent absences, conflicts, inability to meet deadlines or concentrate, poor performance
- Thoughts of hurting someone, or yourself

If you get assistance early, you can prevent more serious problems from developing. If you delay seeking help because of avoidance or stigma, your problems may actually cause you to lose your job, your relationships, and your happiness. Mental and emotional problems can be managed or treated, and early detection is essential.

Many of the common reactions to experience in a war zone are also symptoms of more serious problems such as PTSD. In PTSD, however, they're much more intense and troubling, and they don't go away. If these symptoms don't decrease over a few months, or if they continue to cause significant problems in your daily life, it's time to seek treatment from a professional.

Chapter 36

Recent Research on PTSD

Using brain imaging to track the effects of treatment of posttraumatic stress disorder (PTSD), scientists have identified a brain circuit on which a frequently used and effective psychotherapy (prolonged exposure) acts to quell symptoms. The findings help explain why the neural circuit identified is a promising target for additional treatment development, including brain stimulation therapies.

In an accompanying paper, the authors also report that they have identified hallmarks in brain activity of people with PTSD that predict who will benefit from treatment.

In prolonged exposure treatment for patients with PTSD, trained therapists use deliberate and careful exposure to images, situations, or cues that evoke traumatic memories. The object of the therapy is to reduce fearful associations with these trauma cues and replace them with a sense of safety and control over emotional reactions. The treatment can be very effective, but it has not been clear how it changes brain processes to have a beneficial effect on symptoms.

Amit Etkin, M.D., Ph.D., at Stanford University School of Medicine, led a team of scientists collaborating on this work. The study enrolled 66 individuals with PTSD; all underwent functional magnetic resonance brain imaging (fMRI) at rest and while carrying out tasks that engage different aspects of emotional response and regulation.

This chapter includes text excerpted from "Imaging Pinpoints Brain Circuits Changed by PTSD Therapy," National Institute of Mental Health (NIMH), July 18, 2017.

By tracking blood flow, fMRI reveals areas of the brain that are active. Scientists monitor regional brain activity while a subject is carrying out a given task. Participants were then randomly assigned either to treatment with exposure therapy or a waitlist. All then had fMRI scans either following treatment or, if assigned to waitlist, after a comparable waiting period.

In participants who received exposure therapy, there were changes in activation observed in a part of the brain nearest the front of the cortex—the seat of higher-order brain function, including thought and decision making—when they were doing a reappraisal task which instructed them to reduce their level of distress by interpreting or seeing a negative picture (such as a gruesome scene) differently. The posttreatment changes in the frontopolar cortex were only observed during this task, not with two other tasks that required participants to simply react to emotional cues (such as fearful expression faces), or sort conflicting emotional information (for example if they viewed a fearful face labeled happy).

The magnitude of the changes in brain activation observed was greater in participants who had improved to a greater extent in a clinical test of PTSD symptoms. Imaging also revealed an increase in connectivity between the frontopolar cortex and two other brain regions, providing a fuller picture of a brain circuit that exposure therapy acts on. To probe the nature of the connections between these brain regions, the investigators applied magnetic pulses (transcranial magnetic stimulation or TMS) to the frontopolar cortex of healthy subjects; the stimulation deactivated the "downstream" brain areas, confirming a functional connection between the two areas.

The frontopolar area of the cortex plays a role in cognitive flexibility, the ability of the brain to shift between different aims and strategies. The team probed whether PTSD treatment changed patterns of activity in this brain circuit at rest by acquiring fMRI scans of subjects while they let their minds wander. In those who had received therapy, there was more varied, changing activity than in those who had not been treated. The investigators suggest that this variability is a signature of flexibility in mental processes.

In an accompanying paper, this team reports that brain activation patterns observed in conjunction with certain behavioral tasks can predict who will benefit from exposure therapy; by selecting the most informative measures, the team could predict with more than 95 percent accuracy who would experience improvement in symptoms. As with the posttreatment findings, brain activation patterns were seen when TMS was used to probe brain responses prior to treatment paralleled those seen with combined fMRI and behavioral tests. In those study participants who would benefit most from therapy, both sets of tests suggested that the prefrontal cortex exerted a greater regulatory effect on an emotional center in the brain (the amygdala).

Tellingly, the elements of brain activation that predicted therapeutic effect were not the same as those that reflected positive effects posttreatment. The brain circuit identified here that predicted whether someone would benefit from therapy was different from the one that changed when therapy was effective, an insight into how multiple circuits may be involved in processes underlying therapeutic change. An important aspect of this study was the use of multiple behavioral tests used to probe brain activation and the inclusion of a control (untreated) group for comparison, allowing the investigators to pinpoint meaningful changes in brain activity and link them, with confidence, to therapy. "This study provides a solid footing for understanding mechanisms so we can start working towards matching people to the treatment most likely to work for them and develop novel therapeutics for directly targeting brain therapy," said lead author Etkin. "By grounding psychotherapy in brain mechanisms, we can also hopefully decrease stigma, an invisible barrier to care that is so prevalent in psychiatric disorders and prevents people from getting the care that would benefit them."

One motivation for this work is that understanding the biology of a psychosocial intervention can provide information on which to base the design of direct brain circuit interventions, like TMS. Tools like TMS could also be used in a targeted way to enhance (or even enable) the beneficial effects of psychotherapy. "Perhaps the best way to inform and motivate the development of novel brain stimulation-based treatment by necessity comes through studying psychotherapy, the oldest and most interpersonal treatment we have in psychiatry," said Etkin.

The work is in keeping with National Institute of Mental Health's (NIMH) efforts to foster research aimed at developing a circuit-based understanding of brain function and psychiatric disorders; Etkin points out that this work shows how the therapeutic effects of psychosocial treatments for brain disorders are, like medication and brain stimulation techniques, grounded in biology.

Part Four

Treating Stress-Related Disorders

Chapter 37

Warning Signs and Risk Factors for Emotional Distress

It is common to feel stress symptoms before or after a crisis. Natural and human-caused disasters can have a devastating impact on people's lives because they sometimes cause physical injury, damage to property, or the loss of a home or place of employment. Anyone who sees or experiences this can be affected in some way. Most stress symptoms are temporary and will resolve on their own in a fairly short amount of time. However, for some people, particularly children and teens, these symptoms may last for weeks or even months and may influence their relationships with families and friends. Common warning signs of emotional distress include:

- Eating or sleeping too much or too little
- Pulling away from people and things
- Having low or no energy
- Having unexplained aches and pains, such as constant stomachaches or headaches

---

This chapter includes text excerpted from "Warning Signs and Risk Factors for Emotional Distress," Substance Abuse and Mental Health Services Administration (SAMHSA), July 20, 2016.

- Feeling helpless or hopeless
- Excessive smoking, drinking, or using drugs, including prescription medications
- Worrying a lot of the time; feeling guilty but not sure why
- Thinking of hurting or killing yourself or someone else
- Having difficulty readjusting to home or work life

For those who have lived through a natural or human-caused disaster, the anniversary of the event may renew feelings of fear, anxiety, and sadness. Certain sounds, such as sirens, can also trigger emotional distress. These and other environmental sensations can take people right back to the disaster, or cause them to fear that it's about to happen again. These "trigger events" can happen at any time.

Warning Signs and Risk Factors for Children and Teens

Children are often the most vulnerable of those impacted during and after a disaster. According to the National Child Traumatic Stress Network (NCTSN), a growing body of research has established that children as young as infancy may be affected by events that threaten their safety or the safety of their parents or caregivers.

Disasters are unfamiliar events that are not easily understood by children, who can find them emotionally confusing and frightening. During the time of turmoil, they may be left with a person unfamiliar to them and provided with limited information. Some warning signs of distress in children ages 6–11 include:

- Withdrawing from playgroups and friends
- Competing more for the attention of parents and teachers
- Being unwilling to leave home
- Being less interested in schoolwork
- Becoming aggressive
- Having added conflict with peers or parents
- Having difficulty concentrating

For teens, the impact of disasters varies depending on how much of a disruption the disaster causes their family or community. Teens ages 12–18 are likely to have physical complaints when under stress or be less interested in schoolwork, chores, or other responsibilities.

Although some teens may compete vigorously for attention from parents and teachers after a disaster, they also may:

- Become withdrawn
- Resist authority
- Become disruptive or aggressive at home or in the classroom
- Experiment with high-risk behaviors such as underage drinking or prescription drug misuse and abuse

Children and teens most at risk for emotional distress include those who:

- Survived a previous disaster
- Experienced temporary living arrangements, loss of personal property, and parental unemployment in a disaster
- Lost a loved one or friend involved in a disaster

Most young people simply need additional time to experience their world as a secure place again and receive some emotional support to recover from their distress. The reactions of children and teens to a disaster are strongly influenced by how parents, relatives, teachers, and caregivers respond to the event. They often turn to these individuals for comfort and help. Teachers and other mentors play an especially important role after a disaster or other crisis by reinforcing normal routines to the extent possible, especially if new routines have to be established.

Warning Signs and Risk Factors for Adults

Adults impacted by disaster are faced with the difficult challenge of balancing roles as first responders, survivors, and caregivers. They are often overwhelmed by the sheer magnitude of responsibility and immediate task of the crisis response and recovery at hand. They must also take the time to address their own physical and emotional needs as well as those of their family members and community.

Warnings signs of stress in adults may include:

- Crying spells or bursts of anger
- Difficulty eating

- Losing interest in daily activities
- Increasing physical distress symptoms such as headaches or stomach pains
- Fatigue
- Feeling guilty, helpless, or hopeless
- Avoiding family and friends

Adults most at risk of experiencing severe emotional stress and posttraumatic stress disorder (PTSD) include those with a history of:

- Exposure to other traumas, including severe accidents, abuse, assault, combat, or rescue work
- Chronic medical illness or psychological disorders
- Chronic poverty, homelessness, or discrimination
- Recent or subsequent major life stressors or emotional strain, such as single parenting

Adults most at risk for emotional stress include:

- Those who survived a previous disaster
- Those who lost a loved one or friend involved in a disaster
- Those who lack economic stability and/or knowledge of the English language
- Older adults that may lack mobility or independence

As with children and teens, adults also need time to get back into their normal routine. It is important that people try to accept whatever reactions they have related to the disaster. Take every day one-at-a-time and focus on taking care of your own disaster-related needs and those of your family.

Warning Signs and Risk Factors for First Responders and Recovery Workers

First responders and recovery workers include:

- Firefighters, police officers, emergency medical technicians, 911 operators, and other fire, emergency, and medical personnel
- Military service men and women

- Clergy
- Staff and volunteers serving with disaster-relief organizations, including sheltering, animal rescue, food service, and crisis counseling

First responders and recovery workers are not only physically and emotionally tested during an emergency, but they also may have loved ones in the area for whom they are concerned. They also are often the last to seek help for work-related stress.

Warnings signs of stress in responders and recovery workers may include:

- Experiencing a rapid heart rate, palpitations, muscle tensions, headaches, and tremors
- Feeling fear or terror in life-threatening situations or perceived danger, as well as anger and frustration
- Being disoriented or confused, having difficulty solving problems, and making decisions
- Engaging in problematic or risky behaviors, such as taking unnecessary risks, failing to use personal protective equipment, or refusing to follow orders or leave the scene
- Becoming irritable or hostile in social situations, resorting to blaming, and failing to support teammates

First responders and recovery workers most at risk for emotional distress include those who have experienced:

- Prolonged separation from loved ones
- Life-threatening situations
- Previous deployments that caused disruptions in home or work life
- Trauma from having witnessed or been exposed in some way to difficult stories of survival or loss

For first responders, being prepared for the job and strengthening stress management skills before a disaster assignment is the best protection from stress. Responder stress can be diminished by practicing for the disaster role, developing a personal toolkit of stress management skills, and preparing themselves and loved ones for a disaster.

Intimate Partner or Family Violence

Disasters can be extremely disruptive to individual families and community routines, leading to stress and inviting all types of violent behavior, including intimate partner violence or family violence. Women and girls can be particularly at risk. Following a disaster, resources for reporting violent crimes may be temporarily suspended or unavailable. For women and girls who have experienced intimate partner violence, sexual violence, or family violence, this can further heighten their sense of isolation and vulnerability.

Before, during, and after a disaster, what may seem like fighting between intimate partners or family members may actually be a symptom of a larger pattern of abuse. Further, during the response and recovery phase after a disaster, the risk for violence against women and girls becomes greater. These disaster survivors may become displaced from their homes and moved to shelters or temporary housing, where they encounter overcrowded, co-ed living conditions and a lack of security, among other things.

Chapter 38

Finding and Choosing a Therapist

Finding a Therapist[1]

Good treatments for posttraumatic stress disorder (PTSD) are available. Here are some suggestions for finding a therapist, counselor, or mental healthcare provider who can help your recovery.

Things to Consider

- Make sure the provider has experience treating people who have experienced a trauma.
- Try to find a provider who specializes in evidence-based medications for PTSD or effective psychotherapy for PTSD (e.g., cognitive behavioral therapy (CBT); cognitive processing therapy (CPT); prolonged exposure therapy (PE); or eye movement desensitization and reprocessing (EMDR)).
- Find out what type(s) of insurance the provider accepts and what you will have to pay (out-of-pocket costs) for care.

This chapter includes text excerpted from documents published by two public domain sources. Text under the headings marked 1 are excerpted from "Finding a Therapist," U.S. Department of Veterans Affairs (VA), October 27, 2015; Text under the headings marked 2 are excerpted from "Choosing a Therapist," U.S. Department of Veteran Affairs (VA), August 14, 2015.

First Steps

- Contact your family doctor to ask for a recommendation. You can also ask friends and family if they can recommend someone.
- If you have health insurance, call to find out which mental health providers your insurance company will pay for. Your insurance company may require that you choose a provider from among a list they maintain.

Finding a Provider by Phone

In addition to the numbers listed above, you can also find a therapist, counselor, or mental health provider in the following ways:

- Some mental health services are listed in the phone book. In the Government pages, look in the "County Government Offices" section, and find "Health Services (Dept. of)" or "Department of Health Services (DoHS)." "Mental Health" will be listed.
- In the yellow pages, mental health providers are listed under "counseling," "psychologists," "social workers," "psychotherapists," "social and human services," or "mental health."
- You can also call the psychology department of a local college or university.

Choosing a Therapist[2]

There are a many things to consider when choosing a therapist. Some practical issues are location, cost, and what insurance the therapist accepts. Other issues include the therapist's background, training, and the way he or she works with people. Your therapist should explain the therapy, how long treatment is expected to last, and how to tell if it is working. The information below can help you choose a therapist who is right for you.

Questions to Ask before Therapy[2]

Here is a list of questions you may want to ask a possible therapist:

- What is your education? Are you licensed? How many years have you been practicing?
- What are your special areas of practice?

- Have you ever worked with people who have been through trauma? Do you have any special training in posttraumatic stress disorder (PTSD) treatment?
- What kinds of PTSD treatments do you use? Have they been proven effective in dealing with my kind of problem or issue? How much therapy would you recommend?
- Do you prescribe medications?
- What are your fees? (Fees are usually based on a 45–50 minute session.) Do you have any discounted fees?
- What types of insurance do you accept? Do you file insurance claims? Do you contract with any managed care organizations? Do you accept Medicare or Medicaid insurance?

These questions are just guidelines. In the end, your choice of a therapist will be based on many factors. Think about your comfort with the person as well as his or her qualifications and experience treating PTSD. And keep in mind the importance of evidence-based, trauma-focused treatments like cognitive processing therapy (CPT), prolonged exposure (PE), and eye movement desensitization and reprocessing (EMDR).

Making Your Therapy a Good "Fit"[2]

In PTSD treatment or any mental health therapy, you work together with your therapist to get better. A good "fit" between a therapist and a patient can make a difference. You will want to choose a therapist you are comfortable with so that you can get better. This means you should feel like you can ask questions that help you understand treatment and your progress in therapy.

The most effective PTSD treatments are time-limited, usually lasting 10–12 weeks. If you are not getting better or if you feel your therapist is not a good fit for you, look for someone else to work with. Sometimes it takes a few tries to find just the right therapist. This is not unusual and your therapist should be understanding. If you are getting treatment at the U.S. Department of Veterans Affairs (VA), a patient advocate can help you if this issue arises.

Help for Veterans[1]

- All VA Medical Centers and many VA clinics provide PTSD care.

- Some VA centers have specialty programs for PTSD. Use the VA PTSD Program Locator to find a VA PTSD program.
- Vet Centers provide readjustment counseling to Veterans and their families after war. Find a Vet Center near you.
- VA Medical Centers and Vet Centers are also listed in the phone book. In the Government pages, look under "United States Government Offices." Then look for "Veterans Affairs, Dept of." In that section, look under "Medical Care" and "Vet Centers – Counseling and Guidance."

Paying for Therapy[1]

If you have health insurance, check to see what mental health services are covered. Medicare, Medicaid, and most major health plans typically cover a certain number of mental health counseling sessions per year. Note that you may have a small additional amount you will have to pay, called a copayment (or copay). Call your insurance company to see what they cover so you won't be surprised by a big bill. If you don't have health insurance that will cover your therapy, you may still be able to get counseling, even if you can't afford to pay full price. Many community mental health centers have sliding scales that base your fee on what you are able to pay.

Chapter 39

Psychotherapies for Stress-Related Disorders

Psychotherapy (sometimes called "talk therapy") is a term for a variety of treatment techniques that aim to help a person identify and change troubling emotions, thoughts, and behavior. Most psychotherapy takes place with a licensed and trained mental healthcare professional and a patient meeting one on one or with other patients in a group setting.

Someone might seek out psychotherapy for different reasons:

- You might be dealing with severe or long-term stress from a job or family situation, the loss of a loved one, or relationship or other family issues. Or you may have symptoms with no physical explanation: changes in sleep or appetite, low energy, a lack of interest or pleasure in activities that you once enjoyed, persistent irritability, or a sense of discouragement or hopelessness that won't go away.
- A health professional may suspect or have diagnosed a condition such as depression, bipolar disorder, posttraumatic stress or other disorder and recommended psychotherapy as a first treatment or to go along with medication.

This chapter includes text excerpted from "Psychotherapies," National Institute of Mental Health (NIMH), November 2016.

- You may be seeking treatment for a family member or child who has been diagnosed with a condition affecting mental health and for whom a health professional has recommended treatment.

An exam by your primary care practitioner can ensure there is nothing in your overall health that would explain your or a loved one's symptoms.

What to Consider When Looking for a Therapist

Therapists have different professional backgrounds and specialties. There are resources at the end of this material that can help you find out about the different credentials of therapists and resources for locating therapists. There are many different types of psychotherapy. Different therapies are often variations on an established approach, such as cognitive behavioral therapy (CBT). There is no formal approval process for psychotherapies as there is for the use of medications in medicine. For many therapies, however, research involving large numbers of patients has provided evidence that treatment is effective for specific disorders. These "evidence-based therapies (EBT)" have been shown in research to reduce symptoms of depression, anxiety, and other disorders. The particular approach a therapist uses depends on the condition being treated and the training and experience of the therapist. Also, therapists may combine and adapt elements of different approaches.

One goal of establishing an evidence base for psychotherapies is to prevent situations in which a person receives therapy for months or years with no benefit. If you have been in therapy and feel you are not getting better, talk to your therapist, or look into other practitioners or approaches. The object of therapy is to gain relief from symptoms and improve quality of life.

Once you have identified one or more possible therapists, a preliminary conversation with a therapist can help you get an idea of how treatment will proceed and whether you feel comfortable with the therapist. Rapport and trust are important. Discussions in therapy are deeply personal and it's important that you feel comfortable and trusting with the therapist and have confidence in his or her expertise. Consider asking the following questions:

- What are the credentials and experience of the therapist? Does he or she have a specialty?
- What approach will the therapist take to help you? Does he or she practice a particular type of therapy? What can the therapist

tell you about the rationale for the therapy and the evidence base?

- Does the therapist have experience in diagnosing and treating the age group (for example, a child) and the specific condition for which treatment is being sought? If a child is the patient, how will parents be involved in treatment?
- What are the goals of therapy? Does the therapist recommend a specific time frame or a number of sessions? How will progress be assessed and what happens if you (or the therapist) feel you aren't starting to feel better?
- Will there be homework?
- Are medications an option? How will medications be prescribed if the therapist is not an M.D.?
- Are our meetings confidential? How can this be assured?

Psychotherapies and Other Treatment Options

Psychotherapy can be an alternative to medication or can be used along with other treatment options, such as medications. Choosing the right treatment plan should be based on a person's individual needs and medical situation and under a mental health professional's care. Even when medications relieve symptoms, psychotherapy and other interventions can help a person address specific issues. These might include self-defeating ways of thinking, fears, problems with interactions with other people, or dealing with situations at home and at school or with employment.

Elements of Psychotherapy

A variety of different kinds of psychotherapies and interventions have been shown to be effective for specific disorders. Psychotherapists may use one primary approach, or incorporate different elements depending on their training, the condition being treated, and the needs of the person receiving treatment.

Here are examples of the elements that psychotherapies can include:

- Helping a person become aware of ways of thinking that may be automatic but are inaccurate and harmful. (An example might be someone who has a low opinion of his or her own abilities.) The therapist helps the person find ways to question these thoughts, understand how they affect emotions and behavior, and try ways to change self-defeating patterns. This approach is central to CBT.

- Identifying ways to cope with stress.
- Examining in depth a person's interactions with others and offering guidance with social and communication skills, if needed.
- Relaxation and mindfulness techniques.
- Exposure therapy for people with anxiety disorders. In exposure therapy, a person spends brief periods, in a supportive environment, learning to tolerate the distress of certain items, ideas, or imagined scenes cause. Over time the fear associated with these things dissipates.
- Tracking emotions and activities and the impact of each on the other.
- Safety planning can include helping a person recognize warning signs, and thinking about coping strategies, such as contacting friends, family, or emergency personnel.
- Supportive counseling to help a person explore troubling issues and provide emotional support.

eHealth

The telephone, Internet, and mobile devices have opened up new possibilities for providing interventions that can reach people in areas where mental health professionals may not be easily available, and can be at hand 24/7. Some of these approaches involve a therapist providing help at a distance, but others—such as web-based programs and cell phone apps—are designed to provide information and feedback in the absence of a therapist. Some approaches that use electronic media to provide help for mental health-related conditions have been shown by research to be helpful in some situations, others not as yet. The American Psychological Association (APA) has information to consider before choosing online therapy. It is important to note that, as with all care for conditions affecting mental health, the treatment needs to be appropriate for the condition and the individual. eHealth approaches may be helpful in some situations, including as a support with other in-person treatment, but may not be appropriate or effective as a substitute for in-person care.

Taking the First Step

The symptoms of mental disorders can have a profound effect on someone's quality of life and ability to function. Treatment can address symptoms as well as assist someone experiencing severe or ongoing stress. Some of the reasons that you might consider seeking out psychotherapy include:

- Overwhelming sadness or helplessness that doesn't go away
- Serious, unusual insomnia or sleeping too much
- Difficulty focusing on work, or carrying out other everyday activities
- Constant worry and anxiety
- Drinking to excess or any behavior that harms self or others
- Dealing with a difficult transition, such as a divorce, children leaving home, job difficulties, or the death of someone close
- Children's behavior problems that interfere with school, family, or peers

Seeking help is not an admission of weakness, but a step towards understanding and obtaining relief from distressing symptoms.

Finding a Therapist

Many different professionals offer psychotherapy. Examples include psychiatrists, psychologists, social workers, counselors, and psychiatric nurses. Information on the credentials of providers is available from the National Alliance on Mental Illness (NAMI). Your health plan may have a list of mental health practitioners who participate in the plan. Other resources on the "Help for Mental Illnesses" page can help you look for reduced cost health services. The resources listed there include links to help find reduced cost treatment. When talking with a prospective therapist, ask about treatment fees, whether the therapist participates in insurance plans, and whether there is a sliding scale for fees according to income.

Chapter 40

Medications for Stress-Related Disorders

Medications can play a role in treating several mental disorders and conditions. Treatment may also include psychotherapy (also called "talk therapy") and brain stimulation therapies (less common). In some cases, psychotherapy alone may be the best treatment option. Choosing the right treatment plan should be based on a person's individual needs and medical situation, and under a mental health professional's care. The National Institute of Mental Health (NIMH), a federal research agency, does not provide medical advice or referrals.

Understanding Your Medications

If you are prescribed a medication, be sure that you:

- Tell the doctor about all medications and vitamin supplements you are already taking
- Remind your doctor about any allergies and any problems you have had with medicines
- Understand how to take the medicine before you start using it and take your medicine as instructed

---

This chapter includes text excerpted from "Mental Health Medications," National Institute of Mental Health (NIMH), October 2016.

- Don't take medicines prescribed for another person or give yours to someone else
- Call your doctor right away if you have any problems with your medicine or if you are worried that it might be doing more harm than good. Your doctor may be able to adjust the dose or change your prescription to a different one that may work better for you
- Report serious side effects to the U.S. Food and Drug Administration (FDA) MedWatch Adverse Event Reporting program online (www.fda.gov/Safety/MedWatch) or by phone

Antidepressants

Antidepressants are medications commonly used to treat depression. Antidepressants are also used for other health conditions, such as anxiety, pain, and insomnia. Although antidepressants are not FDA-approved specifically to treat attention deficit hyperactivity disorder (ADHD), antidepressants are sometimes used to treat ADHD in adults. The most popular types of antidepressants are called selective serotonin reuptake inhibitors (SSRIs). Examples of SSRIs include:

- Fluoxetine
- Citalopram
- Sertraline
- Paroxetine
- Escitalopram

Other types of antidepressants are serotonin and norepinephrine reuptake inhibitors (SNRIs). SNRIs are similar to SSRIs and include venlafaxine and duloxetine.

Another antidepressant that is commonly used is bupropion. Bupropion is a third type of antidepressant which works differently than either SSRIs or SNRIs. Bupropion is also used to treat seasonal affective disorder (SAD) and to help people stop smoking. SSRIs, SNRIs, and bupropion are popular because they do not cause as many side effects as older classes of antidepressants, and seem to help a broader group of depressive and anxiety disorders. Older antidepressant medications include tricyclics, tetracyclics, and monoamine oxidase inhibitors (MAOIs). For some people, tricyclics, tetracyclics, or MAOIs may be the best medications.

How Do People Respond to Antidepressants?

According to a research review by the Agency for Healthcare Research and Quality (AHRQ), all antidepressant medications work about as well as each other to improve symptoms of depression and to keep depression symptoms from coming back. For reasons not yet well understood, some people respond better to some antidepressant medications than to others.

Therefore, it is important to know that some people may not feel better with the first medicine they try and may need to try several medicines to find the one that works for them. Others may find that a medicine helped for a while, but their symptoms came back. It is important to carefully follow your doctor's directions for taking your medicine at an adequate dose and over an extended period of time (often 4–6 weeks) for it to work.

Once a person begins taking antidepressants, it is important to not stop taking them without the help of a doctor. Sometimes people taking antidepressants feel better and stop taking the medication too soon, and the depression may return. When it is time to stop the medication, the doctor will help the person slowly and safely decrease the dose. It's important to give the body time to adjust to the change. People don't get addicted (or "hooked") on these medications, but stopping them abruptly may also cause withdrawal symptoms.

What Are the Possible Side Effects of Antidepressants?

Some antidepressants may cause more side effects than others. You may need to try several different antidepressant medications before finding the one that improves your symptoms and that causes side effects that you can manage. The most common side effects listed by the FDA include:

- Nausea and vomiting
- Weight gain
- Diarrhea
- Sleepiness
- Sexual problems

Call your doctor right away if you have any of the following symptoms, especially if they are new, worsening, or worry you:

- Thoughts about suicide or dying

- Attempts to commit suicide
- New or worsening depression
- New or worsening anxiety
- Feeling very agitated or restless
- Panic attacks
- Trouble sleeping (insomnia)
- New or worsening irritability
- Acting aggressively, being angry, or violent
- Acting on dangerous impulses
- An extreme increase in activity and talking (mania)
- Other unusual changes in behavior or mood

Combining the newer SSRI or SNRI antidepressants with one of the commonly-used "triptan" medications used to treat migraine headaches could cause a life-threatening illness called "serotonin syndrome." A person with serotonin syndrome may be agitated, have hallucinations (see or hear things that are not real), have a high temperature, or have unusual blood pressure changes. Serotonin syndrome is usually associated with the older antidepressants called MAOIs, but it can happen with the newer antidepressants as well, if they are mixed with the wrong medications. Antidepressants may cause other side effects that were not included in this list. To report any serious adverse effects associated with the use of antidepressant medicines, please contact the FDA MedWatch program (www.fda.gov/Safety/MedWatch).

Antianxiety Medications

Antianxiety medications help reduce the symptoms of anxiety, such as panic attacks, or extreme fear and worry. The most common antianxiety medications are called benzodiazepines. Benzodiazepines can treat generalized anxiety disorder (GAD). In the case of panic disorder or social phobia (social anxiety disorder), benzodiazepines are usually second-line treatments, behind SSRIs or other antidepressants. Benzodiazepines used to treat anxiety disorders include:

- Clonazepam
- Alprazolam
- Lorazepam

Short half-life (or short-acting) benzodiazepines (such as Lorazepam) and beta-blockers are used to treat the short-term symptoms of anxiety. Beta-blockers help manage physical symptoms of anxiety, such as trembling, rapid heartbeat, and sweating that people with phobias (an overwhelming and unreasonable fear of an object or situation, such as public speaking) experience in difficult situations.

Taking these medications for a short period of time can help the person keep physical symptoms under control and can be used "as needed" to reduce acute anxiety. Buspirone (which is unrelated to the benzodiazepines) is sometimes used for the long-term treatment of chronic anxiety. In contrast to the benzodiazepines, buspirone must be taken every day for a few weeks to reach its full effect. It is not useful on an "as-needed" basis.

How Do People Respond to Antianxiety Medications?

Antianxiety medications such as benzodiazepines are effective in relieving anxiety and take effect more quickly than the antidepressant medications (or buspirone) often prescribed for anxiety. However, people can build up a tolerance to benzodiazepines if they are taken over a long period of time and may need higher and higher doses to get the same effect. Some people may even become dependent on them. To avoid these problems, doctors usually prescribe benzodiazepines for short periods, a practice that is especially helpful for older adults, people who have substance abuse problems and people who become dependent on medication easily. If people suddenly stop taking benzodiazepines, they may have withdrawal symptoms or their anxiety may return. Therefore, benzodiazepines should be tapered off slowly.

What Are the Possible Side Effects of Antianxiety Medications?

Like other medications, antianxiety medications may cause side effects. Some of these side effects and risks are serious. The most common side effects for benzodiazepines are drowsiness and dizziness. Other possible side effects include:

- Nausea
- Blurred vision
- Headache
- Confusion

- Tiredness
- Nightmares

Tell your doctor if any of these symptoms are severe or do not go away:

- Drowsiness
- Dizziness
- Unsteadiness
- Problems with coordination
- Difficulty thinking or remembering
- Increased saliva
- Muscle or joint pain
- Frequent urination
- Blurred vision
- Changes in sex drive or ability

If you experience any of the symptoms below, call your doctor immediately:

- Rash
- Hives
- Swelling of the eyes, face, lips, tongue, or throat
- Difficulty breathing or swallowing
- Hoarseness
- Seizures
- Yellowing of the skin or eyes
- Depression
- Difficulty speaking
- Yellowing of the skin or eyes
- Thoughts of suicide or harming yourself
- Difficulty breathing

Common side effects of beta-blockers include:

- Fatigue

- Cold hands
- Dizziness or light-headedness
- Weakness

Beta-blockers generally are not recommended for people with asthma or diabetes because they may worsen symptoms related to both. Possible side effects from buspirone include:

- Dizziness
- Headaches
- Nausea
- Nervousness
- Lightheadedness
- Excitement
- Trouble sleeping

Antianxiety medications may cause other side effects that are not included in the lists above. To report any serious adverse effects associated with the use of these medicines, please contact the FDA MedWatch program (www.fda.gov/Safety/MedWatch).

Stimulants

As the name suggests, stimulants increase alertness, attention, and energy, as well as elevate blood pressure, heart rate, and respiration. Stimulant medications are often prescribed to treat children, adolescents, or adults diagnosed with ADHD. Stimulants used to treat ADHD include:

- Methylphenidate
- Amphetamine
- Dextroamphetamine
- Lisdexamfetamine dimesylate

Stimulants are also prescribed to treat other health conditions, including narcolepsy, and occasionally depression (especially in older or chronically medically ill people and in those who have not responded to other treatments).

How Do People Respond to Stimulants?

Prescription stimulants have a calming and "focusing" effect on individuals with ADHD. Stimulant medications are safe when given under a doctor's supervision. Some children taking them may feel slightly different or "funny." Some parents worry that stimulant medications may lead to drug abuse or dependence, but there is little evidence of this when they are used properly as prescribed. Additionally, research shows that teens with ADHD who took stimulant medications were less likely to abuse drugs than those who did not take stimulant medications.

What Are the Possible Side Effects of Stimulants?

Stimulants may cause side effects. Most side effects are minor and disappear when dosage levels are lowered. The most common side effects include:

- Difficulty falling asleep or staying asleep
- Loss of appetite
- Stomach pain
- Headache

Less common side effects include:

- Motor tics or verbal tics (sudden, repetitive movements or sounds)
- Personality changes, such as appearing "flat" or without emotion

Call your doctor right away if you have any of these symptoms, especially if they are new, become worse, or worry you. Stimulants may cause other side effects that are not included in the list above. To report any serious adverse effects associated with the use of stimulants, please contact the FDA MedWatch program (www.fda.gov/Safety/MedWatch).

Antipsychotics

What Are Antipsychotics?

Antipsychotic medicines are primarily used to manage psychosis. The word "psychosis" is used to describe conditions that affect the mind, and in which there has been some loss of contact with reality, often including delusions (false, fixed beliefs) or hallucinations (hearing or seeing things that are not really there). It can be a symptom of a physical condition such as drug abuse or a mental disorder such as schizophrenia, bipolar disorder, or very severe depression (also known as "psychotic depression"). Antipsychotic medications are often used in combination with other medications to treat delirium, dementia, and mental health conditions, including:

- Attention deficit hyperactivity disorder (ADHD)
- Severe depression
- Eating disorders
- Posttraumatic stress disorder (PTSD)
- Obsessive-compulsive disorder (OCD)
- Generalized anxiety disorder (GAD)

Antipsychotic medicines do not cure these conditions. They are used to help relieve symptoms and improve quality of life. Older or first-generation antipsychotic medications are also called conventional "typical" antipsychotics or "neuroleptics." Some of the common typical antipsychotics include:

- Chlorpromazine
- Haloperidol
- Perphenazine
- Fluphenazine

Second generation medications are also called "atypical" antipsychotics. Some of the common atypical antipsychotics include:

- Risperidone
- Olanzapine
- Quetiapine
- Ziprasidone
- Aripiprazole
- Paliperidone
- Lurasidone

According to a 2013 research review by the Agency for Healthcare Research and Quality (AHRQ), typical and atypical antipsychotics both work to treat symptoms of schizophrenia and the manic phase of bipolar disorder. Several atypical antipsychotics have a "broader spectrum" of action than the older medications, and are used for treating bipolar depression or depression that has not responded to an antidepressant medication alone.

How Do People Respond to Antipsychotics?

Certain symptoms, such as feeling agitated and having hallucinations, usually go away within days of starting an antipsychotic medication. Symptoms like delusions usually go away within a few weeks, but the full effects of the medication may not be seen for up to six weeks. Every patient responds differently, so it may take several trials of different antipsychotic medications to find the one that works best.

Some people may have a relapse—meaning their symptoms come back or get worse. Usually, relapses happen when people stop taking their medication, or when they only take it sometimes. Some people stop taking the medication because they feel better or they may feel that they don't need it anymore, but no one should stop taking an antipsychotic medication without talking to his or her doctor.

When a doctor says it is okay to stop taking a medication, it should be gradually tapered off—never stop suddenly. Many people must stay on an antipsychotic continuously for months or years in order to stay well; treatment should be personalized for each individual.

What Are the Possible Side Effects of Antipsychotics?

Antipsychotics have many side effects (or adverse events) and risks. The FDA lists the following side effects of antipsychotic medicines:

- Drowsiness
- Dizziness
- Restlessness
- Weight gain (the risk is higher with some atypical antipsychotic medicines)
- Dry mouth
- Constipation
- Nausea

- Vomiting
- Blurred vision
- Low blood pressure
- Uncontrollable movements, such as tics and tremors (the risk is higher with typical antipsychotic medicines)
- Seizures
- A low number of white blood cells, which fight infections

A person taking an atypical antipsychotic medication should have his or her weight, glucose levels, and lipid levels monitored regularly by a doctor. Typical antipsychotic medications can also cause additional side effects related to physical movement, such as:

- Rigidity
- Persistent muscle spasms
- Tremors
- Restlessness

Long-term use of typical antipsychotic medications may lead to a condition called tardive dyskinesia (TD). TD causes muscle movements, commonly around the mouth, that a person can't control. TD can range from mild to severe, and in some people, the problem cannot be cured. Sometimes people with TD recover partially or fully after they stop taking typical antipsychotic medication. People who think that they might have TD should check with their doctor before stopping their medication. TD rarely occurs while taking atypical antipsychotics. Antipsychotics may cause other side effects that are not included in this list above. To report any serious adverse effects associated with the use of these medicines, please contact the FDA MedWatch program (www.fda.gov/Safety/MedWatch).

Mood Stabilizers

Mood stabilizers are used primarily to treat bipolar disorder, mood swings associated with other mental disorders, and in some cases, to augment the effect of other medications used to treat depression. Lithium, which is an effective mood stabilizer, is approved for the treatment of mania and the maintenance treatment of bipolar disorder. A number of cohort studies describe antisuicide benefits of lithium for individuals on long-term maintenance. Mood stabilizers work by decreasing abnormal activity in the brain and are also sometimes used to treat:

- Depression (usually along with an antidepressant)
- Schizoaffective disorder
- Disorders of impulse control
- Certain mental illnesses in children

Anticonvulsant medications are also used as mood stabilizers. They were originally developed to treat seizures, but they were found to help control unstable moods as well. One anticonvulsant commonly used as a mood stabilizer is valproic acid (also called divalproex sodium). For some people, especially those with "mixed" symptoms of mania and depression or those with rapid-cycling bipolar disorder, valproic acid may work better than lithium. Other anticonvulsants used as mood stabilizers include:

- Carbamazepine
- Lamotrigine
- Oxcarbazepine

What Are the Possible Side Effects of Mood Stabilizers?

Mood stabilizers can cause several side effects, and some of them may become serious, especially at excessively high blood levels. These side effects include:

- Itching, rash
- Excessive thirst
- Frequent urination
- Tremor (shakiness) of the hands
- Nausea and vomiting
- Slurred speech
- Fast, slow, irregular, or pounding heartbeat
- Blackouts
- Changes in vision
- Seizures

- Hallucinations (seeing things or hearing voices that do not exist)
- Loss of coordination
- Swelling of the eyes, face, lips, tongue, throat, hands, feet, ankles, or lower legs

If a person with bipolar disorder is being treated with lithium, he or she should visit the doctor regularly to check the lithium levels his or her blood, and make sure the kidneys and the thyroid are working normally. Lithium is eliminated from the body through the kidney, so the dose may need to be lowered in older people with reduced kidney function. Also, loss of water from the body, such as through sweating or diarrhea, can cause the lithium level to rise, requiring a temporary lowering of the daily dose. Although kidney functions are checked periodically during lithium treatment, actual damage of the kidney is uncommon in people whose blood levels of lithium have stayed within the therapeutic range.

Mood stabilizers may cause other side effects that are not included in this list. To report any serious adverse effects associated with the use of these medicines, please contact the FDA MedWatch program (www.fda.gov/Safety/MedWatch). Some possible side effects linked anticonvulsants (such as valproic acid) include:

- Drowsiness
- Dizziness
- Headache
- Diarrhea
- Constipation
- Changes in appetite
- Weight changes
- Back pain
- Agitation
- Mood swings
- Abnormal thinking
- Uncontrollable shaking of a part of the body
- Loss of coordination
- Uncontrollable movements of the eyes

- Blurred or double vision
- Ringing in the ears
- Hair loss

These medications may also:

- Cause damage to the liver or pancreas, so people taking it should see their doctors regularly
- Increase testosterone (a male hormone) levels in teenage girls and lead to a condition called polycystic ovarian syndrome (a disease that can affect fertility and make the menstrual cycle become irregular)

Medications for common adult health problems, such as diabetes, high blood pressure, anxiety, and depression may interact badly with anticonvulsants. In this case, a doctor can offer other medication options.

Special Groups: Children, Older Adults, Pregnant Women

All types of people take psychiatric medications, but some groups have special needs, including:

- Children and adolescents
- Older adults
- Women who are pregnant or who may become pregnant

Children and Adolescents

Many medications used to treat children and adolescents with mental illness are safe and effective. However, some medications have not been studied or approved for use with children or adolescents. Still, a doctor can give a young person an FDA-approved medication on an "off-label" basis. This means that the doctor prescribes the medication to help the patient even though the medicine is not approved for the specific mental disorder that is being treated or for use by patients under a certain age. Remember:

- It is important to watch children and adolescents who take these medications on an "off-label" basis
- Children may have different reactions and side effects than adults

- Some medications have current FDA warnings about potentially dangerous side effects for younger patients

In addition to medications, other treatments for children and adolescents should be considered, either to be tried first, with medication added later if necessary, or to be provided along with medication. Psychotherapy, family therapy, educational courses, and behavior management techniques can help everyone involved cope with disorders that affect a child's mental health.

Older Adults

People over 65 have to be careful when taking medications, especially when they're taking many different drugs. Older adults have a higher risk for experiencing bad drug interactions, missing doses, or overdosing. Older adults also tend to be more sensitive to medications. Even healthy older people react to medications differently than younger people because older people's bodies process and eliminate medications more slowly. Therefore, lower or less frequent doses may be needed for older adults.

Before starting a medication, older people and their family members should talk carefully with a physician about whether a medication can affect alertness, memory, or coordination, and how to help ensure that prescribed medications do not increase the risk of falls. Sometimes memory problems affect older people who take medications for mental disorders. An older adult may forget his or her regular dose and take too much or not enough. A good way to keep track of medicine is to use a seven-day pill box, which can be bought at any pharmacy.

At the beginning of each week, older adults and their caregivers fill the box so that it is easy to remember what medicine to take. Many pharmacies also have pillboxes with sections for medications that must be taken more than once a day.

Women Who Are Pregnant or Who May Become Pregnant

The research on the use of psychiatric medications during pregnancy is limited. The risks are different depending on which medication is taken, and at what point during the pregnancy the medication is taken. Decisions on treatments for all conditions during pregnancy should be based on each woman's needs and circumstances, and based on a careful weighing of the likely benefits and risks of all available options, including psychotherapy (or "watchful waiting" during part or all of the pregnancy), medication, or a combination of the two. While no medication is considered perfectly safe for all women at all stages of pregnancy, this must be balanced for each woman against the fact that untreated serious mental disorders themselves can pose a risk to a pregnant woman and her developing fetus.

Medications should be selected based on available scientific research, and they should be taken at the lowest possible dose. Pregnant women should have a medical professional who will watch them closely throughout their pregnancy and after delivery. Most women should avoid certain medications during pregnancy. For example, Mood stabilizers are known to cause birth defects. Benzodiazepines and lithium have been shown to cause "floppy baby syndrome," in which a baby is drowsy and limp, and cannot breathe or feed well. Benzodiazepines may cause birth defects or other infant problems, especially if taken during the first trimester.

According to research, taking antipsychotic medications during pregnancy can lead to birth defects, especially if they are taken during the first trimester and in combination with other drugs, but the risks vary widely and depend on the type of antipsychotic taken. The conventional antipsychotic haloperidol has been studied more than others, and has been found not to cause birth defects. Research on some of the atypical antipsychotics is ongoing.

Antidepressants, especially SSRIs, are considered to be safe during pregnancy. However, antidepressant medications do cross the placental barrier and may reach the fetus. Birth defects or other problems are possible, but they are very rare. The effects of antidepressants on childhood development remain under study.

Studies have also found that fetuses exposed to SSRIs during the third trimester may be born with "withdrawal" symptoms such as breathing problems, jitteriness, irritability, trouble feeding, or hypoglycemia (low blood sugar). Most studies have found that these symptoms in babies are generally mild and short-lived, and no deaths have been reported. Risks from the use of antidepressants need to be balanced with the risks of stopping medication; if a mother is too depressed to care for herself and her child, both may be at risk for problems.

In 2004, the FDA issued a warning against the use of certain antidepressants in the late third trimester. The warning said that doctors may want to gradually taper pregnant women off antidepressants in the third trimester so that the baby is not affected. After a woman delivers, she should consult with her doctor to decide whether to return to a full dose during the period when she is most vulnerable to postpartum depression.

After the baby is born, women and their doctors should watch for postpartum depression, especially if a mother stopped taking her medication during pregnancy. In addition, women who nurse while taking psychiatric medications should know that a small amount of the medication passes into the breast milk. However, the medication may or may not affect the baby depending on the medication and when it is taken. Women taking psychiatric medications and who intend to breastfeed should discuss the potential risks and benefits with their doctors.

Chapter 41

Complementary and Alternative Medicine Therapies

Chapter Contents

Section 41.1

Acupuncture

This section contains text excerpted from the following sources: Text beginning with the heading "What Is Acupuncture?" is excerpted from "Acupuncture: In Depth," National Center for Complementary and Integrative Health (NCCIH), January 2016; Text under the heading "Acupuncture May Help Symptoms of Posttraumatic Stress Disorder" is excerpted from "Acupuncture May Help Symptoms of Posttraumatic Stress Disorder," National Center for Complementary and Integrative Health (NCCIH), September 3, 2014. Reviewed June 2018.

What Is Acupuncture?

Acupuncture is a technique in which practitioners stimulate specific points on the body—most often by inserting thin needles through the skin. It is one of the practices used in traditional Chinese medicine (TCM).

What the Science Says about the Effectiveness of Acupuncture

Results from a number of studies suggest that acupuncture may help ease types of pain that are often chronic such as low-back pain, neck pain, and osteoarthritis (OA)/knee pain. It also may help reduce the frequency of tension headaches and prevent migraine headaches. Therefore, acupuncture appears to be a reasonable option for people with chronic pain to consider. However, clinical practice guidelines are inconsistent with recommendations about acupuncture. The effects of acupuncture on the brain and body and how best to measure them are only beginning to be understood. Current evidence suggests that many factors—like expectation and belief—that are unrelated to acupuncture needling may play important roles in the beneficial effects of acupuncture on pain.

What the Science Says about Safety and Side Effects of Acupuncture

Relatively few complications from using acupuncture have been reported. Still, complications have resulted from use of nonsterile needles and improper delivery of treatments. When not delivered properly, acupuncture can cause serious adverse effects, including infections, punctured organs, collapsed lungs, and injury to the central nervous system. The U.S. Food and Drug Administration (FDA) regulates acupuncture needles as medical devices for use by licensed practitioners and requires that needles be manufactured and labeled according to certain standards. For example, the FDA requires that needles be sterile, nontoxic, and labeled for single use by qualified practitioners only.

NCCIH-Funded Research

National Center for Complementary and Integrative Health (NCCIH) funds research to evaluate acupuncture's effectiveness for various kinds of pain and other conditions, and to further understand how the body responds to acupuncture and how acupuncture might work. Some NCCIH-supported studies are looking at:

- If acupuncture can reduce the frequency of hot flashes associated with menopause
- Whether acupuncture can reduce pain and discomfort that may accompany chemotherapy
- Objectively determining if actual acupuncture is more effective than simulated acupuncture or usual care for pain relief, and (if so) by how much

More to Consider

- Don't use acupuncture to postpone seeing a healthcare provider about a health problem.
- If you decide to visit an acupuncturist, check his or her credentials. Most states require a license, certification, or registration to practice acupuncture; however, education and training standards and requirements for obtaining these vary from state to state. Although a license does not ensure quality of care, it does indicate that the practitioner meets certain standards regarding the knowledge and use of acupuncture. Most states require a diploma from the National Certification Commission for Acupuncture and Oriental Medicine (NCCAOM) for licensing.
- Some conventional medical practitioners—including physicians and dentists—practice acupuncture. In addition, national

acupuncture organizations (which can be found through libraries or by searching the Internet) may provide referrals to acupuncturists. When considering practitioners, ask about their training and experience.

- Ask the practitioner about the estimated number of treatments needed and how much each treatment will cost. Some insurance companies may cover the costs of acupuncture, while others may not.
- Help your healthcare providers give you better coordinated and safe care by telling them about all the health approaches you use. Give them a full picture of what you do to manage your health.

Acupuncture May Help Symptoms of Posttraumatic Stress Disorder (PTSD)

A pilot study shows that acupuncture may help people with post-traumatic stress disorder (PTSD). PTSD is an anxiety disorder that can develop after exposure to a terrifying event or ordeal in which grave physical harm occurred or was threatened. Traumatic events that may trigger PTSD include violent personal assaults, natural or human-caused disasters, accidents, or military combat.

Michael Hollifield, M.D., and colleagues conducted a clinical trial examining the effect of acupuncture on the symptoms of PTSD. The researchers analyzed depression, anxiety, and impairment in 73 people with a diagnosis of PTSD. The participants were assigned to receive either acupuncture or group cognitive behavioral therapy (CBT) over 12 weeks, or were assigned to a wait-list as part of the control group. The people in the control group were offered treatment or referral for treatment at the end of their participation.

The researchers found that acupuncture provided treatment effects similar to group CBT; both interventions were superior to the control group. Additionally, treatment effects of both the acupuncture and the group therapy were maintained for 3 months after the end of treatment. The limitations of the study are consistent with preliminary research. For example, this study had a small group of participants that lacked diversity, and the results do not account for outside factors that may have affected the treatments' results.

Section 41.2

Aromatherapy

This section contains text excerpted from "Aromatherapy and Essential Oils (PDQ®)–Patient Version," National Cancer Institute (NCI), February 23, 2018.

What Is Aromatherapy?

Aromatherapy is the use of essential oils from plants to improve the mind, body, and spirit. It is used by patients with cancer to improve quality of life and reduce stress, anxiety, nausea, and vomiting caused by cancer and its treatment. Aromatherapy may be used with other complementary treatments like massage therapy and acupuncture, as well as with standard treatments, for symptom management.

Essential oils (also known as volatile oils) are the fragrant (aromatic) part found in many plants, often under the surface of leaves, bark, or peel. The fragrance is released if the plant is crushed or a special steam process is used. There are many essential oils used in aromatherapy, including those from Roman chamomile, geranium, lavender, tea tree, lemon, ginger, cedarwood, and bergamot. Each plant's essential oil has a different chemical makeup that affects how it smells, how it is absorbed, and how it affects the body. Essential oils are very concentrated. For example, it takes about 220 pounds of lavender flowers to make about 1 pound of essential oil. The aroma of essential oils fades away quickly when left open to air.

How Is Aromatherapy Given or Taken?

Aromatherapy is used in several ways.

- **Indirect inhalation:** The patient breathes in an essential oil by using a room diffuser, which spreads the essential oil through the air, or by placing drops nearby.
- **Direct inhalation:** The patient breathes in an essential oil by using an individual inhaler made by floating essential oil drops on top of hot water.
- **Massage:** In aromatherapy massage, one or more essential oils are diluted into a carrier oil and massaged into the skin.

Essential oils may also be mixed with bath salts and lotions, or applied to bandages. There are some essential oils used to treat specific conditions. However, the types of essential oils used and the ways they are combined may vary, depending on the experience and training of the aromatherapist.

Have Any Preclinical (Laboratory or Animal) Studies Been Done Using Aromatherapy?

In laboratory studies, tumor cells are used to test a substance to find out if it is likely to have any anticancer effects. In animal studies, tests are done to see if a drug, procedure, or treatment is safe and effective in animals. Laboratory and animal studies are done before a substance is tested in people. Laboratory and animal studies have tested the effects of essential oils.

Have Any Clinical Trials (Research Studies with People) of Aromatherapy Been Done?

Clinical trials of aromatherapy have studied its use in the treatment of anxiety, nausea, vomiting, and other health-related conditions in cancer patients. No studies of aromatherapy used to treat cancer have been published in a peer-reviewed scientific journal. Studies of aromatherapy massage or inhalation have had mixed results. There have been some reports of improved mood, anxiety, sleep, nausea, and pain. Other studies reported that aromatherapy showed no change in symptoms.

A trial of 103 cancer patients studied the effects of massage compared to massage with Roman chamomile essential oil. A decrease in anxiety and improved symptoms were noted in the group that had a massage with essential oil. The group that had massage only did not have the same benefit.

A study of inhaled ginger essential oil in women receiving chemotherapy for breast cancer showed improvements in acute nausea, but no improvement in vomiting or chronic nausea. A study of inhaled bergamot essential oil in children and adolescents at the time of stem cell infusion reported an increase in anxiety and nausea and no effect on pain. In a study of adult patients at the time of stem cell infusion, tasting or smelling sliced oranges was more effective at reducing nausea, retching, and coughing than inhaling an orange essential oil. A study of tea tree essential oil as a topical treatment to clear antibiotic-resistant

MRSA (methicillin-resistant *Staphylococcus aureus*) bacteria from the skin of hospital patients found that it was as effective as the standard ointment.

Have Any Side Effects or Risks Been Reported from Aromatherapy?

Safety testing on essential oils shows very few side effects or risks when they are used as directed. Most essential oils have been approved as ingredients in food and fragrances and are labeled as GRAS (generally recognized as safe) by the U.S. Food and Drug Administration (FDA). Swallowing large amounts of essential oils is not recommended.

Allergic reactions and skin irritation may occur when essential oils are in contact with the skin for long periods of time. Sun sensitivity may occur when citrus or other essential oils are applied to the skin before going out in the sun. Lavender and tea tree essential oils have been found to have effects similar to estrogen (female sex hormone) and also block or decrease the effect of androgens (male sex hormones). Applying lavender and tea tree essential oils to the skin over a long period of time was linked in one study to breast growth in boys who had not yet reached puberty.

Section 41.3

Biofeedback

"Biofeedback," © 2018 Omnigraphics.
Reviewed June 2018.

What Is Biofeedback?

Biofeedback is a type of therapy that helps people control certain body functions that otherwise take place involuntarily, such as blood pressure, heart rate, skin temperature, and muscle tension. The biofeedback technique works on the principle that by harnessing the power of one's mind, a person can be aware of the processes taking place inside their body, and this can give them more control over their health. With biofeedback, electrodes or sensors are attached to the skin. These help receive information about the body, measure processes, and display the results on a monitor. Using this information, a biofeedback therapist can help a person learn how the heart rate or blood pressure can be controlled. The individual then uses the monitor to see his or her progress and eventually will be able to achieve success without it. The therapy is said to prevent or treat conditions such as high blood pressure, chronic pain, migraine headaches, and urinary incontinence.

Biofeedback Methods

Depending on the individual's need, a biofeedback therapist recommends the appropriate course of action. Some biofeedback therapies include:

- **Brainwave.** This method uses scalp sensors attached to an electroencephalograph (EEG) to monitor brain waves.
- **Breathing.** Breathing patterns and respiration rate are observed by placing bands around the abdomen and chest during respiration.
- **Muscle.** Electromyography (EMG) is used to measure muscle tension. This involves placing sensors over skeletal muscles to monitor electrical activity.
- **Heart rate.** An electrocardiograph (ECG) measures the heart rate and its variability. This method of feedback uses sensors placed on the chest, wrist, or lower torso.
- **Temperature.** Blood flow to the skin is measured using sensors attached to the fingers or feet.
- **Sweat glands.** Sweat gland activity and skin perspiration are measured by an electrodermograph (EDG) by attaching sensors to the fingers, palm, or wrist.

How Does Biofeedback Work?

Biofeedback is known to promote relaxation and help relieve stress. Researchers are not sure how the method works; however, people who have undergone treatment report benefiting greatly from biofeedback therapy. When the body is under stress, certain internal processes, like blood pressure and heart rate, tend to become overactive. Biofeedback promotes relaxation, and many scientists believe that this is the key to stress reduction and other health benefits. A biofeedback therapist can help an individual learn to reduce stress through mental exercises and physical relaxation techniques.

A Biofeedback Session

A typical biofeedback session involves attaching electrodes to an individual's skin. The electrodes send signals to a monitor that displays the current heart rate, breathing rate, skin temperature, blood pressure, muscle activity, and perspiration. If the individual is under stress, muscles tighten, heart rate becomes faster, blood pressure rises, sweating increases, and breathing quickens. When the monitor displays variation from normal rates, the biofeedback therapist trains the individual to manage these functions through various mental and physical relaxation techniques. This eventually helps the individual bring involuntary internal body functions under his or her control outside of the therapy session.

The following are some of the types of relaxation techniques used in biofeedback therapy:

- **Progressive muscle relaxation.** Tightening and relaxing different muscle groups.
- **Mindfulness meditation.** Negative emotions are purged by refocusing thought processes.
- **Guided imagery.** Focusing on a specific calming image makes one feel more relaxed.
- **Deep breathing.** A breathing exercise intended to promote a sense of well-being.

Benefits of Biofeedback

Proponents of biofeedback cite many of its benefits that can be used to manage both physical and mental issues. Biofeedback therapy is found to be most effective for conditions influenced by stress, such as eating and learning disorders, bedwetting, and muscle spasms. Other problems that can be helped by biofeedback include asthma, incontinence, irritable bowel syndrome (IBS), constipation, high blood pressure, chronic pain, anxiety, depression, diabetes, headaches, and the effects of chemotherapy. Researchers have found that biofeedback has also helped improve intelligence and behavior in children, reportedly including attention deficit hyperactivity disorder (ADHD) and autism. Some people prefer biofeedback to other types of therapy since it is noninvasive and reduces the need for medication.

Biofeedback method is more useful and effective in children. For instance, EEG neurofeedback (especially when combined with cognitive therapy) has been found to improve behavior and intelligence scores in children with ADHD and autism. Abdominal pain can be relieved by biofeedback combined with a fiber-rich diet. Migraine and chronic tension headaches among children and teens can be relieved or controlled by thermal biofeedback.

Risks of Biofeedback

Biofeedback is generally considered safe, and research has not revealed any side effects. A consultation with a primary healthcare provider is a good idea before beginning therapy since biofeedback may not be for everyone. For example, some people with existing serious mental health issues might not find this form of treatment to be beneficial.

References

1. "Biofeedback," Mayo Clinic, January 3, 2018.
2. Kiefer, David, MD. "Overview of Biofeedback," WebMD, August 1, 2016.
3. Ehrlich, D. Steven, NMD. "Biofeedback," University of Maryland Medical Center (UMMC), November 6, 2015.
4. "Biofeedback," Healthline, January 11, 2016.
5. Nordqvist, Joseph. "Biofeedback," *Medical News Today*, January 10, 2017.

Section 41.4

Herbal Supplements May Improve Stress Symptoms

This section contains text excerpted from "Herbals, Complementary Medicines, and Nutritional Supplements," U.S. Department of Veterans Affairs (VA), July 2007. Reviewed June 2018.

What Is Herbal Therapy?

Herbs have been used in medicine for as long as people have been on earth. The use of herbal therapies has been recorded in ancient Greece, Egypt, Rome, India, Russia, and China. Many modern medicines came from Native American remedies. There are many examples of drugs used today that are from plants. They may come from the plant's leaves, roots, flowers or fruits. Digoxin is a good example of a drug that comes from a plant source. Digoxin is used to treat problems with heart rhythms or heart failure. Psyllium, the ingredient in Metamucil© used to add fiber to a patient's diet, is also a natural product. Taxol®, made from a type of tree bark, is used to treat cancer. Herbal therapy has been gaining popularity in the United States as a compliment to "conventional medicine." In many other countries herbs are already regulated by the government and available by prescription.

Things to Know before You Use Herbals or Other Complementary Medicines

Complementary medicines are considered food supplements. The U.S. Food and Drug Administration (FDA) does not control herbal therapies, vitamins or other complementary medicines. This means no government agency is checking to be sure that these products are safe or effective. Unlike traditional drugs, no testing needs to be done before a company can claim their product is effective.

Complementary medicines or supplements are not safe for all people. Most will have some effect on your body, possibly one you weren't planning on. You may have an allergic or a toxic reaction. The complementary medicine may interfere with your prescribed medicines. Before starting any new treatment, you should know the risks and benefits. Discuss any medicine, herbal or otherwise, with your healthcare provider before using.

How Should I Choose a Herbal Product?

Discuss your choice with your healthcare provider. Then look for brands that standardize their product. This means that the same amount of herb is in each dose. Avoid products that do not list the ingredients and their strengths on the label. The label should list the scientific name of the product, a lot or batch number, the date the product was manufactured, and the expiration date. Only buy products from a reputable source.

Where Can I Get More Information about Complementary Therapies?

There are many sources of information on complementary therapies. Be sure to get your information from a neutral source, not advertising by a manufacturer.

Your first source of medical information should always be your healthcare providers. Physicians, nurses, physician's assistants, and pharmacists are all good people to ask.

Some Biologicals Used to Treat Stress

Kava

Kava is a drink of the South Pacific that was first introduced to the modern world by Captain James Cook. Since then, kava has been served to officials visiting the South Pacific, including Presidents and Pope John Paul II. Most commonly, kava is served as a tea made of the dried roots.

Uses

Treatment for nervousness, restlessness, and stress.

How It Works

It is believed it works in a similar way to the drugs Valium® or Xanax®.

Dose

An extract of 55–70 percent kavalactones is the current standard. The daily dose of kava should be 140–210 mg in 2–3 doses. It has also been noticed that fresh kava, not usually available in America, is the most effective.

Safety

When used on a regular basis, kava can cause a dry scaly rash on the palms of the hands and the soles of the feet. It may also cause the skin, hair or nails to turn yellow. Some patients may be allergic to kava.

Kava can cause a feeling of giddiness. Patients taking kava should not drive or operate heavy machinery. Patients should not drink alcohol or take other drugs for treating stress when using kava. Some people have been arrested for driving under the influence of kava. Kava should be avoided in patients with liver problems.

*Lavender**

Lavender is native to the Mediterranean region, the Arabian Peninsula, and Russia. It is grown in Europe, the United States, and Australia. Lavender has a long history of use to boost appetite and mood, as well as relieve gastrointestinal problems and anxiety. It was also used in ancient Egypt as part of the process for mummifying bodies. At present, people use lavender as a dietary supplement for anxiety, stress, depression, intestinal problems, and pain. People also apply it to the skin for hair loss, pain, and for improving emotional health. People may also inhale a lavender vapor to help sleep, to reduce pain, and for agitation related to dementia. Tea can be made from lavender leaves. A vapor for inhalation can be made by mixing lavender oil (an essential oil) with boiling water. Lavender oil is used for massage and in baths. Lavender is also found in capsules and liquid extracts.

What Have We Learned?

- Many studies have investigated lavender's effectiveness for a number of conditions, such as pain, anxiety, stress, and overall well-being, but several were small and of poor quality.
- There is little scientific evidence of lavender's effectiveness for most health uses.
- Studies on lavender for anxiety have shown mixed results.

What Do We Know about Safety?

- Topical use of diluted lavender oil is generally considered safe for most adults, but reports suggest it can cause skin irritation.

- There's not enough evidence to determine its safety when inhaled as aromatherapy.
- Some evidence suggests that some topical applications containing lavender oil may affect sex hormone activity.
- Lavender oil may be poisonous if taken by mouth.
- Lavender extracts may cause stomach upset, joint pain, or headache.

**Text excerpted from "Lavender," National Center for Complementary and Integrative Health (NCCIH), November 30, 2016.*

Valerian

Valerian is a plant native to Europe and Asia; it also grows in North America. Valerian has been used medicinally since the times of early Greece and Rome; Hippocrates wrote about its uses. Historically, valerian was used to treat nervousness, trembling, headaches, and heart palpitations. At present, valerian is used as a dietary supplement for insomnia, anxiety, and other conditions such as depression and menopause symptoms. The roots and rhizomes (underground stems) of valerian are used to make capsules, tablets, and liquid extracts, as well as teas.

What Have We Learned?

- The evidence on whether valerian is helpful for sleep problems is inconsistent.
- There's not enough evidence to allow any conclusions about whether valerian can relieve anxiety, depression, or menopausal symptoms.

What Do We Know about Safety?

- Studies suggest that valerian is generally safe for use by most healthy adults for short periods of time.
- No information is available about the long-term safety of valerian or its safety in children younger than age 3, pregnant women, or nursing mothers.
- Few side effects have been reported in studies of valerian. Those that have occurred include headache, dizziness, itching, and digestive disturbances.

- Because it is possible (though not proven) that valerian might have a sleep-inducing effect, it should not be taken along with alcohol or sedatives.

Section 41.5

Massage Therapy

This section contains text excerpted from "Massage Therapy for Health Purposes," National Center for Complementary and Integrative Health (NCCIH), June 2016.

What Is Massage Therapy?

The term "massage therapy" includes many techniques, and the type of massage given usually depends on your needs and physical condition.

- Massage therapy dates back thousands of years. References to massage appear in ancient writings from China, Japan, India, and Egypt.
- In general, massage therapists work on muscle and other soft tissue to help you feel better.
- In Swedish massage, the therapist uses long strokes, kneading, deep circular movements, vibration, and tapping.
- Sports massage combines techniques of Swedish massage and deep tissue massage to release chronic muscle tension. It's adapted to the needs of athletes.
- Myofascial trigger point therapy focuses on trigger points—areas that are painful when pressed and are associated with pain elsewhere in the body.
- Massage therapy is sometimes done using essential oils as a form of aromatherapy.

What the Science Says about the Effectiveness of Massage

A lot of the scientific research on massage therapy is preliminary or conflicting, but much of the evidence points toward beneficial effects on pain and other symptoms associated with a number of different conditions. Much of the evidence suggests that these effects are short term and that people need to keep getting massages for the benefits to continue.

Researchers have studied the effects of massage for many conditions. Some that they have studied more extensively are the following

Pain

- A 2008 research review and 2011 National Center for Complementary and Integrative Health (NCCIH)-funded clinical trial concluded that massage may be useful for chronic low-back pain.
- Massage may help with chronic neck pain, a 2009 NCCIH-funded clinical trial reported.
- Massage may help with pain due to osteoarthritis (OA) of the knee, according to a 2012 NCCIH-funded study.
- Studies suggest that for women in labor, massage provided some pain relief and increased their satisfaction with other forms of pain relief, but the evidence isn't strong, a 2012 review concluded.

Cancer

Numerous research reviews and clinical studies have suggested that at least for the short term, massage therapy for cancer patients may reduce pain, promote relaxation, and boost mood. However, the National Cancer Institute (NCI) urges massage therapists to take specific precautions with cancer patients and avoid massaging:

- Open wounds, bruises, or areas with skin breakdown
- Directly over the tumor site
- Areas with a blood clot in a vein
- Sensitive areas following radiation therapy.

Mental Health

- A 2010 meta-analysis of 17 clinical trials concluded that massage therapy may help to reduce depression.
- Brief, twice-weekly yoga and massage sessions for 12 weeks were associated with a decrease in depression, anxiety, and back and leg pain in pregnant women with depression, a 2012 NCCIH-funded clinical trial showed. Also, the women's babies weighed more than babies born to women who didn't receive the therapy.
- However, a 2013 research review concluded that there's not enough evidence to determine if massage helps pregnant mothers with depression.
- A 2010 review concluded that massage may help older people relax.
- For generalized anxiety disorder, massage therapy was no better at reducing symptoms than providing a relaxing environment and deep breathing lessons, according to a small, 2010 NCCIH-supported clinical trial.

Fibromyalgia (FM)

A 2010 review concluded that massage therapy may help temporarily reduce pain, fatigue, and other symptoms associated with fibromyalgia, but the evidence is not definitive. The authors noted that it's important that the massage therapist not cause pain.

Headaches

Clinical trials on the effects of massage for headaches are preliminary and only somewhat promising.

Human Immunodeficiency Virus (HIV)/Acquired Immunodeficiency Syndrome (AIDS)

Massage therapy may help improve the quality of life for people with human immunodeficiency virus (HIV) or acquired immunodeficiency syndrome (AIDS), a 2010 review of four small clinical trials concluded.

Infant Care

Massaging preterm infants using moderate pressure may improve weight gain, a 2010 review suggested. There isn't enough evidence to know if massage benefits healthy infants who are developing normally, a 2013 review determined.

Other Conditions

Researchers have studied massage for the following but it's still unclear if it helps:

- Behavior of children with autism or autism spectrum disorders
- Immune function in women with breast cancer
- Anxiety and pain in patients following heart surgery
- Quality of life and glucose levels in people with diabetes
- Lung function in children with asthma.

What the Science Says about the Safety and Side Effects of Massage Therapy

Massage therapy appears to have few risks when performed by a trained practitioner. However, massage therapists should take some precautions in people with certain health conditions.

- In some cases, pregnant women should avoid massage therapy. Talk with your healthcare provider before getting a massage if you're pregnant.
- People with some conditions such as bleeding disorders or low blood platelet counts should avoid having forceful and deep tissue massage. People who take anticoagulants (also known as blood thinners) also should avoid them. Massage should not be done in any potentially weak area of the skin, such as wounds.
- Deep or intense pressure should not be used over an area where the patient has a tumor or cancer, unless approved by the patient's healthcare provider.

NCCIH-Funded Research

NCCIH-sponsored studies have investigated the effects of massage on a variety of conditions including

- The effects of an 8-week course of Swedish massage compared to usual care on pain and function in adults with OA of the knee
- Whether massage helps with generalized anxiety disorder

- The effect of massage therapy on cancer-related fatigue
- How massage therapy and progressive muscle relaxation compare for reducing chronic low-back pain in patients referred from primary care practices
- The frequency and length of massages needed to address neck pain.

Training, Licensing, and Certification

In the United States, 44 states and the District of Columbia (D.C.) regulate massage therapists. Cities, counties, or other local governments also may regulate massage. Training standards and requirements for massage therapists vary greatly by state and locality. Most states that regulate massage therapists require them to have a minimum of 500 hours of training from an accredited training program. The National Certification Board for Therapeutic Massage and Bodywork (NCBTMB) certifies practitioners who pass a national examination and fulfill other requirements.

More to Consider

- Do not use massage therapy to replace conventional care or to postpone seeing a healthcare provider about a medical problem.
- If you have a medical condition and are unsure whether massage therapy would be appropriate for you, discuss your concerns with your healthcare provider, who may also be able to help you select a massage therapist.
- Ask about the training, experience, and credentials of the massage therapist you are considering. Also ask about the number of treatments that might be needed, the cost, and insurance coverage.
- For more tips on finding a complementary health practitioner, such as a massage therapist, see the National Center for Complementary and Integrative Health's (NCCIH) webpage—How To Find a Complementary Health Practitioner (nccih.nih.gov/health/howtofind.htm).
- Tell all your healthcare providers about any complementary and integrative health approaches you use. Give them a full picture of what you do to manage your health. This will ensure coordinated and safe care.

Section 41.6

Meditation

This section contains text excerpted from "Meditation: In Depth," National Center for Complementary and Integrative Health (NCCIH), April 2016.

What Is Meditation?

Meditation is a mind and body practice that has a long history of use for increasing calmness and physical relaxation, improving psychological balance, coping with illness, and enhancing overall health and well-being. Mind and body practices focus on the interactions among the brain, mind, body, and behavior.

There are many types of meditation, but most have four elements in common: a quiet location with as few distractions as possible; a specific, comfortable posture (sitting, lying down, walking, or in other positions); a focus of attention (a specially chosen word or set of words, an object, or the sensations of the breath); and an open attitude (letting distractions come and go naturally without judging them).

What the Science Says about the Effectiveness of Meditation

Many studies have investigated meditation for different conditions, and there's evidence that it may reduce blood pressure as well as symptoms of irritable bowel syndrome and flare-ups in people who have had ulcerative colitis (UC). It may ease symptoms of anxiety and depression, and may help people with insomnia.

Meditation can help these conditions:

- Pain
- For high blood pressure
- For irritable bowel syndrome (IBS)
- For ulcerative colitis (UC)
- For anxiety, depression, and insomnia
- For smoking cessation
- Other conditions

Meditation and the Brain

Some research suggests that meditation may physically change the brain and body and could potentially help to improve many health problems and promote healthy behaviors. In a 2012 study, researchers compared brain images from 50 adults who meditate and 50 adults who don't meditate. Results suggested that people who practiced meditation for many years have more folds in the outer layer of the brain. This process (called gyrification) may increase the brain's ability to process information.

A 2013 review of three studies suggest that meditation may slow, stall, or even reverse changes that take place in the brain due to normal aging. Results from a 2012 National Center for Complementary and Integrative Health (NCCIH)-funded study suggest that meditation can affect activity in the amygdala (a part of the brain involved in processing emotions), and that different types of meditation can affect the amygdala differently even when the person is not meditating.

Research about meditation's ability to reduce pain has produced mixed results. However, in some studies, scientists suggest that meditation activates certain areas of the brain in response to pain.

What the Science Says about Safety and Side Effects of Meditation

Meditation is generally considered to be safe for healthy people. People with physical limitations may not be able to participate in certain meditative practices involving movement. People with physical health conditions should speak with their healthcare providers before starting a meditative practice, and make their meditation instructor aware of their condition. There have been rare reports that meditation could cause or worsen symptoms in people with certain psychiatric problems like anxiety and depression. People with existing mental health conditions should speak with their healthcare providers before starting a meditative practice, and make their meditation instructor aware of their condition.

NCCIH-Funded Research

NCCIH-supported studies are investigating meditation for:

- Teens experiencing chronic, widespread pain, such as from fibromyalgia (FM)

- Stress reduction for people with multiple sclerosis (MS)
- Posttraumatic stress disorder (PTSD), headaches, reducing blood pressure.

More to Consider

- Don't use meditation to replace conventional care or as a reason to postpone seeing a healthcare provider about a medical problem.
- Ask about the training and experience of the meditation instructor you are considering.
- Tell all your healthcare providers about any complementary or integrative health approaches you use. Give them a full picture of what you do to manage your health. This will help ensure coordinated and safe care.

Section 41.7

Spirituality May Alleviate Distress

This section contains text excerpted from "Talking about Spiritual and Religious Factors in Wellness," Substance Abuse and Mental Health Services Administration (SAMHSA), September 16, 2017.

Defining Spirituality/Religion

Spirituality/Religion and its role in promoting physical and behavioral health have been embraced in many public health settings as an important tool to promote wellness. Harold Koenig, a well known researcher in spirituality and health, writes that "religion" involves the beliefs, practices, and rituals related to the sacred; and that "spirituality" is more difficult to define, but is generally considered more personal and something "people define for themselves that is largely free of the rules, regulations, and responsibilities associated with religion." The use of the term spirituality in healthcare has grown from attempts to be more inclusive in pluralistic healthcare settings, and to address the needs both of religious and nonreligious people. Researchers working on this important topic often use the terms religion—where religion is a multidimensional construct not limited to institutional forms of religion—and spirituality synonymously.

Spirituality/Religion in the Lives of People with Behavioral Health Disorders: Why Is It Important for Providers to Consider?

There are a number of reasons why providers should consider talking about spirituality with individuals with behavioral health disorders. Most importantly, studies have shown that individuals with higher spirituality and religiosity levels had an 18 percent reduction in mortality rates.

Symptom Management

Individuals who identify as being religious or spiritual report lower rates of psychiatric conditions such as depression and anxiety. Not only that, individuals who identify as being religious or spiritual report experience improved health outcomes with chronic conditions such and cardiovascular disease and type-2 diabetes, which decreases the risk of premature mortality.

Spirituality and Recovery from Serious Mental Illness

Spirituality/religion is an important part of recovery for individuals with serious mental illness; and many persons would like treatment providers to be made aware of their spiritual beliefs and have this information considered as a part of their treatment planning. To date, the systematic research published in the mental health literature does not support the argument that religious involvement usually has an adverse effect on mental health and recovery. Rather in general, studies find that religious involvement is related to better coping with stress and less depression, suicide, anxiety, and substance abuse.

Spirituality and Social Support

A significant number of individuals living with psychiatric disabilities report that they have used religion to help them cope. Religious beliefs can provide a sense of meaning and purpose during difficult life circumstances. Unlike many other coping resources, religion is available to anyone at any time, regardless of financial, social, physical, or mental circumstances. Accessing religion can also create opportunities for building support networks, which may be helpful in dealing with the stressors individuals living with behavioral health conditions encounter.

Spirituality and Culture

Cultural factors may influence how individuals seek support and access services. For example, individuals experiencing a behavioral health crisis may be more likely to seek support from faith-based organizations. Consequently, it is important to consider religious and faith-based organizations as valued partners. In other words, considering cultural factors such as spirituality/religion can improve engagement and retention.

Strategies for Talking about Spirituality/Religion with Individuals with Serious Mental Illness

Focus on Meaning

As noted earlier, people may use terms such as Spirituality and Religion interchangeably. Relying on a particular definition may not be the most successful strategy for engaging individuals with serious mental illness. However, engaging people in conversations about the strategies they use to find a sense of meaning and purpose in life and maintain a sense of hope when faced with adversity (overlapping concepts in spirituality, religion, and faith) can create an opportunity for more open dialogue between individuals being served and providers.

Make Use of Existing Resources

Tools such as Cultural Activation Prompts (CAPs) can help. Created by the Nathan Kline Institute (NKI) Center of Excellence in Culturally Competent Mental Health, CAPs is a tool for promoting cultural activation. It includes a list of 15 cues for consumers to use to convey information to caregivers on what culturally matters to them in receiving care. Through the use of CAPs, individuals receiving services can learn strategies for starting a cultural conversation with their caregivers and providers, including but not limited to their religious/spiritual beliefs. Providers can explore the CAPs, too, and actively work to integrate the tool into service provision.

Be Understanding and Communicative

When talking with the individuals you serve about spirituality, it's important to be understanding. Understanding entails knowing that the spiritual beliefs of the individual you're working with may not be in alignment with your own, while also understanding the myriad of different belief systems that exist. Not only are there a number of belief systems, religions, and faiths, but people exist at different developmental stages of their own spiritual journeys. You may meet an individual who has never considered spiritual wellness as a component of their well-being, whereas another may be a lifetime follower of a particular faith. Be mindful and understanding of these differences and strive to make recommendations or suggestions that meet the individual where they are. This communication can help foster a sense of inclusion. Even if you do not share the same beliefs as the individual you're working with, listen to them share and cooperate to make relevant treatment plans or goals for achieving optimal health and well-being. Clinicians need to be aware of the religious and spiritual activities of the individuals they serve, and appreciate their value as a resource for healthy mental and social functioning.

Section 41.8

Yoga

This section contains text excerpted from "Yoga: In Depth," National Center for Complementary and Integrative Health (NCCIH), June 2013. Reviewed June 2018.

Yoga is a mind and body practice with historical origins in ancient Indian philosophy. Like other meditative movement practices used for health purposes, various styles of yoga typically combine physical postures, breathing techniques, and meditation or relaxation. This section provides basic information about yoga, summarizes scientific research on effectiveness and safety, and suggests sources for additional information.

Key Facts

Studies in people with chronic low-back pain suggest that a carefully adapted set of yoga poses may help reduce pain and improve function (the ability to walk and move). Studies also suggest that practicing yoga (as well as other forms of regular exercise) might have other health benefits such as reducing heart rate and blood pressure, and may also help relieve anxiety and depression. Other research suggests yoga is not helpful for asthma, and studies looking at yoga and arthritis have had mixed results.

People with high blood pressure, glaucoma, or sciatica, and women who are pregnant should modify or avoid some yoga poses. Ask a trusted source (such as a healthcare provider or local hospital) to recommend a yoga practitioner. Contact professional organizations for the names of practitioners who have completed an acceptable training program. Tell all your healthcare providers about any complementary health approaches you use. Give them a full picture of what you do to manage your health. This will help ensure coordinated and safe care.

About Yoga

Yoga in its full form combines physical postures, breathing exercises, meditation, and a distinct philosophy. There are numerous styles of yoga. Hatha yoga, commonly practiced in the United States and Europe, emphasizes postures, breathing exercises, and meditation. Hatha yoga styles include Ananda, Anusara, Ashtanga, Bikram, Iyengar, Kripalu, Kundalini, Viniyoga, and others.

Side Effects and Risks

- Yoga is generally low-impact and safe for healthy people when practiced appropriately under the guidance of a well-trained instructor.
- Overall, those who practice yoga have a low rate of side effects, and the risk of serious injury from yoga is quite low. However, certain types of stroke, as well as pain from nerve damage, are among the rare possible side effects of practicing yoga.
- Women who are pregnant and people with certain medical conditions, such as high blood pressure, glaucoma (a condition in which fluid pressure within the eye slowly increases and may damage the eye's optic nerve), and sciatica (pain, weakness,

numbing, or tingling that may extend from the lower back to the calf, foot, or even the toes), should modify or avoid some yoga poses.

Use of Yoga for Health in the United States

According to the 2007 National Health Interview Survey (NHIS), which included a comprehensive survey on the use of complementary health approaches by Americans, yoga is the sixth most commonly used complementary health practice among adults. More than 13 million adults practiced yoga in the previous year, and between the 2002 and 2007 NHIS, use of yoga among adults increased by 1 percent (or approximately 3 million people). The 2007 survey also found that more than 1.5 million children practiced yoga in the previous year. Many people who practice yoga do so to maintain their health and well-being, improve physical fitness, relieve stress, and enhance quality of life. In addition, they may be addressing specific health conditions, such as back pain, neck pain, arthritis, and anxiety.

What the Science Says about Yoga

Current research suggests that a carefully adapted set of yoga poses may reduce low-back pain and improve function. Other studies also suggest that practicing yoga (as well as other forms of regular exercise) might improve quality of life; reduce stress; lower heart rate and blood pressure; help relieve anxiety, depression, and insomnia; and improve overall physical fitness, strength, and flexibility. But some research suggests yoga may not improve asthma, and studies looking at yoga and arthritis have had mixed results.

- One National Center for Complementary and Integrative Health (NCCIH)-funded study of 90 people with chronic low-back pain found that participants who practiced Iyengar yoga had significantly less disability, pain, and depression after 6 months.
- In a 2011 study, also funded by NCCIH, researchers compared yoga with conventional stretching exercises or a self-care book in 228 adults with chronic low-back pain. The results showed that both yoga and stretching were more effective than a self-care book for improving function and reducing symptoms due to chronic low-back pain.
- Conclusions from another 2011 study of 313 adults with chronic or recurring low-back pain suggested that 12 weekly yoga classes resulted in better function than usual medical care.

However, studies show that certain health conditions may not benefit from yoga.

- A 2011 systematic review of clinical studies suggests that there is no sound evidence that yoga improves asthma.
- A 2011 review of the literature reports that few published studies have looked at yoga and arthritis, and of those that have, results are inconclusive. The two main types of arthritis—osteoarthritis (OA) and rheumatoid arthritis (RA)—are different conditions, and the effects of yoga may not be the same for each. In addition, the reviewers suggested that even if a study showed that yoga helped osteoarthritic finger joints, it may not help osteoarthritic knee joints.

Training, Licensing, and Certification

There are many training programs for yoga teachers throughout the country. These programs range from a few days to more than 2 years. Standards for teacher training and certification differ depending on the style of yoga. There are organizations that register yoga teachers and training programs that have complied with a certain curriculum and educational standards. For example, one nonprofit group (the Yoga Alliance) requires at least 200 hours of training, with a specified number of hours in areas including techniques, teaching methodology, anatomy, physiology, and philosophy. Most yoga therapist training programs involve 500 hours or more. The training standards of the International Association of Yoga Therapists (IAYT) are competency-based and require at least 800 hours after a basic 200 hours teacher training program.

If You Are Considering Practicing Yoga

- Do not use yoga to replace conventional medical care or to postpone seeing a healthcare provider about pain or any other medical condition.
- If you have a medical condition, talk to your healthcare provider before starting yoga.
- Ask a trusted source (such as your healthcare provider or a nearby hospital) to recommend a yoga practitioner. Find out about the training and experience of any practitioner you are considering.

- Everyone's body is different, and yoga postures should be modified based on individual abilities. Carefully selecting an instructor who is experienced with and attentive to your needs is an important step toward helping you practice yoga safely. Ask about the physical demands of the type of yoga in which you are interested and inform your yoga instructor about any medical issues you have.
- Carefully think about the type of yoga you are interested in. For example, hot yoga (such as Bikram yoga) may involve standing and moving in humid environments with temperatures as high as 105°F. Because such settings may be physically stressful, people who practice hot yoga should take certain precautions. These include drinking water before, during, and after a hot yoga practice and wearing suitable clothing. People with conditions that may be affected by excessive heat, such as heart disease, lung disease, and a prior history of heatstroke may want to avoid this form of yoga. Women who are pregnant may want to check with their healthcare providers before starting hot yoga.
- Tell all your healthcare providers about any complementary health approaches you use. Give them a full picture of what you do to manage your health. This will help ensure coordinated and safe care.

NCCIH-Funded Research

Research on yoga for conditions such as low-back pain, depression, stress, blood pressure, and insomnia is ongoing. NCCIH is currently supporting research on how practicing yoga may affect:

- Diabetes risk
- Human immunodeficiency virus (HIV)
- Immune function
- Forms of arthritis
- Menopausal symptoms
- Multiple sclerosis (MS)
- Posttraumatic stress disorder (PTSD)
- Smoking cessation

Chapter 42

Treating Depression

Depression (major depressive disorder or clinical depression) is a common but serious mood disorder. It causes severe symptoms that affect how you feel, think, and handle daily activities, such as sleeping, eating, or working. To be diagnosed with depression, the symptoms must be present for at least two weeks.

Treatment Options for Depression

Depression, even the most severe cases, can be treated. The earlier that treatment can begin, the more effective it is. Depression is usually treated with medications, psychotherapy, or a combination of the two. If these treatments do not reduce symptoms, electroconvulsive therapy (ECT) and other brain stimulation therapies may be options to explore.

Medications

Antidepressants are medicines that treat depression. They may help improve the way your brain uses certain chemicals that control mood or stress. You may need to try several different antidepressant medicines before finding the one that improves your symptoms and has manageable side effects. A medication that has helped you or a close family member in the past will often be considered.

This chapter includes text excerpted from "Depression," National Institute of Mental Health (NIMH), February 2018.

Antidepressants take time—usually 2–4 weeks to work, and often, symptoms such as sleep, appetite, and concentration problems improve before mood lifts, so it is important to give medication a chance before reaching a conclusion about its effectiveness. If you begin taking antidepressants, do not stop taking them without the help of a doctor. Sometimes people taking antidepressants feel better and then stop taking the medication on their own, and the depression returns. When you and your doctor have decided it is time to stop the medication, usually after a course of 6–12 months, the doctor will help you slowly and safely decrease your dose. Stopping them abruptly can cause withdrawal symptoms.

In some cases, children, teenagers, and young adults under 25 may experience an increase in suicidal thoughts or behavior when taking antidepressants, especially in the first few weeks after starting or when the dose is changed. This warning from the U.S. Food and Drug Administration (FDA) also says that patients of all ages taking antidepressants should be watched closely, especially during the first few weeks of treatment. If you are considering taking an antidepressant and you are pregnant, planning to become pregnant, or breastfeeding, talk to your doctor about any increased health risks to you or your unborn or nursing child.

You may have heard about an herbal medicine called St. John's wort. Although it is a top-selling botanical product, the FDA has not approved its use as an over-the-counter (OTC) or prescription medicine for depression, and there are serious concerns about its safety (it should never be combined with a prescription antidepressant) and effectiveness. Do not use St. John's wort before talking to your healthcare provider. Other natural products sold as dietary supplements, including omega-3 fatty acids and S-adenosylmethionine (SAMe), remain under study but have not yet been proven safe and effective for routine use.

Psychotherapies

Several types of psychotherapy (also called "talk therapy" or, in a less specific form, counseling) can help people with depression. Examples of evidence-based approaches specific to the treatment of depression include cognitive behavioral therapy (CBT), interpersonal therapy (IPT), and problem-solving therapy (PST).

Brain Stimulation Therapies

If medications do not reduce the symptoms of depression, electroconvulsive therapy (ECT) may be an option to explore. Based on the latest research:

- ECT can provide relief for people with severe depression who have not been able to feel better with other treatments.
- Electroconvulsive therapy can be an effective treatment for depression. In some severe cases where a rapid response is necessary or medications cannot be used safely, ECT can even be a first-line intervention.
- Once strictly an inpatient procedure, today ECT is often performed on an outpatient basis. The treatment consists of a series of sessions, typically three times a week, for 2–4 weeks.
- ECT may cause some side effects, including confusion, disorientation, and memory loss. Usually, these side effects are short term, but sometimes memory problems can linger, especially for the months around the time of the treatment course. Advances in ECT devices and methods have made modern ECT safe and effective for the vast majority of patients. Talk to your doctor and make sure you understand the potential benefits and risks of the treatment before giving your informed consent to undergoing ECT.
- ECT is not painful, and you cannot feel the electrical impulses. Before ECT begins, a patient is put under brief anesthesia and given a muscle relaxant. Within one hour after the treatment session, which takes only a few minutes, the patient is awake and alert.

Other types of brain stimulation therapies used to treat medicine-resistant depression include repetitive transcranial magnetic stimulation (rTMS) and vagus nerve stimulation (VNS). Other types of brain stimulation treatments are under study. If you think you may have depression, start by making an appointment to see your doctor or healthcare provider. This could be your primary care practitioner or a health provider who specializes in diagnosing and treating mental health conditions.

Beyond Treatment: Things You Can Do

Here are other tips that may help you or a loved one during treatment for depression:

- Try to be active and exercise
- Set realistic goals for yourself
- Try to spend time with other people and confide in a trusted friend or relative
- Try not to isolate yourself, and let others help you

- Expect your mood to improve gradually, not immediately
- Postpone important decisions, such as getting married or divorced, or changing jobs until you feel better. Discuss decisions with others who know you well and have a more objective view of your situation
- Continue to educate yourself about depression

Join a Study

What Are Clinical Trials?

Clinical trials are research studies that look at new ways to prevent, detect, or treat diseases and conditions, including depression. During clinical trials, some participants receive treatments under study that might be new drugs or new combinations of drugs, new surgical procedures or devices, or new ways to use existing treatments. Other participants (in the "control group") receive a standard treatment, such as a medication already on the market, an inactive placebo medication, or no treatment. The goal of clinical trials is to determine if a new test or treatment works and is safe. Although individual participants may benefit from being part of a clinical trial, participants should be aware that the primary purpose of a clinical trial is to gain new scientific knowledge so that others may be better helped in the future.

How Do I Find a Clinical Trials at National Institute of Mental Health (NIMH) on Depression?

Doctors at The National Institute of Mental Health (NIMH) are dedicated to mental health research, including clinical trials of possible new treatments as well as studies to understand the causes and effects of depression. The studies take place at the National Institute of Health (NIH) Clinical Center (CC) in Bethesda, Maryland and require regular visits. After the initial phone interview, you will come to an appointment at the clinic and meet with one of our clinicians.

How Do I Find a Clinical Trial Near Me?

To search for a clinical trial near you, you can visit ClinicalTrials.gov (www.clinicaltrials.gov). This is a searchable registry and results database of federally and privately supported clinical trials conducted in the United States and around the world. This information should be used in conjunction with advice from health professionals.

Chapter 43

Treating Anxiety Disorders

Occasional anxiety is a normal part of life. You might feel anxious when faced with a problem at work, before taking a test, or making an important decision. But anxiety disorders involve more than temporary worry or fear. For a person with an anxiety disorder, the anxiety does not go away and can get worse over time. The feelings can interfere with daily activities such as job performance, school work, and relationships. There are several different types of anxiety disorders. Examples include generalized anxiety disorder, panic disorder, and social anxiety disorder. Anxiety disorders are generally treated with psychotherapy, medication, or both.

Psychotherapy

Psychotherapy or "talk therapy" can help people with anxiety disorders. To be effective, psychotherapy must be directed at the person's specific anxieties and tailored to his or her needs. A typical "side effect" of psychotherapy is temporary discomfort involved with thinking about confronting feared situations.

Cognitive Behavioral Therapy (CBT)

CBT is a type of psychotherapy that can help people with anxiety disorders. It teaches a person different ways of thinking, behaving,

---

This chapter includes text excerpted from "Anxiety Disorders," National Institute of Mental Health (NIMH), March 2016.

and reacting to anxiety-producing and fearful situations. CBT can also help people learn and practice social skills, which is vital for treating social anxiety disorder. Two specific stand-alone components of CBT used to treat social anxiety disorder are cognitive therapy and exposure therapy. Cognitive therapy focuses on identifying, challenging, and then neutralizing unhelpful thoughts underlying anxiety disorders.

Exposure therapy focuses on confronting the fears underlying an anxiety disorder in order to help people engage in activities they have been avoiding. Exposure therapy is used along with relaxation exercises and/or imagery. One study, called a meta-analysis because it pulls together all of the previous studies and calculates the statistical magnitude of the combined effects, found that cognitive therapy was superior to exposure therapy for treating social anxiety disorder. CBT may be conducted individually or with a group of people who have similar problems. Group therapy is particularly effective for social anxiety disorder. Often "homework" is assigned for participants to complete between sessions.

Self-Help or Support Groups

Some people with anxiety disorders might benefit from joining a self-help or support group and sharing their problems and achievements with others. Internet chat rooms might also be useful, but any advice received over the Internet should be used with caution, as Internet acquaintances have usually never seen each other and false identities are common. Talking with a trusted friend or member of the clergy can also provide support, but it is not necessarily a sufficient alternative to care from an expert clinician.

Stress-Management Techniques

Stress management techniques and meditation can help people with anxiety disorders calm themselves and may enhance the effects of therapy. While there is evidence that aerobic exercise has a calming effect, the quality of the studies is not strong enough to support its use as treatment. Since caffeine, certain illicit drugs, and even some over-the-counter (OTC) cold medications can aggravate the symptoms of anxiety disorders, avoiding them should be considered. Check with your physician or pharmacist before taking any additional medications. The family can be important in the recovery of a person with an anxiety disorder. Ideally, the family should be supportive but not help perpetuate their loved one's symptoms.

Medications

Medication does not cure anxiety disorders but often relieves symptoms. Medication can only be prescribed by a medical doctor (such as a psychiatrist or a primary care provider), but a few states allow psychologists to prescribe psychiatric medications. Medications are sometimes used as the initial treatment of an anxiety disorder, or are used only if there is insufficient response to a course of psychotherapy.

In research studies, it is common for patients treated with a combination of psychotherapy and medication to have better outcomes than those treated with only one or the other. The most common classes of medications used to combat anxiety disorders are antidepressants, antianxiety drugs, and beta-blockers. Be aware that some medications are effective only if they are taken regularly and those symptoms may recur if the medication is stopped.

Antidepressants

Antidepressants are used to treat depression, but they also are helpful for treating anxiety disorders. They take several weeks to start working and may cause side effects such as headache, nausea, or difficulty sleeping. The side effects are usually not a problem for most people, especially if the dose starts off low and is increased slowly over time.

Note: Although antidepressants are safe and effective for many people, they may be risky for children, teens, and young adults. A "black box" warning—the most serious type of warning that a prescription can carry—has been added to the labels of antidepressants. The labels now warn that antidepressants may cause some people to have suicidal thoughts or make suicide attempts. For this reason, anyone taking an antidepressant should be monitored closely, especially when they first start taking the medication.

Antianxiety Medications

Antianxiety medications help reduce the symptoms of anxiety, panic attacks, or extreme fear and worry. The most common antianxiety medications are called benzodiazepines. Benzodiazepines are first-line treatments for generalized anxiety disorder. With panic disorder or social phobia (social anxiety disorder), benzodiazepines are usually second-line treatments, behind antidepressants.

Beta-Blockers

Beta-blockers, such as propranolol and atenolol, are also helpful in the treatment of the physical symptoms of anxiety, especially social anxiety. Physicians prescribe them to control rapid heartbeat, shaking, trembling, and blushing in anxious situations. Choosing the right medication, medication dose, and treatment plan should be based on a person's needs and medical situation, and done under an expert's care. Only an expert clinician can help you decide whether the medication's ability to help is worth the risk of a side effect. Your doctor may try several medicines before finding the right one. You and your doctor should discuss:

- How well medications are working or might work to improve your symptoms
- Benefits and side effects of each medication
- Risk for serious side effects based on your medical history
- The likelihood of the medications requiring lifestyle changes
- Costs of each medication
- Other alternative therapies, medications, vitamins, and supplements you are taking and how these may affect your treatment
- How the medication should be stopped. Some drugs can't be stopped abruptly but must be tapered off slowly under a doctor's supervision.

Join a Study

Clinical trials are research studies that look at new ways to prevent, detect, or treat diseases and conditions, including anxiety disorders. During clinical trials, treatments might be new drugs or new combinations of drugs, new surgical procedures or devices, or new ways to use existing treatments. The goal of clinical trials is to determine if a new test or treatment works and is safe. Although individual participants may benefit from being part of a clinical trial, participants should be aware that the primary purpose of a clinical trial is to gain new scientific knowledge so that others may be better helped in the future.

Note: Decisions about whether to apply for a clinical trial and which ones are best suited for a given individual are best made in collaboration with your licensed health professional.

Clinical Trials at National Institutes of Health (NIH)

Scientists at the National Institutes of Health (NIH) campus conduct research on numerous areas of study, including cognition, genetics, epidemiology, and psychiatry. The studies take place at NIH Clinical Center (CC) in Bethesda, Maryland, and require regular visits. After the initial phone interview, you will come to an appointment at the clinic and meet with a clinician.

How Do I Find a Clinical Trial Near Me?

To find a clinical trial near you, you can visit ClinicalTrials.gov (www.clinicaltrials.gov). This is a searchable registry and results database of federally and privately supported clinical trials conducted in the United States and around the world. ClinicalTrials.gov gives you information about a trial's purpose, who may participate, locations, and phone numbers. This information should be used in conjunction with advice from health professionals.

Chapter 44

Treating Bipolar Disorder

Bipolar disorder, also known as manic-depression, is a treatable psychiatric disorder marked by extreme changes in mood, thoughts, behaviors, activity, and sleep. A person with bipolar disorder will experience intense emotional states or "mood episodes," shifting from mania to depression. The ups and downs experienced by someone with bipolar disorder are very different from the normal ups and downs that most people experience from time to time. These changes in mood can last for hours, days, weeks, or months. In between these extremes, the person's mood may be normal.

Treatment

There are a variety of medications and therapies available to those suffering from bipolar disorder. Medications can help reduce symptoms and are recommended as the first-line treatment for bipolar disorder. Individuals with bipolar disorder can also learn to manage their symptoms and improve their functioning with psychosocial treatment and rehabilitation. Research has shown that the treatments listed here are effective for people with bipolar disorder. They are considered to be evidence-based practice.

This chapter includes text excerpted from "What Is Bipolar Disorder?" U.S. Department of Veterans Affairs (VA), July 15, 2014. Reviewed June 2018.

Medication

Mood stabilizers, antipsychotic, and antidepressant medications are frequently utilized in the treatment of bipolar disorder.

Psychoeducation

Psychoeducation provides patients with an understanding of their illness and the most effective ways of treating symptoms and preventing relapse. Psychoeducation covers topics such as the nature and course of bipolar disorder, the importance of active involvement in treatment, the potential benefits and adverse effects of various treatment options, identification of early signs of relapse, and behavior changes that reduce the likelihood of relapse.

Cognitive Behavioral Therapy (CBT)

Cognitive behavioral therapy (CBT) is a blend of two therapies: cognitive therapy and behavioral therapy. Cognitive therapy focuses on a person's thoughts and beliefs and how they influence a person's mood and actions. CBT aims to change a person's way of thinking to be more adaptive and healthy. Behavioral therapy focuses on a person's actions and aims to change unhealthy behavior patterns. CBT is used as an adjunct to medical treatment and includes psychoeducation about the disorder as well as problem-solving techniques.

Individuals learn to identify what triggers episodes of the illness, which can reduce the chance of relapse. This can help individuals with bipolar disorder minimize the types of stress that can lead to a hospitalization. CBT also helps individuals learn how to identify maladaptive thoughts, logically challenge them, and replace them with more adaptive thoughts. CBT further targets depressive symptoms by encouraging patients to schedule pleasurable activities. Individuals who receive both CBT and medication treatment have better outcomes than those who do not receive CBT as an adjunctive treatment. CBT may be done one-on-one or in a group setting.

Interpersonal and Social Rhythm Therapy (IPSRT)

In interpersonal and social rhythm therapy (IPSRT), patients first learn to recognize the relationship between their circadian rhythms and daily routines, and their mental health symptoms. IPSRT then focuses on stabilizing sleep/wake cycles, maintaining regular patterns of daily activities (i.e., sleeping, eating, exercise, and other stimulating activities), and addressing potential problems that may disrupt these routines. This often involves resolving current interpersonal problems and developing strategies to prevent such problems from recurring in the future. When combined with medication, IPSRT can help individuals increase their targeted lifestyle routines and reduce both depressive and manic symptoms.

Family-Based Services

Mental illness affects the whole family. Family services teach families to work together towards recovery. In family-based services, the family and clinician meet to discuss problems the family is experiencing. Families then attend educational sessions where they will learn basic facts about mental illness, coping skills, communication skills, problem-solving skills, and ways to work with one another toward recovery.

Individuals with bipolar disorder who participate in family interventions along with taking medication have fewer relapses, longer time between relapses, better medication adherence, less severe mood symptoms, and increased positive communication between family members. There is a range of family programs available to fit the specific needs of each family. Some families benefit from just a few sessions, while more intensive services are especially helpful for families that are experiencing high levels of stress and tension and for individuals with bipolar disorder who are chronically symptomatic or prone to relapse. Generally, these longer-term interventions last 6–9 months and can be conducted in single family or multi-family formats.

Social Skills Training (SST)

Many people with bipolar disorder have difficulties with social skills. Social skills training (SST) aims to correct these deficits by teaching skills to help express emotion and communicate more effectively so individuals are more likely to achieve their goals, develop relationships, and live independently. Social skills are taught in a very systematic way using behavioral techniques, such as modeling, role-playing, positive reinforcement, and shaping.

Illness Self-Management

Components of illness self-management include psychoeducation, coping skills training, relapse prevention, and social skills training. Individuals learn about their psychiatric illness, their treatment choices, medication adherence strategies, and coping skills to deal with stress and symptoms. Relapse prevention involves recognizing situations that might trigger symptoms, tracking warning signs and symptoms of relapse, and developing a plan to cope with triggers and warning signs to prevent relapse. This treatment approach also teaches individuals social skills in order to improve the quality of their relationships with others.

Assertive Community Treatment (ACT)

Assertive community treatment (ACT) is an approach that is most effective for individuals with the greatest service needs, such as those with a history of multiple hospitalizations or those who are homeless. In ACT, the person receives treatment from an interdisciplinary team of usually 10–12 professionals, including case managers, a psychiatrist, several nurses and social workers, vocational specialists, substance abuse treatment specialists, and peer specialists.

The team provides coverage 24 hours a day, 7 days per week, and limits caseloads to ensure a high staff to client ratio, usually 1 staff member for every 10 clients. Services provided in ACT include: case management, comprehensive treatment planning, crisis intervention, medication management, individual supportive therapy, substance abuse treatment, rehabilitation services (e.g., supported employment), and peer support. The U.S. Department of Veterans Affairs (VA) version of this program is called Mental Health Intensive Case Management (MHICM).

Psychosocial Interventions for Alcohol and Substance Use Disorders (SUDs)

Many individuals with bipolar disorder also struggle with an alcohol or substance use disorder. Co-occurring disorders are best treated concurrently, meaning that treatment for bipolar disorder should be integrated with the treatment for the alcohol or drug problem. Integrated treatment includes motivational enhancement and cognitive behavioral interventions. Integrated treatments are effective at reducing substance use, preventing relapse, and keeping individuals in treatment longer. These interventions can be delivered one-on-one or in a group format.

Supported Employment

Research shows that about 70 percent of adults with severe mental illness want to work and about 60 percent can be successfully employed through supported employment. Supported employment is a program designed to help people with severe mental illness find and keep competitive employment. The approach is characterized by a focus on competitive work, a rapid job search without prevocational training, and continued support once a job is obtained. Employment specialists work with individuals to identify their career goals and skills. Case managers and mental health providers work closely with employment specialist to provide support during the job seeking and keeping process.

Psychosocial Interventions for Weight Management

Weight gain is a significant and frustrating side effect of some medications used to treat the symptoms of bipolar disorder. Weight gain can lead to problems such as diabetes and hypertension, making it a serious health issue for many individuals. Resources to support weight loss are available. Weight programs generally last 3 months or longer and include education about nutrition and portion control. Participants learn skills to monitor their daily food intake and activity levels, have regular weigh-ins, and set realistic and attainable personal wellness goals. Participation in such a program can help prevent additional weight gain and lead to modest weight loss. The VA's version of this program is called MOVE! It is offered in a supportive group setting.

Mood Stabilizers: What You Should Know

- Bipolar disorder is regarded as a medical disorder (like diabetes). Mood stabilizers are usually the first choice to treat bipolar disorder. Except for lithium, many of these medications are anticonvulsants. Anticonvulsant medications are usually used to treat seizures, but they also help control mood.
- Research has found that mood stabilizers are effective for treating the symptoms of bipolar disorder, but it is not clear exactly how they work. Brain chemicals called neurotransmitters (chemical messengers) are believed to regulate mood. It is thought that lithium may affect the activity of two of these neurotransmitters, serotonin and dopamine. Anticonvulsants are believed to work by increasing the neurotransmitter, GABA (gamma-Aminobutyric acid), which has a calming effect on the brain. It is also believed that they decrease glutamate, which is an excitatory neurotransmitter.

- All mood-stabilizing medications must be taken as prescribed. After achieving the desired, effective dose of a mood stabilizer, it may take an additional 1–2 weeks before you can expect to see improvement in manic symptoms. It may take up to 4 weeks for depressive symptoms to lessen. It is important that you don't stop taking your medication because you think it's not working. Give it time!
- You and your doctor have a lot of choices of medications, and it is hard to know which one may work best for you. Sometimes the mood-stabilizing medication you first try may not lead to improvements in symptoms. This is because each person's brain chemistry is unique; what works well for one person may not do as well for another. Be open to trying a different medication or combination of medications in order to find a good fit. Let your doctor know if your symptoms have not improved or have worsened, and do not give up searching for the right medication!
- Once you have responded to medication treatment, it is important to continue taking your medication as prescribed. In general, it is necessary for individuals with bipolar disorder to continue taking mood-stabilizing medications for extended periods of time (at least 2 years). Discontinuing treatment earlier may lead to a relapse of symptoms if you have had a number of episodes of mania or depression, your doctor may recommend longer-term treatment. If episodes of mania or depression occur while on mood stabilizers, your doctor may add other medications to be taken for shorter periods of time. To prevent symptoms from returning or worsening, do not abruptly stop taking your medications, even if you are feeling better, as this may result in a relapse. You should only stop taking your medication under your doctor's supervision. If you want to stop taking your medication, talk to your doctor about how to correctly stop.
- Here is a safe rule of thumb if you miss a dose of your mood-stabilizing medication: if it has been 3 hours or less from the time you were supposed to take your medication, take your medication. If it has been more than 3 hours after the dose should have been taken, just skip the forgotten dose and resume taking your medication at the next regularly scheduled time. Never double up on doses of your mood stabilizer to "catch up" on those you have forgotten.

- Mood-stabilizing medications can interact with other medications to create potentially serious health consequences. Be sure to tell your doctor about all the medications you are taking, including prescription medications, over-the-counter (OTC) medications, herbal supplements, vitamins, and minerals.
- Like all medications, mood-stabilizing medications can have side effects. In many cases, these side effects are mild and tend to diminish with time. Many people have few or no side effects, and the side effects people typically experience are tolerable and subside within a few days. Your doctor will discuss some common side effects with you. Check with your doctor if any of the common side effects persist or become bothersome. If you experience side effects, talk to your doctor before making any decisions about discontinuing treatment.
- In rare cases, these medications can cause severe side effects. Contact your doctor immediately if you experience one or more severe symptoms.

Mood-Stabilizing Medications

- Lithium (Eskalith or Lithobid)
- Valproate/Valproic Acid/Divalproex Sodium (Depakote or Depakene)
- Carbamazepine (Equetro or Tegretol)
- Lamotrigine (Lamictal)
- Oxcarbazepine (Trileptal)
- Gabapentin (Fanatrex, Gabarone, Horizant, or Neurontin)
- Topiramate (Topamax or Topiragen)

Side Effects of Lithium

Common side effects of lithium: acne; fine hand tremor; increased thirst; nausea; low thyroid hormone (associated with brittle hair, low energy, and sensitivity to cold temperatures); rash; weight gain.

Lithium toxicity is a serious condition caused by having too much lithium in your system. For this reason, your doctor will require you to do periodic blood tests to ensure that lithium is not impacting your kidney or thyroid functioning. In addition, use of certain pain medications (such as ibuprofen) or physical activity with significant sweating can cause your lithium level to increase.

You should talk to your doctor about how to exercise safely. Some signs of lithium toxicity include new onset of nausea, vomiting, diarrhea, headache, loss of coordination, slurred speech, nystagmus (abnormal eye movements), dizziness, seizure, confusion, increased thirst, and worsening tremors. You should contact your doctor right away if you experience any of these symptoms.

Side Effects of Anticonvulsants

Common side effects of anticonvulsants: appetite change; dizziness; double vision; headache; irritability; loss of balance/coordination; nausea; sedation; vomiting; weight gain or loss. Lamotrigine and Carbamazepine may affect white blood cells, the liver, and other organs. Individuals prescribed these medications will need to have their blood checked periodically to make sure the medications are not impacting their organs in a negative way.

Lamotrigine and Carbamazepine can also cause a serious skin rash that should be reported to your doctor immediately. In some cases, this rash can cause permanent disability or be life threatening. The risk for getting this rash can be minimized by very slowly increasing your dose of lamotrigine. This rash occurs to a lesser extent with Carbamazepine although the risk is higher for individuals of Asian ancestry, including South Asian Indians. Anticonvulsant medications may increase suicidal thinking and behaviors. Close monitoring for new or worsening symptoms of depression, suicidal thoughts or behavior, or any unusual changes in mood or behavior is advised.

Antipsychotic Medications: What You Should Know

- Antipsychotic medications are sometimes used for treatment when individuals are in a manic episode or a depressive episode. They vary in their effectiveness for treating these episodes. Your doctor will help you choose the best one for you.
- All antipsychotic medications must be taken as prescribed. Their effects can sometimes be noticed within the same day of the first dose. However, the full benefit of the medication may not be realized until after a few weeks of treatment. It is important that you don't stop taking your medication because you think it's not working. Give it time!

- Like mood stabilizers, the antipsychotic medication you try first may not lead to improvements in symptoms. It may be necessary to try another medication or combination of medications. Talk to your doctor if your symptoms do not improve.
- Once you have responded to treatment, it is important to continue taking your medication as prescribed to prevent your symptoms from coming back or worsening. Do not abruptly stop taking your medications, even if you are feeling better as this may result in a relapse. Medication should only be stopped under your doctor's supervision. If you want to stop taking your medication, talk to your doctor about how to correctly stop.
- Most antipsychotics are prescribed once daily. If you forget to take your medication, do not double up the next day to "catch up" on the dose you missed. If your medication is prescribed to be taken twice a day, and you forget to take a dose, a rule of thumb is: if it has been 6 hours or less from the time you were supposed to take your medication, go ahead and take your medication. If it is more than 6 hours after the missed dose should have been taken, just skip the forgotten dose and resume taking your medication at the next regularly scheduled time. Never double up on doses of your antipsychotic to "catch up" on those you have forgotten.
- Some antipsychotic medications are available as long-acting injectables. Use of injectable medications is one strategy that can be used for individuals who regularly forget to take their medication.
- Like all medications, antipsychotic medications can have side effects. In many cases, they are mild and tend to diminish with time. Many people have few or no side effects, and the side effects people typically experience are tolerable and subside within a few days. Your doctor will discuss some common side effects with you. Check with your doctor if any of the common side effects persist or become bothersome. If you experience side effects, talk to your doctor before making any decisions about discontinuing treatment.
- In rare cases, these medications can cause severe side effects. Contact your doctor immediately if you experience one or more severe symptoms.

Antipsychotic Medications

These are sometimes referred to as conventional, typical or first-generation antipsychotic medications:

- Chlorpromazine (Thorazine)
- Fluphenazine (Prolixin)
- Haloperidol (Haldol)
- Loxapine (Loxitane or Loxapac)
- Perphenazine (Trilafon)
- Thiothixene (Navane)
- Trifluoperazine (Stelazine)

These are sometimes referred to as atypical or second-generation antipsychotic medications:

- Aripiprazole (Abilify)
- Asenapine (Saphris)
- Clozapine (Clozaril)
- Iloperidone (Fanapt)
- Lurasidone (Latuda)
- Olanzapine (Zyprexa)
- Paliperidone (Invega)
- Quetiapine (Seroquel)
- Risperidone (Risperdal)
- Ziprasidone (Geodon)

Long-Acting Injectable Antipsychotic Medications

Certain antipsychotic medications are available as long-acting injectables. These medications are given every two to four weeks. Some patients find these more convenient because they don't have to take the medications daily. The side effects of these medications are similar to their oral counterparts.

- Fluphenazine (Prolixin decanoate)
- Haloperidol (Haldol decanoate)

- Olanzapine (Zyprexa Relprevv)
- Paliperidone (Sustena)
- Risperidone (Risperdal Consta)

Side Effects of Antipsychotic Medications

Some individuals experience side effects that mimic symptoms of Parkinson disease (PD), which are called parkinsonian or extrapyramidal symptoms. These include tremor, shuffling walk, and muscle stiffness. A related side effect is akathisia, which is a feeling of internal restlessness. Additionally, prolonged use of antipsychotics may cause tardive dyskinesia, a condition marked by involuntary muscle movements in the face and body.

An uncommon, but serious side effect is called neuroleptic malignant syndrome (NMS). These symptoms include high fever, muscle rigidity, and irregular heart rate or blood pressure. Contact your doctor immediately if any of these symptoms appear. People taking antipsychotic medications can also experience a variety of other side effects including: unusual dreams; blank facial expression; blurred vision; breast enlargement or pain; breast milk production; constipation; decreased sexual performance in men; diarrhea; dizziness or fainting when you sit up or stand up; difficulty urinating; drowsiness; dry mouth; excessive saliva; missed menstrual periods; mood changes; nausea; nervousness; restlessness and sensitivity to the sun.

Weight gain, changes in blood sugar regulation, and changes in blood levels of lipids (cholesterol and triglycerides) are common with some antipsychotics. Therefore, your doctor will check your weight and blood chemistry on a regular basis. If you have a scale at home, it would be helpful to regularly check your own weight. Each of these medications differs in their risk of causing these side effects. If you start to gain weight, talk to your doctor. It may be recommended that you switch medications or begin a diet and exercise program.

Clozapine can cause agranulocytosis, which is a loss of the white blood cells that help a person fight off infection. Therefore, people who take clozapine must get their white blood cell counts checked frequently. This very serious condition is reversible if clozapine is discontinued. Despite this serious side effect, clozapine remains the most effective antipsychotic available and can be used safely if monitoring occurs at the appropriate time intervals.

Antidepressant Medications: What You Should Know

- Antidepressant medications are sometimes used to treat symptoms of depression in bipolar disorder. Individuals who are prescribed antidepressants are usually required to take a mood-stabilizing medication at the same time to reduce the risk of switching from depression to mania or hypomania.
- Research has found that antidepressants are effective for treating depression, but it is not clear exactly how they work. Brain chemicals called neurotransmitters (chemical messengers) are believed to regulate mood. Antidepressant medications work to increase the following neurotransmitters: serotonin, norepinephrine, and/or dopamine.
- All antidepressants must be taken as prescribed for 3–4 weeks before you can expect to see positive changes in your symptoms. It is important that you don't stop taking your medication because you think it's not working. Give it time!
- Like mood stabilizers, the antidepressant you try first may not lead to improvements in mood. It may be necessary to try another medication or combination of medications. Talk to your doctor if your symptoms do not improve.
- Once you have responded to treatment, it is important to continue taking your medication to prevent your symptoms from coming back or worsening. Do not abruptly stop taking your medication, even if you are feeling better, as this may result in a relapse. Medication should only be stopped under your doctor's supervision. If you want to stop taking your medication, talk to your doctor about how to correctly stop.
- Here is a safe rule of thumb if you miss a dose of your antidepressant medication: if it has been 3 hours or less from the time you were supposed to take your medication, take your medication. If it has been more than 3 hours after the dose should have been taken, just skip the forgotten dose and resume taking your medication at the next regularly scheduled time. Never double up on doses of your antidepressant to "catch up" on those you have forgotten.
- Like all medications, antidepressants can have side effects. In many cases, they are mild and tend to diminish with time. Many people have few or no side effects, and the side effects people typically experience are tolerable and subside within a few days.

Your doctor will discuss some common side effects with you. Check with your doctor if any of the common side effects persist or become bothersome. If you experience side effects, talk to your doctor before making any decisions about discontinuing treatment. In rare cases, these medications can cause severe side effects. Contact your doctor immediately if you experience one or more severe symptoms.

- There are five different classes of antidepressant medications.

Antidepressant Class 1: Selective Serotonin Reuptake Inhibitors (SSRIs)

SSRIs are the most commonly prescribed class of antidepressants because they tend to have the fewest side effects. SSRIs increase the level of serotonin by inhibiting reuptake of the neurotransmitter.

- Fluoxetine (Prozac)
- Citalopram (Celexa)
- Sertraline (Zoloft)
- Paroxetine (Paxil)
- Escitalopram (Lexapro)

Common side effects for SSRIs: abnormal dreams; anxiety; blurred vision; constipation; decreased sexual desire or ability; diarrhea; dizziness; drowsiness; dry mouth; flu-like symptoms (e.g., fever, chills, muscle aches); flushing; gas; increased sweating; increased urination; lightheadedness when you stand or sit up; loss of appetite; nausea; nervousness; runny nose; sore throat; stomach upset; stuffy nose; tiredness; trouble concentrating; trouble sleeping; yawning; vomiting; weight loss.

Antidepressant Class 2: Serotonin and Norepinephrine Reuptake Inhibitors (SNRIs)

SNRIs are similar to SSRIs in that they increase levels of serotonin in the brain. They also increase norepinephrine in the brain to improve mood.

- Venlafaxine (Effexor)
- Duloxetine (Cymbalta)
- Desvenlafaxine (Pristiq)

Common side effects for SNRIs: anxiety; blurred vision; changes in taste; constipation; decreased sexual desire or ability; diarrhea; dizziness; drowsiness; dry mouth; fatigue; flushing; headache; increased sweating; loss of appetite; nausea; nervousness; sore throat; stomach upset; trouble sleeping; vomiting; weakness; weight loss; yawning.

Antidepressant Class 3: Atypical Antidepressants

In addition to targeting serotonin and/or norepinephrine, atypical antidepressants may also target dopamine. They also tend to have fewer side effects than the older classes of medication listed below (antidepressant Classes 4 and 5). The common side effects differ for each of the medications in this class of antidepressants.

Bupropion (Wellbutrin)

Common side effects: Constipation; dizziness; drowsiness; dry mouth; headache; increased sweating; loss of appetite; nausea; nervousness; restlessness; taste changes; trouble sleeping; vomiting; weight changes.

Mirtazapine (Remeron)

Common side effects: Constipation; dizziness; dry mouth; fatigue; increased appetite; low blood pressure; sedation; weight gain.

Trazodone (Desyrel)

Common side effects: blurred vision; constipation; decreased appetite; dizziness; drowsiness; dry mouth; general body discomfort; headache; light-headedness; muscle aches/pains; nausea; nervousness; sleeplessness; stomach pain; stuffy nose; swelling of the skin; tiredness; tremors.

Nefazodone (Serzone)

Common side effects: abnormal dreams; abnormal skin sensations; changes in taste; chills; confusion; constipation; decreased concentration; decreased sex drive; diarrhea; dizziness; drowsiness; dry mouth; fever; frequent urination; headache; incoordination; increased appetite; increased cough; indigestion; lightheadedness; memory loss; mental confusion; ringing in the ears; sleeplessness; sore throat; swelling of the hands and feet; tremor; urinary retention; urinary tract infection; vaginal infection; weakness.

Antidepressant Class 4: Tricyclics and Tetracyclics (TCAs and TECAs)

This is an older class of antidepressants that also work by increasing levels of serotonin and norepinephrine in the brain. These medications are good alternatives if the newer medications are ineffective.

- Amitriptyline (Elavil or Endep)
- Amoxapine (Asendin)
- Clomipramine (Anafranil)
- Desipramine (Norpramin or Pertofrane)
- Doxepin (Sinequan or Adapin)
- Imipramine (Tofranil)
- Nortriptyline (Pamelor)
- Protriptyline (Vivactil)
- Trimipramine (Surmontil)
- Maprotiline (Ludiomil)

Common side effects for the TCAs: abnormal dreams; anxiety or nervousness; blurred vision; change in appetite or weight; changes in blood pressure; change in sexual desire or ability; clumsiness; confusion; constipation; decreased memory or concentration; dizziness; drowsiness; dry mouth; excess sweating; excitement; headache; heartburn; indigestion; nausea; nightmares; pounding in the chest; pupil dilation; restlessness; sleeplessness; stuffy nose; swelling; tiredness; tremors; trouble sleeping; upset stomach; urinary retention; vomiting; weakness.

Antidepressant Class 5: Monoamine Oxidase Inhibitors (MAOIs)

MAOIs are an older class of antidepressants that are not frequently used because of the need to follow a special diet to avoid potential side effects. However, these medications can be very effective. These drugs work by blocking an enzyme called monoamine oxidase, which breaks down the brain chemicals serotonin, norepinephrine, and dopamine.

When taking MAOIs, it is important to follow a low "tyramine" diet, which avoids foods such as cheeses, pickles, and alcohol, and to avoid some over-the-counter (OTC) cold medications. Most people can adopt to a low tyramine diet without much difficulty. Your doctor will provide a complete list of all food, drinks, and medications to avoid.

- Phenelzine (Nardil)
- Tranylcypromine (Parnate)
- Selegiline (Emsam) patch

Common side effects for MAO/MAOIs: blurred vision; changes in sexual function; diarrhea, gas, constipation, or upset stomach; difficulty swallowing or heartburn; dizziness, lightheadedness or fainting; drowsiness; dry mouth; headache; nausea, muscle pain or weakness; purple blotches on the skin; rash, redness, irritation, or sores in the mouth (if you are taking the orally disintegrating tablets); sleeping problems; stomach pain, tiredness; tremors; twitching; unusual muscle movements; vomiting, unusual dreams; upset stomach; weakness.

Chapter 45

Coping with Traumatic Stress Reactions

What Is a Traumatic Event?[1]

Most everyone has been through a stressful event in his or her life. When the event, or series of events, causes a lot of stress, it is called a traumatic event. Traumatic events are marked by a sense of horror, helplessness, serious injury, or the threat of serious injury or death. Traumatic events affect survivors, rescue workers, and the friends and relatives of victims who have been involved. They may also have an impact on people who have seen the event either firsthand or on television.

What Are Some Common Responses?[1]

A person's response to a traumatic event may vary. Responses include feelings of fear, grief and depression. Physical and behavioral responses include nausea, dizziness, and changes in appetite and sleep pattern as well as withdrawal from daily activities. Responses

---

This chapter includes text excerpted from documents published by two public domain sources. Text under headings marked 1 are excerpted from "Coping with a Traumatic Event," Centers for Disease Control and Prevention (CDC), March 1, 2003. Reviewed June 2018; Text under headings marked 2 are excerpted from "Coping with Traumatic Stress Reactions," U.S. Department of Veterans Affairs (VA), August 14, 2015.

to trauma can last for weeks to months before people start to feel normal again.

Most people report feeling better within three months after a traumatic event. If the problems become worse or last longer than one month after the event, the person may be suffering from posttraumatic stress disorder (PTSD).

Know That Recovery Is a Process[2]

Following exposure to a trauma most people experience stress reactions. Understand that recovering from the trauma is a process and takes time. Knowing this will help you feel more in control.

- Having an ongoing response to the trauma is normal.
- Recovery is an ongoing, daily process. It happens little by little. It is not a matter of being cured all of a sudden.
- Healing doesn't mean forgetting traumatic events. It doesn't mean you will have no pain or bad feelings when thinking about them.
- Healing may mean fewer symptoms and symptoms that bother you less.
- Healing means more confidence that you will be able to cope with your memories and symptoms. You will be better able to manage your feelings.

Positive Coping Actions[2]

Certain actions can help to reduce your distressing symptoms and make things better. Plus, these actions can result in changes that last into the future. Here are some positive coping methods:

Learn about Trauma and Posttraumatic Stress Disorder (PTSD)

It is useful for trauma survivors to learn more about common reactions to trauma and about posttraumatic stress disorder (PTSD). Find out what is normal. Find out what the signs are that you may need assistance from others. When you learn that the symptoms of PTSD are common, you realize that you are not alone, weak, or crazy. It helps to know your problems are shared by hundreds of thousands of others.

When you seek treatment and begin to understand your response to trauma, you will be better able to cope with the symptoms of PTSD.

Talk to Others for Support

When survivors talk about their problems with others, something helpful often results. It is important not to isolate yourself. Instead make efforts to be with others. Of course, you must choose your support people with care. You must also ask them clearly for what you need. With support from others, you may feel less alone and more understood. You may also get concrete help with a problem you have.

Practice Relaxation Methods

Try some different ways to relax, including:

- Muscle relaxation exercises
- Breathing exercises
- Meditation
- Swimming, stretching, yoga
- Prayer
- Listening to quiet music
- Spending time in nature

While relaxation techniques can be helpful, in a few people they can sometimes increase distress at first. This can happen when you focus attention on disturbing physical sensations and you reduce contact with the outside world. Most often, continuing with relaxation in small amounts that you can handle will help reduce negative reactions. You may want to try mixing relaxation in with music, walking, or other activities.

Distract Yourself with Positive Activities

Pleasant recreational or work activities help distract a person from his or her memories and reactions. For example, art has been a way for many trauma survivors to express their feelings in a positive, creative way. Pleasant activities can improve your mood, limit the harm caused by PTSD, and help you rebuild your life.

Talking to Your Doctor or a Counselor about Trauma and PTSD

Part of taking care of yourself means using the helping resources around you. If efforts at coping don't seem to work, you may become fearful or depressed. If your PTSD symptoms don't begin to go away or get worse over time, it is important to reach out and call a counselor who can help turn things around. Your family doctor can also refer you to a specialist who can treat PTSD. Talk to your doctor about your trauma and your PTSD symptoms. That way, he or she can take care of your health better. Many with PTSD have found treatment with medicines to be helpful for some symptoms. By taking medicines, some survivors of trauma are able to improve their sleep, anxiety, irritability, and anger. It can also reduce urges to drink or use drugs.

Coping with the Symptoms of Posttraumatic Stress Disorder (PTSD)[2]

Here are some direct ways to cope with these specific PTSD symptoms:

Unwanted Distressing Memories, Images, or Thoughts

- Remind yourself that they are just that, memories.
- Remind yourself that it's natural to have some memories of the trauma(s).
- Talk about them to someone you trust.
- Remember that, although reminders of trauma can feel overwhelming, they often lessen with time.

Sudden Feelings of Anxiety or Panic

Traumatic stress reactions often include feeling your heart pounding and feeling lightheaded or spacey. This is usually caused by rapid breathing. If this happens, remember that:

- These reactions are not dangerous. If you had them while exercising, they most likely would not worry you.
- These feelings often come with scary thoughts that are not true. For example, you may think, "I'm going to die," "I'm having a heart attack," or "I will lose control." It is the scary thoughts that make these reactions so upsetting.

- Slowing down your breathing may help
- The sensations will pass soon and then you can go on with what you were doing

Each time you respond in these positive ways to your anxiety or panic, you will be working toward making it happen less often. Practice will make it easier to cope.

Feeling Like the Trauma Is Happening Again (Flashbacks)

- Keep your eyes open. Look around you and notice where you are.
- Talk to yourself. Remind yourself where you are, what year you're in, and that you are safe. The trauma happened in the past, and you are in the present.
- Get up and move around. Have a drink of water and wash your hands.
- Call someone you trust and tell them what is happening
- Remind yourself that this is a common response after trauma
- Tell your counselor or doctor about the flashback(s)

Dreams and Nightmares Related to the Trauma

- If you wake up from a nightmare in a panic, remind yourself that you are reacting to a dream. Having the dream is why you are in a panic, not because there is real danger now.
- You may want to get up out of bed, regroup, and orient yourself to the here and now
- Engage in a pleasant, calming activity. For example, listen to some soothing music.
- Talk to someone if possible
- Talk to your doctor about your nightmares. Certain medicines can be helpful.

Difficulty Falling or Staying Asleep

- Keep to a regular bedtime schedule.
- Avoid heavy exercise for the few hours just before going to bed.

- Avoid using your sleeping area for anything other than sleeping or sex
- Avoid alcohol, tobacco, and caffeine. These harm your ability to sleep.
- Do not lie in bed thinking or worrying. Get up and enjoy something soothing or pleasant. Read a calming book, drink a glass of warm milk or herbal tea, or do a quiet hobby.

Irritability, Anger, and Rage

- Take a time out to cool off or think things over. Walk away from the situation.
- Get in the habit of exercise daily. Exercise reduces body tension and relieves stress.
- Remember that staying angry doesn't work. It actually increases your stress and can cause health problems.
- Talk to your counselor or doctor about your anger. Take classes in how to manage anger.
- If you blow up at family members or friends, find time as soon as you can to talk to them about it. Let them know how you feel and what you are doing to cope with your reactions.

Difficulty Concentrating or Staying Focused

- Slow down. Give yourself time to focus on what it is you need to learn or do.
- Write things down. Making "to do" lists may be helpful.
- Break tasks down into small doable chunks
- Plan a realistic number of events or tasks for each day
- You may be depressed. Many people who are depressed have trouble concentrating. Again, this is something you can discuss with your counselor, doctor, or someone close to you.

Trouble Feeling or Expressing Positive Emotions

- Remember that this is a common reaction to trauma. You are not doing this on purpose. You should not feel guilty for something you do not want to happen and cannot control.

- Make sure to keep taking part in activities that you enjoy or used to enjoy. Even if you don't think you will enjoy something, once you get into it, you may well start having feelings of pleasure.
- Take steps to let your loved ones know that you care. You can express your caring in little ways: write a card, leave a small gift, or phone someone and say hello.

When Should You Contact Your Doctor or Mental Health Professional?[1]

About half of those with PTSD recover within three months without treatment. Sometimes symptoms do not go away on their own or they last for more than three months. This may happen because of the severity of the event, direct exposure to the traumatic event, seriousness of the threat to life, the number of times an event happened, a history of past trauma, and psychological problems before the event.

You may need to consider seeking professional help if your symptoms are severe enough during the first month to interfere a lot with your family, friends, and job. If you suspect that you or someone you know has PTSD talk with a healthcare provider or call your local mental health clinic.

Chapter 46

Treating PTSD

Chapter Contents

Section 46.1

Helping a Family Member Who Has PTSD

This section includes text excerpted from "Helping a Family Member Who Has PTSD," U.S. Department of Veteran Affairs (VA), August 13, 2015.

When someone has posttraumatic stress disorder (PTSD), it can change family life. The person with PTSD may act differently and get angry easily. He or she may not want to do things you used to enjoy together. You may feel scared and frustrated about the changes you see in your loved one. You also may feel angry about what's happening to your family, or wonder if things will ever go back to the way they were. These feelings and worries are common in people who have a family member with PTSD. It is important to learn about PTSD so you can understand why it happened, how it is treated, and what you can do to help. But you also need to take care of yourself. Changes in family life are stressful, and taking care of yourself will make it easier to cope.

How Can I Help?

You may feel helpless, but there are many things you can do. Nobody expects you to have all the answers.

Here are ways you can help:

- Learn as much as you can about PTSD. Knowing how PTSD affects people may help you understand what your family member is going through. The more you know, the better you and your family can handle PTSD.
- Offer to go to doctor visits with your family member. You can help keep track of medicine and therapy, and you can be there for support.
- Tell your loved one you want to listen and that you also understand if he or she doesn't feel like talking.
- Plan family activities together, like having dinner or going to a movie.
- Take a walk, go for a bike ride, or do some other physical activity together. Exercise is important for health and helps clear your mind.

- Encourage contact with family and close friends. A support system will help your family member get through difficult changes and stressful times.

Your family member may not want your help. If this happens, keep in mind that withdrawal can be a symptom of PTSD. A person who withdraws may not feel like talking, taking part in group activities, or being around other people. Give your loved one space, but tell him or her that you will always be ready to help.

How Can I Deal with Anger or Violent Behavior?

Your family member may feel angry about many things. Anger is a normal reaction to trauma, but it can hurt relationships and make it hard to think clearly. Anger also can be frightening. If anger leads to violent behavior or abuse, it's dangerous. Go to a safe place and call for help right away. Make sure children are in a safe place as well. It's hard to talk to someone who is angry. One thing you can do is set up a time-out system. This helps you find a way to talk even while angry. Here's one way to do this:

- Agree that either of you can call a time-out at any time.
- Agree that when someone calls a time-out, the discussion must stop right then.
- Decide on a signal you will use to call a time-out. The signal can be a word that you say or a hand signal.
- Agree to tell each other where you will be and what you will be doing during the time-out. Tell each other what time you will come back.

While you are taking a time-out, don't focus on how angry you feel. Instead, think calmly about how you will talk things over and solve the problem.

After you come back:

- Take turns talking about solutions to the problem. Listen without interrupting.
- Use statements starting with "I" such as "I think" or "I feel." Using "you" statements can sound accusing.
- Be open to each other's ideas. Don't criticize each other.
- Focus on things you both think will work. It's likely you will both have good ideas.
- Together, agree which solutions you will use.

How Can I Communicate Better?

You and your family may have trouble talking about feelings, worries, and everyday problems. Here are some ways to communicate better:

- Be clear and to the point.
- Be positive. Blame and negative talk won't help the situation.
- Be a good listener. Don't argue or interrupt. Repeat what you hear to make sure you understand, and ask questions if you need to know more.
- Put your feelings into words. Your loved one may not know you are sad or frustrated unless you are clear about your feelings.
- Help your family member put feelings into words. Ask, "Are you feeling angry? Sad? Worried?"
- Ask how you can help.
- Don't give advice unless you are asked.

If your family is having a lot of trouble talking things over, consider trying family therapy. Family therapy is a type of counseling that involves your whole family. A therapist helps you and your family communicate, maintain good relationships, and cope with tough emotions. During therapy, each person can talk about how a problem is affecting the family. Family therapy can help family members understand and cope with PTSD. Your health professional or a religious or social services organization can help you find a family therapist who specializes in PTSD.

How Can I Take Care of Myself?

Helping a person with PTSD can be hard on you. You may have your own feelings of fear and anger about the trauma. You may feel guilty because you wish your family member would just forget his or her problems and get on with life. You may feel confused or frustrated because your loved one has changed, and you may worry that your family life will never get back to normal.

All of this can drain you. It can affect your health and make it hard for you to help your loved one. If you're not careful, you may get sick yourself, become depressed, or burn out and stop helping your loved one. To help yourself, you need to take care of yourself and have other people help you.

Care for yourself:

- Don't feel guilty or feel that you have to know it all. Remind yourself that nobody has all the answers. It's normal to feel helpless at times.
- Don't feel bad if things change slowly. You cannot change anyone. People have to change themselves.
- Take care of your physical and mental health. If you feel yourself getting sick or often feel sad and hopeless, see your doctor.
- Don't give up your outside life. Make time for activities and hobbies you enjoy. Continue to see your friends.
- Take time to be by yourself. Find a quiet place to gather your thoughts and "recharge."
- Get regular exercise, even just a few minutes a day. Exercise is a healthy way to deal with stress.
- Eat healthy foods. When you are busy, it may seem easier to eat fast food than to prepare healthy meals. But healthy foods will give you more energy to carry you through the day.
- Remember the good things. It's easy to get weighed down by worry and stress. But don't forget to see and celebrate the good things that happen to you and your family.

Get Help

During difficult times, it is important to have people in your life who you can depend on. These people are your support network. They can help you with everyday jobs, like taking a child to school, or by giving you love and understanding.

You may get support from:

- Family members
- Friends, coworkers, and neighbors
- Members of your religious or spiritual group
- Support groups
- Doctors and other health professionals

Section 46.2

PTSD Medication and Treatment

This section contains text excerpted from the following sources: Text under the heading "Medications for Posttraumatic Stress Disorder (PTSD) " is excerpted from "Medications for PTSD," U.S. Department of Veterans Affairs (VA), December 7, 2017; Text under the heading "Treatment of PTSD" is excerpted from "Treatment of PTSD," U.S. Department of Veterans Affairs (VA), August 18, 2017.

Medications for Posttraumatic Stress Disorder (PTSD)

Medications that have been shown to be helpful in treating posttraumatic stress disorder (PTSD) symptoms are some of the same medications also used for symptoms of depression and anxiety. These are antidepressants, called SSRIs (selective serotonin reuptake inhibitors) and SNRIs (serotonin-norepinephrine reuptake inhibitors).

The four antidepressants effective for treating PTSD are:

SSRIs:

- Sertraline (Zoloft)
- Paroxetine (Paxil)
- Fluoxetine (Prozac)

SNRIs:

- Venlafaxine (Effexor)

Note: Medications have two names: a brand name (for example, Zoloft) and a generic name (for example, Sertraline).

How Do They Work?

PTSD may be related to changes in the brain that are linked to our ability to manage stress. People with PTSD appear to have different amounts of certain chemicals (called neurotransmitters) in the brain than people without PTSD. SSRIs and SNRIs are believed to treat PTSD by putting these brain chemicals back in balance.

What Can I Expect?

To receive medications for PTSD, you'll need to meet with a provider who can prescribe these medications to you. Many different types of providers, including your family doctor and even some nurses and physician assistants, can prescribe antidepressant medications for PTSD. You and your provider can work together to decide which antidepressant medication may be best for you. In general, the four different SSRIs and SNRIs listed above appear to work equally well for PTSD.

Once you fill your prescription, you will begin taking a pill at regular time(s) each day. It may take a few weeks before you notice the effects of the medication. It is important to continue to take it even if you do not notice changes right away. You will meet with your provider every few months or so. Your provider will monitor your response to the medication (including side effects) and change your dose, if needed.

What Are the Risks?

The risks of taking SSRIs and SNRIs are mild to moderate side effects such as upset stomach, sweating, headache, and dizziness. Some people have sexual side effects, such as decreased desire to have sex or difficulty having an orgasm. Some side effects are short term, though others may last as long as you are taking the medication.

Will I Talk in Detail about My Trauma?

No, you will not need to talk about the details of your trauma. However, your provider may ask for some basic information about your trauma—like the type of trauma and when it happened—when you first meet.

Will I Have Homework?

No, you will just need to take your medication as prescribed.

How Long Does Treatment Last?

You may start to feel better in about 4–6 weeks. You will need to keep taking the medication to keep getting the benefits.

Treatment of PTSD

Effective treatments for PTSD include different types of psychotherapy (talk therapy) or medication.

Trauma-Focused Psychotherapies

Trauma-focused psychotherapies are the most highly recommended type of treatment for PTSD. "Trauma-focused" means that the treatment focuses on the memory of the traumatic event or its meaning. These treatments use different techniques to help you process your traumatic experience. Some involve visualizing, talking, or thinking about the traumatic memory. Others focus on changing unhelpful beliefs about the trauma. They usually last about 8–16 sessions. The trauma-focused psychotherapies with the strongest evidence are:

- **Prolonged exposure (PE).** Teaches you how to gain control by facing your negative feelings. It involves talking about your trauma with a provider and doing some of the things you have avoided since the trauma.
- **Cognitive processing therapy (CPT).** Teaches you to reframe negative thoughts about the trauma. It involves talking with your provider about your negative thoughts and doing short writing assignments.
- **Eye-movement desensitization and reprocessing (EMDR).** Helps you process and make sense of your trauma. It involves calling the trauma to mind while paying attention to a back-and-forth movement or sound (like a finger waving side to side, a light, or a tone).

There are other types of trauma-focused psychotherapy that are also recommended for people with PTSD. These include:

- **Brief eclectic psychotherapy (BEP).** A therapy in which you practice relaxation skills, recall details of the traumatic memory, reframe negative thoughts about the trauma, write a letter about the traumatic event, and hold a farewell ritual to leave trauma in the past.
- **Narrative exposure therapy (NET).** Developed for people who have experienced trauma from ongoing war, conflict, and organized violence. You talk through stressful life events in order (from birth to the present day) and put them together into a story.
- **Written narrative exposure.** Involves writing about the trauma during sessions. Your provider gives instructions on the writing assignment, allows you to complete the writing alone, and then returns at the end of the session to briefly discuss any reactions to the writing assignment.
- **Specific cognitive behavioral therapies (CBTs) for PTSD.** Include a limited number of psychotherapies shown to work

for PTSD where the provider helps you learn how to change unhelpful behaviors or thoughts.

Suggested Treatments: Treatments with Some Research Support

Some psychotherapies do not focus on the traumatic event, but do help you process your reactions to the trauma and manage symptoms related to PTSD. The research behind these treatments is not as strong as the research supporting trauma-focused psychotherapies (listed above). However, these psychotherapies may be a good option if you are not interested in trauma-focused psychotherapy, or if it is not available:

- **Stress inoculation training (SIT).** A cognitive behavioral therapy (CBT) that teaches skills and techniques to manage stress and reduce anxiety.
- **Present-centered therapy (PCT).** Focuses on current life problems that are related to PTSD.
- **Interpersonal psychotherapy (IPT).** Focuses on the impact of trauma on interpersonal relationships.

Other Treatments: Treatments That Do Not yet Have Research Support

There may be other options available such as certain complementary and integrative medicine approaches (like yoga, meditation, or acupuncture), biological treatments (like hyperbaric oxygen therapy or transcranial magnetic stimulation), or online treatment programs. These treatments do not have strong research behind them at this time, but you and your doctor can discuss the benefits and risks of these options to determine whether or not they are right for you.

No one treatment is right for everyone. You can discuss treatment options with your healthcare provider, and determine which ones are best for you based on the benefits, risks, and side effects of each treatment. Some people are uncomfortable with the idea of seeking treatment because of concerns with stigma or worries about having to talk about difficult life experiences. However, treatment provides the opportunity to improve symptoms, personal and professional relationships, and quality of life.

Chapter 47

Preventing Suicide

Suicide is a major public health concern. Over 40,000 people die by suicide each year in the United States; it is the 10th leading cause of death overall. Suicide is complicated and tragic but it is often preventable. Knowing the warning signs for suicide and how to get help can help save lives.

Signs and Symptoms

The behaviors listed below may be signs that someone is thinking about suicide.

- Talking about wanting to die or wanting to kill themselves
- Talking about feeling empty, hopeless, or having no reason to live
- Making a plan or looking for a way to kill themselves, such as searching online, stockpiling pills, or buying a gun
- Talking about great guilt or shame
- Talking about feeling trapped or feeling that there are no solutions
- Feeling unbearable pain (emotional pain or physical pain)
- Talking about being a burden to others

This chapter includes text excerpted from "Suicide Prevention," National Institute of Mental Health (NIMH), March 2017.

- Using alcohol or drugs more often
- Acting anxious or agitated
- Withdrawing from family and friends
- Changing eating and/or sleeping habits
- Showing rage or talking about seeking revenge
- Taking great risks that could lead to death, such as driving extremely fast
- Talking or thinking about death often
- Displaying extreme mood swings, suddenly changing from very sad to very calm or happy
- Giving away important possessions
- Saying goodbye to friends and family
- Putting affairs in order, making a will

If these warning signs apply to you or someone you know, get help as soon as possible, particularly if the behavior is new or has increased recently. One resource is the National Suicide Prevention Lifeline (NSPL), 800-273-TALK (800-273-8255). The Lifeline is available 24 hours a day, 7 days a week. The deaf and hard of hearing can contact the Lifeline via TTY at 800-799-4889.

Risk Factors

Suicide does not discriminate. People of all genders, ages, and ethnicities can be at risk. Suicidal behavior is complex and there is no single cause. In fact, many different factors contribute to someone making a suicide attempt. But people most at risk tend to share certain characteristics. The main risk factors for suicide are:

- Depression, other mental disorders, or substance abuse disorder
- Certain medical conditions
- Chronic pain
- A prior suicide attempt
- Family history of a mental disorder or substance abuse
- Family history of suicide
- Family violence, including physical or sexual abuse

- Having guns or other firearms in the home
- Having recently been released from prison or jail
- Being exposed to others' suicidal behavior, such as that of family members, peers, or celebrities

Many people have some of these risk factors but do not attempt suicide. It is important to note that suicide is not a normal response to stress. Suicidal thoughts or actions are a sign of extreme distress, not a harmless bid for attention, and should not be ignored.

Often, family and friends are the first to recognize the warning signs of suicide and can be the first step toward helping an at-risk individual find treatment with someone who specializes in diagnosing and treating mental health conditions.

Do Gender and Age Affect Suicide Risk?

Men are more likely to die by suicide than women, but women are more likely to attempt suicide. Men are more likely to use deadlier methods, such as firearms or suffocation. Women are more likely than men to attempt suicide by poisoning. The most recent figures released by the Center for Disease Control and Prevention (CDC) show that the highest rate of suicide deaths among women is found between ages 45–64, while the highest rate for men occurs at ages 75+. Children and young adults also are at risk for suicide. Suicide is the second leading cause of death for young people ages 15–34.

What about Different Racial / Ethnic Groups?

The CDC reports that among racial and ethnic groups, American Indians and Alaska Natives tend to have the highest rate of suicides, followed by non-Hispanic Whites. African Americans tend to have the lowest suicide rate, while Hispanics tend to have the second lowest rate.

Treatments and Therapies

Research has shown that there are multiple risk factors for suicide and that these factors may vary with age, gender, physical and mental well-being, and with individual experiences. Treatments and therapies for people with suicidal thoughts or actions will vary as well. National Institute of Mental Health (NIMH) has focused research on strategies that have worked well for mental health conditions related to suicide such as depression and anxiety.

Psychotherapies

Multiple types of psychosocial interventions have been found to be beneficial for individuals who have attempted suicide. These types of interventions may prevent someone from making another attempt. Psychotherapy, or "talk therapy," is one type of psychosocial intervention and can effectively reduce suicide risk.

One type of psychotherapy is called cognitive behavioral therapy (CBT). CBT can help people learn new ways of dealing with stressful experiences through training. CBT helps individuals recognize their own thought patterns and consider alternative actions when thoughts of suicide arise.

Another type of psychotherapy, called dialectical behavior therapy (DBT), has been shown to reduce the rate of suicide among people with borderline personality disorder, a serious mental illness characterized by unstable moods, relationships, self-image, and behavior. A therapist trained in DBT helps a person recognize when his or her feelings or actions are disruptive or unhealthy, and teaches the skills needed to deal better with upsetting situations.

Medication

Some individuals at risk for suicide might benefit from medication. Doctors and patients can work together to find the best medication or medication combination, as well as the right dose.

Clozapine is an antipsychotic medication used primarily to treat individuals with schizophrenia. However, it is the only medication with a specific U.S. Food and Drug Administration (FDA) indication for reducing the risk of recurrent suicidal behavior in patients with schizophrenia or schizoaffective disorder who are at risk for ongoing suicidal behavior. Because many individuals at risk for suicide often have psychiatric and substance use problems, individuals might benefit from medication along with psychosocial intervention.

If you are prescribed a medication, be sure you:

- Talk with your doctor or a pharmacist to make sure you understand the risks and benefits of the medications you're taking.
- Do not stop taking a medication without talking to your doctor first. Suddenly stopping a medication may lead to "rebound" or worsening of symptoms. Other uncomfortable or potentially dangerous withdrawal effects also are possible.
- Report any concerns about side effects to your doctor right away. You may need a change in the dose or a different medication.

- Report serious side effects to the FDA MedWatch Adverse Event Reporting program online (www.fda.gov/Safety/MedWatch/default.htm) or by phone at 800-332-1088. You or your doctor may send a report.

Other medications have been used to treat suicidal thoughts and behaviors but more research is needed to show the benefit for these options.

Five Action Steps for Helping Someone in Emotional Pain

1. **Ask:** "Are you thinking about killing yourself?" It's not an easy question but studies show that asking at-risk individuals if they are suicidal does not increase suicides or suicidal thoughts.
2. **Keep them safe:** Reducing a suicidal person's access to highly lethal items or places is an important part of suicide prevention. While this is not always easy, asking if the at-risk person has a plan and removing or disabling the lethal means can make a difference.
3. **Be there:** Listen carefully and learn what the individual is thinking and feeling. Findings suggest acknowledging and talking about suicide may in fact reduce rather than increase suicidal thoughts.
4. **Help them connect:** Save the NSPL's number in your phone so it's there when you need it: 800-273-TALK (800-273-8255). You can also help make a connection with a trusted individual like a family member, friend, spiritual advisor, or mental health professional.
5. **Stay connected:** Staying in touch after a crisis or after being discharged from care can make a difference. Studies have shown the number of suicide deaths goes down when someone follows up with the at-risk person.

More Ideas

Instant access: It may be helpful to save several emergency numbers to your cell phone. The ability to get immediate help for yourself or for a friend can make a difference.

- The phone number for a trusted friend or relative

- The nonemergency number for the local police department
- The Crisis Text Line: 741741
- The National Suicide Prevention Lifeline (NSPL): 800-273-TALK (800-273-8255).

Social media: Knowing how to get help for a social media friend can save a life. Contact the social media site directly if you are concerned about a friend's updates or dial 911 in an emergency.

Ongoing Research

In order to know who is most at risk and to prevent suicide, scientists need to understand the role of long-term factors (such as childhood experiences) as well as more immediate factors like mental health and recent life events. Researchers also are looking at how genes can either increase risk or make someone more resilient to loss and hardships.

If You Know Someone in Crisis

Call the toll-free NSPL at 800-273-TALK (800-273-8255), 24 hours a day, 7 days a week. The service is available to everyone. The deaf and hard of hearing can contact the Lifeline via TTY at 800-799-4889. All calls are confidential. Contact social media outlets directly if you are concerned about a friend's social media updates or dial 911 in an emergency.

Part Five

Stress Management

Chapter 48

The Basics of Preventing and Managing Stress

Not all stress is bad. But chronic (ongoing) stress can lead to health problems. Preventing and managing chronic stress can lower your risk for serious conditions like heart disease, obesity, high blood pressure, and depression.

You can prevent or reduce stress by:

- Planning ahead
- Deciding which tasks need to be done first
- Preparing for stressful events

Some stress is hard to avoid. You can find ways to manage stress by:

- Noticing when you feel stressed
- Taking time to relax
- Getting active and eating healthy
- Talking to friends and family

This chapter includes text excerpted from "Manage Stress," Office of Disease Prevention and Health Promotion (ODPHP), U.S. Department of Health and Human Services (HHS), March 20, 2018.

What Are the Signs of Stress?

When people are under stress, they may feel:

- Worried
- Angry
- Irritable
- Depressed
- Unable to focus

Stress also affects the body. Physical signs of stress include:

- Headaches
- Back pain
- Problems sleeping
- Upset stomach
- Weight gain or loss
- Tense muscles
- Frequent or more serious colds

Stress is different for everyone.

What Causes Stress?

Change is often a cause of stress. Even positive changes, like having a baby or getting a job promotion, can be stressful. Stress can be short term or long term.

Common causes of short-term stress:

- Needing to do a lot in a short amount of time
- Experiencing many small problems in the same day, like a traffic jam or running late
- Getting lost
- Having an argument

Common causes of long-term stress:

- Problems at work or at home
- Money problems

- Caring for someone with a serious illness
- Chronic (ongoing) illness
- Death of a loved one

What Are the Benefits of Managing Stress?

Over time, chronic stress can lead to health problems. Managing stress can help you:

- Sleep better
- Control your weight
- Get sick less often
- Feel better faster when you do get sick
- Have less neck and back pain
- Be in a better mood
- Get along better with family and friends

Tips for Preventing and Managing Stress

Being prepared and feeling in control of your situation might help lower your stress. Follow these 9 tips for preventing and managing stress.

1. **Plan your time**

   Think ahead about how you are going to use your time. Write a to-do list and figure out what's most important—then do that thing first. Be realistic about how long each task will take.

2. **Prepare yourself**

   Prepare ahead of time for stressful events like a job interview or a hard conversation with a loved one.

   - Stay positive.
   - Picture what the room will look like and what you will say.
   - Have a backup plan.

3. **Relax with deep breathing or meditation**

   Deep breathing and meditation are 2 ways to relax your muscles and clear your mind

- Find out how easy it is to use deep breathing to relax
- Try meditating for a few minutes today

4. **Relax your muscles**

   Stress causes tension in your muscles. Try stretching or taking a hot shower to help you relax.

5. **Get active**

   Regular physical activity can help prevent and manage stress. It can also help relax your muscles and improve your mood.

   - Aim for 2 hours and 30 minutes a week of physical activity. Try going for a bike ride or taking a walk.
   - Be sure to exercise for at least 10 minutes at a time.
   - Do strengthening activities—like crunches or lifting weights—at least 2 days a week.

6. **Eat healthy**

   Give your body plenty of energy by eating healthy foods—including vegetables, fruits, and lean sources of protein.

7. **Drink alcohol only in moderation**

   Avoid using alcohol or other drugs to manage stress. If you choose to drink, drink only in moderation. This means no more than 1 drink a day for women and no more than 2 drinks a day for men.

8. **Talk to friends and family**

   Tell your friends and family if you are feeling stressed. They may be able to help. Learn how friends and family can help you feel less stressed.

9. **Get help if you need it**

   Stress is a normal part of life. But if your stress doesn't go away or keeps getting worse, you may need help. Over time, stress can lead to serious problems like depression or anxiety.

   - If you are feeling down or hopeless, talk to a doctor about depression.
   - If you are feeling anxious, find out how to get help for anxiety.

- If you have lived through an unsafe event, find out about treatment for posttraumatic stress disorder (PTSD).

A mental health professional (like a psychologist or social worker) can help treat these conditions with talk therapy (called psychotherapy) or medicine. Lots of people need help dealing with stress—it's nothing to be ashamed of!

Chapter 49

Developing Resilience: The Most Important Defense against Stress

Resilience refers to the ability of an individual, family, or community to cope with adversity and trauma, and adapt to challenges or change. Trauma can occur as a result of violence, abuse, neglect, loss, and other emotionally harmful experiences. Traumatic and toxic stressors such as physical abuse, exposure to domestic or community violence, and depending on parents with mental and/or substance use disorders, tend to cluster in families. Often when one stressor is present, others are present as well.

Becoming More Resilient

Can we learn to be more resilient? Could sensitive or less resilient individuals become hardier? In this modern age of hypersensitivity, when even the simplest of issues become major or easy tasks become insurmountable, people have learned to give up instead of plowing on through the problem. The answer to the first question is a resounding

---

This chapter contains text excerpted from the following sources: Text in this chapter begins with excerpts from "Trauma Resilience Resources," Substance Abuse and Mental Health Services Administration (SAMHSA), November 22, 2016; Text beginning with the heading "Becoming More Resilient" is excerpted from "Becoming More Resilient," Federal Bureau of Investigation (FBI), October 1, 2012. Reviewed June 2018.

yes. Remember your years in school? You probably had physical training or played sports, and the coach would push you past your comfort level to achieve greater results. As you found, you could endure. Or, do you recall, perhaps, growing up with just the basic necessities, playing outside, having no fast food or television, walking to and from school, and working in your yard because you were told to do so? This was the beginning of resilience.

Granted, when a person faces a problem, it often seems big to them at that moment. For some of us looking at the same issue, we cannot imagine why the individual sees it as so large. And, there's the rub—we differ in how we cope with stressful situations. Resilience comes from understanding yourself and how you react to your environment. It can change how you handle setbacks. Being more resilient can affect how enthusiastically you approach challenges. It can improve how you think during conflicts or stressful periods. Resilience can help you learn from past difficulties and derive knowledge and meaning from those setbacks and failures. Responding effectively to adversity, overcoming obstacles, getting through normal daily hassles, and dealing with life-altering events form the cornerstone of resilience.

Proactive use of resilience allows you the ability to seek out new experiences that will enrich your life. With this said, you need to understand yourself first. How? Introspection is the first step in understanding what you can or cannot do and your level of endurance at a mental, personal, and emotional level.

Areas of Focus

Emotional Intelligence

Emotional intelligence is a form of social intelligence that employs the skill of awareness, or being "clued in," to monitor one's own and others' emotions, discriminate among them, and, in the end, use the information to guide one's own thinking and actions. Several subcategories relating to both intrapersonal and interpersonal skills are important in understanding how it works.

Self-awareness involves observing yourself and recognizing a feeling as it happens. Self-regulation entails handling feelings appropriately; realizing what is behind a feeling; and finding ways to address fear, anxiety, anger, and sadness. Motivation includes channeling emotions in the service of a goal, controlling emotions, delaying gratification, and stifling impulses. Empathy involves remaining sensitive to others' feelings and concerns, taking their perspective, and appreciating the differences in how people feel about things. Social skills include managing emotions in others, embodying social competence, and handling relationships.

Self-Awareness

- **Emotional awareness:** recognizing emotions and their effects
- **Accurate self-assessment:** knowing personal strengths and limits
- **Self-confidence:** having a strong sense of self-worth and capabilities, a basic belief in the ability to do what is needed to produce a desired outcome

Self-Regulation

- **Self-control:** keeping disruptive emotions and impulses in check
- **Trustworthiness:** maintaining standards of honesty and integrity
- **Conscientiousness:** taking responsibility for personal performance
- **Adaptability:** learning to be flexible in handling change
- **Innovation:** being comfortable with novel ideas, approaches, and new information

Motivation

- **Achievement drive:** striving to improve or meet a standard of excellence
- **Commitment:** aligning with the goals of the group or organization
- **Initiative:** becoming ready to act on opportunities
- **Optimism:** maintaining persistence in pursuing goals despite obstacles and setbacks and aligning with hope—a predictor of success (e.g., I am able to motivate myself to try and try again in the face of setbacks. I like to push the limits of my ability. Under pressure, I rarely feel helpless. I easily can set negative feelings aside when called on to perform.)

Empathy

- **Understanding others:** sensing other people's feelings and perspectives and taking an active interest in their concerns
- **Developing others:** detecting other individuals' development needs and bolstering their abilities
- **Leveraging diversity:** cultivating opportunities through different kinds of people
- **Maintaining political awareness:** reading a group's emotional currents and power relationships (e.g., I am effective at listening to other people's problems. I rarely get angry at people who come around and bother me with foolish questions. I am adept at reading people's feelings by their facial expressions. I easily can "put myself into other people's shoes.")

Social Skills

- **Influence:** wielding effective tactics for persuasion
- **Communication:** listening openly and sending convincing messages
- **Leadership:** inspiring and guiding individuals and groups
- **Change catalyst:** initiating or managing change
- **Building bonds:** nurturing instrumental relationships
- **Collaboration and cooperation:** working with others toward shared goals
- **Team capabilities:** creating group synergy in pursuing collective goals

Your emotional resilience can improve and strengthen through understanding yourself better and improving your emotional intelligence. We all are born with different coping mechanisms; in fact, some of us have none. Emotional intelligence gives us the ability to, finally, become a more resilient person.

Visualization

Think about becoming mentally and emotionally tougher. Look to other people for examples of mental and emotional toughness. For instance, when I was a boy, I admired John Wayne and wanted to emulate his confidence, strength, and fortitude. Although he was an actor, the character traits he exuded made me want to be strong like him. The point? Seeing is believing; start acting like a more resilient person, and, eventually, you also will start to believe it. According to one expert, "It's not that less resilient people are lacking some kind of 'coping gene' or anything like that. Indeed, they have the power within to become just as resilient as their more intuitively resilient counterparts simply by training their minds to think more positively and then learning how to change their behaviors to reflect their new, more positive attitudes." You need to make a personal paradigm shift from being hopeless, hapless, and helpless to become stronger, tougher, and harder.

Positive Psychology

Your mental outlook or mood affects how you behave and interact with the world. Start seeing the good in things, the brighter side of life and the little enjoyments along the way that cheer you up. To this end, positive psychology—the study of the human condition and how people live and interact with their environment—focuses on cultivating personality strengths and honing an optimistic approach to life, rather than on cataloging human frailty and disease, which has served too long as the focus of psychology. Traditional psychology focused on atypical or dysfunctional people with mental illness, emotional problems, personality disorders, or other psychological issues and, in the end, how to treat them. By contrast, positive psychology, a relatively new field, examines how ordinary people can become happier and more fulfilled.

Cognitive Restructuring

Another way to become a more resilient person is through a process called cognitive restructuring—in short, changing a perception from a negative interpretation to a neutral or positive one and, in turn, making it less stressful. Cognitive restructuring also is known as reappraisal, relabeling, and reframing. Individuals acquire irrational or illogical cognitive interpretations or beliefs about themselves or their environment. The extent to which these beliefs are irrational is important and equals the amount of emotional distress experienced by the person.

Chapter 50

Supporting a Friend or Family Member with Mental Health Problems

Anyone can experience mental health problems. Friends and family can make all the difference in a person's recovery process.

You can help your friend or family member by recognizing the signs of mental health problems and connecting them to professional help. Talking to friends and family about mental health problems can be an opportunity to provide information, support, and guidance. Learning about mental health issues can lead to:

- Improved recognition of early signs of mental health problems
- Earlier treatment
- Greater understanding and compassion

If a friend or family member is showing signs of a mental health problem or reaching out to you for help, offer support by:

- Finding out if the person is getting the care that he or she needs and wants—if not, connect him or her to help

---

This chapter includes text excerpted from "For Friends and Family Members," MentalHealth.gov, U.S. Department of Health and Human Services (HHS), September 26, 2017.

- Expressing your concern and support
- Reminding your friend or family member that help is available and that mental health problems can be treated
- Asking questions, listening to ideas, and being responsive when the topic of mental health problems come up
- Reassuring your friend or family member that you care about him or her
- Offering to help your friend or family member with everyday tasks
- Including your friend or family member in your plans—continue to invite him or her without being overbearing, even if your friend or family member resists your invitations
- Educating other people so they understand the facts about mental health problems and do not discriminate
- Treating people with mental health problems with respect, compassion, and empathy

How to Talk about Mental Health

Do you need help starting a conversation about mental health? Try leading with these questions and make sure to actively listen to your friend or family member's response.

- I've been worried about you. Can we talk about what you are experiencing? If not, who are you comfortable talking to?
- What can I do to help you to talk about issues with your parents or someone else who is responsible and cares about you?
- What else can I help you with?
- I am someone who cares and wants to listen. What do you want me to know about how you are feeling?
- Who or what has helped you deal with similar issues in the past?
- Sometimes talking to someone who has dealt with a similar experience helps. Do you know of others who have experienced these types of problems who you can talk with?
- It seems like you are going through a difficult time. How can I help you to find help?
- How can I help you find more information about mental health problems?

- I'm concerned about your safety. Have you thought about harming yourself or others?

When talking about mental health problems:

- Know how to connect people to help.
- Communicate in a straightforward manner.
- Speak at a level appropriate to a person's age and development level (preschool children need fewer details as compared to teenagers).
- Discuss the topic when and where the person feels safe and comfortable.
- Watch for reactions during the discussion and slow down or back up if the person becomes confused or looks upset.

Sometimes it is helpful to make a comparison to a physical illness. For example, many people get sick with a cold or the flu, but only a few get really sick with something serious like pneumonia. People who have a cold are usually able to do their normal activities. However, if they get pneumonia, they will have to take medicine and may have to go to the hospital.

Similarly, feelings of sadness, anxiety, worry, irritability, or sleep problems are common for most people. However, when these feelings get very intense, last for a long period of time, and begin to interfere with school, work, and relationships, it may be a sign of a mental health problem. And just like people need to take medicine and get professional help for physical conditions, someone with a mental health problem may need to take medicine and/or participate in therapy in order to get better.

Get Help for Your Friend or Family Member

Seek immediate assistance if you think your friend or family member is in danger of harming themselves. You can call a crisis line or the NSPL at 800-273-TALK (800-273-8255).

Chapter 51

How to Say No: Asserting Yourself Can Reduce Stress

Many of us are faced with stress every day, but we might not know how to deal with it. It is important to learn how to handle stress because it can affect our performance and relationships in our work and home. At work, stress can lead to distraction and cause an unfortunate accident. At home, stress can put a strain on family relationships.

Stress usually occurs when there are changes in our lives and we feel that we don't have enough resources to deal with those changes and demands. Which of the following do you think causes stress: getting married, winning the lottery, or having an argument? It is all of them. Stress can occur not only from negative life experiences, but also from positive ones. People react and deal with stress differently, but common stress symptoms include upset stomach, fatigue, tight neck muscles, irritability, and headaches. Some people react to stress by eating or drinking too much, losing sleep or smoking cigarettes.

This chapter contains text excerpted from the following sources: Text in this chapter begins with excerpts from "Controlling Stress," U.S. Department of Energy (DOE), July 1, 2010. Reviewed June 2018; Text under the heading "Learning to Say No" is excerpted from "The National Service Stress Survival Guide," Corporation for National and Community Service (CNCS), December 6, 2006. Reviewed June 2018; Text beginning with the heading "Assertive Communication Relieves Stress" is excerpted from "Learning to Be Assertive," U.S. Department of State (DOS), October 13, 2003. Reviewed June 2018.

Stress may also make you more susceptible to illnesses, including the common cold, ulcers, and some cancers.

The first step to managing stress is to identify your "stressors"; those things that are making you react. Stressors may not only be events that cause you to feel sad, frightened, anxious or happy. You can cause stress through your thoughts, feelings and expectations.

Everyone has to deal with life's problems. A key to dealing with the big and little everyday stressors is coping with stress in a positive way.

- **Acceptance.** Many of us worry about things we have no control over. For example, a family illness, a great deal of change at work, or finding out that your basketball team lost. One way to manage stress is to accept when things are beyond your control. It may be helpful to think positive thoughts such as, "Someday I'll laugh about this," or "It's a learning experience."
- **Attitude.** Try to focus on the positive side of situations. Ask yourself, "What good can come out of this?" "What can I learn from this situation?" and "How can I handle this better when it comes up again?" Solutions come easier when you focus on the positive and your stress level will be reduced.
- **Perspective.** We often worry about things that never happen. Keep things in perspective by asking yourself, "How important is this situation?" "Can I do anything about it?" "In five years, will I even remember it happened?"

Think about the situations in your life that cause you stress. Are they important or unimportant? Are they controllable or uncontrollable? If they are controllable events, you can take action to change the situation; if they are uncontrollable, you can use your skills in acceptance, attitude, and perspective to reduce the stress.

Learning to Say No

- **Define your limits, then say "no!"** Define how you take charge of your time and space and get in touch with your feelings. You don't have to save the world today or do it all yourself.
- **Delegate.** Don't be afraid to hand off tasks to coworkers.
- **Sharpen your time management skills.** Use the time you have beneficially to reach your goals. Get out that planner.

- **Live by lists.** Make lists of daily tasks and activities. Use it as your guide.
- **Don't procrastinate.** Procrastination causes stress and the stressful byproducts of guilt, anger, and low self-esteem.
- **Take time** away when you need it.

Assertive Communication Relieves Stress

How we engage in conversation often affects the results of the communication or interaction. There are three styles of communication: Passive; Assertive; and Aggressive

- **Passive communicators** are those who would avoid confrontation and problems. They tend to be more easily manipulated by others, and they frequently lack self-confidence and give in easily to others in disagreements. Those of us who are "People Persons" often use this style to avoid conflict.
- **Assertive communicators** will usually face their problems directly. They tend to be respected and have a reputation for stating their point of view or opinion. Others usually know what these people are thinking. Frequently they will be seen as exuding self-confidence. The "Learned Expert" personality and "Practical Managers" have little difficulty being assertive. Their communications tend to be clear and to the point.
- **Aggressive communicators** are those who often would prefer to take advantage of others. Often, they have little respect for others and sometimes for themselves. They can be openly hostile. When angered the "Practical Managers and Learned Experts" can easily become very aggressive. "Creative Problem Solvers" can at times demonstrate a form of aggressive communication which is nonhostile but very intense. Because they often won't take "no" for an answer, "Creative Problem Solvers" try to use their charm to manipulate others.

A good reason to encourage appropriately assertive communications is to reduce the levels of stress experienced in the communication experience. Studies indicate that passive and aggressive communicators both feel more stress than do assertive communicators. Aggressive communicators experience the most stress!

Ten Tips to Improve Assertion Skills

1. It is OK to say "no." You do not have to not have to offer excuses or to justify your behavior to most people.
2. It is OK to make mistakes. In fact it is good to make mistakes. If you are not making mistakes you may not be taking appropriate risks. There are jobs, hobbies and lifestyles that expect you to take risks to develop new ideas or solutions. Making mistakes is OK. Just don't make the same mistake more than once if you can help it!
3. Ultimately you are the final and absolute judge of your own behavior.
4. When you have given your answer and someone asks you the same question again, Calmly repeat yourself over and over and over and over and over and over and over... again.
5. When asserting yourself, keep your language clear, simple and focused. Don't say things like, "No thank you, I don't think I will have any of that." That comment invites the host to say "Are you sure?" Just say "No thank you!"
6. There is an assertion technique called Fogging. It involves you acknowledging criticism and verifying feelings. You begin by agreeing with the person. "Well, I certainly think eight hours of homework is too much also. It is important that you have time for yourself, so what I am willing to do is to assign two hours of homework every night of the week. This way you will get all the calculus information you need to pass the final exam." And ten hours of calculus homework!!!!!
7. Appropriate Assertion is a learned behavior. Practice assertion skills in school, at work and at home. Role play the times and circumstances where others might take advantage of your less assertive nature. Practice does not make perfect. Practice makes permanent. By practicing at home you will be able to say assertive things when appropriate. Practice saying exactly what you want to communicate. Use the words, the tone, the inflection, the volume. Role-playing is a powerful assertion management tool!
8. Having many unfinished tasks hanging over your head can be distracting and lead to passivity. Seek closure on unfinished business. Decide when you can the first time. Don't drag

things out. When you know the answer give it. When you have decided, ACT!

9. When giving an "I" Message, delivering bad news or just protecting your rights, give the problems to the owner. Don't complain about calculus homework to the French teacher.

10. When appropriate seek a support group of similar minded friends or acquaintances. Joining in a support network helps to reaffirm positive self-images and your connection with a larger community. Support groups prove that you are normal after all and may even help to alleviate stress.

Chapter 52

Mindfulness-Based Stress Reduction Techniques

Practise Mindfulness Regularly

Mindfulness is a way to be fully aware in the present moment of physical sensations, emotions, and thoughts, but without judging them. Regular daily practice of stress management techniques will allow you to deal with your stress in a healthier way.

Mindfulness-based stress reduction (MBSR) techniques have been proven to reduce stress and stress-related conditions in Veterans. They can reduce anxiety, improve attention and memory, and help manage chronic pain. These techniques center on being fully aware in the present moment without judgment

- **Mindfulness meditation.** The intention of mindfulness meditation is to be fully aware of what is going on in the present moment without any judgment.
- **Compassion meditation.** This meditation can lower stress and stress hormone levels and raise self-esteem. You can improve self-compassion by working on unhelpful thoughts and by practicing this meditation.

This chapter includes text excerpted from "Manage Stress Workbook," U.S. Department of Veterans Affairs (VA), June 2014. Reviewed June 2018.

- **Body scan meditation.** This meditation is deeply relaxing and can help you become more accepting of areas of pain or discomfort.
- **Mindful eating exercise.** This exercise helps you to practice mindfulness with something you do every day eating. You will learn how to increase your awareness while eating, which can increase mindfulness and improve your eating habits overall.
- **Progressive muscle relaxation.** This exercise can help you become aware of muscle tension, so you can release it when needed.
- **Mindfulncss circle.** This will help you to return to mindful awareness throughout your day.

If you find these techniques helpful, you can speak with your primary care/Program of Assertive Community Treatment (PACT) team to find stress management programs that might be available in your area.

Mindfulness Meditation

To anchor yourself in the present, focus on your breath as you inhale and exhale. Breathing mindfully does not involve a conscious changing of your breath.

1. Set aside a 1–5 minute period of time, and tell yourself that you will not engage your thoughts during that time. As thoughts pop up, just notice them and let them go.
2. As you notice your mind thinking about things, try to let those thoughts go without judging them and return your attention to the experience of breathing. The point is not to stop having thoughts. The point of this meditation is to become more aware of your thoughts without automatically engaging them.

If focusing on your breath does not work to bring you into the present moment, you can focus on anything in the present, such as sounds, a picture you like, or a candle flame, so long as you don't have to think about it.

Compassion Meditation

1. First, take a few deep, cleansing breaths and ground yourself in the present.

2. As you breathe deeply, focus on your heart and visualize softness, warmth, and compassion glowing in your chest. Repeat these phrases to yourself: "May I be happy. May I be well. May I be safe. May I be peaceful and at ease."

3. After a minute or two, visualize extending this energy to include somebody you care deeply about. Now repeat the phrases, filling in the person's name. For example, "May my wife be happy. May my wife be well. May my wife..."

4. Next, visualize extending the energy to somebody you feel neutrally about. Repeat the phrases with his or her name. For example, "May the cashier at the store be happy. May the cashier be well. May the cashier...."

5. Now extend the energy to somebody for whom you have negative feelings. Repeat the phrases with his or her name.

6. Finally, visualize extending this energy to the rest of the world.

As you become comfortable with this practice, try extending the length of time you spend at each stage, increasing the overall time spent on the meditation.

Body Scan Meditation

The body scan meditation can help you become more accepting of areas of pain or discomfort and not tense in response to them, which can make the discomfort worse.

To practice the body scan meditation, get into a comfortable position. You might lie down on the floor or in bed with a pillow under your head. Take a few deep, grounding breaths and gently bring your awareness to the present.

1. Pay attention to a specific body part, such as your left foot. As you breathe deeply, scan that part of your body for sensations. Notice the sensations you feel, but try not to get lost in thought. Gradually let your focus move to different body parts—each leg, your hips, stomach, chest, hands, arms, and head.

2. Practice mindfulness meditation with your focus on your body. Become aware of your mind's tendency to get lost in thought. When you notice this happening, just let the thought go and

gently redirect your attention back to your body. Try not to engage in the content of the thoughts.

If you have any pain or discomfort, just notice it, accept it, and continue scanning. Continue to scan each part of your body in this way until you have scanned your whole body.

Mindful Eating Exercise

Mindful eating is an ongoing practice, but it starts with three simple steps.

1. Become aware of the physical characteristics of food. Make each bite a mindful bite. Think of your mouth as being a magnifying glass, able to zoom in. Imagine magnifying each bite 100 percent. Pay close attention to your senses. Use your tongue to feel the texture of your food and to gauge the temperature. Take a whiff of the aroma. Ask yourself, "How does it really taste? What does it feel like in my mouth? Is this something I really want? Does it satisfy my taste buds? Is my mind truly present when I take a bite so that I experience it fully?"
2. Become aware of repetitive habits and the process of eating. Notice how you eat. Fast? Slow? Do you put your fork down between bites? Are you stuck in any mindless habits, such as eating a snack at the same time each day, multi-tasking while you eat, or eating the same foods over and over again?

   Ask yourself the following questions: "Do I have any ingrained habits concerning how I snack? When I pick up my fork, what stands in the way of eating wisely?"
3. Become aware of mindless eating triggers. Look for specific cues that prompt you to start and stop eating. Is your kitchen a hot spot for snacking? Do feelings such as stress, discomfort, or boredom lead to a food binge? Do judgmental thoughts like "I'm an idiot!" trigger mindless eating?

Become an expert on the emotional buttons that trigger you to eat when you aren't physically hungry. When you know your triggers, you can anticipate and respond to them.

Ask yourself, "What am I feeling right before I mindlessly snack? Is my environment, emotional state, or dining companion helping or hurting my efforts to eat wisely?"

Progressive Muscle Relaxation (PMR)

Progressive muscle relaxation (PMR) exercises will help you recognize when your muscles are tense and teach you how to return your muscles to a relaxed state.

1. Breathe normally and let your body just 'be.' Take note of how your body feels from your toes to your head. Does any of your body feel tense, stiff, or achy?
2. Close your eyes and notice how your toes feel. Tightly curl your toes to the point where you feel tension, as if trying to squeeze a small ball between your toes and the ball of your feet. Hold this toe curl for 10 seconds. Release your curl and let your toes spread. Notice how your toes feel when they are free from tension.
3. Next, repeat this cycle of tensing and relaxing with your calves. Next, do your thighs. Move up the body. Repeat with your hands, then arms, and then the muscles of your upper back and shoulders. Finally, tense and relax your neck and face.
4. After you complete tensing and relaxing each muscle in the body, breathe in through your nose and hold your breath for five seconds. Slowly and gently breathe out through your mouth. Open your eyes and notice how your muscles—your feet, calves, thighs, fists, arms, upper back, neck, and face—feel when relaxed.

Mindfulness Circle

Mindfulness practice doesn't have to be limited to focusing on your breath. You can do almost anything mindfully. Try practicing mindfulness with one of the activities below or one of your own. Be aware of your breath, senses, thoughts, and feelings as you perform the activity. Consider your posture, your mood, how quickly you move, what is going on around you, and your level of tension.

Try being mindful while doing these everyday actions:

- Washing hands
- Stopping at a red light
- Looking at a clock or your watch
- Washing dishes

- Brushing your teeth
- Taking a shower
- Dressing and undressing
- Walking

Dealing with Distractions during Meditation

The purpose of meditation is not to concentrate on your breath or to achieve a perfectly still and serene mind. The goal of meditation is to achieve uninterrupted mindfulness. Being distracted is normal; it's how our minds work. When you sit down to concentrate on your breath, don't be upset when your mind wanders from the subject of meditation. Instead, simply observe the distraction mindfully. Whenever you are distracted away from your breath as you meditate, briefly switch your attention to the distraction. Make the distraction a temporary object of meditation, but only temporary. Your breath should remain your primary focus.

Switch your attention to the distraction only long enough to notice certain things about it. What is it? How strong is it? How long does it last? Return your attention to your breath as soon as you have wordlessly answered these questions.

The first step to changing something is seeing it the way it really is—these questions can free you from what is distracting you and give you insight into its nature. It's important to tune into the distraction without getting stuck on it.

When you begin using this technique, you will probably have to do it with words. Ask your questions in words and answer in words. Soon you will be able to dispense with the use of words altogether. As the mental habits are established, you will be able to simply note the distraction, note the qualities of the distraction, and then return your focus to your breath.

A distraction can be anything: a sound, a sensation, an emotion, a fantasy. Whatever it is, don't try to repress it or force it out of your mind. Just observe it mindfully and wordlessly. When you do, it will fade by itself. Don't fight your distracting thoughts, even if they have popped up before. Any energy you give toward resistance makes the distraction that much stronger. Just observe your distractions mindfully, and return your focus to your breathing. Refuse to feed your distractions with your own fear, anger, and greed, and they will eventually go away. Be patient and persistent. While mindfulness disarms distractions, it may take many times to break the hold of deep-seated thought patterns.

Chapter 53

Healthy Habits to Combat Stress

Chapter Contents

Section 53.1

Your Guide to Healthy Sleep

This section includes text excerpted from "Healthy Sleep," MedlinePlus, National Institutes of Health (NIH), April 26, 2017.

What Is Sleep?

While you are sleeping, you are unconscious, but your brain and body functions are still active. Sleep is a complex biological process that helps you process new information, stay healthy, and feel rested.

During sleep, your brain cycles through five stages: Stage 1, 2, 3, 4, and rapid eye movement (REM) sleep. Different things happen during each stage. For example, you have a different pattern of brain waves during each one. Your breathing, heart, and temperature may be slower or faster in some stages. Certain phases of sleep help you:

- Feel rested and energetic the next day
- Learn information, get insight, and form memories
- Give your heart and vascular system a rest
- Release more growth hormone, which helps children grow. It also boosts muscle mass and the repair of cells and tissues in children and adults.
- Release sex hormones, which contributes to puberty and fertility
- Keep from getting sick or help you get better when you are sick, by creating more cytokines (hormones that help the immune system fight various infections)

You need all of the stages to get a healthy sleep.

How Much Sleep Do I Need?

The amount of sleep you need depends on several factors, including your age, lifestyle, health, and whether you have been getting enough sleep recently. The general recommendations for sleep are:

- **Newborns:** 16–18 hours a day
- **Preschool-aged children:** 11–12 hours a day
- **School-aged children:** At least 10 hours a day

- **Teens:** 9–10 hours a day
- **Adults (including the elderly):** 7–8 hours a day

During puberty, teenagers' biological clocks shift, and they are more likely to go to bed later than younger children and adults, and they tend to want to sleep later in the morning. This delayed sleep-wake rhythm conflicts with the early-morning start times of many high schools and helps explain why most teenagers do not get enough sleep.

Some people think that adults need less sleep as they age. But there is no evidence to show that seniors can get by with less sleep than people who are younger. As people age, however, they often get less sleep or they tend to spend less time in the deep, restful stage of sleep. Older people are also more easily awakened.

And it's not just the number of hours of sleep you get that matters. The quality of the sleep you get is also important. People whose sleep is frequently interrupted or cut short might not get enough of certain stages of sleep. If you are wondering whether you are getting enough sleep, including quality sleep, ask yourself:

- Do you have trouble getting up in the morning?
- Do you have trouble focusing during the day?
- Do you doze off during the day?

If you answered yes to these three questions, you should work on improving your sleep.

What Are the Health Effects of Not Getting Enough Sleep?

Sleep is important for overall health. When you don't get enough sleep (sleep deprivation), it does more than just make you feel tired. It can affect your performance, including your ability to think clearly, react quickly, and form memories. This may cause you to make bad decisions and take more risks. People with sleep deprivation are more likely to get into accidents.

Sleep deprivation can also affect your mood, leading to:

- Irritability
- Problems with relationships, especially for children and teenagers

- Depression
- Anxiety

It can also affect your physical health. Research shows that not getting enough sleep, or getting poor-quality sleep, increases your risk of:

- High blood pressure
- Heart disease
- Stroke
- Kidney disease
- Obesity
- Type 2 diabetes

Not getting enough sleep can also mean that you don't get enough of the hormones that help children grow and help adults and children build muscle mass, fight infections, and repair cells. Sleep deprivation magnifies the effect of alcohol. A tired person who drinks too much alcohol will be more impaired than a well-rested person.

How Can I Get Better Sleep?

You can take steps to improve your sleep habits. First, make sure that you allow yourself enough time to sleep. With enough sleep each night, you may find that you're happier and more productive during the day.

To improve your sleep habits, it also may help to:

- Go to bed and wake up at the same time every day
- Avoid caffeine, especially in the afternoon and evening
- Avoid nicotine
- Exercise regularly, but don't exercise too late in the day
- Avoid alcoholic drinks before bed
- Avoid large meals and beverages late at night
- Don't take a nap after 3 p.m.
- Relax before bed, for example by taking a bath, reading, or listening to relaxing music
- Keep the temperature in your bedroom cool

- Get rid of distractions such as noises, bright lights, and a TV or computer in the bedroom. Also, don't be tempted to go on your phone or tablet just before bed.
- Get enough sunlight exposure during the day
- Don't lie in bed awake; if you can't sleep for 20 minutes, get up and do something relaxing
- See a doctor if you have continued trouble sleeping. You may have a sleep disorder, such as insomnia or sleep apnea. In some cases, your doctor may suggest trying over-the-counter (OTC) or prescription sleep aid. In other cases, your doctor may want you to do a sleep study, to help diagnose the problem.

If you are a shift worker, it can be even harder to get a good sleep. You may also want to:

- Take naps and increase the amount of time available for sleep
- Keep the lights bright at work
- Limit shift changes so your body clock can adjust
- Limit caffeine use to the first part of your shift
- Remove sound and light distractions in your bedroom during daytime sleep (for example, use light-blocking curtains)

Section 53.2

Exercise Can Help Control Stress

This section contains text excerpted from the following sources: Text in this section begins with excerpts from "Benefits of Exercise," MedlinePlus, National Institutes of Health (NIH), August 30, 2017; Text under the heading "What Being Active Does for Your Mental Health" is excerpted from "Why Physical Activity Is Important," girlshealth.gov, Office on Women's Health (OWH), March 27, 2015; Text under the heading "Deep Breathing Exercise" is excerpted from "Manage Stress Workbook," U.S. Department of Veterans Affairs (VA), June 2014. Reviewed June 2018.

We have all heard it many times before—regular exercise is good for you, and it can help you lose weight. But if you are like many Americans, you are busy, you have a sedentary job, and you haven't yet changed your exercise habits. The good news is that it's never too late to start. You can start slowly, and find ways to fit more physical activity into your life. To get the most benefit, you should try to get the recommended amount of exercise for your age. If you can do it, the payoff is that you will feel better, help prevent or control many diseases, and likely even live longer.

What Are the Health Benefits of Exercise?

Regular exercise and physical activity may:

- **Help you control your weight.** Along with diet, exercise plays an important role in controlling your weight and preventing obesity. To maintain your weight, the calories you eat and drink must equal the energy you burn. To lose weight, you must use more calories than you eat and drink.
- **Reduce your risk of heart diseases.** Exercise strengthens your heart and improves your circulation. The increased blood flow raises the oxygen levels in your body. This helps lower your risk of heart diseases such as high cholesterol, coronary artery disease, and heart attack. Regular exercise can also lower your blood pressure and triglyceride levels.
- **Help your body manage blood sugar and insulin levels.** Exercise can lower your blood sugar level and help your insulin work better. This can cut down your risk for metabolic syndrome and type 2 diabetes. And if you already have one of those diseases, exercise can help you to manage it.

- **Help you quit smoking.** Exercise may make it easier to quit smoking by reducing your cravings and withdrawal symptoms. It can also help limit the weight you might gain when you stop smoking.
- **Improve your mental health and mood.** During exercise, your body releases chemicals that can improve your mood and make you feel more relaxed. This can help you deal with stress and reduce your risk of depression.
- **Help keep your thinking, learning, and judgment skills sharp as you age.** Exercise stimulates your body to release proteins and other chemicals that improve the structure and function of your brain.
- **Strengthen your bones and muscles.** Regular exercise can help kids and teens build strong bones. Later in life, it can also slow the loss of bone density that comes with age. Doing muscle-strengthening activities can help you increase or maintain your muscle mass and strength.
- **Reduce your risk of some cancers**, including colon, breast, uterine, and lung cancer.
- **Reduce your risk of falls.** For older adults, research shows that doing balance and muscle-strengthening activities in addition to moderate-intensity aerobic activity can help reduce your risk of falling.
- **Improve your sleep.** Exercise can help you to fall asleep faster and stay asleep longer.
- **Improve your sexual health.** Regular exercise may lower the risk of erectile dysfunction (ED) in men. For those who already have ED, exercise may help improve their sexual function. In women, exercise may increase sexual arousal.
- **Increase your chances of living longer.** Studies show that physical activity can reduce your risk of dying early from the leading causes of death, like heart disease and some cancers.

How Can I Make Exercise a Part of My Regular Routine?

- **Make everyday activities more active.** Even small changes can help. You can take the stairs instead of the elevator. Walk down the hall to a coworker's office instead of sending an email. Wash the car yourself. Park further away from your destination.

- **Be active with friends and family.** Having a workout partner may make you more likely to enjoy exercise. You can also plan social activities that involve exercise. You might also consider joining an exercise group or class, such as a dance class, hiking club, or volleyball team.
- **Keep track of your progress.** Keeping a log of your activity or using a fitness tracker may help you set goals and stay motivated.
- **Make exercise more fun.** Try listening to music or watching TV while you exercise. Also, mix things up a little bit—if you stick with just one type of exercise, you might get bored. Try doing a combination of activities.
- **Find activities that you can do even when the weather is bad.** You can walk in a mall, climb stairs, or work out in a gym even if the weather stops you from exercising outside.

What Being Active Does for Your Mental Health

Did you know being physically active can affect how good you feel? It also can affect how well you do your tasks, and even how pleasant you are to be around. That's partly because physical activity gets your brain to make "feel-good" chemicals called endorphins. Regular physical activity may help you by:

- Reducing stress
- Improving sleep
- Boosting your energy
- Reducing symptoms of anxiety and depression
- Increasing your self-esteem
- Making you feel proud for taking good care of yourself
- Improving how well you do at school

Deep Breathing Exercise

Deep breathing is one of the fastest ways that you can regain control over stress.

1. Start by sitting down in a comfortable place that's free from distraction. Uncross your legs, put both feet on the floor, and

rest your hands in your lap. Pay attention to how this position feels and let your mind and body just "be" for a few moments.

2. Close your eyes and notice the pattern of your breath as you inhale and exhale. It may be soft or loud, slow or quick, or shallow or deep. Make a mental note of your breath before you start relaxing with deep breathing. Just breathe naturally for a few moments, taking slow and deep breaths in through your nose and then breathing out through your mouth.
3. Now hold your breath for 5 seconds after you inhale, and for another 5 seconds after you exhale. Continue breathing in this rhythm for a few moments.
4. Breathe naturally for a moment. Now place both of your hands on top of your stomach and try to notice how your belly rises with each inhale and falls with each exhale. Notice your breath moving in and out again from your belly, to your chest, and gently out through your mouth. Continue breathing naturally.
5. This time say, "Relax" silently or aloud after each time you exhale.
6. Repeat this exercise for 1–5 minutes.

Section 53.3

Dealing with Stress and Smoking

This section includes text excerpted from "How to Deal with Stress," Smokefree.gov, U.S. Department of Health and Human Services (HHS), February 28, 2017.

Dip Isn't the Answer

It can be helpful to know that dip isn't a good way to deal with stress and bad moods. Check out some reasons why:

- The relief you might feel from dip only lasts a short time. As soon as you start to feel stressed or down again, you'll want to dip.

- Dip doesn't solve your problem—it just hides it. The cause of your stress or bad mood isn't going away because of dip.
- Using dip causes more stress than it relieves. Studies show that a person's stress levels tend to go down after quitting tobacco.

Things That Can Help You Deal with Your Emotions

Here are a few ideas to get you started:

- **Move your body.** If you're feeling down, think about getting active. Any kind of physical activity can help. Try taking a walk, going to the gym, or joining a team sport. It might be hard to get motivated at first because feeling down can drain your energy. But if you stick with it, physical activity can help you feel better.
- **Spend time with people you care about.** Getting support from the important people in your life can be key to helping you feel better. Focus on spending time with people who make you feel good about yourself and want to help you stay tobacco-free. If you're feeling down, you might want to spend more time alone. That's normal, but just talking with someone you trust can help boost your mood.
- **Build healthy habits.** Being physically run down can make it harder to deal with a bad mood. Take care of yourself—eat regularly, get enough sleep, and build in time for fun and healthy activities, like lifting weights or going fishing with a friend.

Look out for Signs of Depression

Feeling sad after you quit dip is normal. If you are feeling extreme sadness, you may need help from a professional. It is common for people who are feeling depressed to think about hurting themselves or dying. If you or someone you know is having these feelings, you can get help now. Call a 24-hour crisis center at 800-273-TALK (800-273-8255) or 800-SUICIDE (800-784-2433) for free, private help or dial 911. The Substance Abuse and Mental Health Services Administration (SAMHSA)—a part of the U.S. Department of Health and Human Services (HHS)—runs both crisis centers.

Section 53.4

Quick Stress Relief: Engage Your Senses

This section includes text excerpted from "The Basics of Quick Stress Relief: Engage Your Senses," U.S. Department of Veterans Affairs (VA), May 12, 2015.

There are countless techniques for preventing stress. Yoga and meditation work wonders for improving our coping skills. But who can take a moment to chant or meditate during a job interview or a disagreement with your spouse? For these situations, you need something more immediate and accessible. That's when quick stress relief comes to the rescue.

The speediest way to stamp out stress is by engaging one or more of your senses—your sense of sight, sound, taste, smell, touch, or movement—to rapidly calm and energize yourself.

Remember exploring your senses in elementary school? Grownups can take a tip from grade school lessons by revisiting the senses and learning how they can help us prevent stress overload. Use the following exercises to identify the types of stress-busting sensory experiences that work quickly and effectively for you.

Sights

If you're a visual person, try to manage and relieve stress by surrounding yourself with soothing and uplifting images. You can also try closing your eyes and imagining the soothing images. Here are a few visually-based activities that may work as quick stress relievers:

- Look at a cherished photo or a favorite memento.
- Bring the outside indoors; buy a plant or some flowers to enliven your space.
- Enjoy the beauty of nature–a garden, the beach, a park, or your own backyard.
- Surround yourself with colors that lift your spirits.
- Close your eyes and picture a situation or place that feels peaceful and rejuvenating.

Sound

Are you sensitive to sounds and noises? Are you a music lover? If so, stress-relieving exercises that focus on your auditory sense may work particularly well. Experiment with the following sounds, noting how quickly your stress levels drop as you listen.

- Sing or hum a favorite tune. Listen to uplifting music.
- Tune in to the soundtrack of nature-crashing waves, the wind rustling the trees, birds singing.
- Buy a small fountain, so you can enjoy the soothing sound of running water in your home or office.
- Hang wind chimes near an open window.

Smell and Scents

If you tend to zone out or freeze when stressed, surround yourself with smells that are energizing and invigorating. If you tend to become overly agitated under stress, look for scents that are comforting and calming.

- Light a scented candle or burn some incense.
- Lie down in sheets scented with lavender.
- Smell the roses-or another type of flower.
- Enjoy the clean, fresh air in the great outdoors.
- Spritz on your favorite perfume or cologne.

Touch

Experiment with your sense of touch, playing with different tactile sensations. Focus on things you can feel that are relaxing and renewing. Use the following suggestions as a jumping off point:

- Wrap yourself in a warm blanket.
- Pet a dog or cat.
- Hold a comforting object (a stuffed animal, a favorite memento).
- Soak in a hot bath.
- Give yourself a hand or neck massage.
- Wear clothing that feels soft against your skin.

Taste

Slowly savoring a favorite treat can be very relaxing, but mindless stress eating will only add to your stress and your waistline. The key is to indulge your sense of taste mindfully and in moderation. Eat slowly, focusing on the feel of the food in your mouth and the taste on your tongue:

- Chew a piece of sugarless gum.
- Indulge in a small piece of dark chocolate.
- Sip a steaming cup of coffee or tea or a refreshing cold drink.
- Eat a perfectly ripe piece of fruit.
- Enjoy a healthy, crunchy snack (celery, carrots, or trail mix).

Movement

If you tend to shut down when you're under stress, stress-relieving activities that get you moving may be particularly helpful. Anything that engages the muscles or gets you up and active can work. Here are a few suggestions:

- Run in place or jump up and down.
- Dance around.
- Stretch or roll your head in circles.
- Go for a short walk.
- Squeeze a rubbery stress ball.

The Power of Imagination

Sensory-rich memories can also quickly reduce stress. After drawing upon your sensory toolbox becomes a habit, another approach is to learn to simply imagine vivid sensations when stress strikes. Believe it or not, the mere memory of your baby's face will have the same calming or energizing effects on your brain as seeing her photo. So if you can recall a strong sensation, you'll never be without access to your quick stress relief toolbox.

Chapter 54

Stressful Situations: Tips for Coping

Chapter Contents

Section 54.1

Aggressive Driving

This section includes text excerpted from "VHA Driver Safety—VA 7350," U.S. Department of Veterans Affairs (VA), September 9, 2017.

When other drivers are acting out behind the wheel, it is commonly referred to as aggressive driving. It is best to avoid aggravating the situation. What can you do to control anger behind the wheel? Avoid aggravating the situation. We can't predict what another driver may do. Let that hostile driver go by and get ahead so that we can control the situation.

Stress is another mental condition that is dangerous to everyone's driving safety—our own safety and the safety of others around us. It comes from letting other matters—such as deadlines—take priority over our driving. It's one thing to know the importance of being emotionally in control in driving situations, but it is much more difficult to do the right thing when we suddenly find ourselves in such situations. What we need to have working for us is a plan for gaining control when our emotions are affecting our driving. We all have stressful obligations in our lives, but smart drivers realize that a collision or violation is only going to increase their stress.

Aggressive Driving versus Road Rage

Aggressive driving is:

1. Driving in a bold, selfish, or pushy manner without regard for the rights or safety of other drivers.
2. A ticketable offense.

Road rage is:

1. Using a vehicle as a weapon with intent to do harm
2. Physical assault of a person or vehicle as a result of a traffic incident
3. A criminal offense.

Reduce your own aggressive driving behavior and avoid confrontations with other aggressive drivers by taking and maintaining self-control.

Every decision you make has consequences, both positive and negative. You need not give up control of your driving to the actions of others or to random emotions.

Remember—the only person who can control your behavior behind the wheel is you. Other drivers may make you mad, but only you have the power to make your own decisions.

Reduce Stress and Aggression behind the Wheel

- Remember—driving is not a win or lose situation.
- The only winners are those drivers who reach their destination safely.
- Don't worry about the behavior of other drivers, concentrate on driving safely.
- Aggressive driving only leads to more aggressive driving.
- Show courtesy to other drivers; give them the benefit of the doubt. The more courtesy a driver shows, the more he or she gets back.
- Avoid driving when angry, upset, or overly tired.
- Plan your trip with enough time so you don't feel rushed.
- Use the time to relax instead of focusing on hurrying to a destination. Let it be personal time spent in a personal space. Listen to music or think about something pleasant.
- Personalize the other drivers.
- Don't forget that every driver is someone's family member or friend.

Three Steps to Regain Control

If you find that you are becoming aggravated or are choosing unsafe, aggressive behaviors, try using these three steps:

1. **Reflect.** Ask yourself: "Why am I feeling this way or choosing this behavior? Is this something I can control?"
2. **Reframe the situation.** Create a more positive and safe situation. For example: "It could be worse."
3. **Refocus.** Think about something else, not the situation (s) that are causing you stress.

Section 54.2

Caregiver Stress

This section includes text excerpted from "Caregiver Stress," Office on Women's Health (OWH), U.S. Department of Health and Human Services (HHS), March 2, 2018.

Caregivers care for someone with an illness, injury, or disability. Caregiving can be rewarding, but it can also be challenging. Stress from caregiving is common. Women especially are at risk for the harmful health effects of caregiver stress. These health problems may include depression or anxiety. There are ways to manage caregiver stress.

What Is a Caregiver?

A caregiver is anyone who provides care for another person in need, such as a child, an aging parent, a husband or wife, a relative, friend, or neighbor. A caregiver also may be a paid professional who provides care in the home or at a place that is not the person's home. People who are not paid to give care are called informal caregivers or family caregivers. The family caregiver often has to manage the person's daily life. This can include helping with daily tasks like bathing, eating, or taking medicine. It can also include arranging activities and making health and financial decisions.

Who Are Caregivers?

Most Americans will be informal caregivers at some point during their lives. A survey found that 36 percent of Americans provided unpaid care to another adult with an illness or disability in the past year. That percentage is expected to go up as the proportion of people in the United States who are elderly increases. Also, changes in healthcare mean family caregivers now provide more home-based medical care. Nearly half of family caregivers in the survey said they give injections or manage medicines daily. Also, most caregivers are women. And nearly three in five family caregivers have paid jobs in addition to their caregiving.

What Is Caregiver Stress?

Caregiver stress is due to the emotional and physical strain of caregiving. Caregivers report much higher levels of stress than people who are not caregivers. Many caregivers are providing help or are "on call" almost all day. Sometimes, this means there is little time for work or other family members or friends. Some caregivers may feel overwhelmed by the amount of care their aging, sick or disabled family member needs. Although caregiving can be very challenging, it also has its rewards. It feels good to be able to care for a loved one. Spending time together can give new meaning to your relationship. Remember that you need to take care of yourself to be able to care for your loved one.

Who Gets Caregiver Stress?

Anyone can get caregiver stress, but more women caregivers say they have stress and other health problems than men caregivers. And some women have a higher risk for health problems from caregiver stress, including those who:

- **Care for a loved one who needs constant medical care and supervision.** Caregivers of people with Alzheimer disease or dementia are more likely to have health problems and to be depressed than caregivers of people with conditions that do not require constant care
- **Care for a spouse.** Women who are caregivers of spouses are more likely to have high blood pressure, diabetes, and high cholesterol and are twice as likely to have heart disease as women who provide care for others, such as parents or children

Women caregivers also may be less likely to get regular screenings, and they may not get enough sleep or regular physical activity.

What Are the Signs and Symptoms of Caregiver Stress?

Caregiver stress can take many forms. For instance, you may feel frustrated and angry one minute and helpless the next. You may make mistakes when giving medicines. Or you may turn to unhealthy behaviors like smoking or drinking too much alcohol.

Other signs and symptoms include:

- Feeling overwhelmed
- Feeling alone, isolated, or deserted by others
- Sleeping too much or too little

- Gaining or losing a lot of weight
- Feeling tired most of the time
- Losing interest in activities you used to enjoy
- Becoming easily irritated or angered
- Feeling worried or sad often
- Having headaches or body aches often

Talk to your doctor about your symptoms and ways to relieve stress. Also, let others give you a break. Reach out to family, friends, or a local resource.

How Does Caregiver Stress Affect My Health?

Some stress can be good for you, as it helps you cope and respond to a change or challenge. But long-term stress of any kind, including caregiver stress, can lead to serious health problems.

Some of the ways stress affects caregivers include:

- **Depression and anxiety.** Women who are caregivers are more likely than men to develop symptoms of anxiety and depression. Anxiety and depression also raise your risk for other health problems, such as heart disease and stroke.
- **Weak immune system.** Stressed caregivers may have weaker immune systems than noncaregivers and spend more days sick with the cold or flu. A weak immune system can also make vaccines such as flu shots less effective. Also, it may take longer to recover from surgery.
- **Obesity.** Stress causes weight gain in more women than men. Obesity raises your risk for other health problems, including heart disease, stroke, and diabetes.
- **Higher risk for chronic diseases.** High levels of stress, especially when combined with depression, can raise your risk for health problems, such as heart disease, cancer, diabetes, or arthritis.
- **Problems with short-term memory or paying attention.** Caregivers of spouses with Alzheimer disease are at higher risk for problems with short-term memory and focus.

Caregivers also report symptoms of stress more often than people who are not caregivers.

What Can I Do to Prevent or Relieve Caregiver Stress?

Taking steps to relieve caregiver stress helps prevent health problems. Also, taking care of yourself helps you take better care of your loved one and enjoy the rewards of caregiving.

Here are some tips to help you prevent or manage caregiver stress:

- **Learn ways to better help your loved one.** Some hospitals offer classes that can teach you how to care for someone with an injury or illness.
- **Find caregiving resources in your community to help you.** Many communities have adult daycare services or respite services to give primary caregivers a break from their caregiving duties.
- **Ask for and accept help.** Make a list of ways others can help you. Let helpers choose what they would like to do. For instance, someone might sit with the person you care for while you do an errand. Someone else might pick up groceries for you.
- **Join a support group for caregivers.** You can find a general caregiver support group (link is external) or a group with caregivers who care for someone with the same illness or disability as your loved one. You can share stories, pick up caregiving tips, and get support from others who face the same challenges as you do.
- **Get organized.** Make to-do lists, and set a daily routine.
- **Take time for yourself.** Stay in touch with family and friends, and do things you enjoy with your loved ones.
- **Take care of your health.** Find time to be physically active on most days of the week, choose healthy foods, and get enough sleep.
- **See your doctor for regular checkups.** Make sure to tell your doctor or nurse you are a caregiver. Also, tell her about any symptoms of depression or sickness you may have.

If you work outside the home and are feeling overwhelmed, consider taking a break from your job. Under the federal Family and Medical Leave Act (FMLA), eligible employees can take up to 12 weeks of unpaid leave per year to care for relatives. Ask your human resources office about your options.

What Caregiving Services Can I Find in My Community?

Caregiving services include:

- Meal delivery
- Home healthcare services, such as nursing or physical therapy
- Nonmedical home care services, such as housekeeping, cooking, or companionship
- Making changes to your home, such as installing ramps or modified bathtubs
- Legal and financial counseling
- Respite care, which is substitute caregiving (someone comes to your home, or you may take your loved one to an adult day care center or day hospital)

The National Eldercare Locator, a service of the U.S. Administration on Aging (AOA), can help you find caregiving services in your area.

How Can I Pay for Home Healthcare and Other Caregiving Services?

Medicare, Medicaid, and private insurance companies will cover some costs of home healthcare. Other costs you will have to pay for yourself.

- If the person who needs care has insurance, check with the person's insurance provider to find out what's included in the plan.
- If the person who needs care has Medicare, find out what home health services are covered.
- If the person who needs care has Medicaid, coverage of home health services vary between states. Check with your state's Medicaid program to learn what the benefits are.

If you or the person who needs caregiving also needs health insurance, learn about services covered under Marketplace plans at HealthCare.gov.

Section 54.3

Socioeconomic Hardship and Stress

This section contains text excerpted from the following sources: Text in this section begins with excerpts from "Socioeconomic Indicators That Matter for Population Health," Centers for Disease Control and Prevention (CDC), March 30, 2012. Reviewed June 2018; Text under the heading "Insights on Childhood Stress" is excerpted from "Insights on Childhood Stress: What Does It Mean for Children in Poverty?" Office of Policy Development and Research (PD&R), U.S. Department of Housing and Urban Development (HUD), February 9, 2015.

Increasing research and policy attention is being given to how the socioeconomic environment influences health. We define socioeconomic environment as a place with geographically defined boundaries that also has economic, educational, social, cultural, and political characteristics.

The socioeconomic environment shapes resources, opportunities, and exposures (positive and negative). Theoretically, the neighborhood socioeconomic environment could influence health outcomes either directly or indirectly. Direct effects on health include injuries from crime or environmental hazards or illness from socially patterned toxic exposures. In addition, many aspects of the neighborhood socioeconomic environment—including poverty and discrimination—can be considered stressors. Chronic exposure to social stressors can elevate the body's stress response (via neural, neuroendocrine, and immune systems) and produce "allostasis," a physiologic state that in the long run causes changes in the immune system and brain that can lead to disease through a variety of biological mechanisms. Other putative mechanisms linking socioeconomic environment and health are indirect, such as differential access to key resources like employment opportunities (which strongly influence income), food, housing, and healthcare services.

Insights on Childhood Stress

The negative lifelong effects of adversity and toxic stress in early childhood are well documented. Existing research indicates that children from low-income families face more stressors than children living in advantaged circumstances. Key findings from research across various sectors indicate the need for multifaceted, collaborative research on childhood stress. Neuroscientists suggest that the negative biomedical consequences of childhood stress are detrimental. Public health research indicates that childhood hardship leads to negative health outcomes and ultimately can impact larger systems such as family units, neighborhoods, and communities. In addition, research suggests that social programs can significantly affect health outcomes and success later in life. Taken collectively, these studies indicate the need for more research to prevent childhood stress and reduce the risk of negative outcomes in adulthood. Current research on childhood stress across various sectors overlaps and demonstrates similar findings. Although these research fields are not traditionally linked, they convey strikingly similar discoveries and conclusions.

The Neuroscience of Childhood Stress

Children are exposed to various stressors throughout their development, ranging from typical events such as a vaccination to toxic situations such as a habitually unsafe living environment. The brain responds to these stressors by initiating a neurochemical and hormonal cascade that coordinates the stress response and, when the stressor is no longer present, rapidly returns biological systems back to baseline. Under typical circumstances, this stress response is an important part of normal development; it facilitates adaptation and protection in a process known as allostasis. After prolonged exposure to toxic stressors, however, the stress response system becomes hyperactive and maladaptive, promoting inflammation that can damage both brain and body. This cumulative systemic wear and tear, known as allostatic load, can be measured using biomarkers that circulate in the blood, such as inflammatory cytokines. Science is just beginning to uncover the numerous ways that damage caused by toxic stressors, such as those associated with poverty, food insecurity, and unstable housing, can disrupt the delicate process of brain development in children. Evidence suggests that toxic stress may change the structure and function of neural systems important for cognition, emotional regulation, and prosocial behavior, thereby altering the typical trajectory of the brain development, and leading to poor mental and physical health.

Public Health and Childhood Stress

Childhood poverty is associated with adverse effects on health, educational success, and economic well-being later in life. Hardships associated with persistent poverty leave low-income children more vulnerable to stressors. One of the most prevalent yet preventable types of stressors, material hardships, comes in three forms: food insecurity, unstable or crowded housing, and inability to afford home heating or cooling. In 2011, a study in *Pediatrics* highlighted the development of a cumulative index based on food, housing, and energy insecurity as a predictor of the health of young children. Among more than 7,000 participants, multivariate analyses showed a significant association between the cumulative hardship index and children's adjusted odds of wellness. As determined by overall measures of wellness, children who experienced multiple poverty-related hardships had significantly worse health outcomes. Severe hardship had a significantly greater impact on health outcomes than moderate hardship, which in turn had a significantly greater impact than no hardship. Moving forward, researchers must consider how to alleviate these remediable stressors. Investments in home visiting, early education, and public benefit programs could potentially mitigate correctable material hardships.

More than four decades of sociological stress research suggests similar findings regarding the adverse effects of stress and hardship on health. Generational stress, like generational poverty, sustains and widens the health gap between advantaged and disadvantaged social groups. For example, research suggests that stressors proliferate across the life course. Stressful childhood events often generate stressful experiences during young adulthood, leading to more stressors during adulthood. Adults who report multiple traumatic events during childhood report increased recent and lifetime stress levels. Stressors also proliferate across generations. Parental stressors—in particular, the stress of persistent poverty, often manifest in children. Parents under stress give less warmth and support to their children, elevating their children's distress and often leading to behavioral problems and poor educational performance. Systematically, stress proliferation processes are important because they sustain and accelerate social disadvantage across generations.

Current Research

A study recently published in *Proceedings of the National Academy of Sciences* investigated whether a psychosocial intervention focused on improving parenting skills, strengthening family relationships, and building youth competencies could reduce inflammation (a biological indicator of stress) in African Americans of low socioeconomic status from rural Georgia. Researchers recruited 19-year-old youths who had participated in a study of the Strong African American Families

(SAAF) Program 8 years before. The original SAAF study enrolled families with 11-year-old children into a randomized controlled trial to test how well a family-centered intervention could enhance regulated, communicative parenting and youth independence. The follow-up study enrolled 272 youths from the earlier SAAF study, 173 of whom had been in the original treatment group that received the psychosocial intervention and 99 of whom had been in the original control group. To assess inflammation, researchers took blood draws from both groups to measure levels of inflammatory cytokines, which provided a measure of allostatic load. The results indicated the treatment group had significantly lower levels of allostatic load than did the control group and that reduced inflammation was partially mediated by improved parenting in these families. Moreover, the youths living in the most disadvantaged circumstances experienced the greatest reduction in inflammation. These findings suggest that psychosocial interventions focused on enhanced family communication and nurturing parenting, such as SAAF, may help reduce stress.

Section 54.4

Holiday Stress

This section includes text excerpted from "Managing Holiday Stress," National Oceanic and Atmospheric Administration (NOAA), U.S. Department of Commerce (DOC), 2011. Reviewed June 2018.

This section provides tips for alleviating holiday-related tension before the pressures of the season become too difficult to manage.

Tips for Managing Holiday Stress

Consider the following:

- **Make a "to-do" list.** List the tasks that need to be done in order of their importance.
- **Don't overcommit.** Don't say yes to every holiday invitation. Pick the events and activities that are most important to you, and say no to others.

- **Get organized.** Keep all of your appointments clearly marked on one calendar and update it regularly.
- **Use downtime to your advantage.** Cook and freeze meals for the week; fill your car with gas; take care of your laundry/dry cleaning; write holiday cards; shop; etc.
- **Simplify tasks.** Purchase food that is easy to prepare, combine errands into one trip, and set aside a block of time to do tasks (e.g., returning telephone calls, paying bills, etc.).
- **Ask for help.** If you are in charge of holiday meals, consider making it potluck or enlist the help of your family and/or friends.
- **Find "down" time.** Whether it's taking a bubble bath or exercising, make time to relax, re-energize and refresh your body and mind.
- **Enjoy time with your loved ones.** It is easy to get caught up in the fast pace of the holiday season; take time out to spend quality time with family and friends.

Tips for Holiday Traveling

- **Make travel plans early.** Book airline flights and make reservations early to cut down on stress—and possibly save money.
- **Allow plenty of travel time.** Given the heavy volume of travelers, expect delays. Arrive early to avoid long lines, overbooked reservations, and to cut down on stress.
- **Anticipate traffic jams.** During the holidays, traffic volume is at its heaviest. Plan to carpool during the holidays to cut down on traffic, or bring along some music or books on cassette to help pass the time.

Tips for Holiday Shopping and Gift Giving

Finding, buying and wrapping holiday gifts can add stress to your daily schedule and your finances. Here are some tips for alleviating the stress of holiday shopping:

- **Shop early.** One of the greatest sources of holiday stress is last-minute shopping. Crowded malls, bumper-to-bumper traffic and packed parking lots can make shopping stressful. Create shopping lists before you go to the store, or try catalog or Internet shopping to save time and avoid crowds and long lines.

- **Be creative.** The money spent on gifts during the holiday season can overwhelm both you and your budget. To cut down on expenses, organize a gift swap with family or friends; bake homemade cookies or candy; or make cards, gifts or crafts.
- **Wrap gifts as you buy them.** Instead of waiting for the last minute to wrap and decorate your gifts, do a little bit at a time.
- **Write out holiday cards in advance.** If you send holiday cards, start early or do a few each night to make it more manageable.
- **Mail presents and cards early.** If you need to send gifts, mail them ahead of time to ensure they arrive on time.

Taking Care of Yourself during the Holidays

In addition to staying organized, your best weapon for combating stress is maintaining healthy habits. Here are some suggestions for taking care of yourself during the holidays:

- **Get plenty of sleep.** In trying to keep up with your hectic holiday schedule, it can be difficult to get enough sleep. Remember that getting enough rest will help you stay alert and have enough energy to do all of the activities you enjoy.
- **Eat well.** Food is an integral part of every holiday tradition, but it is important to eat the foods you enjoy in moderation. Though you don't have to skip holiday treats altogether, avoid overeating which may make you feel sluggish and full.
- **Strive to be healthy.** Stress can cause a multitude of physical symptoms, including tension headaches, backaches, migraines, muscle cramps, difficulty sleeping and eating, etc. To help combat these symptoms, be sure to drink plenty of water, avoid excessive alcohol and get enough exercise.

Grieving during the Holidays

If you have lost a loved one, grieving can intensify during holiday times—which can also add to the stress. Even though no one can take away your grief at these times, there are things you can do to make the holidays without your loved one less stressful.

- **Be honest about your feelings.** Decide how much celebrating you can handle and what feels most comfortable for you. For example, will you really be able to handle the responsibility of the annual family dinner? Do your best to surround yourself with people who wish to support you in what you need.
- **Make changes if necessary.** If you wish to continue the family traditions, do so; if you wish to make changes, that is okay, too. Visit friends or relatives for a holiday or anniversary instead of hosting others; open presents on Christmas morning as opposed to Christmas Eve; vary the timing of Chanukah gift giving; etc.

Holiday stress can be even more intense coupled with work or volunteer responsibilities. If possible, take time off from work or volunteer obligations to spend some time preparing for the holidays—and enjoying them. If you are unable to take time off, do your best to keep your to-do list manageable at home and do not over commit to personal responsibilities (cooking, entertaining, etc.) that will be too time-consuming and stressful.

- **Help others.** Helping others can be a great way to heal your own pain. Volunteer, spend time with others less fortunate, or donate to charities.
- **Remember your loved one in a special way.** Perhaps include his or her name in a prayer before you eat; light a candle to symbolize your loved one's place at the table; or read aloud a poem. If it offers you comfort, reminisce with friends and family about your loved one or look through photo albums and scrapbooks.
- **Do your best to be positive.** Feel gratitude for the things that are going well in your life (health, job, friends, family, etc.). Remind yourself that you are allowed to experience joy and happiness. These feelings are not disrespectful to your loved one.
- **Recognize stress signals.** Learn to recognize your stress signals and alleviate contributors to your stress. If, for example, you are suffering from unusual or increased physical ailments, your body may be sending you signals that you are stressed. Note—If stress turns into severe anxiety and/or depression, seek professional help immediately.

Section 54.5

Work Stress

This section includes text excerpted from "Stress at Work," Centers for Disease Control and Prevention (CDC), September 15, 2017.

The ways that work processes are structured and managed, called "work organization," can directly heighten or alleviate workers' on-the-job stress. Studies suggest that work organization also may have a broad influence on worker safety and health, and may contribute to occupational injury, work-related musculoskeletal disorders, cardiovascular disease, and even may intensify other occupational health concerns (such as complaints about indoor air quality).

Who's at Risk?

One-fourth to one-third of U.S. workers report high levels of stress at work. Americans spend 8 percent more time on the job than they did 20 years ago (47 hours per week on average), and 13 percent also work a second job. Two-fifths (40%) of workers say that their jobs are very stressful, and more than one-fourth (26%) say they are "often burned out or stressed" by their work.

Can It Be Prevented?

Yes. As widespread corporate and government restructuring continues to have an effect on workers in today's rapidly changing economy, it is important to recognize that stress does not have to be 'just part of the job.' Work stress can be prevented through changes in the work organization and use of stress management, with an emphasis on work organization changes as a primary step.

The Bottom Line

- Work-related stress is a real problem that can negatively impact health and safety.
- Identifying stressful aspects of work can help in devising strategies for reducing or eliminating workplace stress. Some strategies include: clearly defining worker roles and responsibilities, improving communication, and making sure workers participate in decisions about their jobs.

Section 54.6

Managing Stress after a Disaster or Other Traumatic Event

This section includes text excerpted from "Tips for Survivors of a Disaster or Other Traumatic Event: Managing Stress," Substance Abuse and Mental Health Services Administration (SAMHSA), 2013. Reviewed June 2018.

If you were involved in a disaster such as a hurricane, flood, or even terrorism, or another traumatic event like a car crash, you may be affected personally regardless of whether you were hurt or lost a loved one. You can be affected just by witnessing a disaster or other traumatic event. It is common to show signs of stress after exposure to a disaster or other traumatic event, and it is important to monitor your physical and emotional health.

Possible Reactions to a Disaster or Other Traumatic Event

Try to identify your early warning signs of stress. Stress usually shows up in the four areas shown below, but everyone should check for any unusual stress responses after a disaster or other traumatic event. Below are some of the most common reactions.

You may feel emotionally:

- Anxious or fearful
- Overwhelmed by sadness
- Angry, especially if the event involved violence
- Guilty, even when you had no control over the traumatic event
- Heroic, like you can do anything
- Like you have too much energy or no energy at all
- Disconnected, not caring about anything or anyone
- Numb, unable to feel either joy or sadness

You may have physical reactions, such as:

- Having stomach aches or diarrhea
- Having headaches or other physical pains for no clear reason

- Eating too much or too little
- Sweating or having chills
- Getting tremors (shaking) or muscle twitches
- Being jumpy or easily startled

After the Event: Managing Your Tasks

If you've been involved in a disaster or other traumatic event, a number of tasks likely require your attention fairly urgently. First, make sure you are not injured, as sometimes survivors don't realize they've been physically hurt until many hours later. If you realize you've been injured, seek medical treatment before you do anything else. If you need to find a safe place to stay, work on that task next. Make sure to let a family member or friend know where you are and how to reach you. Secure your identification and any other papers you may need, such as insurance, bank, property, and medical records. Completing one task at a time may help you feel like you are gaining back some control, so make a list of the most important things you need to do. Remember to be patient with yourself. Take deep breaths or gently stretch to calm yourself before you tackle each task. Plan to do something relaxing after working for a while.

You may have behavioral reactions, such as:

- Having trouble falling asleep, staying asleep, sleeping too much, or trouble relaxing
- Noticing an increase or decrease in your energy and activity levels
- Feeling sad or crying frequently
- Using alcohol, tobacco, illegal drugs or even prescription medication in an attempt to reduce distressing feelings or to forget
- Having outbursts of anger, feeling really irritated and blaming other people for everything
- Having difficulty accepting help or helping others
- Wanting to be alone most of the time and isolating yourself

You may experience problems in your thinking, such as:

- Having trouble remembering things

- Having trouble thinking clearly and concentrating
- Feeling confused
- Worrying a lot
- Having difficulty making decisions
- Having difficulty talking about what happened or listening to others

Practical Tips for Relieving Stress

These stress management activities seem to work well for most people. Use the ones that work for you.

- Talk with others who understand and accept how you feel. Reach out to a trusted friend, family member, or faith-based leader to explore what meaning the event may have for you. Connect with other survivors of the disaster or other traumatic events and share your experience.
- Body movement helps to get rid of the buildup of extra stress hormones. Exercise once daily or in smaller amounts throughout the day. Be careful not to lift heavy weights. You can damage your muscles if you have too much adrenaline in your system. If you don't like exercise, do something simple, like taking a walk, gently stretching, or meditating.
- Take deep breaths. Most people can benefit from taking several deep breaths often throughout the day. Deep breathing can move stress out of your body and help you to calm yourself. It can even help stop a panic attack.
- Listen to music. Music is a way to help your body relax naturally. Play music timed to the breath or to your heartbeat. Create a relaxing playlist for yourself and listen to it often.
- Pay attention to your physical self. Make sure to get enough sleep and rest each day. Don't leave resting for the weekend. Eat healthy meals and snacks and make sure to drink plenty of water. Avoid caffeine, tobacco, and alcohol, especially in large amounts. Their effects are multiplied under stress and can be harmful, just making things worse.
- Use known coping skills. How did you handle past traumatic events like a car crash or the death of a loved one? What helped

then (e.g., spent time with family, went to a support group meeting)? Try using those coping skills now.

When Your Stress Is Getting the Best of You

Know that distressing feelings about a disaster or traumatic event usually fade over time (2–4 weeks after the event) as you get back to routines—and especially if you have engaged in some ways to help yourself. Try to use some of these tips several times a week.

Chapter 55

Other Stress Management Strategies

Chapter Contents

Section 55.1

Abdominal Breathing

This section includes text excerpted from "Abdominal Breathing," U.S. Department of Veterans Affairs (VA), July 2013. Reviewed June 2018.

What Is Abdominal Breathing?

The goal of breath-focused relaxation is to shift from quick, shallow chest breathing to deeper, more relaxed abdominal breathing. During times of stress, our natural tendency is to either hold our breath, or to breathe in a shallow, rapid manner. When we are relaxed our breathing is naturally slower and deeper. When stress is chronic, we may habitually breathe shallowly, never really discharging the stale air from our lungs. Holding in your stomach for reasons of vanity also restricts breathing. In order to take a full deep breath, we must allow our diaphragm (the muscle separating our chest cavity from the abdominal cavity below the lungs) to drop down and our abdomen to expand. If we keep our stomach muscles held in tight when we breathe, we restrict the expansion of our lungs and rob our bodies of optimal oxygen. This puts our bodies in a state of alarm that creates the sensation of anxiety. Taking a few slow, deep breaths sends the signal to our body to relax. Deep breathing is also referred to as abdominal breathing, diaphragmatic breathing, or belly breathing. Abdominal breathing is a form of relaxation that you can use any time to help you to calm yourself physically and mentally and in turn, decrease stress.

Instructions for Learning Abdominal Breathing

1. Place one hand, palm side down, on your chest. Place the other hand, palm side down, on your stomach.
2. Breathe in through your nose to a slow count of 3 or 4 (one… two… three… four…). Notice the motion of each hand. When you breathe in, does the hand on your chest move? If so, which way does it move (out/up or in/down) and how much does it move? Does the hand on your stomach move? If so, which way (out or in) and how much?
3. Now exhale through your nose, again to a slow count of 3 or 4. Notice again how each of your hands moves.

For the most relaxing breath, the hand on your chest should move very little while the hand on your stomach pushes out significantly on the inhale (in breath) and goes back in on the exhale (out breath). A common problem is for the chest to inflate on the in breath while the stomach stays still or even sucks in. When this happens, only the upper part of the lungs (the part behind the upper chest) is being used. When a full deep breath is properly taken, the diaphragm muscle drops down into the abdominal cavity to make room for the lungs to expand. As the diaphragm muscle drops down, it pushes the organs in the abdomen forward to make more room for the lungs. That is why the stomach goes out when you take the most relaxing type of breath.

Learning to take abdominal breaths versus chest breathing is a challenge for some people. The following tips can make it easier.

- Imagine yourself filling a medium-sized balloon in your stomach each time you inhale and releasing the air in the balloon when you exhale.
- Breathe in the same amount of air you breathe out.
- It is sometimes easier to first learn abdominal breathing while lying on your back with your hand on your stomach. It is easier to feel the stomach motion in this position versus sitting or standing.
- It is best to only practice a few deep breaths at a time at first. This is because deep breathing can make you feel lightheaded if you aren't used to it. If you begin to feel light-headed, it is just your body's signal that it has had enough practice for now. Return to your normal breathing and practice again later. With practice, you will be able to take a greater number of deep breaths without becoming light headed.
- Start practicing this deep breathing technique when you are calm so you have mastered it and are ready to use it when you are stressed.

Longer Relaxation Exercises

Deep breathing can be expanded into a longer relaxation exercise as well. Two examples are given below:

Three-Part Rhythmic Breathing

Inhale… hold the breath… and then exhale… with the inhale, hold, and exhale each being of equal length. Inhale and exhale completely using the entire length of the lungs. Keep your shoulders and face relaxed while you hold your breath. Use a count that is comfortable for you. Repeat five times.

Breathing with Imagery

For about 30 seconds, simply relax with your eyes closed. Then start to pay attention to your breathing. Let your breathing become slow and relaxed, like a person sleeping. Feel the air entering through your nose with each inhalation, and feel your breath leave as you exhale. Imagine the tension is leaving your body with each out breath.

Now imagine that, as you breathe in, the air comes into your nose and caresses your face like a gentle breeze. As you breathe out, the exhalation carries away the tension from your face. As you breathe slowly in and out, tension gradually leaves your body and you become more and more relaxed.

Now imagine that, as you breathe in, the gentle air enters your nose and spreads relaxation up over the top of your head. As you exhale, imagine the tension leaving this area and passing out of our body. Then imagine the next breath carrying relaxation over your face, your scalp, and both sides of your head. As you exhale, let any tension flow out easily.

If other thoughts come to mind, simply return to paying attention to your breathing. Your breathing is slow and easy, with no effort at all. Let your body relax.

Now let your breath carry relaxation to your neck. As you exhale, tension passes out of your neck and out of your body with the exhaled air. Feel a breath carry relaxation into your shoulders. As you exhale, any tension leaves your shoulders and passes out of your body.

Now one breath at a time, focus your attention on each part of your body from the top down: your upper arms, forearms, hands, chest, back, stomach, hips, thighs, knees, calves, ankles, and feet. Imagine each breath of air carrying relaxation into each part of your body. As you breathe out, let any tension pass out through your nostrils. This exercise takes several minutes. Do it at your own pace. When you have finished, sit quietly for a minute or two more.

Section 55.2

Humor as Stress Relief

This section includes text excerpted from "Laughter Is Important for Wellness," U.S. Department of Veterans Affairs (VA), May 12, 2015.

There are many ways to be or stay emotionally healthy: sleep, healthy diet, exercise, etc. However, sometimes a good laugh can help us take a mental vacation from life's problems and gain some perspective. Aside from the little mental break we get, laughter is good for many other aspects of our lives.

Laughter Is a Prescription Free Medicine for Our Bodies and Minds

Nothing works faster or is more reliable in bringing your mind and body back into balance than a good laugh. Here are some health benefits of laughter:

- Laughter relaxes the whole body. A good, hearty laugh relieves physical tension and stress, leaving your muscles relaxed for up to 45 minutes after.
- Laughter boosts the immune system. Laughter decreases stress hormones and increases immune cells and infection-fighting antibodies, thus improving your resistance to disease.
- Laughter triggers the release of endorphins, the body's natural feel-good chemicals. Endorphins promote an overall sense of well-being and can even temporarily relieve pain.
- Laughter protects the heart. Laughter improves the function of blood vessels and increases blood flow, which can help protect you against a heart attack and other cardiovascular problems.

Laughter and Humor Help You Stay Emotionally Healthy

- Laughter dissolves distressing emotions. You can't feel anxious, angry, or sad when you're laughing.
- Laughter helps you relax and recharge. It reduces stress and increases energy, enabling you to stay focused and accomplish more.

- Humor shifts perspective, allowing you to see situations in a more realistic, less threatening light. A humorous perspective creates psychological distance, which can help you avoid feeling overwhelmed.

Bring More Laughter and Fun into Your Life

Here are some ways to start:

- Smile. Smiling is the beginning of laughter. Like laughter, it's contagious. Pioneers in "laugh therapy," find it's possible to laugh without even experiencing a funny event. The same holds for smiling. When you look at someone or see something even mildly pleasing, practice smiling.
- Count your blessings. Literally make a list. The simple act of considering the good things in your life will distance you from negative thoughts that are a barrier to humor and laughter. When you're in a state of sadness, you have further to travel to get to humor and laughter.
- When you hear laughter, move toward it. Sometimes humor and laughter are private, a shared joke among a small group, but usually not. More often, people are very happy to share something funny because it gives them an opportunity to laugh again and feed off the humor you find in it. When you hear laughter, seek it out and ask, "What's funny?"
- Spend time with fun, playful people. These are people who laugh easily—both at themselves and at life's absurdities—and who routinely find the humor in everyday events. Their playful point of view and laughter are contagious.
- Bring humor into conversations. Ask people, "What's the funniest thing that happened to you today? This week? In your life?"

Today is a great way to start laughing. You can never be too young or too old to enjoy a good laugh. So, find a comic you like, see a comedy movie, tell some jokes with friends, anything you have to do to get out there and laugh, go do it!

Section 55.3

Pet Ownership Reduces Stress

This section contains text excerpted from the following sources: Text in this section begins with excerpts from "Healthy Pets, Healthy People—About Pets and People," Centers for Disease Control and Prevention (CDC), February 2, 2018; Text under the heading "Health Benefits of Human–Animal Interactions" is excerpted from "The Power of Pets," *NIH News in Health*, National Institutes of Health (NIH), February 2018.

Most households in the United States have at least one pet. Studies have shown that the bond between people and their pets can increase fitness, lower stress, and bring happiness to their owners. Some of the health benefits of having a pet include:

- Decreased blood pressure
- Decreased cholesterol levels
- Decreased triglyceride levels
- Decreased feelings of loneliness
- Increased opportunities for exercise and outdoor activities
- Increased opportunities for socialization

Although pets come with many benefits, there's something else you should know: pets sometimes carry harmful germs that can make people sick. The diseases people get from animals are called zoonotic diseases. It is hard to know which animals could be carrying zoonotic diseases, especially since animals carrying these germs can often look healthy and normal. Here are some tips that can help you and your pets stay healthy:

- Take your pet to its veterinarian regularly so it stays in good health.
- Practice good hygiene around your pets so they don't pass germs to you.
- Learn about diseases different types of animals can spread—just in case.

Health Benefits of Human–Animal Interactions

Nothing compares to the joy of coming home to a loyal companion. The unconditional love of a pet can do more than keep you company.

Pets may also decrease stress, improve heart health, and even help children with their emotional and social skills. An estimated 68 percent of U.S. households have a pet. But who benefits from an animal? And which type of pet brings health benefits? Over the past 10 years, National Institutes of Health (NIH) has partnered with the Mars Corporation's WALTHAM Centre for Pet Nutrition to answer questions like these by funding research studies. Scientists are looking at what the potential physical and mental health benefits are for different animals—from fish to guinea pigs to dogs and cats.

Possible Health Effects

Research on human–animal interactions is still relatively new. Some studies have shown positive health effects, but the results have been mixed. Interacting with animals has been shown to decrease levels of cortisol (a stress-related hormone) and lower blood pressure. Other studies have found that animals can reduce loneliness, increase feelings of social support, and boost your mood.

The NIH/Mars Partnership is funding a range of studies focused on the relationships we have with animals. For example, researchers are looking into how animals might influence child development. They're studying animal interactions with kids who have autism, attention deficit hyperactivity disorder (ADHD), and other conditions.

"There's not one answer about how a pet can help somebody with a specific condition," explains Dr. Layla Esposito, who oversees NIH's Human Animal-Interaction Research Program. "Is your goal to increase physical activity? Then you might benefit from owning a dog. You have to walk a dog several times a day and you're going to increase physical activity. If your goal is reducing stress, sometimes watching fish swim can result in a feeling of calmness. So there's no one type fits all."

NIH is funding large-scale surveys to find out the range of pets people live with and how their relationships with their pets relate to health.

"We're trying to tap into the subjective quality of the relationship with the animal—that part of the bond that people feel with animals—and how that translates into some of the health benefits," explains Dr. James Griffin, a child development expert at NIH.

Animals Helping People

Animals can serve as a source of comfort and support. Therapy dogs are especially good at this. They're sometimes brought into hospitals or nursing homes to help reduce patients' stress and anxiety. "Dogs are very present. If someone is struggling with something, they know how to sit there and be loving," says Dr. Ann Berger, a physician and researcher at the NIH Clinical Center (CC) in Bethesda, Maryland. "Their attention is focused on the person all the time."

Berger works with people who have cancer and terminal illnesses. She teaches them about mindfulness to help decrease stress and manage pain. "The foundations of mindfulness include attention, intention, compassion, and awareness," Berger says. "All of those things are things that animals bring to the table. People kind of have to learn it. Animals do this innately."

Researchers are studying the safety of bringing animals into hospital settings because animals may expose people to more germs. A study is looking at the safety of bringing dogs to visit children with cancer. Scientists will be testing the children's hands to see if there are dangerous levels of germs transferred from the dog after the visit.

Dogs may also aid in the classroom. One study found that dogs can help children with ADHD focus their attention. Researchers enrolled two groups of children diagnosed with ADHD into 12-week group therapy sessions. The first group of kids read to a therapy dog once a week for 30 minutes. The second group read to puppets that looked like dogs.

Kids who read to the real animals showed better social skills and more sharing, cooperation, and volunteering. They also had fewer behavioral problems.

Another study found that children with autism spectrum disorder were calmer while playing with guinea pigs in the classroom. When the children spent 10 minutes in a supervised group playtime with guinea pigs, their anxiety levels dropped. The children also had better social interactions and were more engaged with their peers. The researchers suggest that the animals offered unconditional acceptance, making them a calm comfort to the children.

"Animals can become a way of building a bridge for those social interactions," Griffin says. He adds that researchers are trying to better understand these effects and who they might help.

Animals may help you in other unexpected ways. A study showed that caring for fish helped teens with diabetes better manage their disease. Researchers had a group of teens with type 1 diabetes care for a pet fish twice a day by feeding and checking water levels. The caretaking routine also included changing the tank water each week. This was paired with the children reviewing their blood glucose (blood sugar) logs with parents.

Researchers tracked how consistently these teens checked their blood glucose. Compared with teens who weren't given a fish to care for, fish-keeping teens were more disciplined about checking their own blood glucose levels, which is essential for maintaining their health. While pets may bring a wide range of health benefits, an animal may not work for everyone. Studies suggest that early exposure to pets may help protect young children from developing allergies and asthma. But for people who are allergic to certain animals, having pets in the home can do more harm than good.

Helping Each Other

Pets also bring new responsibilities. Knowing how to care for and feed an animal is part of owning a pet. NIH/Mars funds studies looking into the effects of human–animal interactions for both the pet and the person. Remember that animals can feel stressed and fatigued, too. It's important for kids to be able to recognize signs of stress in their pet and know when not to approach. Animal bites can cause serious harm.

"Dog bite prevention is certainly an issue parents need to consider, especially for young children who don't always know the boundaries of what's appropriate to do with a dog," Esposito explains. Researchers will continue to explore the many health effects of having a pet. "We're trying to find out what's working, what's not working, and what's safe—for both the humans and the animals," Esposito says.

Section 55.4

Social Support: Who Can Give It and How to Get It

This section includes text excerpted from "Do Social Ties Affect Our Health?" *NIH News In Health*, National Institutes of Health (NIH), February 2017.

Cuddles, kisses, and caring conversations. These are key ingredients of our close relationships. Scientists are finding that our links to others can have powerful effects on our health. Whether with romantic partners, family, friends, neighbors, or others, social connections can influence our biology and well-being.

Wide-ranging research suggests that strong social ties are linked to a longer life. In contrast, loneliness and social isolation are linked to poorer health, depression, and increased risk of early death.

Studies have found that having a variety of social relationships may help reduce stress and heart-related risks. Such connections might improve your ability to fight off germs or give you a more positive outlook on life. Physical contact—from hand-holding to sex—can trigger release of hormones and brain chemicals that not only make us feel great but also have other biological benefits.

Marriage is one of the most-studied social bonds. "For many people, marriage is their most important relationship. And the evidence is very strong that marriage is generally good for health," says Dr. Janice Kiecolt-Glaser, an expert on health and relationships at Ohio State University (OSU). "But if a relationship isn't going well, it could have significant health-related consequences."

Married couples tend to live longer and have better heart health than unmarried couples. Studies have found that when one spouse improves his or her health behaviors—such as by exercising, drinking or smoking less, or getting a flu shot—the other spouse is likely to do so, too.

When marriages are full of conflict, though, such health benefits may shrink. In National Institute of Health (NIH)-funded studies, Kiecolt-Glaser and her colleagues found that how couples behave during conflict can affect wound healing and blood levels of stress hormones. In a study of more than 40 married couples, the researchers measured changes to body chemistry over a 24-hour period both before and after spouses discussed a conflict. The troublesome topics included money, in-laws, and communication.

"We found that the quality of the discussion really mattered," Kiecolt-Glaser says. Couples who were more hostile to each other showed much larger negative changes, including big spikes in stress hormones and inflammation-related molecules. "In the more well-functioning marriages, couples might acknowledge that they disagree, or find humor in the situation, but they don't get sarcastic or roll their eyes when the other is talking," Kiecolt-Glaser says. In a related study, blister wounds healed substantially more slowly in couples who were nastier to each other than in those who were kinder and gentler during difficult discussions.

Couples with the "double-whammy" of hostile marriages and depression may also be at risk for weight problems. After eating a high-fat meal and discussing a difficult topic, these troubled couples tended to burn fewer calories than less hostile counterparts. "The metabolism in these couples was slower in ways that could account for weight gain across time," Kiecolt-Glaser says. Compared to the kinder couples, the distressed spouses had signs of more fat storage and other risks for heart disease.

The quality of a marriage—whether supportive or hostile—may be especially important to the health of older couples. Dr. Hui Liu at Michigan State University (MSU) studied data on the health and sexuality of more than 2,200 older people, ages 57–85. Good marriage quality, she found, is linked to reduced risk of developing cardiovascular disease, while bad marriage quality is tied to increased risk, particularly in women. "The association between marriage quality and heart health becomes increasingly strong at older ages," Liu says.

Liu and colleagues are also looking at the links between late-life sexuality and health, including whether sex among the very old is beneficial or risky to heart health. "Some people assume that sex isn't important in older ages, so those ages are often overlooked in research studies related to sex," Liu says. "But our studies suggest that for many older people, sex quality and sex life are important to overall quality of life."

In an analysis, Liu and coworkers found that older women who reported having a satisfying sex life were at reduced risk for high blood pressure 5 years later. But the researchers also found that some older men, ages 57–85, were at increased risk for certain heart-related problems after 5 years if they reported having frequent (at least once a week) or extremely enjoyable sex. The reasons for these increased risks aren't clear and are still under study. Experts suggest that older men and women talk with their doctors about concerns related to sexual issues or potential health risks.

Other types of relationships are important, too. These can include friends, family, neighbors, coworkers, clubs, and religious groups. Studies have found that people who have larger and more diverse types of social ties tend to live longer. They also tend to have better physical and mental health than people with fewer such relationships. Social support may be especially protective during difficult times.

Dr. Sheldon Cohen, a psychologist at Carnegie Mellon University (CMU) in Pittsburgh, has been exploring the links between relationships and health for more than 3 decades. In one study, his team exposed more than 200 healthy volunteers to the common cold virus and observed them for a week in a controlled setting. "We found that the more diverse people's social networks—the more types of connections they had—the less likely they were to develop a cold after exposure to the virus," Cohen says. He and his team have since found evidence that people with more types of connections also tend to have better health behaviors (such as not smoking or drinking) and more positive emotions.

The scientists have also been exploring whether simply believing you have strong social support may help protect against the harms of stress. "Long-term conflicts with others are a potent stressor that can affect health. But we've found that its effects are buffered by perceived social support," Cohen says. "People who have high levels of conflict and low levels of social support are much more likely to get sick when exposed to a virus. But those with high conflict and high levels of social support seem protected." In addition, hugging seemed to shield against stress. People who reported having more frequent hugs were less likely to develop an infection after viral exposure.

Social ties can have mixed effects on our health. But overall, research suggests that the benefits of interactions with others can outweigh any risks. "It's generally healthy for people to try to belong to different groups, to volunteer in different ways, and be involved with a church or involved in their neighborhood," Cohen says. "Involvement with other people across diverse situations clearly can have a very potent, very positive effect on health."

Chapter 56

Stress Management for Children, Teens, and Families

Chapter Contents

Section 56.1

Stress Management Tips for Children and Teens

This section includes text excerpted from "Coping with Stress," Centers for Disease Control and Prevention (CDC), January 9, 2018.

Everyone—adults, teens, and even children—experiences stress at times. Stress can be beneficial. It can help people develop the skills they need to deal with possible threatening situations throughout life. Stress is not helpful when it prevents a person from taking care of themselves or their family. You can put problems into perspective by finding healthy ways to cope. Getting the right care and support can help reduce stressful feelings and symptoms.

Stress is a reaction to a situation where a person feels threatened or anxious. Stress can be positive (e.g., preparing for a wedding) or negative (e.g., dealing with a natural disaster). The symptoms may be physical or emotional.

After a traumatic event that is very frightening, people may have strong and lingering reactions. These events may include personal or environmental disasters, or threats with an assault. These strong emotions, may be normal and temporary.

Common reactions to a stressful event can include:

- Disbelief, shock, and numbness
- Feeling sad, frustrated, and helpless
- Fear and anxiety about the future
- Feeling guilty
- Anger, tension, and irritability
- Difficulty concentrating and making decisions
- Crying
- Reduced interest in usual activities
- Wanting to be alone
- Loss of appetite
- Sleeping too much or too little

- Nightmares or bad memories
- Recurring thoughts of the event
- Headaches, back pains, and stomach problems
- Increased heart rate, difficulty breathing
- Smoking or use of alcohol or drugs

Healthy Ways to Cope with Stress

Feeling emotional and nervous or having trouble sleeping and eating can all be normal reactions to stress. Here are some healthy ways you can deal with stress:

- Take care of yourself:
    - Eat healthy, well-balanced meals.
    - Exercise on a regular basis.
    - Get plenty of sleep.
    - Give yourself a break if you feel stressed out.
- Talk to others. Share your problems and how you are feeling and coping with a parent, friend, counselor, doctor, or pastor.
- Avoid drugs and alcohol. These may seem to help with the stress. But in the long run, they create additional problems and increase the stress you are already feeling.
- Take a break. If news events are causing your stress, take a break from listening or watching the news.

Recognize when you need more help. If problems continue or you are thinking about suicide, talk to a psychologist, social worker, or professional counselor.

Helping Youth Cope with Stress

Children and adolescents often struggle with how to cope well with stress. Youth can be particularly overwhelmed when their stress is connected to a traumatic event—like a natural disaster (earthquakes, tornados, wildfires), family loss, school shootings, or community violence. Parents and educators can take steps to provide stability and support that help young people feel better.

Tips for Parents

It is natural for children to worry, especially when scary or stressful events happen in their lives. Talk to your children about these events. This can help put frightening information into a more balanced setting. Monitor what children see and hear about stressful events happening in their lives. Here are some suggestions to help children cope:

- **Maintain a normal routine.** Helping children wake up, go to sleep, and eat meals at regular times provide them a sense of stability. Going to school and participating in typical after-school activities also provide stability and extra support.
- **Talk, listen, and encourage expression.** Create opportunities to have your children talk, but do not force them. Listen to your child's thoughts and feelings and share some of yours. After a traumatic event, it is important for children to feel they can share their feelings and that you understand their fears and worries. Keep having these conversations. Ask them regularly how they feel in a week, in a month, and so on.
- **Watch and listen.** Be alert for any change in behavior. Are children sleeping more or less? Are they withdrawing from friends or family? Are they behaving in any way out of the ordinary? Any changes in behavior, even small ones, may be signs that your child is having trouble and may need support.
- **Reassure.** Stressful events can challenge a child's sense of physical and emotional safety and security. Take opportunities to reassure your child about his or her safety and well-being. Discuss ways that you, the school, and the community are taking steps to keep them safe.
- **Connect with others.** Make an ongoing effort to talk to other parents and your child's teachers about ways to help your child cope. It is often helpful for parents, schools, and health professionals to work together for the well-being of all children in stressful times.

Tips for Kids and Teens

After a traumatic or violent event, it is normal to feel anxious about your safety and security. Even if you were not directly involved, you may worry about whether this type of event may someday affect you. How can you deal with these fears? Start by looking at the tips below for some ideas.

- **Talk to and stay connected to others.** This might be:
    - Parents
    - Relatives
    - Friends
    - Neighbors
    - Teachers
    - Coach
    - School nurse
    - Counselor
    - Family doctor
    - Member of your church or temple

Talking with someone can help you make sense out of your experience and figure out ways to feel better. If you are not sure where to turn, call your local crisis intervention center or a national hotline.

- **Get active.** Go for a walk, play sports, write a play or poem, play a musical instrument, or join an after-school program. Volunteer with a community group that promotes nonviolence or another school or community activity that you care about. These can be positive ways to handle your feelings and to see that things are going to get better.
- **Take care of yourself.** Try to get plenty of sleep, eat right, exercise, and keep a normal routine. By keeping yourself healthy, you will be better able to handle a tough time.
- **Take information breaks.** Pictures and stories about a disaster can increase worry and other stressful feelings. Taking breaks from the news, Internet, and conversations about the disaster can help calm you down.

Tips for School Personnel

Kids and teens experiencing a stressful event, or see it on television, may react with shock, sadness, anger, fear, and confusion. They may be reluctant to be alone or fearful of leaving safe areas such as the house or classroom. School personnel can help their students restore their sense of safety by talking with the children about their fears. Other tips for school personnel include:

- **Reach out and talk.** Create opportunities to have students talk, but do not force them. Try asking questions like, what do you think about these events, or how do you think these things happen? You can be a model by sharing some of your own thoughts as well as correct misinformation. When children talk about their feelings, it can help them cope and to know that different feelings are normal.
- **Watch and listen.** Be alert for any change in behavior. Are students talking more or less? Withdrawing from friends? Acting out? Are they behaving in any way out of the ordinary? These changes may be early warning signs that a student is struggling and needs extra support from the school and family.
- **Maintain normal routines.** A regular classroom and school schedule can provide reassurance and promote a sense of stability and safety. Encourage students to keep up with their schoolwork and extracurricular activities but do not push them if they seem overwhelmed.
- **Take care of yourself.** You are better able to support your students if you are healthy, coping and taking care of yourself first.
    - Eat healthy, well-balanced meals
    - Exercise on a regular basis
    - Get plenty of sleep
    - Give yourself a break if you feel stressed out

Section 56.2

Helping Children Cope with Emergencies

This section includes text excerpted from "Caring for Children in a Disaster—Helping Children Cope with Emergencies," Centers for Disease Control and Prevention (CDC), March 29, 2018.

Regardless of your child's age, he or she may feel upset or have other strong emotions after an emergency. Some children react right away, while others may show signs of difficulty much later. How a child reacts and the common signs of distress can vary according to the child's age, previous experiences, and how the child typically copes with stress.

Children react, in part, on what they see from the adults around them. When parents and caregivers deal with a disaster calmly and confidently, they can provide the best support for their children. Parents can be more reassuring to others around them, especially children, if they are better prepared. People can become more distressed if they see repeated images of a disaster in the media. Early on, consider limiting the amount of exposure you and your loved ones get to media coverage.

Factors That Influence the Emotional Impact on Children in Emergencies

The emotional impact of an emergency on a child depends on a child's characteristics and experiences, the social and economic circumstances of the family and community, and the availability of local resources. Not all children respond in the same ways. Some might have more severe, longer-lasting reactions. The following specific factors may affect a child's emotional response:

- Direct involvement with the emergency
- Previous traumatic or stressful event
- Belief that the child or a loved one may die
- Loss of a family member, close friend, or pet
- Separation from caregivers
- Physical injury
- How parents and caregivers respond

- Family resources
- Relationships and communication among family members
- Repeated exposure to mass media coverage of the emergency and aftermath
- Ongoing stress due to the change in familiar routines and living conditions
- Cultural differences
- Community resilience

What You Can Do to Help Children Cope with a Disaster

Setting a good example for your children by managing your stress through healthy lifestyle choices, such as eating healthy, exercising regularly, getting plenty of sleep, and avoiding drugs and alcohol, is critical for parents and caregivers. When you are prepared, rested, and relaxed you can respond better to unexpected events and can make decisions in the best interest of your family and loved ones.

The following tips can help reduce stress before, during, and after a disaster or traumatic event.

Before

- Talk to your children so that they know you are prepared to keep them safe.
- Review safety plans before a disaster or emergency happens. Having a plan will increase your children's confidence and help give them a sense of control.

During

- Stay calm and reassure your children.
- Talk to children about what is happening in a way that they can understand. Keep it simple and appropriate for each child's age.

After

- Provide children with opportunities to talk about what they went through or what they think about it. Encourage them to share concerns and ask questions.

- You can help your children feel a sense of control and manage their feelings by encouraging them to take action directly related to the disaster. For example, children can help others after a disaster, including volunteering to help the community or family members in a safe environment. Children should NOT participate in disaster cleanup activities for health and safety reasons.
- It is difficult to predict how some children will respond to disasters and traumatic events. Because parents, teachers, and other adults see children in different situations, it is important for them to work together to share information about how each child is coping after a traumatic event.

Common Reactions

The common reactions to distress will fade over time for most children. Children who were directly exposed to a disaster can become upset again; behavior related to the event may return if they see or hear reminders of what happened. If children continue to be very upset or if their reactions hurt their schoolwork or relationships then parents may want to talk to a professional or have their children to talk to someone who specializes in children's emotional needs. Learn more about common reactions to distress:

For Infants to 2-Year-Olds

Infants may become more cranky. They may cry more than usual or want to be held and cuddled more.

For 3- to 6-Year-Olds

Preschool and kindergarten children may return to behaviors they have outgrown. For example, toileting accidents, bed-wetting, or being frightened about being separated from their parents/caregivers. They may also have tantrums or a hard time sleeping.

For 7- to 10-Year-Olds

Older children may feel sad, mad, or afraid that the event will happen again. Peers may share false information; however, parents or caregivers can correct the misinformation. Older children may focus on details of the event and want to talk about it all the time or not want to talk about it at all. They may have trouble concentrating.

For Preteens and Teenagers

Some preteens and teenagers respond to trauma by acting out. This could include reckless driving, and alcohol or drug use. Others may become afraid to leave the home. They may cut back on how much time they spend with their friends. They can feel overwhelmed by their intense emotions and feel unable to talk about them. Their emotions may lead to increased arguing and even fighting with siblings, parents/caregivers or other adults.

For Special Needs Children

Children who need continuous use of a respirator or are confined to a wheelchair or bed may have stronger reactions to a threatened or actual disaster. They might have more intense distress, worry, or anger than children without special needs because they have less control over day-to-day well-being than other people. The same is true for children with other physical, emotional, or intellectual limitations. Children with special needs may need extra words of reassurance, more explanations about the event, and more comfort and other positive physical contacts such as hugs from loved ones.

Section 56.3

Helping Your Child Heal from Trauma

This section includes text excerpted from "Preventing Child Maltreatment and Promoting Well-Being: A Network for Action," Child Welfare Information Gateway, U.S. Department of Health and Human Services (HHS), 2013. Reviewed June 2018.

Trauma is an intense event that threatens or causes harm, either physical or emotional. Trauma can occur as a result of a natural disaster (such as an earthquake or flood), violence, or abuse. Seeing violence happen, even if you are not the victim, also may cause trauma.

Trauma can have a lasting effect on children's brain development. If not addressed, it can lead to trouble with school, relationships, or drugs and alcohol.

What You Might Be Seeing

Children's reactions to trauma vary with age, culture, and personality. Some children show the following signs of trauma:

- Startling easily and having difficulty calming down
- Behaviors common to younger children (e.g., thumb sucking, bed wetting, fear of the dark, clinging to caregivers)
- Tantrums, aggression, or fighting
- Becoming quiet and withdrawn, wanting to be left alone
- Wanting to talk about the traumatic event all the time, or denying that it happened
- Changes in eating or sleeping (sleeping all the time, not sleeping, nightmares)
- Frequent headaches or stomach aches

What You Can Do

Try the following to help your child heal from trauma:

- **Help your child feel safe.** Stay calm and keep a regular routine for meals, play time, and bedtime. Prepare children in advance for any changes or new experiences.
- **Encourage (don't force) children to talk about their feelings.** Tell children it is normal to have many feelings after a trauma. Listen to their stories, take their reactions seriously, correct any misinformation about the traumatic event, and reassure them that what happened was not their fault.
- **Provide extra attention, comfort, and encouragement.** Spending time together as a family may help children feel safe. Younger children may want extra hugs or cuddling. Follow their lead and be patient if they seem needy.
- **Teach children to relax.** Encourage them to practice slow breathing, listen to calming music, or say positive things ("That was scary, but I'm safe now").
- **Be aware of your own response to trauma.** Parents' history of trauma and feelings about their child's experience can influence how they cope. Seek support if you need it.
- **Remember that everyone heals differently from trauma.** Respecting each child's own course of recovery is important.

- **Find help when needed.** If your child's problems last more than a few weeks, or if they get worse rather than better, ask for help. Find a mental health professional who knows proven strategies to help children cope with trauma.

Section 56.4

Helping Children with Disabilities Cope with Disaster and Traumatic Events

This section includes text excerpted from "Safety and Children with Disabilities—Coping with Disaster and Traumatic Events," Centers for Disease Control and Prevention (CDC), September 5, 2017.

When a disaster or traumatic event occurs, such as a natural disaster or violent act, whether accidental or intentional, it can be stressful for people of all ages. Children tend to react to disaster and traumatic events based on their past experiences and what they know of the current situation. Children with disabilities may require extra support from an adult to help them cope with disaster or traumatic events. There are things that adults can do to help children with disabilities cope better with a disaster or traumatic event.

What Can You Do?

The following tips will help reduce stress before, during, and after a disaster or traumatic event.

Before

- As with all children, those with disabilities need to know that they are going to be safe and that they can find a safe place in an emergency.
- Review safety plans before a disaster or emergency happens. Having a plan will increase the child's confidence and help him or her feel under control. For example, a plan should include needed medications or assistance devices.

During

- Stay calm and reassure the child.
- Talk to children about what is happening in a way that they can understand. Keep it simple and consider the child's age and type of disability. For example, it may be hard to know how much information a child with autism is learning through television and conversations. For these children, it is important for adults to look for cues that may provide information on their feelings and fears.

After

- Provide children with opportunities to talk about what they went through or what they think about it. Encourage them to share concerns and ask questions.
- Children who have serious emotional and behavioral problems are at high risk for severe stress after a disaster or traumatic event. In many cases, it may help to maintain as much of a normal routine and environment as possible.
- It is difficult to predict how some children will respond to disasters and traumatic events. Because parents, teachers, and other adults see children in different situations, it is essential that they work together to share information about how the child is coping after a traumatic event.

Section 56.5

Reducing Toxic Stress in Childhood

This section includes text excerpted from "Reducing Toxic Stress in Childhood," Substance Abuse and Mental Health Services Administration (SAMHSA), April 19, 2016.

The American Academy of Pediatrics (AAP) reports that toxic stress during childhood harms an individual's long-term health and well-being. The link between trauma or other adversities during childhood and the risk of developing mental and/or substance use disorders (SUDs), and other hardships later in life is increasingly recognized. Now a growing body of scientific evidence is revealing how physiological changes that occur in children who endure severe, prolonged stress contribute to both mental and physical health conditions later in life.

Andrew Garner, M.D., Ph.D., former chair of the AAP leadership workgroup on early brain and child development, explained that when a child endures severe, unmitigated stress for a long period of time, the body and brain are bathed in cortisol, a hormone that triggers that fight-or-flight response. Normally, this hormone is helpful, allowing individuals to respond quickly in an emergency, but when cortisol levels are chronically elevated it can cause permanent changes in the brain and gene expression. The good news is that support from nurturing adults can mitigate the harmful effects of toxic stress by helping children feel safer and allowing their bodies to turn off the stress response.

"The antidote to toxic stress is safe, stable, and nurturing relationships," Dr. Garner said. He explained that a comforting adult can help young children to turn off this stress response, and older children can be taught healthy strategies for managing stress and their emotions.

The data, along with policy changes associated with health reform that promote wellness, have prompted the AAP to launch a multipronged effort to combat toxic stress during childhood. The AAP is calling on pediatricians to take a multigenerational approach to child health and help parents to better support children in crisis.

"It's tough for pediatricians, because we think of the child as our patient," Dr. Garner explained. "But science tells us we need to consider the family and the community."

For example, if a physician is seeing a child with asthma whose condition is not improving, the physician may assume the family is not following the treatment plan. But a social worker might tell the physician that the family is experiencing homelessness and has been staying in an abandoned house. They lack the transportation and funds to get the child's medications.

"You are not going to address this child's asthma with medications without linking that family with the services they need," Dr. Garner said. Pediatricians may also be afraid to ask families about such hardships because they are not confident they will be able to link them to services.

Building Safety Nets for Families

To help physicians do this, AAP is working to build stronger community safety nets for families experiencing hardships by working with policymakers and social service providers. A newly formed Center for Healthy, Resilient Children at AAP will work to translate the data on toxic stress into medical practice and policy and to build collaborations with early childhood educators and social services, Dr. Garner said.

"There are multiple ways to start bridging," he said. "We really need to have a web that's catching these kids."

He noted that some programs are already working to help pediatricians and social service organizations work together. For example, an organization called Health Leads works with medical clinics where physicians "prescribe" interventions for families like job training, legal advice, housing, or food, alongside traditional medical care. A cadre of about 1,000 college students help to fill those prescriptions by linking the families to appropriate services. Another example is Head Start–Trauma Smart, an early childhood education program that works to meet the needs of children who have experienced trauma or hardships and helps link these youth and their families to medical care and other services.

The foundation of this effort will require more information for parents and caregivers about the health effects of toxic stress on children. Physicians and other medical professionals working with children will have to ramp up efforts to screen families for homelessness and other risk factors. Finally, treatment and services must be in place to help children in need.

A key goal of the AAP's efforts is to empower parents and help them meet their children's basic needs. "I've never met a parent who doesn't want to do a good job," Dr. Garner said. "But it is hard to do when you don't know where you are going to sleep at night, or you are a victim of abuse, or you don't have a job."

Section 56.6

Nature Helps Kids Deal with Stress

This section includes text excerpted from "Teaching and Learning in Nature," U.S. Fish and Wildlife Service (FWS), November 2007. Reviewed June 2018.

The American people, especially children, spend less time playing outdoors than any previous generation. Research shows that our nation's children are suffering from too much time inside. Kids spend an average of 6.5 hours/day with television, computers and video games. In fact, a child is six times more likely to play a video game than to ride a bike. What does this mean? If children are raised with little or no connection to nature, they may miss out on the many health benefits of playing outdoors. Nature is important to children's development—intellectually, emotionally, socially, spiritually, and physically.

Why Include Outdoor Learning in the School Year?

Studies show that schools that use outdoor classrooms and other forms of experiential education produce significant student gains in social studies, science, language arts, and math. One 2005 study by the California Department of Education (CDE) found that students in outdoor science programs improved their science testing scores by 27 percent.

Children in outdoor education settings show improvement in self-esteem, problem solving, and motivation to learn. Children in schoolyards with both green areas and manufactured play areas engage in more creative forms of play and play in groups more cooperatively. Studies at the University of Illinois show that time in natural settings significantly reduces symptoms of attention deficit hyperactivity disorder (ADHD) in children as young as age five. Research also shows that outdoor experiences help reduce negative stress and protect psychological well-being, especially in children undergoing stressful life events.

Who Benefits from Learning Outdoors?

Children develop knowledge and skills as they undertake exciting, real-life projects. By studying science, math and related subjects through outdoor experiences, students can connect to their local environment and become stewards of their community's natural resources. Teachers can use the broad context of the natural world to enliven teaching and learning that can weave through the curriculum from kindergarten through twelfth grade and beyond. Schools can build cohesion within the school, create opportunities for meaningful community involvement and diversify and beautify the schoolyard while highlighting its educational mission. Communities benefit from outdoor community service or service learning projects, afterschool programming, school-community resource connections, and schoolyard habitat and garden/naturalist programs. Community involvement engages students in relevant, place-based education.

What Can It Look Like?

- Primary grades can learn to count and sort natural objects such as seeds, nuts, and cones. They can match colors and go on nature alphabet hikes.
- Upper elementary students can use the outdoors as prompts for language arts activities, building observation skills, mapping the schoolyard and planning and planting a schoolyard habitat.
- Middle school students can engage in physical education activities such as hiking and biking. They can plan and conduct wildlife monitoring projects, litter clean-ups, and invasive plant removal projects.
- High school students can conduct investigations on biotic and abiotic features of a study site, research local wildlife diversity and document habitat conservation issues in their local communities.

How Does Learning in Nature Fit into the School Curriculum?

- A wide array of teaching materials are available that meet specific grade levels and learning objectives. Many are correlated with state and national education standards.
- Students improve their skills in writing, art, computer technology and science as they participate in interdisciplinary learning in a broad context.

- Scientific, inquiry-based research in a meaningful, real-life context creates hands-on learning with practical application and skill building.
- Students can work with peers, other classes, across grades and schools. They can build character traits of responsibility and teamwork, and make important decisions that build confidence and resilience.
- Many effective nature education activities require few special supplies or extra preparation, just a walk outside into nearby nature.

Are Resources Available for Educators?

Educators play a critical role in inspiring young people to have a positive impact on the natural environment. Many new programs and opportunities are opening promising new doors to outdoor conservation education. Professional development opportunities abound! State environmental and outdoor education organizations, science and social studies teachers organizations, state fish and wildlife agencies, and local offices of federal land management agencies offer interactive workshops for teachers designed to build familiarity with and confidence in outdoor learning lessons, activities and teaching methods.

Section 56.7

Parental Stress and Coping

This section includes text excerpted from "Preventing Child Maltreatment and Promoting Well-Being: A Network for Action," Child Welfare Information Gateway, U.S. Department of Health and Human Services (HHS), 2013. Reviewed June 2018.

Everyone has stress, whether it's a bad day at work, car trouble, or simply too many things to do. However, too much stress can make it hard to parent effectively. After a while, your children may show signs of being stressed out, too!

What You Might Be Seeing

Some signs that you are stressed include:

- Feeling angry or irritable a lot of the time
- Feeling hopeless
- Having trouble making decisions
- Crying easily
- Worrying all the time
- Arguing with friends or your partner
- Overeating or not eating enough
- Being unable to sleep or wanting to sleep all the time

A buildup of stress also can contribute to health problems, including allergies, a sore neck or back, headaches, upset stomach, and high blood pressure.

Parental Resilience

Parents who can cope with the stresses of everyday life as well as an occasional crisis have resilience—the flexibility and inner strength to bounce back when things are not going well. Parents with resilience also know how to seek help in times of trouble. Their ability to deal with life's ups and downs serves as a model of coping behavior for their children.

Multiple life stressors, such as a family history of abuse or neglect, physical and mental health problems, marital conflict, substance abuse, and domestic or community violence—and financial stressors such as unemployment, financial insecurity, and homelessness—can reduce a parent's capacity to cope effectively with the typical day-to-day stresses of raising children.

All parents have inner strengths or resources that can serve as a foundation for building their resilience. These may include faith, flexibility, humor, communication skills, problem-solving skills, mutually supportive caring relationships, or the ability to identify and access outside resources and services when needed. All of these qualities strengthen their capacity to parent effectively, and they can be nurtured and developed through concrete skill-building activities or through supportive interactions with others.

What You Can Do

It is important to learn how to manage your stress—for your own sake and for your children. The following suggestions may help:

- **Identify what's making you stressed.** Everyone's stressors are different. Yours might be related to money, work, your surroundings (traffic, crime), your partner, your children's behavior, or health issues.
- **Accept what you cannot change.** Ask yourself, "Can I do anything about it?" If the answer is no, try to focus on something else. If there is something you can do (look for a new job, for example), break it into smaller steps so it doesn't feel overwhelming.
- **Have faith.** Look back at previous times when you have overcome challenges. Think, "This too shall pass." Consider that people who attend church, pray regularly, or practice other forms of spirituality tend to have less stress.
- **Relax!** Try deep breathing, meditation, yoga, or listening to music. Take 30 minutes to play a board game and laugh with your kids.
- **Take care of your health.** Getting enough sleep can make a big difference in your stress level. So can eating healthy foods and getting some exercise.
- **Take time for yourself.** Take a bath, read a book, or pick up a hobby. When you can, hire a babysitter (or trade time with a friend or neighbor) and get out for a few hours.
- **Develop a support network.** Don't be afraid to ask for help. Older children can set the table. Your spouse or partner could take over bedtime a few nights a week. Friends might pick up the kids from school to give you a break.

Part Six

Additional Help and Information

Chapter 57

Glossary of Terms Related to Stress and Stress-Related Disorders

acne: A disorder resulting from the action of hormones and other substances on the skin's oil glands (sebaceous glands) and hair follicles.

acupuncture: Describes a family of procedures involving the stimulation of points on the body using a variety of techniques. The acupuncture technique that has been most often studied scientifically involves penetrating the skin with thin, solid, metallic needles that are manipulated by the hands or by electrical stimulation.

acute: Refers to a disease or condition that has a rapid onset, marked intensity, and short duration.

acute stress disorder (ASD): A mental disorder that can occur in the first month following a trauma. ASD may involve feelings such as not knowing where you are, or feeling as if you are outside of your body.

addiction: A chronic, relapsing disease characterized by compulsive drug seeking and use and by long-lasting changes in the brain.

This glossary contains terms excerpted from documents produced by several sources deemed reliable.

anorexia nervosa: An eating disorder caused by a person having a distorted body image and not consuming the appropriate calorie intake resulting in severe weight loss.

anticonvulsant: A drug or other substance used to prevent or stop seizures or convulsions. Also called antiepileptic.

antidepressant: Medication used to treat depression and other mood and anxiety disorders.

antipsychotic: Medication used to treat psychosis.

anxiety: An abnormal sense of fear, nervousness, and apprehension about something that might happen in the future.

anxiety disorder: Any of a group of illnesses that fill people's lives with overwhelming anxieties and fears that are chronic and unremitting. Anxiety disorders include panic disorder, obsessive-compulsive disorder, posttraumatic stress disorder, phobias, and generalized anxiety disorder.

arousal: A traumatic reaction that makes a person feel nervous and on edge. The trauma memory might be so intense that it is hard to sleep or focus the mind. Some people become more jumpy or quick to anger. Others feel like they have to be more on guard.

aura: A warning of a migraine headache. Usually visual, it may appear as flashing lights, zigzag lines, or a temporary loss of vision, along with numbness or trouble speaking.

avoidance: One of the symptoms of posttraumatic stress disorder (PTSD). Those with PTSD avoid situations and reminders of their trauma.

binge eating disorder (BED): An eating disorder caused by a person being unable to control the need to overeat.

biofeedback: A method of learning to voluntarily control certain body functions such as heartbeat, blood pressure, and muscle tension with the help of a special machine. This method can help control pain.

bipolar disorder: A disorder that causes severe and unusually high and low shifts in mood, energy, and activity levels as well as unusual shifts in the ability to carry out day-to-day tasks. Also known as manic depression.

body image: How a person feels about how she or he looks.

body mass index (BMI): A measure of body fat based on a person's height and weight.

borderline personality disorder (BPD): A serious mental illness marked by unstable moods, behavior, and relationships.

broken heart syndrome: A condition in which extreme stress can lead to heart muscle failure. The failure is severe, but often short term.

bulimia nervosa: An eating disorder caused by a person consuming an extreme amount of food all at once followed by self-induced vomiting or other purging.

caregiver: Anyone who provides help to another person in need. Usually, the person receiving care has a condition such as dementia, cancer, or brain injury and needs help with basic daily tasks.

chronic: Refers to a disease or condition that persists over a long period of time.

clinical trial: A scientific study using human volunteers (also called participants) to look at new ways to prevent, detect, or treat disease. Treatments might be new drugs or new combinations of drugs, new surgical procedures or devices, or new ways to use existing treatments.

cluster headache: Sudden, extremely painful headaches that occur in a closely grouped pattern several times a day and at the same times over a period of weeks.

cognition: Conscious mental activities (such as thinking, communicating, understanding, solving problems, processing information, and remembering) that are associated with gaining knowledge and understanding.

cognitive behavioral therapy (CBT): A blend of two therapies—cognitive therapy (CT) and behavioral therapy. CT focuses on a person's thoughts and beliefs, how they influence a person's mood and actions, and aims to change a person's thinking to be more adaptive and healthy. Behavioral therapy focuses on a person's actions and aims to change unhealthy behavior patterns.

cognitive impairment: Experiencing difficulty with cognition. Examples include having trouble paying attention, thinking clearly or remembering new information.

comorbidity: The existence of two or more illnesses in the same person. These illnesses can be physical or mental.

complementary and alternative medicine (CAM): A term for medical products and practices that are not part of standard medical care.

coronary heart disease (CHD): A disease in which a waxy substance called plaque builds up inside the coronary arteries. These arteries supply oxygen-rich blood to your heart muscle.

cortisol: A hormone made by the adrenal cortex (the outer layer of the adrenal gland). It helps the body use glucose (a sugar), protein, and fats. Cortisol made in the laboratory is called hydrocortisone. It is used to treat many conditions, including inflammation, allergies, and some cancers. Cortisol is a type of glucocorticoid hormone.

counselor: A person who usually has a master's degree in counseling and has completed a supervised internship.

delusions: Beliefs that have no basis in reality.

depression: Lack of interest or pleasure in daily activities, sadness, and feelings of worthlessness or excessive guilt that are severe enough to interfere with working, sleeping, studying, eating, and enjoying life.

dialectical behavior therapy (DBT): It is a form of cognitive cognitive behavioral therapy (CBT) used to treat people with suicidal thoughts and actions and borderline personality disorder (BPD). The term "dialectical" refers to a philosophic exercise in which two opposing views are discussed until a logical blending or balance of the two extremes—the middle way—is found.

disorder: An abnormality in mental or physical health.

dissociative disorder: A complex mental process known as dissociation allows children and adults to cope with a traumatic experience. "Dissociation" can take many forms, such as "blocking out" a painful experience from memory or feeling detached or "not in" one's own body.

dopamine: A brain chemical, classified as a neurotransmitter, found in regions of the brain that regulate movement, emotion, motivation, and pleasure.

early intervention: Diagnosing and treating a mental illness when it first develops.

eating disorders: Eating disorders, such as anorexia nervosa, bulimia nervosa, and binge-eating disorder, involve serious problems with eating. This could include an extreme decrease of food or severe overeating, as well as feelings of distress and concern about body shape or weight.

electroconvulsive therapy (ECT): A treatment for severe depression that is usually used only when people do not respond to medications and psychotherapy. ECT involves passing a low-voltage electric current through the brain. The person is under anesthesia at the time of treatment.

employee assistance programs (EAPs): Worksite-based programs and/or resources designed to benefit both employers and employees. EAPs help businesses and organizations address productivity issues by helping employees identify and resolve personal concerns that affect job performance.

epinephrine: A hormone and neurotransmitter. Also called adrenaline.

evidence-based practice: Treatments that are supported by clinical research.

family education/support: This part of coordinated specialty care teaches family and friends about first episode psychosis and helps them support the client's recovery. Family and friends are involved in the client's treatment as much as possible, and as long as it is consistent with the client's wishes.

fatigue: A condition marked by extreme tiredness and inability to function due lack of energy. Fatigue may be acute or chronic.

gastritis: A condition in which the stomach lining—known as the mucosa—is inflamed, or swollen.

hallucinations: Hearing, seeing, touching, smelling, or tasting things that are not real.

hormone: Substance produced by one tissue and conveyed by the bloodstream to another to effect a function of the body, such as growth or metabolism.

hypertension: Also called high blood pressure, it is having blood pressure greater than 0 over 90 mmHg (millimeters of mercury). Long-term high blood pressure can damage blood vessels and organs, including the heart, kidneys, eyes, and brain.

inpatient: Healthcare treatment for someone who is admitted to a hospital.

insomnia: Not being able to sleep.

interpersonal therapy (IPT): Most often used on a one-on-one basis to treat depression or dysthymia (a more persistent but less severe form of depression).

intervention: An action intended to help treat or cure a condition.

long-acting injectable (drugs): A shot of medication administered once or twice a month. The shot is an alternative to taking a daily dose of medication.

magnetic resonance imaging (MRI): An imaging technique that uses magnetic fields to take pictures of the structure of the brain.

mania: Feelings of intense mental and physical hyperactivity, elevated mood, and agitation.

massage therapy: Encompasses many different techniques. In general, therapists press, rub, and otherwise manipulate the muscles and other soft tissues of the body. They most often use their hands and fingers, but may use their forearms, elbows, or feet.

meditation: A mind and body practice. There are many types of meditation, most of which originated in ancient religious and spiritual traditions. Some forms of meditation instruct the practitioner to become mindful of thoughts, feelings, and sensations and to observe them in a nonjudgmental way.

mental illness: A health condition that changes a person's thinking, feelings, or behavior (or all three) and that causes the person distress and difficulty in functioning.

migraine: A medical condition that usually involves a very painful headache, usually felt on one side of the head. Besides intense pain, migraine also can cause nausea and vomiting and sensitivity to light and sound. Some people also may see spots or flashing lights or have a temporary loss of vision.

mood disorders: Mental disorders primarily affecting a person's mood.

neurotransmitters: A chemical produced by neurons to carry messages from one nerve cell to another.

obsessive-compulsive disorder (OCD): An anxiety disorder in which a person suffers from obsessive thoughts and compulsive actions, such as cleaning, checking, counting, or hoarding. The person becomes trapped in a pattern of repetitive thoughts and behaviors that are senseless and distressing but very hard to stop.

osteoarthritis (OA): A painful, degenerative joint disease that often involves the hips, knees, neck, lower back, or small joints of the hands.

outpatient: Healthcare treatment given to individuals who are not admitted to a hospital.

over-the-counter (OTC) medicine: All these terms refer to medicine that you can buy without a prescription. They are safe and effective when you follow the directions on the label and as directed by your healthcare professional. Also known as OTC or nonprescription medicine.

panic disorder: An anxiety disorder in which a person suffers from sudden attacks of fear and panic. The attacks may occur without a known reason, but many times they are triggered by events or thoughts that produce fear in the person, such as taking an elevator or driving. Symptoms of the attacks include rapid heartbeat, chest sensations, shortness of breath, dizziness, tingling, and feeling anxious.

parasympathetic nervous system: The part of the nervous system that slows the heart, dilates blood vessels, decreases pupil size, increases digestive juices, and relaxes muscles in the gastrointestinal tract.

phobia: An intense fear of something that poses little or no actual danger. Examples of phobias include fear of closed-in places, heights, escalators, tunnels, highway driving, water, flying, dogs, and injuries involving blood.

postpartum depression: Postpartum depression is when a new mother has a major depressive episode within one month after delivery.

posttraumatic stress disorder (PTSD): A disorder that develops after exposure to a highly stressful event (e.g., wartime combat, physical violence, or natural disaster). Symptoms include sleeping difficulties, hypervigilance, avoiding reminders of the event, and re-experiencing the trauma through flashbacks or recurrent nightmares.

psoriasis: A chronic autoimmune skin disease that speeds up the growth cycle of skin cells.

psychiatrist: A medical doctor (MD) who specializes in treating mental diseases. A psychiatrist evaluates a person's mental health along with his or her physical health and can prescribe medications.

psychiatry: The branch of medicine that deals with identifying, studying, and treating mental, emotional, and behavioral disorders.

psychoeducation: Learning about mental illness and ways to communicate, solve problems, and cope.

psychologist: A mental health professional who has received specialized training in the study of the mind and emotions. A psychologist usually has an advanced degree such as a Ph.D.

psychosis: Conditions that affect the mind, where there has been some loss of contact with reality. When someone becomes ill in this way it is called a psychotic episode. During a period of psychosis, a persons thoughts and perceptions are disturbed and the individual may have difficulty understanding what is real and what is not. Symptoms of psychosis include delusions (false beliefs) and hallucinations (seeing or hearing things that others do not see or hear). Other symptoms include incoherent or nonsense speech, and behavior that is inappropriate for the situation. A person in a psychotic episode may also experience depression, anxiety, sleep problems, social withdrawal, lack of motivation, and difficulty functioning overall.

psychosocial interventions: Nonmedication therapies for people with mental illness and their families. Therapies include psychotherapy, coping skills, training and supported employment, and education services.

psychotherapy: A treatment method for mental illness in which a mental health professional (psychiatrist, psychologist, counselor) and a patient discuss problems and feelings to find solutions. Psychotherapy can help individuals change their thought or behavior patterns or understand how past experiences affect current behaviors.

recovery: The process by which people with mental illness return or begin to work, learn, and participate in their communities. For some individuals and their families, recovery means the ability to live a fulfilling and productive life.

resilience: Refers to the ability to successfully adapt to stressors, maintaining psychological well-being in the face of adversity. It's the ability to "bounce back" from difficult experiences.

schizoaffective disorder: A mental condition that causes both a loss of contact with reality (psychosis) and mood problems (depression or mania).

schizophrenia: A severe mental disorder that appears in late adolescence or early adulthood. People with schizophrenia may have hallucinations, delusions, loss of personality, confusion, agitation, social withdrawal, psychosis, and/or extremely odd behavior.

selective serotonin reuptake inhibitors (SSRIs): A group of medications used to treat depression. These medications cause an increase in the amount of the neurotransmitter serotonin in the brain.

serotonin: A neurotransmitter that regulates many functions, including mood, appetite, and sensory perception.

social phobia: A strong fear of being judged by others and of being embarrassed. This fear can be so strong that it gets in the way of going to work or school or doing other everyday things.

stigma: A negative stereotype about a group of people.

stress response: When a threat to life or safety triggers a primal physical response from the body, leaving a person breathless, heart pounding, and mind racing. From deep within the brain, a chemical signal speeds stress hormones through the bloodstream, priming the body to be alert and ready to escape danger. Concentration becomes more focused, reaction time faster, and strength and agility increase. When the stressful situation ends, hormonal signals switch off the stress response and the body returns to normal.

supported employment/education (SEE): Part of coordinated specialty care, SEE services help clients return to work or school and achieve personal goals. Emphasis is on rapid placement in a work or school setting, combined with coaching and support to ensure success.

sympathetic nervous system: The part of the body that increases heart rate, blood pressure, breathing rate, and pupil size. It also causes blood vessels to narrow and decreases digestive juices.

syndrome: A group of symptoms or signs that are characteristic of a disease.

tension-type headache (TTH): A primary headache that is band-like or squeezing and does not worsen with routine activity. It may be brought on by stress.

trauma: A life-threatening event, such as military combat, natural disasters, terrorist incidents, serious accidents, or physical or sexual assault in adult or childhood.

X-ray: A type of high-energy radiation. In low doses, X-rays are used to diagnose diseases by making pictures of the inside of the body.

yoga: A mind and body practice with origins in ancient Indian philosophy. The various styles of yoga typically combine physical postures, breathing techniques, and meditation or relaxation.

Chapter 58

Directory of Organizations for People with Stress-Related Disorders

Government Agencies That Provide Information about Stress-Related Disorders

Centers for Disease Control and Prevention (CDC)
1600 Clifton Rd.
Atlanta, GA 30329-4027
Toll-Free: 800-CDC-INFO (800-232-4636)
Phone: 404-639-3311
Website: www.cdc.gov
E-mail: cdcinfo@cdc.gov

Federal Emergency Management Agency (FEMA)
500 C St. S.W.
Washington, DC 20472
Toll-Free: 800-621-FEMA (800-621-3362)
Phone: 202-646-2500
Website: www.fema.gov

Resources in this chapter were compiled from several sources deemed reliable; all contact information was verified and updated in June 2018.

Healthfinder®
National Health Information Center (NHIC)
200 Independence Ave. S.W.
Washington, DC 20201
Fax: 301-984-4256
Website: www.healthfinder.gov
E-mail: healthfinder@nhic.org

National Cancer Institute (NCI)
NCI Office of Communications and Education
9609 Medical Center Dr.
BG 9609 MSC 9760
Bethesda, MD 20892-9760
Toll-Free: 800-4-CANCER (800-422-6237)
Website: www.cancer.gov
E-mail: cancergovstaff@mail.nih.gov

National Center for Posttraumatic Stress Disorder (NCPTSD)
VA Medical Center (116D)
215 N. Main St.
White River Junction, VT 05009
Phone: 802-296-6300
Fax: 802-296-5135
Website: www.ptsd.va.gov
E-mail: ncptsd@va.gov

National Heart, Lung, and Blood Institute (NHLBI)
31 Center Dr.
Bldg. 31
Bethesda, MD 20892
Phone: 301-592-8573
Fax: 301-592-8563
Website: www.nhlbi.nih.gov
E-mail: nhlbiinfo@nhlbi.nih.gov

National Institute of Allergy and Infectious Diseases (NIAID)
Office of Communications and Government Relations (OCGR)
5601 Fishers Ln.
MSC 9806
Bethesda, MD 20892-9806
Toll-Free: 866-284-4107
Phone: 301-496-5717
Toll-Free TDD: 800-877-8339
Fax: 301-402-3573
Website: www.niaid.nih.gov

National Institute of Arthritis and Musculoskeletal and Skin Diseases (NIAMS)
National Institutes of Health (NIH)
31 Center Dr.
Bldg. 31 Rm. 4C02
Bethesda, MD 20892-2350
Toll-Free: 877-22-NIAMS (877-226-4267)
Phone: 301-496-8190
Fax: 301-480-2814
Website: www.niams.nih.gov
E-mail: niamsinfo@mail.nih.gov

National Institute of Neurological Disorders and Stroke (NINDS)
NIH Neurological Institute
P.O. Box 5801
Bethesda, MD 20824
Toll-Free: 800-352-9424
Phone: 301-496-5751
Website: www.ninds.nih.gov

National Institute on Aging (NIA)
31 Center Dr. MSC 2292
Bldg. 31 Rm. 5C27
Bethesda, MD 20892
Toll-Free: 800-222-2225
Toll-Free TTY: 800-222-4225
Website: www.nia.nih.gov

National Institute on Alcohol Abuse and Alcoholism (NIAAA)
5635 Fishers Ln.
Bethesda, MD 20892-9304
Toll-Free: 888-MY-NIAAA (888-69-64222)
Phone: 301-443-3860
Website: www.niaaa.nih.gov
E-mail: niaaaweb-r@exchange.nih.gov

National Institute on Drug Abuse (NIDA)
Office of Science Policy and Communications (OSPC)
6001 Executive Blvd.
Rm. 5213 MSC 9561
Bethesda, MD 20892
Phone: 301-443-1124
Website: www.drugabuse.gov

National Institute on Mental Health (NIMH)
Science Writing, Press, and Dissemination Branch
6001 Executive Blvd.
Rm. 6200 MSC 9663
Bethesda, MD 20892-9663
Toll-Free: 866-615-6464
Phone: 301-443-4513
TTY: 301-443-8431
Fax: 301-443-4279
Website: www.nimh.nih.gov
E-mail: nimhinfo@nih.gov

National Institutes of Health (NIH)
9000 Rockville Pike
Bethesda, MD 20892
Phone: 301-496-4000
TTY: 301-402-9612
Website: www.nih.gov
E-mail: NIHinfo@od.nih.gov

National Women's Health Information Center (NWHIC)
Office on Women's Health (OWH)
200 Independence Ave. S.W.
Washington, DC 20201
Toll-Free: 800-994-9662
Website: www.womenshealth.gov/office-womens-health

Substance Abuse and Mental Health Services Administration (SAMHSA)
5600 Fishers Ln.
Rockville, MD 20857
Toll-Free: 877-SAMHSA-7 (877-726-4727)
Toll-Free TTY: 800-487-4889
Fax: 240-221-4292
Website: www.samhsa.gov
E-mail: samhsainfo@samhsa.hhs.gov

U.S. Food and Drug Administration (FDA)
10903 New Hampshire Ave.
Silver Spring, MD 20993
Toll-Free: 888-INFO-FDA (888-463-6332)
Website: www.fda.gov

U.S. National Library of Medicine (NLM)
8600 Rockville Pike
Bethesda, MD 20894
Toll-Free: 888-FIND-NLM (888-346-3656)
Phone: 301-594-5983
Fax: 301-402-1384
Website: www.nlm.nih.gov
E-mail: custserv@nlm.nih.gov

Private Agencies That Provide Information about Stress-Related Disorders

American Academy of Child and Adolescent Psychiatry (AACAP)
3615 Wisconsin Ave. N.W.
Washington, DC 20016-3007
Phone: 202-966-7300
Fax: 202-464-0131
Website: www.aacap.org

American Academy of Experts in Traumatic Stress (AAETS)
127 Echo Ave.
Miller Place, NY 11764
Phone: 631-543-2217
Fax: 631-543-6977
Website: www.aaets.org
E-mail: info@aaets.org

American Academy of Family Physicians (AAFP)
11400 Tomahawk Creek Pkwy
Leawood, KS 66211-2680
Toll-Free: 800-274-2237
Phone: 913-906-6000
Fax: 913-906-6075
Website: www.aafp.org

American Association of Suicidology (AAS)
5221 Wisconsin Ave. N.W.
Washington, DC 20015
Toll-Free: 800-273-TALK (800-273-8255)
Phone: 202-237-2280
Fax: 202-237-2282
Website: www.suicidology.org

American Foundation for Suicide Prevention (AFSP)
120 Wall St.
29th Fl.
New York, NY 10005
Toll-Free: 888-333-AFSP
(888-333-2377)
Phone: 212-363-3500
Fax: 212-363-6237
Website: www.afsp.org
E-mail: info@afsp.org

American Heart Association (AHA)
National Center
7272 Greenville Ave.
Dallas, TX 75231
Toll-Free: 800-AHA-USA-1
(800-242-8721)
Phone: 214-570-5978
Website: www.heart.org

American Institute for Cognitive Therapy
136 E. 57th St.
Ste. 1101
New York, NY 10022
Phone: 212-308-2440
Website: www.
cognitivetherapynyc.com

American Institute of Stress (AIS)
220 Adams Dr.
Ste. 280 – #224
Weatherford, TX 76086
Phone: 682-239-6823
Website: www.stress.org
E-mail: info@stress.org

American Massage Therapy Association (AMTA)
500 Davis St.
Ste. 900
Evanston, IL 60201
Toll-Free: 877-905-0577
Phone: 847-864-0123
Fax: 847-864-5196
Website: www.amtamassage.org
E-mail: info@amtamassage.org

American Medical Association (AMA)
330 N. Wabash Ave.
Ste. 39300
Chicago, IL 60611-5885
Toll-Free: 800-621-8335
Website: www.ama-assn.org

American Music Therapy Association (AMTA)
8455 Colesville Rd.
Ste. 1000
Silver Spring, MD 20910
Phone: 301-589-3300
Fax: 301-589-5175
Website: www.musictherapy.org
E-mail: info@musictherapy.org

American Psychological Association (APA)
750 First St. N.E.
Washington, DC 20002-4242
Toll-Free: 800-374-2721
Phone: 202-336-5500
TDD: 202-336-6123
Website: www.apa.org

Anxiety Disorders Association of America (ADAA)
8701 Georgia Ave.
Ste. 412
Silver Spring, MD 20910
Phone: 240-485-1001
Fax: 240-485-1035
Website: www.adaa.org

Association for Behavioral and Cognitive Therapies (ABCT)
305 Seventh Ave.
16th Fl.
New York, NY 10001
Phone: 212-647-1890
Fax: 212-647-1865
Website: www.abct.org

Association of Traumatic Stress Specialists (ATSS)
5000 Old Buncombe Rd.
Ste. 27-11
Greenville, SC 29617
Phone: 864-294-4337
Website: www.atss.info

Biofeedback Certification International Alliance (BCIA)
5310 Ward Rd., Ste. 201
Arvada, CO 80002
Phone: 720-502-5829
Website: www.bcia.org
E-mail: info@bcia.org

Cleveland Clinic
9500 Euclid Ave.
Cleveland, OH 44195
Toll-Free: 800-223-2273
Website: my.clevelandclinic.org

Depression and Bipolar Support Alliance (DBSA)
55 E. Jackson Blvd., Ste. 490
Chicago, IL 60604
Toll-Free: 800-826-3632
Fax: 312-642-7243
Website: www.dbsalliance.org

Family Caregiver Alliance (FCA)
101 Montgomery St.
Ste. 2150
San Francisco, CA 94104
Toll-Free: 800-445-8106
Phone: 415-434-3388
Website: www.caregiver.org
E-mail: info@caregiver.org

Freedom From Fear
308 Seaview Ave.
Staten Island, NY 10305
Phone: 718-351-1717
Website: www.freedomfromfear.org
E-mail: help@freedomfromfear.org

Imagery International
816 E. Fourth Ave.
San Mateo, CA 94401
Toll-Free: 866-494-9985
Phone: 650-766-9402
Website: imageryinternational.wildapricot.org
E-mail: office@imageryinternational.com

International Society for Traumatic Stress Studies (ISTSS)
One Parkview Plaza
Ste. 800
Oakbrook Terrace, IL 60181
Phone: 847-686-2234
Fax: 847-686-2251
Website: www.istss.org
E-mail: info@istss.org

Iraq and Afghanistan Veterans of America (IAVA)
633 Third Ave.
Sixth Fl.
New York, NY 10017
Phone: 212-982-9699
Fax: 917-591-0387
Website: www.iava.org

March of Dimes
1275 Mamaroneck Ave.
White Plains, NY 10605
Phone: 914-997-4488
Website: www.marchofdimes.org

Mental Health America (MHA)
500 Montgomery St.
Ste. 820
Alexandria, VA 22314
Toll-Free: 800-969-6642
Phone: 703-684-7722
Fax: 703-684-5968
Website: www.mentalhealthamerica.net

National Alliance for Caregiving (NAC)
4720 Montgomery Ln.
Ste. 205
Bethesda, MD 20814
Phone: 301-718-8444
Fax: 301-951-9067
Website: www.caregiving.org
E-mail: info@caregiving.org

National Alliance on Mental Illness (NAMI)
3803 N. Fairfax Dr.
Ste. 100
Arlington, VA 22203
Toll-Free: 800-950-NAMI (800-950-6264)
Phone: 703-524-7600
Website: www.nami.org

National Child Traumatic Stress Network (NCCTS)
11150 W. Olympic Blvd.
Ste. 650
Los Angeles, CA 90064
Phone: 310-235-2633
Fax: 310-235-2612
Website: www.nctsn.org

National Eating Disorders Association (NEDA)
200 W. 41st St.
Ste. 1203
New York, NY 10036
Toll-Free: 800-931-2237
Phone: 212-575-6200
Fax: 212-575-1650
Website: www.nationaleatingdisorders.org
E-mail: info@nationaleatingdisorders.org

National Headache Foundation (NHF)
820 N. Orleans
Ste. 201
Chicago, IL 60610-3131
Toll-Free: 888-NHF-5552
(888-643-5552)
Phone: 312-274-2650
Website: headaches.org
E-mail: info@headaches.org

National Multiple Sclerosis Society (NMSS)
733 Third Ave.
Third Fl.
New York, NY 10017
Toll-Free: 800-344-4867
Phone: 212-463-7787
Fax: 212-986-7981
Website: www.nationalmssociety.org
E-mail: info@msnyc.org

National Organization for Victim Assistance (NOVA)
510 King St., Ste. 424
Alexandria, VA 22314
Toll-Free: 800-TRY-NOVA
(800-879-6682)
Phone: 703-535-6682
Fax: 703-535-5500
Website: www.trynova.org

National Psoriasis Foundation (NPF)
6600 S.W. 92nd Ave., Ste. 300
Portland, OR 97223-7195
Toll-Free: 800-723-9166
Phone: 503-244-7404
Fax: 503-245-0626
Website: www.psoriasis.org
E-mail: getinfo@psoriasis.org

National Sleep Foundation (NSF)
1010 N. Glebe Rd.
Ste. 420
Arlington, VA 22201
Phone: 202-347-3471
Fax: 202-347-3472
Website: www.sleepfoundation.org
E-mail: education@sleepfoundation.org

Nemours Foundation Center for Children's Health Media
1600 Rockland Rd.
Wilmington, DE 19803
Toll-Free: 800-416-4441
Phone: 302-651-4046
Website: www.nemours.org/locations/wilmington-ai-dupont-childrens-hospital.html
E-mail: pr@KidsHealth.org

PsychCentral
55 Pleasant St.
Ste. 207
Newburyport, MA 01950
Website: www.psychcentral.com
E-mail: talkback@psychcentral.com

Rape, Abuse, and Incest National Network (RAINN)
1220 L St. N.W.
Ste. 505
Washington, DC 20005
Toll-Free: 800-656-HOPE
(800-656-4673)
Phone: 202-544-1034
Website: www.rainn.org
E-mail: info@rainn.org

Sidran Traumatic Stress Institute
P.O. Box 436
Brooklandville, MD 21022-0436
Phone: 410-825-8888
Fax: 410-825-8888
Website: www.sidran.org

Social Anxiety Association
Website: www.socialphobia.org

Suicide Awareness Voices of Education (SAVE)
8120 Penn Ave. S.
Ste. 470
Bloomington, MN 55431
Toll-Free: 800-273-8255
Phone: 952-946-7998
Website: www.save.org

Transcendental Meditation (TM) Program
Toll-Free: 888-LEARN-TM (888-532-7686)
Website: www.tm.org

World Federation for Mental Health (WFMH)
P.O. Box 807
Occoquan, VA 22125
Website: www.wfmh.global

Yoga Alliance
1560 Wilson Blvd.
Ste. 700
Arlington, VA 22209
Toll-Free: 888-921-YOGA (888-921-9642)
Website: www.yogaalliance.org

Yoga Journal
Toll-Free: 800-600-9642
Phone: 386-246-0197
Website: www.yogajournal.com

Index

Index

Page numbers followed by 'n' indicate a footnote. Page numbers in *italics* indicate a table or illustration.

A

C

D

F

I

J

K

L

O

P